REFIGURING PROSE STYLE

REFIGURING PROSE STYLE

Possibilities for Writing Pedagogy

Edited by
T. R. JOHNSON
TOM PACE

UTAH STATE UNIVERSITY PRESS
Logan, Utah

Utah State University Press
Logan, Utah 84322

Printed on acid-free paper

Cover design by Barbara Yale-Read

Library of Congress Cataloging-in-Publication Data

Refiguring prose style : possibilities for writing pedagogy / edited by T. R. Johnson and Tom Pace.
    p. cm.
 Includes bibliographical references and index.
 ISBN 0-87421-621-4 (pbk. : alk. paper)
 1. English language–Rhetoric–Study and teaching. 2. English language–Style–Study and teaching. 3. Interdisciplinary
approach in education. 4. Report writing–Study and teaching. I. Johnson, T. R., 1964- II. Pace, Tom, 1969-
 PE1404.R3824 2005
 808'.042'0711–dc22
                        2005017802

CONTENTS

INTRODUCTION

T. R. Johnson and Tom Pace

It happens all the time: someone will use the word style and, at least slightly, the conversation will stumble. Rather more than most words, style means different things to different people. For some, style is always individualized and works in counterpoint to the surrounding community ("I like your style!"); for others, style is just the opposite—it refers to a broad, collective system of symbolic patterns, something like a discourse, even a worldview ("That whole style is so eighties!"). For still others, especially writing teachers, style calls to mind a rather old-fashioned mandate to get students to write more "clearly" and, as such, it partners with grammar as a similar sort of fussiness about "surface" technicalities; for yet others, style refers to something else entirely, perhaps the element of language that crosses into music, the realm of rhythm and balance that opens, in turn, into a mysterious realm of ineffable, intersubjective energies, as when we're powerfully drawn to a text but cannot explain why ("I don't know—the style just grabs me!"). Perhaps this last definition of style—style-as-music—explains why, in most writing classrooms, the discussion of style doesn't often get much beyond vague feelings about how this or that passage "sounds." Style, in short, seems to mean a number of things, perhaps so many that, at last, it means nothing at all.

Or, more likely, style is the elephant in the classroom and in our scholarly field that we constantly pretend isn't there. From the long, historical perspective, style would seem to be precisely such an elephant, for not only is style one of the five canons of classical rhetoric—the others being invention, arrangement, memory, and delivery—it can often subsume these others. Obviously, ideas about delivery and arrangement are intertwined with matters of style, and memory is, too, given how the carefully stylized language we associate with poetry originally served as an aid to memory: orators, in short, can remember their speeches more readily if the speeches are stylized according to principles of balance, rhythm, repetition, and so on (see Havelock 1982; Ong 1982).

But not only does style seem to contain arrangement, delivery, and memory, this elephant, in ways perhaps not so obvious, can also swallow up invention. Aristotle, for example, who otherwise goes to great lengths to oppose the production of knowledge (what he calls dialectics) to issues of language, describes style in Book III of *Rhetoric* in terms of "liveliness" and the value of surprising the audience so that the content seems new and spontaneously invented. And he seems close to fusing style and invention when, in his section on style, he asserts: "[W]hatever words create knowledge in us are the pleasantest" (Aristotle 1991, III.10 244). A similar tendency to link style and invention appears in Cicero's *De Inventione*, where he roundly asserts that "wisdom without eloquence does little for the good of states . . . [and] eloquence without wisdom is generally highly disadvantageous" (Cicero 1949, 3). For another rhetorician of ancient Rome, Quintilian, the purpose of an education in rhetoric is to achieve *facilitas*, or "fullness of expression"—which is derived from a stockpile of expressive patterns and possibilities, a kind of stylistic repertoire that enables one to develop arguments on any subject. For each of these primary figures in the history of rhetoric, then, style is that part of rhetoric that threatens to take over the whole—not just the whole of rhetoric, but perhaps all of our activities of knowing.

Which perhaps is part of why rhetoricians have so often tried to restrict, even erase this elephant—and we've done so, most often, by idealizing so-called clarity. Quintilian, for example, in addition to his concept of *facilitas*, discussed style in terms of standards of correctness, which in turn are features of moral character (the goal of rhetoric being the "the good man speaking well"). And, as Kathryn Flannery has recently argued, this particular way of imagining style has long served to diminish—often quite drastically—style's possibilities. In *The Emperor's New Clothes* (1995), she argues that style is always a conveyer of larger cultural values and that there is no such thing as a naturally "good" style. Rather, the particular style sanctioned by socially powerful groups is often defined as good or proper. She notes that since the late Renaissance, the objective or "transparent" style popularized by scientists in the Royal Society has been encouraged by most Western educational institutions, especially in the United States. The upshot: most readers value plain prose because they've been taught and conditioned to read and trust that type of writing as clear and sincere (Flannery 1995, 21). She insists that literacy education in the United States has the institutional role of teaching the plain style to the masses, while literature, with its premium on artifice, remains privileged discourse. To resist this either-or agenda, Flannery argues, requires a rhetorical conception of style that valorizes artifice and a range of styles for everyone.

A closely related and quite eloquent argument arises in Peter Elbow's recent opinion piece in *College English* called "The Cultures of Literature and Composition: What Could Each Learn from the Other?" Too often, Elbow suggests, teachers of composition see imaginative, figurative language as somehow special or additional, something over and beyond the norm of straightforward, discursive language. And his response: "I'd argue that we can't harness students' strongest linguistic or even cognitive powers unless we see imaginative and metaphorical language as the norm—basic or primal" (Elbow 2002, 536). Elbow laments, too, the way the field of rhetoric and composition has undervalued verbal sophistication—"elegance and irony and indirection"—in its quest to serve in practical ways the ordinary, workaday needs of students. What we need, he insists, is an approach to prose that honors "playfulness, style, pleasure—even adornment and artifice" (543).

Not so long ago, teachers of composition did in fact pay considerable attention to questions of how to craft sentences, but that interest has all but vanished. As Robert Connors (2000) argues, the 1970s saw a robust enthusiasm for sentence combining, imitation, and Francis Christensen's generative rhetoric. But, in the early 1980s, as composition moved into the major phase of its professionalization, this sort of pedagogy seemed to lack the sort of high theoretical basis then becoming fashionable and, rooted as it was in exercises, the pedagogy didn't offer students the sort of meaningful rhetorical context that seemed indispensable to nurturing their abilities. The result, of course, is that many of today's composition teachers aren't teaching style much at all and, if we do, we often do so merely to enhance the "clarity" of student prose. And we certainly aren't talking about it much in the pages of our scholarly journals and books.

Thus the need for a book such as *Refiguring Prose Style: Possibilities for Writing Pedagogy*. We want to move the field beyond the dichotomies that have impoverished its understanding of style. In fact, we follow Kate Ronald and Hephzibah Roskelly, who lament the way that "composition continues to define itself by separating its work into competing identities and categories of opposition" (1989, 1–2). They argue that while categorization is understandable in a field as complex and often contradictory as composition studies, many of these "categories tend to harden, to become exclusionary rather than revisionary" (2). A perfect example of this is the way our field situates style: it belongs with so much current-traditional old-hat, rather than the future; empty, tedious classroom exercises rather than complex, rhetorical experimentation; a sign of pedantry rather than an exciting tool for meaning making and a focus for critical thinking. Operating from the same desire as Ronald and Roskelly to move "farther along" and cut through often-divisive categories, this collection argues that style should be refigured and, as such, become a kind of bridge by which we can lead our students—and each other—beyond counterproductive binaries, such as those between form and content, composition and literature, and between teaching writing as a service course and as tool for critical and creative thinking.

Hence, *Refiguring Prose Style: Possibilities for Writing Pedagogy.* Part I explores the recent history of composition studies, the ways it has figured and all but effaced the whole question of prose style. Part II takes to heart Elbow's suggestion that composition and literature, particularly as conceptualized in the context of creative writing courses, have something to learn from each other. Part III sketches practical classroom procedures for heightening students' abilities to engage style, and part IV explores new theoretical frameworks for defining this vital and much-neglected territory. We hope that the essays assembled here—focusing as they do on historical, aesthetic, practical, and theoretical issues—will awaken composition studies to the possibilities of style, and, in turn, rejuvenate a great many classrooms

PART I: WHAT HAPPENED: THE RISE AND FALL OF STYLISTICS IN COMPOSITION

Introduction

Tom Pace

Since the early 1980s, many teachers of composition have associated the teaching of style with a naïve, product-oriented pedagogy that emphasizes standards of form and rules of usage and that relies on exercises stripped of rhetorical context. One of the primary reasons for the decline of style as a key component of composition scholarship and pedagogy over the last twenty years is a misunderstanding of style in rhetoric and composition's history. The standard narrative held that process pedagogy supplanted current-traditional rhetoric, and that process, in turn, was supplanted by social constructionist and critical pedagogy. At every step, the profession pointed to an emphasis on style as a key sign that a particular pedagogy was deficient. For instance, when process began to supplant current-traditional methods, many of these histories tell us, it did so, in part, by arguing that current-traditionalism was interested in "mere" style—that is, on the surface correctness of the finished product, with no attention given to invention and revision. Likewise, as social constructionist theorists began to criticize process-oriented pedagogy, they suggested that the process approach was too interested in an expressivist, individual style, as celebrated by Donald Murray, Janet Emig, and Peter Elbow, and neglected the way factors of context and community shape meaning far more powerfully than any particular feature of the author's individual voice.

In this section, composition scholars explore the history of style in composition, how style became a neglected part of the field's scholarship and classroom practices, and ultimately how, within this history, style might undergo a certain renaissance today. Tom Pace, in "Style and the Renaissance of Composition Studies," rereads the work of Edward P. J. Corbett, Francis Christensen, and Winston Weathers to critique the widely held notions that their work naïvely separates form and content and wholly neglects critical and creative thinking. In her essay "Where is Style Going? Where Has It Been?" Elizabeth Weiser posits that style has been the victim of the turn from product to process to post-process, and argues that the time is propitious for both ancient and contemporary theories of style to revitalize writing instruction. Rebecca Moore Howard turns her attention to sentence-level pedagogy in her essay "Contextual Stylistics: Breaking Down the Binaries in Sentence-Level Pedagogy" by showing how a return to sentence-level pedagogy does not mean a return to "hegemonic current-traditionalism." Finally, Kathryn Flannery, in "Style Redux," extends and illustrates Howard's point by describing two units of a course she taught called Advanced Prose Style, recounting how her students demonstrated a surprisingly complex understanding of style as multiple sets of choices that lead to stronger, more situated writing. Such a pedagogy is of course a far cry from the current-traditional emphasis on "clarity" and the expressivist emphasis on individual authenticity that, for two decades, so many have assumed are the only outcomes of lessons in style.

1

STYLE AND THE RENAISSANCE OF COMPOSITION STUDIES

Tom Pace

I must say, though, that An Alternative Style *is the only work I've published that has generated hate mail, and the only work I've ever done that was attacked at a national meeting by a colleague who knew I was in the audience.*

—Winston Weathers

Why is it that the one feature most popularly associated with writing is the one most ignored by writing instructors? Many of us who became English majors in college and later pursued careers as professionals in graduate programs did so because of a love for the written word, that feeling of magic and mystery that overcame us when we read a well-crafted sentence or a perfectly placed word in our favorite book, poem, play, or essay. We wanted our writing to achieve at least some semblance of that magic. We wanted our writing to be beautiful, our language to inspire, our words to mean something to someone. For those of us who became English teachers, perhaps we wanted to help others appreciate a well-wrought sentence or paragraph, to arouse others to be moved by beautiful language. Perhaps we wanted our students to appreciate the beauty of the way John Keats describes a centuries-old urn, the way Virginia Woolf describes the winds and waves during a journey to a distant lighthouse, or the way Toni Morrison relates the pain of a young girl upon being thrust into a terrifying world of racism and hate. Or perhaps we wanted our students to recognize the political power of language, its capacity to lead people to social justice—the way Martin Luther King, in a speech on a hot August day, inspired an entire generation to change the world. Whatever our reasons, all of us at one time or another came across words that stirred us enough to want to make that love of language our life's work.

But many writing teachers since the mid-1980s or so have gravitated away from teaching the actual craft of writing interesting sentences, well-chosen words, or finely tuned paragraphs. Many professionals in the field of composition studies have shunned, it seems, the one feature most read-ers and writers associate with good writing—style. While the public, as well as professors outside of English departments, complain loudly about student writers' lack of stylistic grace and control, many writing teachers devote very little of their courses to direct instruction in style or to analy-sis of stylistic choices. Part of the reason why many instructors neglect to introduce their students to style stems from their misunderstanding of the term and its place within rhetorical education.

In a 2002 opinion piece in *College English*, Peter Elbow makes a call for the field of composition and the field of literary studies to learn from, rather than oppose, one another. Elbow hopes that "both cultures could fully accept that a discipline can be even richer and healthier if it lacks a single-vision center. A discipline based on this multiplex model can better avoid either-or thinking and better foster a spirit of productive catholic pluralism" (544). In the course of this argument, he makes a confession: "I miss elegance." He also misses the fun of playing with language that the field of composition, he insists, has lost. Elbow continues: "I'm sad that the composition tradition seems to assume discursive language as the norm and imaginative, metaphorical language as somehow special or marked or additional. I'd argue that we can't harness students' strongest linguistic and even cognitive powers unless we see imaginative and meta-phorical language as the norm—basic or primal" (536).

Elbow, in other words, misses style. He says as much late in the essay when he suggests a list of traits that the field of composition could learn from literary studies: "And what do I wish people in composition could learn from the culture of literature? More honoring of style, playfulness, fun, pleasure, humor. Better writing—and a more pervasive assumption that even in academic writing, even in prose, we can have playfulness, style, pleasure—even adornment and artifice—without being elitist snobs" (543).

Amen.

Elbow is insisting here that studying and teaching style—and playing with language in both scholarship and the classroom—are by no means an exercise in some type of dainty humanism for a few privileged souls, or dull regurgitation of rules. No. Rather, Elbow is suggesting that the study and teaching of style should reside at the very heart of what we should do as composition teachers—instruction in the craft, the skill, and the infinite richness of language. And, I would add, the teaching of style, the playing around with words, the messing around with metaphorical language is conducive, not adverse, to academic writing and to socially responsible writing instruction. But how did the field of composition find itself in this state? What is it about the condition of composition studies at the beginning of the twenty-first century that could lead Elbow to make such a confession? One answer to this question is that compositionists over the last twenty years or so have regarded style as a throwaway element of writing pedagogy, an element that has less to do with knowledge building and more to do with mere surface correctness. Many of these scholars operate within a linear narrative that assumes more complex writing theories supersede less complicated ideas about composing. A review of a key moment in composition and rhetoric's more recent past, the early process movement, will show that their multifaceted approaches to stylistics is not as simplistic as has been previously imagined.

STYLE AND THE EARLY PROCESS MOVEMENT

This desire for disciplinary status in composition studies has led to a tension between the desire to tackle what John C. Gerber, in the very first issue of *College Composition and Communication* (CCC) in 1950, called the "practical needs of the professions" and the desire to elevate its "professional standards" (12). In her essay "Reading—and Rereading—the Braddock Essays," Lisa Ede reflects on the early days of the CCCC conference and of its journal, CCC. Ede recognizes that this tension informed much of the work during the early process years:

> Service to colleagues, students, and society—or progress as a scholarly discipline? Since the inception of the CCCC, many have believed that it is possible and necessary to achieve both goals. Indeed, many have hoped not only to achieve these goals but also to contribute broadly to progressive values and practices—to function, in other words, as agents of social, political, and economic changes. . . . Beliefs such as these have marked the field as transgressive within the academy, even as many in the field have worked to acquire accoutrements of traditional disciplinarity "such" accoutrements as graduate programs and specialized journals, conferences, and associations (all of which have had the effect of extending the scholarly and professional enterprise of composition beyond the domains of the CCCC and CCC) (1999, 11).

Ever since, the field of composition has been working through the tensions among its service mission, its agenda for social reform, and its desire for professional status. The early process movement of the 1960s and 1970s, in many ways, was an attempt "to achieve both goals," as Ede put it. The sense was that in studying how students learned to write, writing teachers could accomplish the two goals at once—one, discover practical, usable pedagogical methods to teach writing more effectively and two, build a body of research and methods of inquiry that could serve as the foundation for composition studies. These two results combined led the way for social reform.

Out of this work, style became an important aspect of writing pedagogy during the days of the early process movement. Style was often seen as a tool of writing instruction in which students could learn various writing strategies and learn to conceive of writing as choice. Certain composition-ists drew from several areas of inquiry to develop pedagogies that used style as a key element of teaching writing: Ken Macrorie wrote a text-book, *Telling Writing* (1970), in which he encouraged students to break out of the routine of writing dull, monotonous prose—which he termed "Engfish" – and stretch their writing legs by using journals and analyzing word choice in an effort to make connections between language use and personal experience; and Peter Elbow published such works as *Writing without Teachers* (1973) and *Writing with Power* (1981), in which he pro-vided numerous writing exercises and prompts in an effort to encourage people to think of themselves as writers, to break through the convention-al roadblocks of traditional grammar instruction and drill exercises, and to write with vividness and magic. In many ways, these teachers were offer-ing alternatives to the tradition-bound constraints of grammar instruction and the focus on surface error that process pedagogy also countered. For these teachers and scholars, the teaching of style formed the centerpiece of writing pedagogy, a type of pedagogy that connected language acquisi-tion to its contexts.

Francis Christensen, for instance, drew from a background in linguis-tics to develop a method of teaching writing that focused on sentence- and paragraph-level writing instruction. Edward P. J. Corbett looked to the recovery of classical rhetorical texts as sources for the teaching of style. And Winston Weathers examined alternative writing styles as a way of teaching students to resist dominant, oppressive forms of language. Although these scholars drew from different sources and backgrounds, they all used studies in style as a gateway for students to become more sophisticated and proficient users of language.

Unfortunately, their work has not always been remembered in that way. In 1991, *The Politics of Writing Instruction: Postsecondary*, edited by Richard Bullock and John Trimbur, appeared. This collection features essays on the political implications of teaching writing in college and offers many examples of classrooms influenced by critical pedagogy. Yet, none of these essays says anything about the teaching of style, or even about the teaching of writing in general. That same year, Patricia Harkin and John Schilb published their collection titled *Contending with Words,* a series of essays that explores the role of composition studies in a postmodern world. As the introduction attests, this collection is "for college and university teachers of English who believe that the study of composition and rhetoric is not merely the service component of the English department, but also an inquiry into cultural values" (1991, 3). Again, nothing on style or on teaching the craft of writing appears in its pages. On the contrary, one of the essays, John Clifford's "The Subject in Discourse," regards the teaching of craft as antithetical to teaching critical pedagogy. Clifford argues that institutions of education, including writing classrooms, are subservient to dominant ideologies. He criticizes such composition textbooks as *St. Martin's Handbook* that make assumptions about apolitical subjectivity based on "romantic" notions of the individual writer. Clifford concludes: "We should do the intellectual work we know best: helping students to read and write and think in ways that both resist domination and exploitation and encourage self consciousness about who they are and can be in the social world" (1991, 51).

What strikes me about Clifford's argument is the dichotomy he establishes between teaching writing as a service and teaching writing as critical literacy. Clifford appears to suggest that teaching skills such as diction, sentence structure, and paragraph organization contradict the goals of teaching students that writing is a site "where hegemony and democracy are contested, where subject positions are constructed, where power and resistance are enacted, where hope for a just society depends on our committed intervention" (1991, 51). If we see style merely as a prescriptive set of colonizing rules—as Clifford argues such books as *St. Martin's Handbook* do—then, yes, it can be very destructive. But style is more than just a set of colonizing rules. Style can find a space within critical pedagogy.

Ten years later, Gary Tate, Amy Ruppier, and Kurt Schick edited a series of essays entitled *A Guide to Composition Pedagogies,* in which the only mention of style comes in William Covino's essay on "Rhetorical Pedagogy." Here, Covino refers to style only in his review of how Ramus placed it under "Rhetoric" as part of his method. These three collections of essays on writing pedagogy ignore completely the teaching of style as a viable element of writing pedagogy in the post-process era.

This dismissal suggests that the teaching of style has been ignored over the last twenty years, with many believing the work of the early process-movement compositionists to be "uncritical" or worse, elitist. But as a rereading of Christensen, Corbett, and Weathers will show, their work in style encourages students to become sophisticated language users and, in some instances, to resist dominant forms of discourse. In some ways, these collections had an unforeseen effect: while they were successful at articulating the political nature of writing instruction, they did so at the expense of lumping some early composition scholars into a collective heap that labeled their work as devoid of contextual concerns. In other words, those of us who came of age in composition and rhetoric graduate programs during the mid- to late 1990s, in the wake of "the social turn," often assumed that the work of scholars such as Christensen, Corbett, and Weathers was oversimplistic, too surface-oriented, and apolitical.

FRANCIS CHRISTENSEN'S GENERATIVE RHETORIC

Francis Christensen was a composition and language scholar who was interested in discovering ways for students to write sentences and para-graphs in the manner of professional writers. His hope was that teachers could introduce the composing of sentences and paragraphs to their students in a fashion that would lead students to generate ideas at the same time that they learn new and varied writing strategies. Christensen called this idea "generative rhetoric," and he developed it in a pair of articles for CCC—"The Generative Rhetoric of the Sentence" (1963) and "The Generative Rhetoric of the Paragraph" (1965)—and later in a longer work, *Notes toward a New Rhetoric* (1967; I cite from the second edition of 1978). Christensen's method of using generative rhetoric to help students develop their style while inventing ideas in their writing at the same time enjoyed a brief period of popularity during the 1960s and 1970s.

"We need," he wrote, " a rhetoric of the sentence that will do more than combine the ideas of primer sentences. We need one that will generate ideas" (1978, 26). Rather than teach students how to develop sentences based on traditional classifications, such as loose, balanced, or periodic sentences, or on traditional grammatical structures—simple, compound, complex—Christensen's method asks students to examine the ideas expressed in the sentences and then rephrase the idea in a more effective way. In "The Generative Rhetoric of the Sentence," Christensen develops the idea of the "cumulative sentence," in which ideas are generated by student writers who add modifying words and phrases to their sentences, either before, after, or within the main clause of the sentence. The words or phrases that modify the base clause can have either a subordinate or coordinate relationship to the base clause. In other words, Christensen sees the sentence not as a simple list of words that convey ideas. The sentence, he says, " is dynamic rather than static, representing the mind thinking." He adds that "the mere form of the sentence generates ideas" (p. 28). For Christensen, therefore, instruction in sentence development is not a static exercise but is the very way writers construct meaning in their texts.

Christensen suggested that students practice studying multiple sentence types to recognize how meaning is developed by the addition of various clauses and clusters. Again, his assumption here is not for students to develop stylistic flourish and confidence in a decontextualized environment. Rather, he stressed that these exercises give students more options for their own compositions, as well as help them develop into stronger readers. In "The Generative Rhetoric of the Sentence," Christensen argues that his exercises go beyond decontextualized drill and provide students with the tools they need to develop confidence in their reading of texts and in their writing:

> What I am proposing carries over of itself into the study of literature. It makes the student a better reader of literature. It helps him thread the syntactical mazes of much mature writing, and it gives him insight into that elusive thing we call style. Last year, a student told me of rereading a book by her favorite author, Willa Cather, and of realizing for the first time why she liked reading her: she could understand and appreciate the style. For some students, moreover, such writing makes life more interesting as well as giving them a way to share their interest with others. When they learn to put concrete details into a sentence, they begin to look at life with more alertness (1978, 37–38).

Here, Christensen makes the connection between instruction in style and instruction in larger, contextual factors that go into language learning. He insists that classroom focus on the stylistics of language allows students to make connections between their writing and their reading and, in the process, leads them to be able to make larger connections that go beyond the classroom.

Christensen's idea of coordinate and subordinate combine to create what he terms "cumulative sentences." In other words, students create new sentences and phrases at the same time they develop new ideas for composition. So, in a very concrete way, Christensen's rhetoric of the sentence is not merely a tool to develop style but is an invention technique as well. His rhetoric encourages student writers to examine their thoughts and the meanings that their words convey. Christensen's ideas provide students with a way to make their writing more textured, more rich, and less threadbare. They will create and make meaning as they write more complex sentences. Christensen points out the difference between teaching the cumulative sentence and teaching the periodic sentence, a type of sentence that combines a number of thoughts and statements in a number of balanced clauses. Christensen notes that the cumulative sentence is a more effective sentence for composition instruction because of its capacity to be used as a tool of invention:

> The cumulative sentence is the opposite of the periodic sentence. It does not represent the idea as conceived, pondered over, reshaped, packaged, and delivered cold. It is dynamic rather than static, representing the mind thinking . . . . The additions stay with the same idea, probing its bearings and implications, exemplifying it or seeking an analogy or metaphor for it. . . . Thus the mere form of the sentence generates ideas. It serves the needs of both writer and reader, the writer by compelling him to examine his thought, the reader by letting him into the writer's thought (28).

As students work and grapple with the base clause by adding modifiers and other clauses to it, they generate ideas. These ideas expand on the basic idea conveyed in the main clause and, in the process, lead students to develop and engage additional ideas. Christensen's rhetoric of the sentence, in many ways, hearkens back to Quintilian's call for *facilitas* with language, because the generative nature of cumulative sentences allow student writers to work with and play around with language in a manner that provides students with numerous options and choices. This generative quality is ethical and political, not merely formal and apolitical.

Here's a student example where additional description, via subordinate clauses, adds to the generative quality of the writing in a way that provides additional options for composing:

the hospital was set for night running,
   smooth and silent, (A + A)
   its normal clatter and hum muffled, (Abs)
   the only sounds heard in the white walled room distant and unreal: (Abs)

> a low hum of voices from the nurses' desk, (NC)
> quickly stifled, (VC)
> the soft squish of rubber-soled shoes on the tiled corridor, (NC)
> starched white cloth rustling against itself, (NC)
> and, outside, the lonesome whine of wind in the country night (NC) and the Kansas dust beating against the windows. (NC). (34)

Here, the student sets the scene for the reader: a hospital at night. One by one, the writer adds additional clauses that not only add description of the setting, but also add possibilities for new ideas and circumstances: the "low hum of voices" introducing characters, the "lonesome whine" suggesting a certain mood and atmosphere, "the Kansas dust" bringing in geographical possibilities. In other words, the student has a long sentence in which a series of events and circumstances can be further invented and developed in a manner that leads the student to more mature compositions and to a more mature style.

Christensen's generative method has not been completely forgotten. It is featured prominently in two popular handbooks for first-time teachers of composition: *The St. Martin's Guide to Teaching Writing*, edited by Robert Connors and Cheryl Glenn (1995), and Erika Lindemann's *A Rhetoric for Writing Teachers* (1995). Both texts feature chapters that introduce composition instructors to teaching style, sentences, and paragraphs. But, while Christensen's rhetoric has found a space in these popular handbooks, it seems to me that his placement in these texts merely reinforces the popular critiques of his work—that his theories about rhetoric succeed for the more mundane, uncritical work of actually teaching writing and have nothing to do with the social context surrounding students' writing experiences. For example, *The St. Martin's Guide* relegates Christensen to the back of its text in a chapter titled "Teaching the Sentence and the Paragraph." This chapter comes after lengthy chapters on invention and arrangement. Their placement of Christensen's rhetoric suggests that his rhetoric of the sentence and paragraph should be reserved for matters of composition outside of invention and arrangement, or other elements where ideas may be discovered. Rather, assumptions at play in *The St. Martin's Guide* hold that Christensen's method is a prescriptive one that teaches students rigid form without exploring the tension between form and content. In *The St. Martin's Guide,* the editors write that Christensen's generative rhetoric reinforces a mechanistic, surface-driven pedagogy:

Should you become uncomfortable with the prescriptive nature of any of the approaches in this chapter, you are not alone. We all may worry that in condensing writing to discrete, mechanical formulas, we are taking away from more than we are giving. But be assured that with continued reading and practice in writing, your students should eventually transcend rigid, formal rules. In the final analysis, a grasp of the rules seldom holds anyone down and, when understood correctly, can help keep one up (Connors and Glenn 1995, 262).

On the one hand, Connors and Glenn recognize that sentence rhetorics like Christensen's are useful in teaching a student to write. On the other hand, they assume that Christensen's methods reinforce "rigid, formal rules," and are "discrete, mechanical formulas" that are to be learned and then quickly advanced upon. Christensen's call for a generative rhetoric of the sentence and the paragraph gets at the very heart of the tension between form and content and, in the process, provides students with tools to develop syntactic maturity while, at the same time, they develop ideas to write about.

EDWARD P. J. CORBETT AND CLASSICAL STYLE

Corbett was among a coterie of scholars who rediscovered and made available to writing teachers classical rhetorical texts during the 1960s and 1970s. His first article for CCC was titled "The Usefulness of Classical Rhetoric" (1963). In his preface to *Classical Rhetoric for the Modern Student,* Corbett connects his interest in classical rhetoric to the preparation of students for civic participation. It is acknowledged that a knowledge of rhetoric helps citizens defend against demagogues and other "exploiters of specious arguments, half-truths, and rank emotional appeals to gain personal advantage rather than to promote the public welfare" (1990, 30).

Style, of course, played a significant role in Corbett's recovery of classical rhetoric. For Corbett, style was not simply a matter of writing pretty language for the sake of artifice but was interwoven with discovering ideas and creating textual choices. In his textbook on rhetoric, Corbett connects style to Aristotle's definition of rhetoric:[1] "Style does provide a vehicle for thought, and style can be ornamental; but style is something more than that. It is another one of the 'available means of persuasion,' another of the means of arousing appropriate emotional response in the audience, and of the means of establishing the proper ethical image" (1990, 381).

He dismissed the notion that style is merely "dressed up thought," and tried to remind the field that classical rhetoricians also rejected the idea that style is mere ornament, noting that "none of the prominent classical rhetoricians—Isocrates, Aristotle, Demetrius, Longinus, Cicero, Quintilian—ever preached such a doctrine" (1990, 381). But again, many in the field did not perceive these classical rhetoricians in this way—due in large part to the types of histories that were being written, as well as composition's desire to define itself differently from its classical predecessors.[2] Corbett understood that how something is written directly affects what is being conveyed in the writing. "A writer must be in command of a variety of styles," Corbett asserted, "in order to draw on the style that is most appropriate to the situation" (1990, 381). He stressed that the modern student could become a better writer by focusing primarily on invention.

In "The Usefulness of Classical Rhetoric" Corbett reminds readers that imitation is not merely slavish copying of someone else's style but rather the study and adaptation of multiple styles that assist students in gathering the "available means."

> Many of our students need exercise in constructing their own sentence patterns. They can be assisted in acquiring this skill by such exercises as merely copying passages of sophisticated prose, constructing their own sentences according to models, varying sentence patterns. The term imitation suggests to some people the attempt to encourage students to acquire someone else's style. Such a view betrays a total misunderstanding of what the rhetoricians meant by imitation and what they hoped to accomplish by it. (1963, 163).

In *Classical Rhetoric for the Modern Student,* Corbett put together a series of imitation exercises to help students develop an eloquent style. The point here is for students to draw from a whole host of prose styles and not focus solely on one style. Here, Corbett echoes the suggestion of Erasmus nearly five hundred years earlier, who implored students at St. Paul's not to imitate Cicero only but to draw from other writers as well. Corbett provides examples from a wide range of authors and prose styles, including the Bible, John Dryden, Edward Gibbon, Mary Wollstonecraft, Abraham Lincoln, James Baldwin, Susan Sontag, Alice Walker, and Toni Morrison, to name only a few. Corbett stresses that students who imitate writers do so with a pen or pencil, copying and imitating the authors slowly, paying attention to the sentence structure and placement of words. He encourages students to focus on a single passage each day, rather than try to cram many different passages into a single day's work. "You must have time to absorb what you have been observing in this exercise," Corbett advises, "and you will not have time to absorb the many lessons to be learned from this exercise if you cram it into a short period" (1990, 476).

After students copy passages, Corbett suggests they move toward imitation proper. He recommends that students begin with simple sentences and work up to more complex sentences and eventually to imitation of entire passages. Corbett wants students to use these imitation exercises to introduce novice writers to the complexity and variety of professional prose styles. "The aim of this exercise," Corbett cautions, "is not to achieve a word-for-word correspondence with the model but rather to achieve an awareness of the variety of sentence structures of which the English language is capable . . . writing such patterns according to models will increase [students'] syntactical resources" (Corbett 1990, 495). Again, Corbett supplies a variety of sample sentences for students to imitate. Corbett also draws from Erasmus's method of expressing an idea in multiple ways. "Devising an alternate expression," Corbett notes, "often involves the choice of different words and different syntactical structures" (498). Here, he models several sentences, showing variations of the sentence patterns as well as an alternate way to express the idea in a different style. Again, the purpose here, much like in copying other authors' prose, is to be introduced to a variety of styles and to practice imitating and studying the sentence structure of various writers.

Corbett's work on style is viewed as part of composition's past that should we should acknowledge but move on from. Many compositionists today regard Corbett's work as part of the preprofessionalization era of composition studies, work that is not as exciting, as innovative, or as complex as the post-process era. I find it interesting, as Connors notes in his introduction to *Style and Statement* (Corbett and Connors 1999), that the individuals who find Corbett's work on style the most relevant are high school and college composition instructors, individuals who struggle every day with teaching students the actual craft of writing. I find this confession interesting because it suggests that the professionalization of rhetoric and composition has led scholars in the field away from the business of teaching writing. Indeed, many of us who came to the field in the mid- to late 1990s assumed Corbett's work on style was part of a distant past that did not speak to the more "complex" issues of composition: postmodern identity, the negotiation of difference, and discourse communities, to name only a few. For example, during my first graduate seminar on the teaching of writing, our instructor introduced us to Corbett's method of analyzing prose style. This method asks students to count the number of sentences in an essay and identify their type—simple, complex, and so on—and count the number of words in each sentence. The rationale behind such an exercise is to determine the readability of a piece of writing and to determine areas for possible revision and editing. As we sat in the seminar listening to the instructor and applying this method to our own writing sample, I noticed most of us—budding composition and rhetoric scholars—resisting this exercise by rolling our eyes, grumbling under our breaths—in general, not taking it very seriously. Later, during our break, one of my class colleagues complained bitterly in the hallway that the exercise was a total waste of time, that it was too hard. At the time, I tended to agree. How does counting sentences help students write? What we failed to understand then, and what many of us still fail to recognize, is that Corbett's pedagogy of style is not some series of surface-oriented exercises, but rather lies at the very heart of what rhetorical education attempts to provide: the ability in individuals to write eloquently and responsibly within numerous contexts, whether they be personal, academic, or public.

Corbett's work on style, and his insistence that style should be taught within the realm of the whole rhetorical canon, came out of his reading and recovery of classical rhetorical texts—namely, Aristotle, Cicero, and Quintilian. His ideas about style have a decidedly Western canonical bent to them and, as a result, Corbett's stylistic exercises do not cross the line into what we might think of as radical or alternative styles. But there is another scholar whose work attempts to break through traditional stylistic boundaries who has gone largely unrecognized for the past ten to fifteen years—Winston Weathers.

WINSTON WEATHERS: AN ALTERNATIVE

Weathers, a writing teacher and scholar from the 1960s and 1970s, overtly sought alternative styles and radical approaches to teaching writing. He published such titles as *A New Strategy of Style* (1978, with Otis Winchester) and *Alternative Style: Options in Composition* (1980). Weathers was interested in exploring a pedagogy of style that would lead students to resist dominant modes of discourse and write alternative prose styles. For Weathers, the teaching of style was itself a revolutionary act, which could lead to critical thinking against dominant forms of communication. One way that Weathers urged writing teachers and students to resist these dominant discourses was through the development of different styles, noting that "we can point out that with the acquisition of a plurality of styles (and we are after pluralities, aren't we? not just the plain style?) the student is equipping himself for a more adaptive way of life within a society increasingly complex and multifaceted" (2000, 295).

He encouraged writing teachers to use style as a tool to break through rigid systems and to teach writing that was more socially responsible, writing that took into consideration multiple styles and not just the socially sanctioned conventional style prevalent in most American writing classrooms. Alternative styles, for Weathers, was a place where most writers—professional and nonprofessional alike—wrote. In a 1996 interview with Wendy Bishop, Weathers reflects on the inspiration for his 1980 book, *An Alternative Style: Options in Composition.*

> I'd long noticed that much of the great literature I was teaching was not written in the traditional straight/linear mode. I'd noticed, too, that out in the "real world," a great many of the messages presented in advertising, publicity, promotion, in personal letters, journals, diaries, and even in more daring book reviews, testimonials, meditations, etc. were using writing techniques that no one in the nation's English departments seemed to be teaching. The Academy occasionally acknowledged the existence of "experimental writing" but never suggested that ordinary writers might also practice something like it. My goal in writing *An Alternative Style* was simply to say to students (and their teachers) that there's more to writing than the style usually found in the Freshman theme, the second semester research report, or the graduate literary essay. (Bishop and Weathers 1996, 76)

Style, for Weathers, is by no means some rigid, cold, mechanistic tool used to teach inflexible conventions of writing. For Weathers, style becomes a place where all people use language in fresh, inventive ways, ways that can be recast and used in socially responsible and democratic contexts. The rigid systems that Weathers recognized in most English departments needed to be challenged. One of those systems, of course, was the tradition of style as a surface-oriented tool of writing instruction that had been reinforced in the history of writing instruction since the Renaissance.

In an article originally published in CCC in 1970, "Teaching Style: A Possible Anatomy," Weathers argued that for the teaching of style to be a viable element of writing pedagogy, instructors must accomplish three tasks:

(1)   make the teaching of style significant and relevant to our students,

(2)   reveal style as a measurable and viable subject matter, and

(3)   make style believable and real as a result of our own stylistic practices (2000, 294).

Weathers's call for a richer pedagogy of style is significant because he assumes an integration of style in all forms of writing instruction and not just a technique for editing or polishing students' prose. For example, he writes that students need a strategy of style so that they can accomplish two objectives in literacy acquisition, by "(1) identifying the categories of style, and (2) describing the constituency of those categories in terms of stylistic material" (2000, 297). In other words, Weathers wants teachers to incorporate the study of style into the larger purpose of writing instruction in a way that allows the student to develop a variety of prose styles to use in multiple rhetorical situations. Weathers follows much of the same ideas about imitation that Corbett learned from the classical rhetoricians and that Erasmus encouraged students in the sixteenth century to practice. "We ask the student to write a sentence or a topic of his own choosing, but following the model he has just studied," Weathers writes. "In this process, the student is asked to recognize, copy, understand, and imitate creatively" (2000, 296–97). For Weathers, style becomes the very way students use language to make meaning in their worlds. The more styles students experiment with, Weathers argues, the more able they are to resist dominant structures of language and use language more democratically.

One of the more telling moments in this article occurs when Weathers associates alternative styles with democracy. Here, Weathers articulates the role that the teaching of style can play in a liberating pedagogy that teaches students to become responsible users of language:

> Style is a gesture of personal freedom against inflexible states of mind; that in a very real way—because it is the art of choice and option—style has something to do with freedom; that as systems—rhetorical or political—become rigid and dictatorial, style is reduced, unable to exist in totalitarian environments. We can reveal to students the connection between democracy and style, saying that the study of style is a part of our democratic and free experience. And finally we can point out that with the acquisition of a plurality of styles (and we are after pluralities, aren't we? not just the plain style?) the student is equipping himself for a more adaptive way of life within a society increasingly complex and multifaceted (2000, 295).

Even though Weathers is counseling writing teachers to resist rigid systems of writing instruction and encourage their students to write in a variety of styles, his caution against the totalitarianism of systems applies to the way histories are embraced and eventually become unyielding systems in their own right. Questioning the received history of style allows current composition scholars to break through a system of instruction that consigns style to a rigid, surface-only concern. Weathers wants the teaching of style to be much more. He argues that teachers of writing can show the connections between style and democracy to their students, encouraging them to practice and study multiple verbalizations. Weathers pushes students to play with multiple styles in a manner that could suggest stretching the boundaries of traditional stylistic grounds. In other words, it may lead them on a path toward recognizing how multiple styles are representative of multiple points of view—indeed, the very essence of democracy.

Weathers wants students to recognize and be able to incorporate a plurality of styles. Such plurality, Weathers insists, is necessary for educating students to become vital participants in a democracy. "We can reveal to students the connection between democracy and style," he writes, "saying that the study of style is part of our democratic and free experience" (2000, 295). Weathers wrote this call for an integrated pedagogy of style during a time when American society was being reminded of its own plurality in the form of the protest against the war in Vietnam, the civil rights movement, and the second-wave feminist movement. Such movements, of course, were particularly popular on college campuses. There, students were searching for ways to connect what they were learning in the classroom with their concerns for social justice. Weathers's call to make style, and writing itself, more relevant in students' lives shows how his work on style was not some exercise in getting students to prettify their language but rather to discover the richness of language and its uses in a democracy. "Many students write poorly and with deplorable styles simply because they do not care," Weathers insists (2000, 295). Weathers simply wanted to make writing more relevant to student experience.

In 1980, Weathers published *An Alternative Style: Options in Composition*. The purpose of this textbook, as Weathers notes in the preface, is to provide student writers with ways to develop a varied prose style. "And so this book," he writes. "Ready to be shared—as we become aware of more mentalities than one (left brain/right brain if nothing else), aware of more compositional goals than one, more life-styles than one, more human chemistries than one, more 'voices' than one" (2000, preface). Weathers wants student writers to be able to move in and out of different writing situations and adjust their writing styles accordingly, without being beholden to any one, dominant mode of writing. "I write for many reasons," he notes, "to communicate many things. And yet, much of what I wish to communicate does not seem to be expressible within the ordinary conventions of composition as I have learned them and mastered them in the long years of my education" (1). In an e-mail conversation with Wendy Bishop, almost twenty years after he published *An Alternative Style,* Weathers echoes his desire for teaching student writers multiple styles. "A good writer—like a good architect—should know how to design and build all kinds of structures: traditional, art deco, baroque, functional, etc," he declares. "Who knows what 'content' requirements will be presented to us day after day? A concern with style is a concern with being prepared to build the best composition we can whatever the content happens to be" (Bishop and Weathers 1996, p.75). And encouraging students to build the best compositions they can forms the focus of Weathers's interest in style.

In *Alternative Style,* Weathers offers a short explanation of his theory of alternative style and a variety of rhetorical devices and strategies that professional writers use to develop new and interesting styles. For Weathers, an alternate style means any type of style that seeks to go beyond tradition-bound notions of "good writing" in the effort to construct the best piece of writing possible. He distinguishes between what he calls Grammar A and Grammar B. Grammar A, according to Weathers, is the "traditional" grammar or instruction in style in most writing classrooms, which "has the characteristics of continuity, order, reasonable progression and sequence, consistency, unity, etc. We are all familiar with these characteristics, for they are promoted in nearly every English textbook and taught by nearly every English teacher" (1980, 6). Grammar B, on the other hand, seeks to expand Grammar A's rigidity and open students to alternative ways to express themselves. "It is a mature and alternate (not experimental) style used by competent writers and offering students of writing a well-tested set of options that, added to the traditional grammar of style, will give them a much more flexible voice, a much greater communication capacity, a much greater opportunity to put into effective language all the things they have to say" (Weathers 1980, 8). Later, Weathers describes a number of characteristics of Grammar B and does so in a manner that allows users of the book to apply them to their own writing—some tricks of the trade, as it were.[3]

What's important to keep in mind about Weathers's theory of Grammar A and Grammar B is that they are not mutually exclusive. Grammar B, for Weathers, is an expansion of Grammar A. He does not want to keep his students away from learning and understanding the dimensions of Grammar A. Not at all. He wants them to be able to break away from the conventions of Grammar A and become more imaginative and creative with their style, based on what the rhetorical constraints are. "Grammar B in no way threatens Grammar A," he insists. "It uses the same stylistic deck of fifty-two cards and embraces the same English language we are familiar with. Acknowledging its existence and discovering how it works and including it in our writing expertise, we simply become better teachers of writing, making a better contribution to the intellectual and emotional lives of our students" (1980, 8). Here, Weathers echoes Aristotle's definition of rhetoric as being the ability to discover the available means of persuasion. Grammar B becomes another of the available means. Playing around with and using crots, for example, allow student writers to find connections among ideas where they may not have looked before. His double-voice technique encourages students to examine ideas from various perspectives, while working on the stylistic features of their writing. Weathers's desire for student writers to develop multiple, even subversive, writing strategies also echoes Erasmus's call for teaching students to express ideas in a variety of ways. Students who incorporate Weathers's suggestions for labyrinthine sentences and sentence fragments, alongside the more traditional sentences of Grammar A, give themselves more options for phrasing ideas in new and interesting ways.

Weathers has largely been forgotten among many rhetoric and composition specialists. Although his essay "Teaching Style: A Possible Anatomy" appears in the latest edition of the perennially popular *The Writing Teacher's Sourcebook* (Corbett, Tate, and Myers 2000), most compositionists have ignored his work. Wendy Bishop notes that his "work didn't seem to be half as influential as I thought it should be" (Weathers and Bishop 1996, 72). His work is rarely, if ever, cited in the pages of CCC or *College English* anymore, and his textbooks are out of print. Graduate programs in composition and rhetoric rarely include Weathers's work as part of the curriculum or reading lists. It almost appears as if Weathers's work has disappeared completely.

Weathers himself tells stories of how the field resisted vehemently his theories and ideas about the teaching of style (see the epigraph to this chapter). Weathers also tells the story of how he was received by his colleagues during his keynote address at the 1982 CCCC convention in San Francisco, a city Bishop, in a delicious moment of irony, calls "the city of alternative styles" (Weathers and Bishop 1996, 79):

It was, in effect, boycotted. I was invited to give the address by Donald Stewart. . . . He had read some of my work, had written about it in an article, which led to some correspondence, which led to the invitation. He was the CCCC program chairman at the time, as I remember. Alas, though the conference attendance was large, I gave the address to about fifty people—in a vast, cavernous Hyatt Regency ballroom that would have held a thousand. It was obvious that the title of the address, or my reputation perhaps, had led vast numbers of people to stay away. (79)

That was twenty years ago, and it seems safe to say that Weathers's reputation has not changed much. My sense is that Weathers has been lumped into a group of compositionists—including Christensen and Corbett—whose work on style and rhetoric runs counter to the goals of critical and creative thinking espoused by the proponents of critical pedagogy.

As the 1970s turned into the 1980s, and social construction theories of composition slowly took precedence in composition programs and on the pages of composition journals, the stylistic and sentence-level pedagogies of Christensen, Corbett, and Weathers came under fire. Robert Connors argues that many of their critics pointed out that sentence-level rhetorics like Christensen's "were quintessentially exercises, context-stripped from what students really wanted to say themselves" (Connors 2000, 115). James Britton, for example, called such writing exercises "dummy runs," and condemned such writing instruction for its lack of contextual awareness, arguing that a student writer should be "called upon to perform a writing task in order (a) to exercise his capacity to perform that kind of task, and/or (b) to demonstrate to the teacher his proficiency in performing [the writing assignment]" (Britton et al., 1975, 104–5). Sabina Thorne Johnson, a contemporary of Christensen, voiced her critique by questioning Christensen's claim that students can generate ideas by merely adding modifiers to their sentences. In her article "Some Tentative Strictures on Generative Rhetoric," Johnson at first praises Christensen's method for offering a "revolution in our assessment of style and in our approach to the teaching of composition" (1969, 159). But later she wonders why Christensen seems to believe that form can generate content. "I don't believe it can, especially if the content is of an analytic or critical nature" (159). Later A. B. Tibbets chimed in on the complaint against Christensen, noting that the generative rhetoric method led students to produce clever sentences but not much else. Tibbets argues:

"What we are generally after in expository writing is accuracy rather than cleverness" (1976, 144). Tibbets assumes here that interesting sentences can't produce interesting ideas. And he says as much later in his article when he notes that effective writing instruction leads students to separate content from form, as well as divide issues from one another (144). Tibbets's assumptions about the split between form and content resonate with the other critiques of Christensen's rhetoric. What most of these critiques assume, however, is that learning to write eloquent and interesting sentences and paragraphs is somehow antithetical to learning to express ideas effectively.

CONCLUSION

During the early process years of the late 1960s and 1970s, the teaching of style, via Christensen's generative rhetoric, Corbett's recovery of classical rhetoric, and the alternative style of Weathers, shared, along with the process movement, prominence across the composition landscape. As compositionists started to investigate more deeply the various social and political contexts that affect how students learn to write, the focus on stylistics became associated with oversimplistic, decontextualized writing pedagogy. The work of such figures as Christensen, Corbett, and Weathers subsequently became associated with this type of "uncritical" pedagogy. But reassessment of these scholars reveals that their work on style and the sentence was done under the assumption that the more stylistic options were available to students, the more likely that students would be able to demonstrate successful rhetorical activity.

2

WHERE IS STYLE GOING? WHERE HAS IT BEEN?

Elizabeth Weiser

Ron Fortune, in a 1989 article in the journal *Style,* wrote: "While style in composition has experienced the decline that several scholars in the field have noted, work currently being done seems to be laying the foundations for its reemergence as a major concern" (527). Fortune analyzed work from 1965, when Louis Milic's foundational article "Theories of Style and Their Implications for the Teaching of Composition" appeared in *College Composition and Communication,* through the "paradigm shift" from product to process orientation that Maxine Hairston chronicled in 1982, to the then cutting-edge use of "style checkers" in word processing discussed by Randy Smye in *Computers and Composition* in 1988. Style, Fortune believed, was on the cusp of developing the two things it most needed to regain its prominent role in the field: a theory that positioned style within a generative process model of composition (that is, a model with a focus on making decisions in the drafting of one's text rather than on the correctness of the finished product), and textbooks that employed a generative model in their approach to style to disseminate the theory-driven practice.

Yet the revolution never happened; the reemergence of style never occurred. At conferences, in the journals, the few discussions of style that appear have titles that imply its loss, such as Sharon Myers's recent "ReMembering the Sentence" (2003), and they routinely begin with a defense of style. As to the two elements, textbooks and a theory, that Fortune believed necessary for style to regain its prominence, Sam Burke Martinez's 1997 dissertation study of forty college composition textbooks found that nearly all of them ignored the innovations in style pedagogy that Fortune referred to in favor of a treatment of style (as "accurate" translation of thought) dating to the nineteenth century (288–89). And by 2000, when Robert Connors published "The Erasure of the Sentence," he could point to the felt absence of a theory of style as a leading cause of style's demise in our classrooms—despite considerable empirical evidence of its practical value (118). In fact, by the time Fortune made his optimistic prediction regarding the resurgence of style, its tide had already turned. The "work currently being done" that Fortune described reached its publication zenith in 1980, when thirteen articles dealing with "style" or "stylistics" appeared in the field's major journal, *College Composition and Communication* (CCC). In the intervening nine years until Fortune's article appeared, the average number of articles declined by two-thirds, and in the decade after that, the average dropped to slightly over one article per year.

What happened? In an effort to uncover some of the answers, I examined back issues of CCC for the thirty years from 1973 to 2003, ranking articles on style by research method (the various subcategories of qualitative and quantitative methodologies) and by rhetorical orientation (reader-based or social-constructionist approaches, writer-based or expressivistic-process approaches, and text-focused or current-traditional approaches). While a number of scholars posit the decline of style as resulting from the rise of process pedagogy and the de-emphasis of attention to product, there has been to date no other study looking at the journals themselves and attempting to chronicle the trajectory of style's reemergence from and then resubmergence into obscurity in the field's professional dialogue. What I found suggests that style has indeed been the victim of a turn from product to process, but in a manner more complex than that simple statement implies. And recent examinations of both ancient and modern theories of style may supply the revitalization it needs at exactly this moment in the history of writing instruction.

The first thing one notices about style is the multitude of perspectives it encompasses. If "Style" were the name over the door of a conference room, the conversations going on inside would be quite varied, even mutually exclusive. We all might recognize some of them. Linguists stand in one knot, arguing about transformational-generative grammar and its effect on free modifiers. Rhetoricians shout that the writer's attention to audience is key, while a subgroup keeps offering to teach schemes and tropes in order to reach that audience. Expressivists form a circle and argue with both groups over their belief that style can be taught at all, particularly in the mechanical manner of classical trope analysis. Feminists and multiculturalists hover nearby reminding the expressivists that the style of individual voices means culturally constructed voices. Grammarians nod silently to each other, secretly gloating at how many current-traditionalists remain in the room while bemoaning the current generation's inability to parse a sentence. Style theorists gather in a corner and dream of a unified theory to tie all the conversations together, while empiricists demand to know what more the theorists could want beyond well-documented studies that prove success. Pedagogues, who had entered the room wanting to share what they thought was a pretty good idea they'd tried out in their classrooms, slip away unnoticed, back into the hallway where the literary theorists read the sign on the door and wonder what all the fuss is about, anyway, since the author is dead.

Elizabeth Rankin, in the theorist gathering, proposed in a 1985 article that the first step toward a "revitalized" theory of style had to be "a broad yet workable definition" (12). This lack of a common definition is obvious to anyone attempting to study style: Martinez, for instance, found that textbook definitions ranged from "style is what makes the same lyric and the same melody sound different when sung by Frank Sinatra and Mick Jagger" to "narrow definitions of style as 'objective' or 'academic'" (1997, 2, 203). Rankin offers the definition found in James McCrimmon's *Writing with a Purpose* (McCrimmon, 1984) as what she considers to be the usual parameters for a professional discussion of style: "the pattern of choices the writer makes in developing his or her purpose. If the choices are consistent, they create a harmony of tone and language that constitutes the style of the work. A description of the style of any piece of writing is therefore an explanation of the means by which the writer achieved his or her purpose" (8).

Is this definition "specific enough to distinguish stylistic considerations from other concerns of the writing process" yet "broad and inclusive enough to account for overlap" between these concerns? (Rankin 1985, 12). Could this definition, in other words, be placed on the door to our imaginary conference room and accommodate everyone inside while keeping out those who wanted to mix up the issues? Apparently not, for the first thing I discovered in my search for style articles published in CCC in the past thirty years is that each of the databases cataloguing the journal indexes "style or stylistics" quite differently. In a search of the ERIC, MLA, and COMPPILE databases for articles that included the keywords "style" or "stylistics," only six of eighty articles were listed in all three sites, and all had "style" or "stylistics" as a part of their title.[1] In addition to including all eighty articles that appeared in any of the three databases, therefore, I also examined each issue of the journal myself, adding another thirty-eight articles that clearly dealt with style issues yet were not included in any database. (All 118 articles are given in the appendix.) Examples of these latter range from Sternglass's "Dialect Features in the Compositions

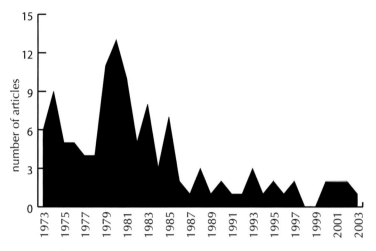

Figure 1. Style Articles per Year, 1973 to 2003.

of Black and White College Students" (1974) to D'Angelo's "The Topic Sentence Revisited" (1986) to Skorczewski's "'Everybody Has Their Own Ideas': Responding to Cliché in Student Writing" (2000). Again, it is clear that "style" as a category is very broad, and the working definition I used for this study, "purposeful attention to language at the sentence level" (a distillation of McCrimmon with a sentence emphasis to distinguish it from form), made it especially so. Thus, with such an inclusive definition of what I would accept as a "style article," it was interesting to find that fewer and fewer articles, as time went on, could fit into the category.

Let us first look at the 118 articles overall. It is clear from figure 1 that the watershed period for the reemergence of style in the professional journals lasted from 1979 to 1985.

During those seven years, nearly half (49 percent, or 58) of all the style articles for the entire thirty years were published. Indeed, if we divide the thirty years studied in half, 80 percent (94) of the articles were published in the first half of the period, from 1973 to 1987. In the past decade, only 13 articles have been published that deal with style in any manner, approximately the same number as were published in 1980 alone. While the total number of articles published per issue in CCC has also declined (as articles have increased dramatically in length), the percentage of style articles has fallen more drastically. For instance, in 1980, 37 percent (13 of 35) of all the articles published in CCC dealt in some way with style. In 2002, 10 percent (2 of 20) dealt with style. In the years 1998 and 1999, no articles whatsoever were written about style. Clearly, stylistic concerns, at least in the professional journal that guides the dialogue, are an obscure topic today.

THE RISE AND FALL OF STYLE

Why has the interest in style lessened? In part the problem springs from an ancient debate. John Gage, in his 1980 article, "Philosophies of Style and Their Implications for Composition," noted that style can be considered simultaneously as a linguistic, a rhetorical, or a philosophical concept. Linguistic concepts of style place an emphasis on grammar norms and deviations; rhetorical concepts place an emphasis on the choice of stylistic devices and their effects on the audience; philosophical concepts place an emphasis on language and the nature of reality. Another way to name these three concepts—and one in keeping with lines of argument that run through the history of style—is to say that linguistic stylists have been chiefly concerned with perspicuity (clarity), rhetorical stylists have been chiefly concerned with kairos (fitness for the occasion), and philosophical stylists have been chiefly concerned with the mimetic or nonmimetic relationship of language to reality. Thus, early rhetors such as Isocrates promised to teach young Athenians the ability to discern the proper mode of speech for their occasion, nineteenth-century rhetors such as Newman and Day taught increasing numbers of middle-class university students the benefits of the "plain style" for business discourse, and twentieth-century rhetors such as Richards and Burke recaptured a lost tradition reaching all the way back to Gorgias of Leontini to argue that style was not the ability to choose words that most accurately mirrored one's thoughts, but was instead the attitude that one brought, unbidden, to any description.

Thus, when, in the mid-1960s, the debate over stylistic pedagogies flared up in composition with the publication of several articles by Milic, the questions he raised represented modern versions of ancient arguments. Milic viewed New Critical pedagogies focusing on the uniqueness of each writer's syntax and diction as a problem for the teaching of style. As Milic wrote, "This curious reluctance to be specific and concrete, to admit that style is first of all made up of certain kinds of linguistic units, betrays a distrust of available methods of discussing style" (1966, 129). We can see here the renewal of the nineteenth-century debate between stylistic linguists such as Henry N. Day and mimetic philosophers such as Walter Pater and J. F. Genung (for more on this, see Crowley 1986). For Milic and his colleagues, the rise of expressivism in the 1970s and 1980s only exacerbated the trend away from style. Such an approach Milic categorized as "monistic," a view of style as the unique and accurate representation of the writer's creative "vision" (1965, 67)—(for examples, see Kelly 1974 or Linn 1975). Those who followed this approach (Peter Elbow is mentioned) and celebrated the writer's "voice" were labeled by Frank D'Angelo as the "new romantics" (D'Angelo, 1975).

In contrast to the monistic, new romantic approach, Milic categorized the other approach to style as "dualistic," dealing with style as a "manner" (1965, 67). Its followers—such as Edward P. J. Corbett—Richard Young (1982) called the "new classicists," and they claimed a tradition dating back to the kairos emphasis of the early rhetors. According to Milic, only this dualistic, new classical view allowed style to be external to the individual, and therefore capable of being learned (and taught). The McCrimmon definition quoted above is an example of the new classical philosophy that style is teachable by determining what experts do and developing tools to help beginners imitate them. The new classicists were responsible for the return not only of rhetorical schemes and tropes (see for an example Graves 1974), but also for such practices as sentence combining and imitation (see Winterowd 1983). According to the standard version of our history, then, style fell into disfavor when expressivist "new romantics" pointed out that not all stylistic decisions were conscious choices and, therefore, not all were teachable because one can only learn what one is conscious of doing (Pringle 1983; Milic "Rhetorical Choice" (1971)—and here we see the initial influence on composition of the twentieth-century nonmimetic philosophers. In fact, expressivists went on to argue, most stylistic decisions were unconscious and, therefore, impossible to teach.

In response to this challenge to the teaching of style, "new classicists" had two options. They could turn to research studies demonstrating the success of their practices, or they could turn to attempts to forge a theory that would systematically explain the success of their rhetorical tropes and sentence combining. Examples of the former begin to crop up in CCC beginning in 1978, with articles including Daiker, Kerek, and Morenberg's "Sentence Combining and Syntactic Maturity in Freshman English" (1978) and Faigley's "Generative Rhetoric as a Way of Increasing Syntactic Fluency" (1979). According to Connors, however, the professionalization of composition within English departments doomed the experimental research that proved the success of new classical pedagogies because such research did not fit within the English (literature) department's antiformalist, antiempiricist, antibehaviorist ideology (2000, 125).

Instead of relying on either textual analysis or quantitative research, then, compositionists within English departments felt pressured to explain their pedagogies via theory, as W. Ross Winterowd demonstrated in a 1983 essay: "Certain teaching methods in composition . . . are widely used, but remain largely unexamined for underlying theory and pedagogical rationale" (80). These attempts at theory formation were less successful, however, for reasons adequately summed up by Mary Hiatt in 1978:

> Stylistic theory itself ranges widely. Some stylisticians hold that style is totally a matter of one individual's writing. . . . Others take an opposing view and maintain that it is possible to describe the characteristics of a group of writers or of writers of a certain era. Stylisticians further differ on whether style is the sum total of the characteristics of the writing or whether it describes in what way the writing departs from a norm. . . . Some theorists also hold that any style can only be adequately described in the context of another style. . . . The state of the theory itself is therefore conflicting and confusing. (222)

In other words, once again the numerous perspectives on the nature of style defied any unifying statement.

Thus, the standard history tells us that the decline of style in the professional dialogue occurred because composition teachers were unable to explain to the satisfaction of their English department colleagues the underpinnings of what they were doing in their classrooms. I wondered about this explanation, however. With composition changing so much as a field from 1973 to today, was the decline in attention to style due only to an inability to theorize classroom pedagogies? Might other factors—changing interests in specific research methodologies, changes in the rhetorical stance of the field—not also play a role? I wondered if:

1. The shift away from empirical or quantitative research methods toward qualitative studies that began with the 1980s reaction to cognitive research methods, together with the literary community's turn away from New Critical formalism, led to a decline in interest in "measuring" stylistic success.
2. The ideological shifts in rhetorical stance from those emphasizing the importance of the text to those emphasizing the importance of the writer to those emphasizing the importance of the audience rendered discussions of style outside the scope of analysis.

What I found suggests that shifts in both methodological preference and rhetorical orientation have worked together to deprive style of much of its institutional authority and intellectual interest.

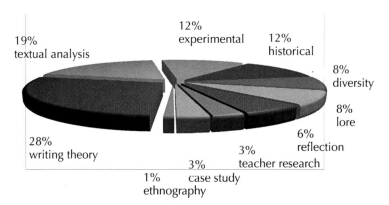

Figure 2. Style Articles, Percentage by Methodology, 1973 to 2003.

SHIFTING METHODOLOGIES

I tested my first hypothesis by classifying all 118 articles dealing with style from the past thirty years of CCC by one of ten broad research methodologies described by Gesa Kirsch and Patricia Sullivan in their *Methods and Methodology in Composition Research* (1992): writing theory, textual analysis, experimental research, historical analysis, diversity critique, teacher research, case study, ethnography, discourse analysis, and cognitive approaches.[2] After examining the articles, I deleted the final two categories (discourse analysis and cognitive) since no essays used these methods, and I added two categories: reflection—exploratory articles based on years of experience discussed in a nontheorized manner—and lore—how-to articles based on localized (and nonempirical) classroom practices. Overall results are presented in figure 2:

What emerges is the fact that almost two-thirds of the articles written on style were produced using one of the two methodological options that our history says were available to new classicists seeking to justify their pedagogies: either recourse to some rhetorical, linguistic, or literary theory (28 percent of all articles), or empiricism (the 19 percent of articles using textual analysis and the 12 percent using experimental research). Another 18 percent of articles relied on disciplinary or institutional history to make their point—either through archival records (historical analysis) or personal recollections (reflection articles). The qualitative classroom- or community-based methodologies (teacher-research, case study, ethnography) were the least likely to be used when discussing style. Thus, it seems at first that quantitative research methods held their own against both theory and qualitative methods.

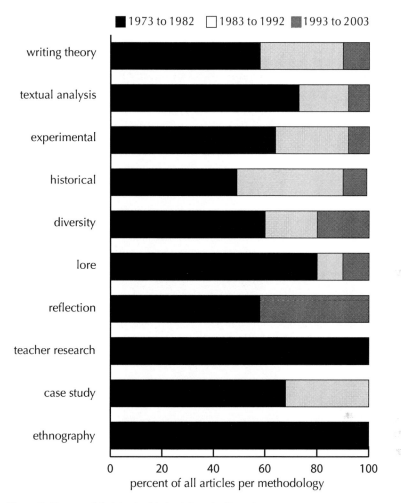

Figure 3. Percent of Articles by Methodology by Decade.

However, when we break down the methodologies by decade, we see a rather different story. Figure 3, which charts what percentage of articles using a particular methodology were written in each decade, demonstrates first that across the board, half or more of all articles using any methodology were written during the decade 1973–82.

The figure also demonstrates that textual analysis in particular grew less popular as the years went on, with very few articles written from 1983 to 2003 (6 of a total 22) using what had at one time been an extremely popular methodology. To a lesser degree, the same can be said for experimental research, particularly in the most recent decade (when only one study was published). Discounting the very small numbers of community-based studies, only lore suffered a larger drop in publication rates from the first to the third decade. This last, of course, speaks to the professionalization of composition as reflected in CCC. As the field matured, the journal accepted fewer and fewer articles based solely on classroom practices. This trend is apparent in the articles themselves, with pieces from the 1980s on that are largely descriptions of pedagogy now self-consciously grounding the classroom practice in theory. Thus, articles such as D'Angelo's 1973 unabashedly lore-based "Imitation and Style" became, by 1988, Arrington's "A Dramatistic Approach to Understanding and Teaching the Paraphrase." The journal's Staffroom Interchange section was undoubtedly created to allow space for lore-based pieces, but it is interesting to note that a typical style-related Staffroom Interchange, Kaufer and Steinberg's 1988 "Economies of Expression: Some Hypotheses" is itself as long as an article and is written from a theoretical perspective. Untheorized how-to descriptions of what works in the classroom had very little place in the principal composition journal after the mid-1980s.

Further examples abound of how style articles published in CCC followed the larger professional trends of English and composition studies. For instance, writing theory was by far the most popular methodology used from 1983 to 1992, with 38 percent of all style articles published employing it—not surprising, considering the "theory wars" then taking place on the literature side of English departments. Textual analysis was at its most popular from 1973 to 1982, when over one-fifth of all articles used its methodology, and historical analysis was equally popular from 1983 to 1992, when rhetorical historiography was fashionable and archival essays such as Woods's "Nineteenth-Century Psychology and the Teaching of Writing" (1985) and literature reviews such as Selzer's "Exploring Options in Composing" (1984) were published. Finally, we can note the surprising popularity of stylistic reflection pieces in the most recent decade. While personal reflection, like lore, was not unusual in the first decade examined, it virtually disappeared in the second. Perhaps it is a sign of the field's increasing confidence in its own stance as a professional discipline that articles such as "Challenging Tradition: A Conversation about Reimagining the Dissertation in Rhetoric and Composition" (The Dissertation Consortium 2001) are again being published.

SHIFTING ORIENTATIONS

I then tested my second hypothesis, that a thirty-year shift in rhetorical emphasis from one element of the communication triangle to another (text to writer to reader) meant a corresponding shift away from stylistic concerns.[3] I posited that the rise of process pedagogies and expressivism would have mandated a focus away from the textual product and onto the writer, and that the later rise of social critique and multiculturalism, as well as the current interest in professional writing, would have similarly shifted focus from writer's intent to reader's reaction. Thus, by a "text-oriented" article, I meant one in which the emphasis of the author was on the words on the page. A classic example would be D'Angelo's "Sacred Cows Make Great Hamburgers: The Rhetoric of Graffiti" (1974), in which his argument was that teachers can use graffiti to teach rhetorical tropes: rather than discussing how students respond to graffiti in the classroom (a writer orientation), D'Angelo focused exclusively on examples of the tropes employed by various graffiti slogans (a textual orientation). By a "writer-oriented" article, I meant one in which the author's focus was on the student writers—their individual (or socially constructed) style, and the effect of particular pedagogies or ideologies on their writing. Linn's "Black Rhetorical Patterns and the Teaching of Composition" (1975) and Raymond's "I-Dropping and Androgyny: The Authorial 'I' in Scholarly Writing" (1993) are examples of the range of this orientation. Finally, by a "reader-oriented" article, I meant one that focused on the reaction of the audience to the writing. Ede's "On Audience and Composition" (1979) is a classic example of this orientation; Beason's "Ethos and Error: How Business People React to Errors" (2002) more recently demonstrates this emphasis. It is important to point out that while certain methodologies more frequently call forth certain orientations (not surprisingly, for example, textual analysis most often focuses on the text), authors are not constrained by methodology to determine their orientation. For instance, Dawn Skorczewski's "'Everybody Has Their Own Ideas:' Responding to Cliché in Student Writing" (2000) and John Dawkins's "Teaching Punctuation as a Rhetorical Tool" (1995) are both textual analyses published in the past ten years, but the former is writer-oriented, the latter reader-oriented. Elizabeth Flynn's "Composing as a Woman" (1988) employs an orientation toward the writer, Terry Myers Zawacki's "Recomposing as a Woman—An Essay in Different Voices" (1992) one

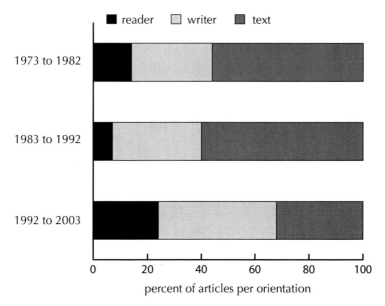

Figure 4. Percent of Articles by Orientation.

toward the text. Other factors than methodology clearly play a role in the author's determination of what aspect of communication to focus on.

Examining the thirty years of articles, I found that, as with methodologies, though a definite shift in rhetorical orientation took place, it does not seem to have transpired exactly as predicted. Of the 118 total articles in CCC, over half (53 percent) were primarily oriented toward the text. Another third (33 percent) were oriented toward the writer, with the final 14 percent oriented toward the reader. Figure 4 breaks this down by decade.

Here we can clearly see that emphases on the reader and writer have increased during the thirty-year period, while the emphasis on the text at first grew but then decreased dramatically in the past decade. How to explain these changes? Considering first the continued increase in articles with a textual orientation even after the movement away from product to process in the larger composition field, it is possible that during the middle decade, when people trained in New Critical formalism were attempting to incorporate more theory into their discussions, they de-emphasized a strict textual analysis in their methodology (as we saw above) but clung to a rhetorical orientation that focused on the text—that is, they theorized about the texts as a way to discuss style. We can see this in articles such as Vande Koppel's "Some Exploratory Discourse on Metadiscourse"

(1985) or Laib's "Conciseness and Amplification" (1990). It is also possible that CCC's editors published such pieces in greater numbers during this decade, as readers also familiarized themselves with theory.

The down-up shift in emphasis on orientation toward the reader is easier to explain: during the first decade, an emphasis on the reader usually meant the teacher (we see this in both Odell's [1973] and Sommers's [1982] identically titled "Responding to Student Writing"). During the middle decade, this orientation toward the teacher gave way to a greater orientation toward the student (articles such as Jensen and DiTiberio's "Personality and Individual Writing Processes" [1984]), and thus away from reader to writer. In the most recent decade, a reader orientation has more often referred not to the teacher but to either the rhetorical audience or a professional audience, with articles such as Beason's "Ethos and Error: How Business People React to Errors" (2002). Finally, an ever-increasing orientation toward the writer reflects the overall emphasis in CCC on student responses to theory and pedagogy.

In interpreting these data, of course, it is important to keep in mind the very small number of style articles published during the past decade—only 11 percent of the thirty-year total and less than 7 percent of all articles published in CCC during the decade. Articles such as Barbara Schneider's "Nonstandard Quotes: Superimpositions and Cultural Maps," which analyzed the rhetorical use of nonstandard quotation marks and argued that students use them to introduce voices "we do not want to recognize" (2002, 188) was one small drop in an ocean of articles in the 2000s that were more like Welch's "'And Now I Know Them': Composing Mutuality in a Service Learning Course" or Hocks's "Understanding Visual Rhetoric in Digital Writing Environments (Hocks, 2003)." In 2001, T. R. Johnson's "School Sucks" noted in its abstract that "this essay explores the ways students experience contemporary writing pedagogy" (620)—a statement that could summarize a majority of the articles currently being published in CCC. Indeed, it is interesting in this light to note Schneider's rhetorical move in orienting her study of quotation mark usage away from the text and toward the reader's reaction and the writer's counterreaction.

CONCLUSION

So what has happened to style? The de-emphasis of the text, both in preferred research methodology and in rhetorical orientation, has led to a tremendous downturn in publishable articles on style. Style has tried to bend with the times, placing greater emphasis on the intentions of writers and the reactions of readers, on diverse classrooms and the application of theories of writing. But the taboo on textual discussion leaves style in rather the same place as two highly political sides of a family getting together for Thanksgiving dinner and agreeing to not discuss politics: what else will they talk about? When we think back to Gage's three philosophies of style—linguistic concepts emphasizing grammar norms and deviations, rhetorical concepts emphasizing choice of devices and their effects on audience, and philosophical concepts emphasizing language and the nature of reality—we see that all three presume some textual emphasis. Rhetorical concepts leave the greatest room for discussions of writer intention and audience reaction, and thus it is not surprising that rhetorical theories are the ones most often applied in contemporary articles on style. When linguistic and philosophical concepts of style are not discussed, however, modern notions fall prey to older lore, just as Martinez (1997) discovered in his study of style discussions in textbooks. In other words, helping students to interpret kairos, the proper discourse for each time and audience, is an important goal, but do we really want to fall back as well on nineteenth-century ideals of clarity or a view of language mirroring reality that ignores the twentieth century?

I believe we can bring back the rest of the conversation—that both ancient and modern rhetoric are already pointing us in the right direction. First, we are recovering ancient pedagogical practices emphasizing the practice of persuasion rather than simply its appropriate consumption. When we emphasize learning "style for" a rhetorical purpose rather than "style of" a studied rhetorical or poetic text, we are taking a first step toward a renewed understanding. Jeffrey Walker's (2000) excellent recent examination of Hellenistic and Second Sophistic rhetorical practices in which schoolboys wrote, memorized, and orated speeches on a variety of topics as a part of a humanistic discourse education points us toward a way to recapture style as integral to the entire process of writing, not as ornamentation to add at the end (if at all). Second, we can tie this practice into our relatively uniform new rhetorical/postmodern theories on the nature of language and reality. Kenneth Burke, for instance, both echoed I. A. Richards and previewed Jacques Derrida when he wrote in *The Philosophy of Literary Form* that critical and imaginative literature provides strategic or stylized answers to the social questions posed by the situations in which it is written. These stylized answers name their situations in ways that contain an attitude toward them—in fact, situations cannot be named without conveying an attitude. There is no neutral language, no "perfect thought" that our students must transfer to the page as accurately and opaquely as possible. Literature provides an especially clear look at the employment of style to name an attitude, but all language is stylized, or attitudinal. Thus we see again that style is much more than an adornment. It becomes the only way we have to name our world.

If style assumed this level of import in our thinking on the writing process, we should indeed see a revitalization of interest. And, in fact, with the proliferation of computer writing, we may be at the kairotic moment for this renewed interest. Steven Johnson, author of *Interface Culture: How New Technology Transforms the Way We Create and Communicate*, describes how his view of the word-thought connection changed with the transition to a computer. With the ability to compose almost as fast as he could frame his thoughts and with no penalties for constant revision, he stopped composing in words, he said, and began to do so in phrases (1997, 142–45). He stopped translating his perfect thoughts into imperfect words and began instead to write his thoughts. Nancy Sommers (1982), in her seminal study of student and experienced writers, found this belief that writing is translating to be common among beginning writers. It is the attitude we have been fighting against for decades, and Johnson's experience suggests that our students' very writing process may now be assisting us.

Connors's and Myers's recent articles in CCC urging the field not to turn its back on proven successes in linguistic style pedagogies; the historical recovery of similar Greco-Roman rhetorical practices; the as-yet unexamined consequences of an increasing number of MFA-trained writers (with their concomitant focus on practice and style) entering the ranks of composition instructors; the confluence of modern rhetoric and literary theory regarding the role of stylized language in naming reality; and now the ubiquity of computer writing, which encourages recursive building of text-thoughts: all these paths converging may well be carrying us toward a renewed conversation in composition in which Gorgias of Leontini can reaffirm that "Logos [the word] is a powerful lord (1990)."

Appendix

ARTICLES SURVEYED, IN CHRONOLOGICAL ORDER

Milic, Louis (1971). Rhetorical Choice and Stylisitic Options: The Conscious and Unconscious Poles. In Chapman, Seymour (ed). *Literary Style: A Symposium.* New York: Oxford UP. 77-88

Minkoff, Harvey, and Sharon Katz. Spoken and Written English: Teaching Passive Grammar. *CCC* 24 (1973): 157–62.

Cain, Betty. Discourse Competence in Nonsense Paralogs. *CCC* 24 (1973): 171–81.

Snipes, Wilson Currin. Oral Composing as an Approach to Writing. *CCC* 24 (1973): 200–5.

D'Angelo, Frank J. Imitation and Style. *CCC* 24 (1973): 283–90.

Hoover, Regina M. Prose Rhythm: A Theory of Proportional Distribution. *CCC* 24 (1973): 366–74.

Odell, Lee. Responding to Student Writing. *CCC* 24 (1973): 394–400.

D'Angelo, Frank J. Sacred Cows Make Great Hamburgers: The Rhetoric of Graffiti. *CCC* 25 (1974): 173–80.

Graves, Richard L. A Primer for Teaching Style. *CCC* 25 (1974): 186–90.

Walpole, Jane Raymon. Eye Dialect in Fictional Dialogue. *CCC* (1974): 191–96.

Kelly, Lou. Is Competent Copyreading a Violation of the Students' Right to Their Own Language? *CCC* 25 (1974): 254–58.

Sternglass, Marilyn S. Dialect Features in the Compositions of Black and White College Students: The Same or Different? *CCC* 25 (1974): 259–63.

Stalker, James C. Written Language as a Dialect of English. *CCC* 25 (1974): 274–76.

Dykeman, Therese B. The Physics of Rhetoric. *CCC* 25 (1974): 382–87.

D'Angelo, Frank J. A Generative Rhetoric of the Essay. *CCC* 25 (1974): 388–96.

Nilsen, Don L. F. The Nature of Implication: or How to Write between the Lines. *CCC* 25 (1974): 417–21.

Kehl, D. G. The Electric Carrot: The Rhetoric of Advertisement. *CCC* 26 (1975): 134–40.

Fleischauer, John F. James Baldwin's Style: A Prospectus for the Classroom. *CCC* 26 (1975): 141–48.

Linn, Michael D. Black Rhetorical Patterns and the Teaching of Composition. *CCC* 26 (1975): 149–53.

Suhor, Charles. Cliches: A Re-assessment. *CCC* 26 (1975): 159–62.

Schulz, Muriel. How Serious is Sex Bias in Language? *CCC* 26 (1975): 163–67.

D'Angelo, Frank (1975) *A Conceptual Theory of Rhetoric.* Cambridge, MA: Winthrop Publishing.

Struck, H. R. Wanted: More Writing Courses for Graduate Students. *CCC* 27 (1976): 192–97.

Weiher, Carol. Sexism in Language and Sex Differences in Language Usage: Which Is More Important? *CCC* 27 (1976): 240–43.

Purdy, Dwight Hilliard. The Lord's Shout: Varieties of Pauline Rhetoric. *CCC* 27 (1976): 248–52.

Nilsen, Don L. F. Clichés, Trite Sayings, Dead Metaphors, and Stale Figures of Speech in Composition Instruction. *CCC* (1976): 278–82.

D'Angelo, Frank J. Notes toward a Semantic Theory of Rhetoric within a Case Grammar Framework. *CCC* 27 (1976): 359–62.

Gorrell, Robert M. Usage as Rhetoric. *CCC* 28 (1977): 20–25.

Kane, Thomas S. "The Shape and Ring of Sentences": A Neglected Aspect of Composition. *CCC* 28 (1977): 38–42.

Rank, Hugh. Mr. Orwell, Mr. Schlesinger, and the Language. *CCC* 28 (1977): 159–65.

De Beaugrande, Robert. Generative Stylistics: Between Grammar and Rhetoric. *CCC* 28 (1977): 240–46.

Daiker, Donald A., Andrew Kerek, and Max Morenberg. Sentence Combining and Syntactic Maturity in Freshman English. *CCC* 29 (1978): 36–41.

Hiatt, Mary P. The Feminine Style: Theory and Fact. *CCC* 29 (1978): 222–26 .

Halloran, S. Michael. On Making Choices, Sartorial and Rhetorical. *CCC* 29 (1978): 369–71.

Taylor, Sheila Ortiz. Women in a Double-Bind: Hazards of the Argumentative Edge. *CCC* 29 (1978): 385–89.

De Beaugrande, Robert. Psychology and Composition. *CCC* 30 (1979): 50–57.

Daugherty, Leo. The English Grapholect and the Introductory Composition Class. *CCC* 30 (1979): 134–40.

Lunsford, Andrea A. Aristotelian vs. Rogerian Argument: A Reassessment. *CCC* 30 (1979): 146–51.

Ross, William T. The Aesthetics of Exposition. *CCC* 30 (1979): 170–75.

Faigley, Lester. Generative Rhetoric as a Way of Increasing Syntactic Fluency. *CCC* 30 (1979): 176–81.

Yoos, George E. An Identity of Roles in Writing and Reading. *CCC* 30 (1979): 245–50.

Walpole, Jane R. Why Must the Passive Be Damned? *CCC* 30 (1979): 251–54.

D'Angelo, Frank J. The Art of Paraphrase. *CCC* 30 (1979): 255–59.

Vitanza, Victor J. A Tagmemic Heuristic for the Whole Composition. *CCC* 30 (1979): 270–74.

Crowley, Sharon. Of Gorgias and Grammatology. *CCC* 30 (1979): 279–84.

Connors, Robert J. The Differences between Speech and Writing: Ethos, Pathos, and Logos. *CCC* 30 (1979): 285–90.

Ede, Lisa S. On Audience and Composition. *CCC* 30 (1979): 291–95.

Flower, Linda, and John R. Hayes. The Cognition of Discovery: Defining a Rhetorical Problem. *CCC* 31 (1980): 21–32.

Nold, Ellen, and Brent Davis. The Discourse Matrix. *CCC* 31 (1980): 141–52.

Knoblauch, C. H. Intentionality in the Writing Process: A Case Study. *CCC* 31 (1980): 153–59.

Kneupper, Charles W. Revising the Tagmemic Heuristic: Theoretical and Pedagogical Considerations. *CCC* 31 (1980): 160–68.

Katula, Richard A., and Richard W. Roth. A Stock Issues Approach to Writing Arguments. *CCC* 31 (1980): 183–96.

Walpole, Jane R. Style as Option. *CCC* 31 (1980): 205–12.

Long, Russell C. Writer-Audience Relationships: Analysis or Invention? *CCC* 31 (1980): 221–26.

Lunsford, Andrea A. The Content of Basic Writers' Essays. *CCC* 31 (1980): 278–90.

Faigley, Lester. Names in Search of a Concept: Maturity, Fluency, Complexity, and Growth in Written Syntax. *CCC* 31 (1980): 291–300.

Freedman, Aviva, and Ian Pringle. Writing in the College Years: Some Indices of Growth. *CCC* 31 (1980): 311–24.

Corbett, Edward P. J. Some Rhetorical Lessons from John Henry Newman. *CCC* 31 (1980): 402–12.

Scott, Fred Newton. Rhetoric Redivia. *CCC* 31 (1980): 413–19.

Bator, Paul. Aristotelian and Rogerian Rhetoric. *CCC* 31 (1980): 427–32.

Moran, Charles. Teaching Writing/Teaching Literature. *CCC* 32 (1981): 21–29.

Klein, Mia. The "Other" Beauty of Martin Luther King, Jr.'s "Letter from Birmingham Jail." *CCC* 32 (1981): 3–37.

Freeman, Donald C. Phenomenal Nominals. *CCC* 32 (1981): 183–88.

Witte, Stephen P., and Lester Faigley. Coherence, Cohesion, and Writing Quality. *CCC* 32 (1981): 189–204.

Brostoff, Anita. Coherence: "Next to" Is Not "Connected to." *CCC* 32 (1981): 278–294.

Broadhead, Glenn J., and James A. Berlin. Twelve Steps to Using Generative Sentences and Sentence Combining in the Composition Classroom. *CCC* 32 (1981): 295–307.

Stotsky, Sandra. The Vocabulary of Essay Writing: Can It Be Taught? *CCC* 32 (1981): 317–26.

Faigley, Lester, and Stephen Witte. Analyzing Revision. *CCC* 32 (1981): 400–7.

Walter, Otis M. The Value of the Classics in Rhetoric. *CCC* 32 (1981): 416–22.

Connors, Robert J. The Rise and Fall of the Modes of Discourse. *CCC* 32 (1981): 444–55.

Vande Kopple, William J. Functional Sentence Perspective, Composition, and Reading. *CCC* 33 (1982): 50–63.

Sommers, Nancy. Responding to Student Writing. *CCC* 33 (1982): 148–56.

Sternglass, Marilyn S. Applications of the Wilkinson Model of Writing Maturity to College Writing. *CCC* 33 (1982): 167–75.

Harwood, John T. Freshman English Ten Years After: Writing in the World. *CCC* 33 (1982): 281–83.

Hoetker, James. Essay Examination Topics and Students' Writing. *CCC* 33 (1982): 377–92.

Hairston, Maxine (1982) The Winds of Change: Thomas Kuhn and the Revolution in the Teaching of Writing. *CCC* 33.1 (76-88).

Crowhurst, Marion. Sentence Combining: Maintaining Realistic Expectations. *CCC* 34 (1983): 62–72.

Holzman, Michael. Scientism and Sentence-Combining. *CCC* 34 (1983): 73–79.

Winterowd, W. Ross. Prolegomenon to Pedagogical Stylistics. *CCC* 34 (1983): 80–90.

Pringle, Ian. Why Teach Style? A Review-Essay. *CCC* 34 (1983): 91–98.

Fahnestock, Jeanne. Semantic and Lexical Coherence. *CCC* 34 (1983): 400–16.

Bamberg, Betty. What Makes a Text Coherent? *CCC* 34 (1983): 417–29.

Stotsky, Sandra. Types of Lexical Cohesion in Expository Writing: Implications for Developing the Vocabulary of Academic Discourse. *CCC* 34 (1983): 430–46.

Sloan, Gary. Transitions: Relationships among T-Units. *CCC* 34 (1983): 447–53.

Selzer, Jack. Exploring Options in Composing. *CCC* 35 (1984): 276–84.

Jensen, George H., and John K. DiTiberio. Personality and Individual Writing Processes. *CCC* 35 (1984): 285–300.

Purves, Alan C. In Search of an Internationally-Valid Scheme for Scoring Compositions. *CCC* 35 (1984): 426–38.

McCrimmon, James (1984) *Writing with a Purpose.* New York: Haughton Mifflin.

Woods, William F. Nineteenth-Century Psychology and the Teaching of Writing. *CCC* 36 (1985): 20–41.

Harned, Jon. The Intellectual Background of Alexander Bain's "Modes of Discourse." *CCC* 36 (1985): 42–50.

Vande Kopple, William J. Some Exploratory Discourse on Metadiscourse. *CCC* 36 (1985): 82–93.

Case, Donald. Processing Professorial Words: Personal Computers and the Writing Habits of University Professors. *CCC* 36 (1985): 317–22.

Peterson, Linda. Repetition and Metaphor in the Early Stages of Composing. *CCC* 36 (1985): 429–43.

Bump, Jerome. Metaphor, Creativity, and Technical Writing. *CCC* 36 (1985): 444–53.

Dowling, H. F., Jr. Imaginative Exposition: Teaching "Creative" Non-Fiction Writing. *CCC* 36 (1985): 454–64.

Stotsky, Sandra. On Learning to Write about Ideas. *CCC* 37 (1986): 276–93.

D'Angelo, Frank J. The Topic Sentence Revisited. *CCC* 37 (1986): 431–41.

Hashimoto, I. Voice as Juice: Some Reservations about Evangelic Composition. *CCC* 38 (1987): 70–80.

Arrington, Phillip. A Dramatistic Approach to Understanding and Teaching the Paraphrase. *CCC* 39 (1988): 185–97.

Rose, Mike. Narrowing the Mind and Page: Remedial Writers and Cognitive Reductionism. *CCC* 39 (1988): 267–302.

Flynn, Elizabeth. Composing as a Woman. *CCC* 39 (1988): 423–35.

Kaufer, David S., and Erwin R. Steinberg. Economies of Expression: Some Hypotheses. *CCC* 39 (1988): 453–57.

Smye, Randy (1988) Style and Usage Software: Mentor Not Judge. *Computers & Composition* 06.1 (47-62).

Beginning Writers: Diverse Voices and Individual Identity. *CCC* 40 (1989): 152–74.

Sloan, Gary. Frequency of Errors in Essays by College Freshmen and by Professional Writers. *CCC* 41 (1990): 299–308.

Laib, Nevin. Conciseness and Amplification. *CCC* 41 (1990): 443–59.

Seitz, James. Composition's Misunderstanding of Metaphor. *CCC* 42 (1991): 288–98.

Zawacki, Terry Myers. Recomposing as a Woman—An Essay in Different Voices. *CCC* 43 (1992): 32–38.

Geisler, Cheryl. Exploring Academic Literacy: An Experiment in Composing." *CCC* 43 (1993): 39–54.

Fleckenstein, Kristie S. An Appetite for Coherence: Arousing and Fulfilling Desires. *CCC* 43 (1993): 81–87.

Raymond, James C. I-Dropping and Androgyny: The Authorial "I" in Scholarly Writing. *CCC* 44 (1993): 478–93.

Lu, Min-Zhan. Professing Multiculturalism: The Politics of Style in the Contact Zone. *CCC* 45 (1994): 442–58.

Bartholomae, David. Writing with Teachers: A Conversation with Peter Elbow. *CCC* 46 (1995): 62–71.

Dawkins, John. Teaching Punctuation as a Rhetorical Tool. *CCC* 46 (1995): 533–48.

Straub, Richard. The Concept of Control in Teacher Response: Defining the Varieties of "Directive" and "Facilitative" Commentary. *CCC* 47 (1996): 223–51.

Lynch, Dennis A. Moments of Argument: Agonistic Inquiry and Confrontational Cooperation. *CCC* 48 (1997): 61–85.

Marshall, Margaret J. Marking the Unmarked: Reading Student Diversity and Preparing Teachers. *CCC* 48 (1997): 231–48.

Connors, Robert J. The Erasure of the Sentence. *CCC* 52 (2000): 96–128.

Skorczewski, Dawn. "Everybody Has Their Own Ideas:" Responding to Cliché in Student Writing. *CCC* 52 (2000): 220–39.

Challenging Tradition: A Conversation about Reimagining the Dissertation in Rhetoric and Composition. *CCC* 52 (2001): 441-54.

Porter, Kevin J. A Pedagogy of Charity: Donald Davidson and the Student-Negotiated Composition Classroom. *CCC* 52 (2001): 574–611.

Dissertation Consortium. *CCC* 52:3 (February 2001) 441-454.

Beason, Larry. Ethos and Error: How Business People React to Errors. *CCC* 53 (2002): 33–64.

Schneider, Barbara. Nonstandard Quotes: Superimpositions and Cultural Maps. *CCC* 54 (2002): 188–207.

Myers, Sharon A. ReMembering the Sentence. *CCC* 54 (2003): 610–28.

Hocks, Mary E. "Understanding Visual Rhetoric in Digital Writing Environments." *CCC* 54.4 (June 2003):629-656.

3

CONTEXTUALIST STYLISTICS: BREAKING DOWN THE BINARIES IN SENTENCE-LEVEL PEDAGOGY

Rebecca Moore Howard

[I]n most of our more illustrious English Departments, departments whose standards of scholarly achievement are the measure for us all, research into why students write badly, what it means to write well or badly, how we can teach anyone to write well, has been at least déclassé, if not an absolute disqualification to any serious academic respect.
—Joseph Williams (1977)

Many students write poorly and with deplorable styles simply because they do not care; their failures are less the result of incapacity than the lack of will.
—Winston Weathers (1970)

Because much of the material online is produced by other students, it is often difficult or impossible for educators to identify plagiarism based on expectations of student-level work.
—"Plagiarism and the Internet" (Turnitin.com, 2003)

The discipline of stylistics has gone through well-documented changes, from formalism through structuralism to contextualism.[1] Through it all, stylisticians have consistently self-identified their methods as descriptive rather than prescriptive. Stylistics, like linguistics, is descriptive, dispassionate, objective.

Most of the twentieth-century interplay of formalism and structuralism is nevertheless hierarchical in its results. Literary texts are highly valued in Western culture; they are considered better than other texts. Regardless of how dispassionate their methods of analysis, when stylisticians endeavor to identify the stylistic qualities that mark a literary text, they are inescapably identifying and justifying the stylistic qualities of what the culture has already identified as the most valuable texts.

Fortunately (it might seem) for composition studies, stylistics has in recent decades moved toward contextualist instead of textualist methods. However, at the time when contextualism began to dominate scholarship in stylistics, compositionists were engaged in a full-scale retreat from sentence-level pedagogy. Compositionists today are comfortable teaching the writing process or positioning the composition classroom as a forum in which to improve society, but many are decidedly uncomfortable about teaching style. Those who do teach it tend to employ textualist methods that are now outdated in stylistics.

This essay traces some of the historical reasons for composition's retreat from style and its consequent failure to take up contextualist stylistics. Equipped with this historical understanding, it may be possible for compositionists to find contextualist means of engaging sentence-level pedagogy and scholarship that advance the current tenets of the field, rather than returning it to a hegemonic current-traditionalism. With contextualist approaches, composition studies could not only recover the third canon of rhetoric but transform it, moving from hegemonic disciplining of students to pedagogical invitations for students to participate in the play of texts.

STYLE IN THE EMERGENCE OF COMPOSITION STUDIES

As the third of the five canons of classical rhetoric, style has a long and honorable history in composition and rhetoric. Even when seventeenth-century Ramistic rhetoric reduced the five canons of rhetoric to two, style (along with delivery) remained. But the scientific ideals of the Royal Society then shrank the options within the canon of style. Gone were the grand, middle, and plain styles of the *Rhetorica ad Herennium;* all that remained was the plain style so well suited to objective, scientific discourse.[2]

With the rhetoric of Hugh Blair's successors came an obsession with style pedagogy. Blair and the "legions" of subsequent textbook writers in his sphere of influence accepted Adam Smith's dictum that "a quality of character was visible in styles of writing."[3] That character was, of course, masculine, heterosexual, European, and upper class.

It was in this context that composition arose as a subject of college instruction. In its early history, which has been well narrated by James Berlin (1984), Robert Connors (1997), and others, style was a grounding principle of composition instruction. This does not necessarily mean that composition classes featured instruction in style, but that style and its crucial component, taste, were measures of writing that informed how composition was taught. Susan Miller (1991) has famously argued that this resulted in composition as carnival: in literature classes, students learned to admire stylistic accomplishment. In composition classes, the absence of stylistic accomplishment marked the grotesque bodies of students, who were instead taught correctness. Whereas Miller's analysis focuses on the larger categories of literature versus composition, W. Ross Winterowd (1998) specifies the role of style: "The rhetorical tradition, central to education for centuries preceding the 1900s, had been vitiated, an architectonic, productive art of public discourse becoming, on the one hand, a doctrine of taste and style in belles lettres, and on the other, management and correctness in composition" (84–85).

The pedagogy of composition had been long established—since the 1880s, when composition became an established requirement in American college curricula. And it had been established with an emphasis on the avoidance of error (Connors 1997, 130). Textualist stylistics fits nicely with this agenda, because it demonstrates the heights to which error-free prose can aspire (in literary texts), the better to demonstrate the depths to which error-ridden prose can sink (in student texts). Imported into the composition classroom, textualist stylistics serves a useful function in gatekeeping. Textualist theories of style, says Richard Bradford,

> share a common assumption: that the stylistic character of a literary text defines it as literature and distinguishes it from the linguistic rules and conventions of non-literary discourse. The theories are textualist in that they perceive the literary text as a cohesive unity of patterns, structures and effects. Textualists record the ways in which literature borrows features from non-literary language but maintain that these borrowings are transformed by the literary stylistics of the text. (1997, 73)

In textualist composition pedagogy, the primary goal of instruction is "clarity," a quality demanded of student texts all and sundry. The clarity valued in composition pedagogy harks back to the four qualities of a persuasive style identified by classical rhetoricians such as Quintilian: correctness, clearness, appropriateness, and ornament. But by the time composition instruction was established in nineteenth-century American colleges, the classical tradition was no longer the informing paradigm. Instead, composition classes demanded clarity in student writing so that teachers could enact a Cartesian scrutiny, dividing students' arguments into their syntactic components, examining the veracity of each component, and then evaluating the whole (Crowley 1990, 34). By 1918, William Strunk's *Elements of Style* uniformly privileged the plain style and its attendant emphasis on clarity, as E. B. White did in his revisions. Gone is Demetrius's appreciation for indirection (1963, II.104). Absent from composition pedagogy are his strategies of ambiguity: "And in truth ambiguity may often add strength. An idea suggested has more weight: simplicity of statement excites contempt" (V.254).

The cultural work accomplished by textualist pedagogy and scholarship in composition and rhetoric is demonstrated in W. Ross Winterowd's 1970 article, "Style: A Matter of Manner." Conducting a stylistic analysis of a student's text, Winterowd observes the student's "ineptness," suggesting a need to "acquir[e] the ability to use a variety of structures as vehicles for his thought—from stylistic exercises." This ability can be cultivated through "the internalization of the 'rules' of grammar," which will give students "the ability to express themselves. . . . The rules should be internalized, however, not through the study of grammar, but through the age-old practice of imitation." This can be accomplished most "economically" through the technique of sentence combining offered by modern linguistics. Winterowd concludes his article with a stylistic analysis of William Faulkner's work, in which of course he observes no ineptness or lack of ability (164–67).

At the time when composition studies emerged as a discipline, the study of style was customarily conducted in this manner, on textualist principles. The beginning of composition instruction is not, however, the beginning of the discipline of composition studies. Although a variety of dates have been advanced for the "birth" of the discipline, I subscribe to the 1960s etiology.[4] That decade is marked by the 1963 publication of Braddock, Lloyd-Jones, and Schoer's *Research in Written Composition* and by the 1966 Dartmouth conference, which, according to Joseph Harris, "symbolized a kind of Copernican shift from a view of English as something you learn about to a sense of it as something you do" (1996, 1). Robert Connors finds the "birth" of composition studies in the 1963 CCCC and its attention to "rhetorical issues" (1997, 205–6) and the subsequent focus on "New Rhetoric" in the October 1963 *College Composition and Communication* (206–7). The 1960s, too, is the decade in which a scholarly basis in linguistics was challenged not only as insufficient but as potentially hegemonic: At the 1969 CCCC convention, the progressive New University Conference held a series of workshops that included a "Workshop on Oppressive Linguistics" (Parks 2000, 133). The NUC was advocating a "process education that moved beyond just 'students' language' to the social environment from which it originated" (135). Historian Stephen Parks continues, "[T]he goal was a reformed society, not a reformed CCCC" (137). Since that time, the progressive, revisionist strain of composition studies has been an important part of disciplinary identity, albeit at times a minority voice. Composition studies today is inseparable from critical pedagogy and its desire to deploy composition pedagogy for social reform, even though by no means do all compositionists endorse that agenda.

The linguistics against which the NUC was reacting was, in the 1960s, an informing precept of composition studies: "In their anxiety to incorporate fresh thinking into the teaching of writing, midcentury composition teachers drew on linguistics partly because of its increasing coherence as a discipline, partly because of its growing status within the professional community, and partly because of the historical connection of grammar with composition" (Crowley 1989, 481). "The best hope for the contribution of linguistics to composition," Crowley continues, "has always lain in its potential to enrich students' mastery of style" (487). This would be accomplished by the objective, descriptive linguistics to which textualist stylisticians, too, adhered. With the emergence of the discipline of composition studies, a division arose between compositionists who subscribed to descriptive linguistics and those who wanted to continue current-traditionalist, prescriptive instruction in usage. The contest took on political overtones, with the descriptive linguists characterized as liberals and the prescriptive compositionists as conservatives (Crowley 1989, 484). Both the Left and the Right recognized that adopting descriptive methods in the composition classroom would upset relations of power. "To put it bluntly, to adopt linguistic methodology was to challenge the authority of teachers to legislate matters of grammar and usage, perhaps even of style" (485). Compositionists worried that good usage would lapse if descriptive linguistics gained the day (486); composition instruction, in other words, should hold the line in the preservation of textual standards and good usage.

The influence of descriptive linguistics nevertheless prompted a variety of interesting, useful approaches to sentence-level composition pedagogy: the generative linguistics of Francis Christensen, the T-unit analyses of Kendall Hunt (1966), the sentence combining of Frank O'Hare (1973), the imitation theories and exercises of Edward P. J. Corbett (Christensen 1971). From its inception, the discipline of composition studies was centrally concerned with issues of sentence-level discourse (Connors 2000, 96–98). But, as Crowley notes, the largest unit of analysis for linguistics is the sentence, which limits its value to composition (1989, 499–500). If composition was ever to be anything more than the carnival to literary studies—if it was ever to do anything more than correct students' errors and try to make their prose look acceptable—it had to move beyond the sentence, even if the approach to the sentence was descriptive rather than prescriptive. When the NUC challenged the hegemony of linguistics, it was not only challenging prescriptive pedagogy but all pedagogy—prescriptive and descriptive alike—that could see no larger than the sentence.

Moving beyond the sentence meant moving beyond linguistics and beyond stylistics, one of the subdisciplines of linguistics. For composition studies to become a discipline, its range of inquiry had to expand. The field had to shake off its obsession with correctness and its subordination to literature. Disavowing an interest in style accomplished both.

SRTOL

"Why did compositionists jump on the process bandwagon in the 1970s and 1980s, seemingly leaving issues of grammar and style and producing final products in the classroom dust?" (Bishop 1995, 177). As Wendy Bishop notes, the process movement was one component of the disciplinary move away from sentence-level pedagogy. In its place, process classrooms focused on "idea and topic generation" and "the recursive nature of the drafting process" (179).

The landmark document in the shift from a linguistic orientation in composition studies was the CCCC document, "Students' Right to Their Own Language" (SRTOL), published in the 1974 *College Composition and Communication*. Parks's (2000) history of that document details the ways in which it arose from larger disciplinary arguments, and Parks also explains how the document affected subsequent scholarship and practice in composition studies. SRTOL took a clear stand on sentence-level issues: "[G]ood speech and good writing ultimately have little to do with traditional notions of surface 'correctness'" (Parks 2000, 12). And it sent powerful signals to teachers: "If we can convince our students that spelling, punctuation, and usage are less important than content, we have removed a major obstacle in their developing the ability to write" (8).

Parks's history unfolds what was for me a revelation: it was never the intention that SRTOL would put an end to sentence-level pedagogy; rather, it was to establish the basis for new pedagogy. When the authors of SRTOL assembled to draft the document, it was with the expectation that another group would then draft guidelines for sound sentence-level pedagogy in the spirit of SRTOL. That second group, however, never completed its work (Parks 2000, 206–10). For those of us who entered the profession just a decade later, no trace of the intended pedagogical reforms was to be found. What remained instead was either a distaste for sentence-level pedagogy or the dogged adherence to the pedagogies that SRTOL had discredited.

The binary choice was a difficult one, and I was surely not the only scholar/practitioner who found herself unable to choose sides. Like many compositionists who received their degrees in the early 1980s, my MA was in linguistics, and much of my doctoral training was there as well. Linguistics was fascinating, compelling. I drew on it every day in my teaching of composition. But my teaching of composition has at the same time always been very politically oriented. From the beginning of my career in composition and rhetoric, I have lived not at the poles of this disciplinary debate, but in the relays between them. After two decades in the field, I find myself increasingly unable to use traditional sentence-level pedagogy—what I will here call "fossil pedagogy"—in my composition classes. Yet I have increasingly felt the need for substantial pedagogical engagement at the sentence level. My search has been for philosophies or techniques that would help me make explicit to and with my students the ways in which linguistic and textual standards function to naturalize social divisions that are in fact based on race, class, gender, sexual preference, and the like. But my search has simultaneously been for pedagogies and techniques that would help me work with my students to arrive at their own well-informed decisions about how much they want to understand and use those textual standards. And of course my search has included both critical and imaginative efforts to find or invent pedagogies that will help students who wish to learn these standards of style and correctness.

Fortunately, others are pursuing compatible lines of inquiry. T. R. Johnson (2003) draws on Lacanian theory to advance a style pedagogy that ruptures the mind/body split, offering authorial pleasure as a principle of composing. Far from self-indulgence, this pleasure is "a feeling of connection with one's audience" (xii), and it is one that empties out the binary within whose poles I struggle. Pleasure, not conflict, informs Johnson's pedagogy. Is it an apolitical escape from institutional hegemony? Is it too individualized in a socially constructed world? Or is it a sound alternative to pedagogy that offers students the choice of roles as heroic resisters of or complicit participants in linguistic hierarchy? Johnson himself anticipates these questions and challenges the belief that alternatives are simply doomed to failure (9). Like Bruce Horner, Johnson seeks to derive strength rather than victimhood from the marginal status of composition in the university, but instead of focusing on "questions of academic knowledge production and the tensions between lore, phenomenology, and ethnography," Johnson investigates how "our marginality impacts our actual classroom practice" (12). The pedagogies that Johnson describes in *A Rhetoric of Pleasure* evidence not only the relationship between authorial pleasure and prose style, but also the pleasure that teachers can draw from a pedagogy of authentic engagement with students.

In her essay "Teaching Grammar for Writers in a Process Workshop Classroom," Wendy Bishop (1995) might seem to be addressing only linguistic correctness and not textual standards. But Bishop advocates teaching "grammar as style," which means teaching alternative forms as well as the rules. Writers, she says, need to understand why they are making textual choices (180–81). Pedagogy would take up this task directly: "Discuss writers' options, ask for suggestions about how texts can be made riskier and more conventional, how style can be altered" (184).

FOSSIL PEDAGOGY

Unfortunately, work such as that of Johnson (2003) and Bishop (1995) is relatively rare in the field. The first century of composition instruction was dominated by an obsession with style and correctness (Purcell and Snowball 1996, 701–2); the past quarter-century, by disdain for it. This does not mean that no compositionists teach style, but that those who do have scant fresh scholarship to draw upon. The severity of the problem is illustrated in the 1994 edition of Gary Tate, Edward P. J. Corbett, and Nancy Myers's *Writing Teacher's Sourcebook:* the four essays in the section "Styles" were first published in 1983 (Connors), 1970 (Weathers), 1985 (Rankin), and 1979 (Ohmann). As Tate and his coeditors surveyed the scholarship for the best work available in 1994 on the topic of style, they could find nothing in the previous decade and instead had to reach back as far as twenty-five years.

Compositionists who teach style must draw primarily on textualist composition scholarship conducted decades ago—scholarship that could not or would not participate in the social turn that composition studies has since taken, nor in the contextualist scholarship that has characterized recent work in stylistics. The textualist composition scholarship of style now functions as fossil pedagogy in composition classrooms—pedagogy focused on the plain style and its hallmark, clarity; pedagogy whose stylistic principles are derived from analysis of literary texts and that thereby positions student writing in negative contrast to literary genius (see, for example, the epigraphs to this chapter); pedagogy that does not position students as critical writers in complex (and sometimes oppressive) social, political, and cultural situations. The very fact that Winston Weathers had to remind his 1970 *College Composition and Communication* readers that they could teach more than the plain style (Tate, Corbett, and Myers 1994, 295) underscores the limitations of textualist style pedagogy. Fossil pedagogy teaches style as a relationship among writer, reader, and text, in which the writer crafts the text so that readers can easily decode information. Two works articulate this philosophy clearly: *The Philosophy of Composition,* by E. D. Hirsch, Jr., and "Defining Complexity," by Joseph Williams, published in 1977 and 1979, respectively. Both works are dedicated to what Hirsch calls "readability." Williams's article offers principles of clarity in sentence structure, with "clarity" being defined in terms of readers' difficulty in processing. Pedagogy, he says, should "lead . . . students to do what we want them to do." What we want them to do is "to become adults who communicate easily and clearly to readers who do not have to struggle to understand what those writers mean" (595).

Williams's assertions about readability fit well with those of Hirsch's book, written two years earlier. The readership for his *The Philosophy of Composition* might have been larger, had Hirsch not then begun writing about cultural literacy. The opposing sides of the canon wars were, in composition and rhetoric, defined by Hirsch's and Patricia Bizzell's (1990) arguments, and his prominent role in those canon wars obscured Hirsch's scholarship on style. They also tainted Hirsch's other work; to cite Hirsch was to align oneself with an individualistic, socially conservative form of cognitivism at a time when the social turn in composition featured Paolo Freire's liberatory pedagogy as foundational.

Nevertheless, Hirsch offers a philosophy of composition that eloquently articulates principles of textualist stylistics as they pertain to composition pedagogy. Acknowledging Richard Lanham's 1974 critique of clarity as the goal of composing, Hirsch instead offers the goal of "communicative efficiency," which he says is not vulnerable to the criticisms that Lanham aimed at clarity (1977, 74–75). Communicative efficiency, Hirsch explains, means "the most efficient communication of any semantic intention, whether it be conformist or individualistic" (75). Readability.

Encoding and decoding. Despite all the composition scholarship that challenges such a simplistic notion of text and composing, the readability principle has endured in style pedagogy—largely because most composition scholarship has in recent decades not reconceptualized style pedagogy but has only attacked it.

Certainly these attacks are warranted. Parks (2000) accuses Joseph Williams of complicity in "pro-corporate education." The charge is based in part on the 1977 "Linguistic Responsibility," in which Williams advocated focusing on "the type of communication skills students will use in the working world" (Parks 2000, 205). From Parks's perspective, Williams "is resituating the English classroom as the supplier of trained workers" (206).

Williams's "Linguistic Responsibility" was published three years after SRTOL but dismisses SRTOL as an "expression of linguistic discontent" (1977, 10). Williams was also part of a movement to revise or disavow SRTOL. In 1981 William Irmscher proposed to then-chair of CCCC Lynn Troyka that a new document replace SRTOL without making the old one look bad.[5] Only one member of the committee (which was chaired by Harold Allen and included Constance Weaver and Richard Rodriguez) wanted no revisions to SRTOL and no new policy. "No one," says Parks, "was arguing that CCCC should not support a student's ability to learn through the use of his or her own language. The issue appeared to be the extent to which the SRTOL could be asked to perform such political work for the CCCC in the new situation of the 1980s" (2000, 212–13). When Allen issued a draft committee report, it affirmed SRTOL but treated it solely as a historical document. The committee tried to liaise with moderate liberals and to "finesse the SRTOL into a conservative era through the politics of pragmatism. Since radical politics will not attract funding, particularly at the local level, it argues, they must be held only as that 'distant goal' in the future" (224). The committee offered a more moderate version of SRTOL that the 1983 Executive Committee chose to accept but not act upon.

In formulating its revisionary report, Allen's committee looked to Joseph Williams's work for guidance. They consulted an unpublished Williams document that promotes teacher authority, calls instruction in Standard Written English a moral responsibility, and extends respect only to "legitimate" language uses of "socially responsible" groups (Parks 2000, 213). Williams's argument, says Parks, erroneously assumes that SRTOL requires abandoning instruction in the standard language (214).

By such means did the liberatory and textualist perspectives in composition become bifurcated. Parks's history provides a context for what might otherwise seem passing references in Williams's work. The reference to SRTOL as an "expression of linguistic discontent" (Williams 1997, 10) becomes a highly charged statement, one that dismisses liberatory pedagogy as the work of malcontents. Williams's remark in the same article that we English teachers "have *always* attempted to teach our students that the conventions of standard written English deserve their *respect*" (11; emphasis added) becomes a historical interpretation that functions as a charge leveled at the SRTOL adherents, who are presumably interrupting the smooth flow of history and contributing to a disrespectful, hence disorderly, society.

And inevitably, adoption of his current textbook, *Style: Ten Lessons in Clarity and Grace* (2002) amounts to a participation, however unwittingly, in those politics of language. In composition pedagogy today, one either teaches fossil pedagogy of style, or one does not teach style at all. And this binary is not simply a choice between current pedagogy and outmoded pedagogy; it is also a political choice.

"[W]hat I have been discussing here is the plainest of the plain styles, discussed in just about the plainest possible of the plainest styles" (Williams 1979, 606). Williams characterizes this plain style as "mature style" and equates it with "clarity and grace" (606). With the plain style as its sole objective and clarity (i.e., readability, communicative efficiency, ease of decoding) as the primary and often sole measure of success, fossil pedagogy is inherently conservative, hence for many compositionists inherently repugnant. Mary Fuller sums it up: "Most of us agree, I expect, that we can anticipate stilted, passionless prose from first-year writers if workshops in finding ideas and developing fluency fall victim to endless lessons in style" (1991, 120).

CONTEXTUALIST STYLISTICS

I not only reject Williams's and Hirsch's philosophy of language,[6] I also reject the notion that my opposition to that philosophy requires my retreat from sentence-level pedagogy. In previous essays (Howard 1996, 2000) I have described some of my own classroom practices in my search for socially responsible sentence-level pedagogy, and in one essay (Howard et al. 2002), I collaborated with others to generate a list of classroom possibilities.

In this essay, I instead explore principles that might help others generate fresh approaches to questions of style, constructing the pedagogies that CCCC never produced in the wake of SRTOL. But I urge that compositionists not succumb to the will to pedagogy, thinking of these issues only in terms of what to teach and how, but also to consider the theoretical issues that help us use composition and rhetoric as means of better understanding (and reforming) the culture in which we live.

I turn to contextualist stylistics for possibilities. Contextualist stylistics, explains Jean Jacques Weber (1996b),[7] is a post-1970s development, part of a larger trend toward contextualization in the field of linguistics. From a contextualist perspective, style is "an effect produced in, by and through the interaction between text and reader" (3). Style is not a feature of text, and it is not the vehicle whereby the reader can correctly decode the sovereign writer's intended meaning.

Weber's survey of contextualist stylistics identifies several trends. First, he says, came speech-act stylistics, with Mary Louise Pratt one of its exemplary practitioners (Pratt 1977) as well as one of its foremost critics (Pratt 1986). Next came linguistic pragmatics, with its attention to "presuppositions and inferences (or implications, implicatures)" (Weber 1996b, 4). Linguistic pragmatics then split into two movements. One is cognitive pragmatics, which attends to means by which readers infer meaning. Cognitive pragmatics avoids the problems of indeterminacy by introducing the universal "principle of relevance, which . . . directs the reader to try and maximize the number of contextual implications while at the same time minimizing the processing costs of deriving them" (5–6). Inescapably, this concern with processing connects with the concerns that E. D. Hirsch, Jr. (1977), and Joseph Williams (2002) have for readability, communicative efficiency, and clarity. Moreover, instead of attending to ideology, cognitive pragmatics focuses on "tropes, especially metaphor and irony" (6).

In contrast, the other movement derived from linguistic pragmatics takes the textual construction of social and political ideologies as a central concern (Weber 1996b, 4). Thus it is to the social pragmatics of contextual stylistics that I turn for principles that might contribute to socially responsible sentence-level inquiry in composition. In Weber's account, social pragmatics is also known as critical linguistics or critical stylistics[8] and includes the work of feminist stylistics.

"Context" is an absent figure in most contemporary writers' handbooks and style textbooks. One exception is Anson and Schwegler's *Longman Handbook* (2003), where context is a consideration when analyzing someone else's text (11–12); another is John Haynes' textbook *Style* (1995), in which context alludes primarily to discourse conventions and readers' expectations (e.g., 9–11).

But the context of contextualism is meant in an expansive, politically astute way, to include "all sorts of sociohistorical, cultural and intertextual factors" (Weber 1996b, 3). Describing the WAC program at Carnegie Mellon, David Kaufer and Richard Young (1993) offer a bridging concept when they say that the Carnegie Mellon writing experts came to embrace a contextualist model of expertise derived from the work of Richard Rorty: "to learn to write is to learn the local contexts in which discourse communities acquire knowledge" (93).

Then in Bruce McComiskey's "Writing in Context" (1997), the idea of context becomes more compelling: If compositionists going to say that their writing classes are preparing students for "real-life" writing, then they must be specific about what this "life" is, what these writing activities will be, and what might be the possible individual and social consequences of "these activities in these future contexts." Students will be living in a postmodern world (30), which McComiskey defines as

> a multiplicity of identifiably distinct though inevitably interdependent communities in which citizens, occupying varied and often contradictory subject positions in institutional power formations, represent their worlds politically through language for audiences (other citizens in different subject positions) who legitimate or delegitimate representations according to localized rhetorical norms. (32)

For this postmodern world, students will need appropriate skills for "participat[ing] in the flow of discourse that generates localized institutional knowledge, i.e., to participate in the discursive practices that characterize and encourage communal democracies" (32). The appropriate pedagogy is one whose goal is "effective participation in radical democracies" (31).

The radical democracy whose development McComiskey wants to foster is not an agenda to which all compositionists would subscribe.[9] "[P]articipat[ing] in the flow of discourse that generates localized institutional knowledge" is, however, a much more widely endorsed agenda. How might contextualized style instruction participate in that project? Richard Bradford's (1997) list of stylistic methodologies that together comprise contextualist stylistics offers possibilities:

> Poststructuralism . . . introduc[es] the reader into the relation between literary and non-literary style, and pos[es] the question of whether the expectations

of the perceiver can determine, rather than simply disclose, stylistic effects and meanings. Feminist critics have examined style less as an enclosed characteristic of a particular text and more as a reflection of the sociocultural hierarchies—predominantly male—which control stylistic habits and methods of interpretation. Similarly, Marxists and new historicists concern themselves with style as an element of the more important agenda of cultural and ideological change and mutation." (13)

Contextual stylistics, including the methodologies that Bradford describes, provides a way of reading texts. These methodologies, however, can also be deployed in teaching the production of text. Contextualist stylistics offers methods that might lead composition students not to acknowledge their inferiority to canonized authors, but to understand how readers construct text-intrinsic authorial ethos; what roles authorial ethos (intrinsic and extrinsic) plays in the effectiveness and success of texts; and how a range of analyses and techniques allows the writer to manipulate the systems of signification through which texts are interpreted. Whether in advanced courses that focus on style or as part of first-year composition, we can, indeed, offer socially responsible sentence-level instruction.

Essential components of such instruction are reflection and reflexivity. By reflection I do not refer to the personal writing that derives from liberal humanist Western pedagogy based in Western Christian traditions (Williams, Bronwyn 2003, 593–94). Rather, I allude to the critical reflection that Chris Gallagher attributes to John Dewey's educational program, a form of reflection that contributes to both personal and social change (2002, 13–14). Ann George describes reflection as a component of Paolo Freire's endeavors to promote "critical consciousness—the ability to define, to analyze, to problematize the economic, political, and cultural forces that shape but, according to Freire, do not completely determine [students'] lives" (93). In contextualist pedagogy, style can become a tool for defining, analyzing, and problematizing cultural forces—most obviously, by teaching rhetorical analysis (see Foss 1995). Turned not to the reception but the production of text, it can become a way for students to understand their own stylistic choices and options, and to see how those choices and options participate in, are constrained by, and have the potential to affect the sociocultural contexts in which they are deployed.

Reflexivity, too, plays an important role in a contextualist style pedagogy. Here I am thinking of feminist standpoint theory as it might apply to the teaching of style.[10] Sandra Harding, a prominent advocate of standpoint theory, explains that feminist research not only investigates the sources of power also acknowledges the positionality of the researcher, averting the objectivity fallacy (1987, 9). Reflexivity in a style course would prompt students not only to engage context as a way of understanding their stylistic options, but also to acknowledge what they learn about themselves and their relation to contexts.

Reflexivity and critical reflection offer a bridge between socially responsible pedagogy and sentence-level instruction. The study of style can significantly contribute to critical pedagogy, and critical methods can rescue compositionists from the binary in which, if they teach on the sentence level, they are necessarily engaged in the task of preparing students for compliant positions in the corporate industrial complex. Stylistic panache can help writers accomplish a wide range of social goals, including the formation of and participation in radical democracy. And the study of style can help writers understand the ways in which language use and language norms naturalize social inequality. A wide range of options and positions between the poles of conservative textualist pedagogy and radical rejection of sentence-level instruction awaits composition studies.

4

STYLE REDUX

Kathryn Flannery

Frustrated, I accused him of censorship; calmly he assured me it was not.
"This is just a matter of style," he said with firmness and finality.
—Patricia Williams, *The Alchemy of Race and Rights*

Patricia Williams begins *The Alchemy of Race and Rights: Diary of a Law Professor* with a "necklace of thoughts on the ideology of style" (1991, 1). As part of her reflection on the relationship between writing and the law, she tells the story of how she was barred entry to a Benetton store "at one o'clock in the afternoon" on a Saturday before Christmas with white customers clearly visible inside. Benetton, like other stores in New York City, had installed a buzzer system under the guise of security: to be admitted to the store, a potential customer had to have a "desirable" face, had to fit a store clerk's notion of a safe customer, and such a notion hinged pointedly and painfully on racial profiling (44–45). The nasty irony was obvious: Benetton, a company that wrapped itself in images of a multicultural, happy, rainbow world, refused to serve Williams's "brown face" (44). Outraged by the store's refusal, Williams turned to writing, first in her journal, then a typed broadside that she taped to Benetton's "big sweater-filled window," and then an essay for a symposium on "Excluded Voices" sponsored by a law review. Despite the apparent concern signaled by the symposium's theme, however, the essay was edited to cut out not only Williams's understandable fury, but any reference to race. Her "meanings" thus turned "stolen and strange," Williams objects to the changes made to her text, but the editor defends the editorial policy: "[I]n a voice gummy with soothing and patience," he explains that while her writing is "nice and poetic" it just does not "advance the discussion of any principle." His editorial interventions are not a matter of censorship, he explains. This is not, in his mind, a matter of disagreeing with Williams's ideas. Rather, erasing race, erasing fury is "just a matter of style" (47–48). Here, through potent story, Williams makes visible the "consequence of an ideology of style rooted in a social text of neutrality" (48).

As Williams makes clear, "just a matter of style" is a blind, an evasion, a cover for ideological interests, a refusal to deal with what's at stake in telling the story this way rather than that. I understand the history of normative style as the history of such acts of dismissal and erasure in the name of neutrality, rationality, or moderation.[1] And yet, as a teacher of writing and reading, I need to ask myself what I am to do with such an understanding. I have to, in other words, call my pedagogical bluff. While ideology critique is visible within English studies and it generates potentially useful knowledge, I have not found critique alone to be pedagogically (or politically) sufficient. I am drawn to Williams's text precisely because it does not rest satisfied with critique alone, but represents a double intervention: at the level of critique, certainly, but also at the level of writing. Williams, in this sense, performs her critique. When, a few years ago, I was asked to teach a course called Advanced Prose Style, I had the opportunity to think through the pedagogical implications of Williams's double move, to imagine what a course grounded in an understanding of the ideology of style could look like, and in particular what sorts of writing it might enable. I wanted the course to work as a semester-long inquiry into the question of style that would also be a semester-long writing workshop. What workable alternatives to "a style rooted in a social text of neutrality" might there be? What would such writing look like? In particular, what might it mean—what might it look like textually—to have a stake in what we write? How might we go about composing such texts? And what possible difference might this difference in writing make?

As Mike Rose has eloquently argued, for students to enter into the intellectual work of the university, they have to have an understanding of what makes a question a question within a given field of inquiry in order to be invested in that inquiry as other than passive witnesses (1989, 192). I thus set out to design a sequence of writing and reading assignments that would begin with problematizing—with an opening exploration of what makes style a question—before moving through a series of instances, or cases, that would allow us to explore the problematic from a number of angles, with the expectation that we would conclude the course with temporary closure, with closure that generates further, more productive questions.[2] Through this spiral sequence, the class and I considered some of the analytical tools that were available for naming and understanding style and we tested those tools to see what they would yield for us not only as readers but as writers who live and act in the world. In this essay, I focus on the opening—or problematizing—unit of the sequence and one particularly fruitful instance or case from the middle unit. This is, however, more than a story about teaching style; it is also the story of how students exceeded the expectations of the course design and pushed my thinking about questions of style.

The course, Advanced Prose Style, had been designed for students planning to go on for a fifth-year secondary education certification program. The course also satisfied an upper-division writing-intensive requirement and attracted students from various majors interested in advanced composition, but not necessarily interested in careers in teaching. Part of the strength of the course, as I saw it, was precisely this mix of students who came with differing investments in writing. No set curriculum or set of texts had heretofore defined the course, but I did understand that I had an obligation to provide opportunities for class members to reflect on pedagogy, on the implications for teaching of our inquiry into the ideology of style. I also assumed that because we all participate in a society that rests—if only (and increasingly) precariously—on a commitment to public education, conversation about learning and about education would not be limited to those with a vocational stake but would involve us all in questions of cultural valuation and concepts of civic responsibility. From the outset, then, the course rested not on the idea that we would come together as neutral parties, but that we were likely to bring multiple and competing concerns to bear on our writing and reading. This was going to be, in other words, a rhetorically dynamic space. To treat style as part of an active rhetorical dynamic, we would have to consider questions of context, convention, audience expectation, as well as writerly aims, commitments and investments, none of which could be pinned down in simple terms.

Here is how I introduced the course:

> Style is a notoriously difficult concept to define. As soon as we begin chasing it down, it eludes our grasp. Is style the arrangement of words and sentences on the page, or a response a reader has to a piece of writing (is style in the eye of the beholder)? Is style what sets one piece of writing apart from another, what makes it distinctive, or is it a way of naming adherence to writerly conventions? This semester, we will try out different approaches to style in order to see what they yield for us as writers and readers. We'll be reading four challenging—perhaps troubling—books, each of which takes a stand, and each of which attempts to stretch the resources of language in order to make some difference in the world. These are committed writers who are interested in

persuading readers to see the world differently, and perhaps more than just seeing differently, persuading us to act differently. Such writing foregrounds the importance of context, purpose, and audience. While each of these books can be said to be stylistically distinctive, their stylistic innovations are in the service of (perhaps indistinguishable from) their persuasive aims. Part of our task as readers, then, will be to consider what is at stake in these books, for whom, under what circumstances. What do we have to do in order to be readers of these texts? Can we see the style of these texts as doing necessary or worthwhile work? We will be writing about the stylistic features of these books; we will also try our hand at composing, taking the books as models to enable our own purposes; and we will also strike out on our own, to stretch our ways of composing, our ways of writing. This is a course that requires a willingness to experiment, to work at the craft of writing, to wrestle with challenging readings, and to come to class prepared to participate actively.

This "first reading" of the course, this introduction—passed out on the first day as part of the syllabus and course policies—is the opening invitation for a semester-long process of inquiry. My introduction was intended as a first step in problematizing what may be taken for granted: what is style? and why should we care?

The course readings—Jonathan Kozol's *Savage Inequalities,* James Agee and Walker Evans's *Let Us Now Praise Famous Men,* Patricia Williams's *The Alchemy of Race and Rights,* and Stephen Jay Gould's *The Mismeasure of Man*—were selected because they each intervene in a public debate, because they each seek to address a larger public beyond the confines of the academy, and because they are to varying degrees stylistically self-conscious. Kozol and Gould address questions directly related to education, but all four texts can be read as "about learning," about how we know what we know and how writing makes visible to ourselves and others what we know. As such these readings are pertinent for a class designed not only for those planning careers in education but for the range of students taking an upper-division writing course, all of whom need to engage in these questions if they are to be citizens. In teaching both literature and composition over the years, I have grounded courses on the belief that students should have opportunities to come to a text without the burden and constraint of my prereading. If inquiry is to be live, rather than canned, I want class members to have the freedom to bring their own questions to a text and in that sense their questions become the driving force in class discussion. Gradually through class talk we would then together build an analytical vocabulary to name the features of text that would enable both reading and writing. While I continue to believe that such an approach to inquiry is necessary and valuable, I have also worried that there is the danger of a certain kind of conservatism in such an approach to the extent that as learners at whatever stage we are all likely to rehearse what we already know, to recognize first or only the forms and textual practices we've become accustomed to seeing. Reading challenging texts is an important step, but it is not by itself enough to defamiliarize familiar, taken-for-granted practices. While composition studies has taught us over the last thirty years or so that drilling students in the "rules" of composing is ineffective at best, I am nonetheless concerned that we risk appearing to withhold usable tools if we create assignments that expect students to intuit or reinvent textual practices for which there are available vocabularies for naming. Advanced Prose Style presented the opportunity to think about an inquiry course in writing and reading that would foreground analytical terminology, making that terminology the object of inquiry, as a way to make more visible and available such ways of understanding discursive practices. But I wanted to make sure that such ways of understanding were treated as under interrogation, rather than an assortment of rules or precepts that would necessarily yield "good" or "effective" writing.

Lydia Fakundiny's "Talking about Style" provided a rich place to begin, not only because she is writing "about" style but because she is exercising, as a writer, stylistic choices. No turgid—or worse, chatty, talk-down-to—handbook prose, Fakundiny offers a flexible analytical vocabulary, and most importantly, she emphasizes writerly choice: "[S]tyle is the realm of choice . . . in language; it is the realm of invention" (1991, 714). Fakundiny centers her discussion of style at the level of the sentence:

> Sentences are what we spend all our time getting in and out of when we write. You can't get away from them any more than a dancer from her own body. Writing is thought moving in sentences, from one to the next. An essay is a stream of sentences if one thinks of discourse as a process—being written or read—or an aggregate of sentences if one considers it as a crafted object, a finished text. Style has to do with the way each sentence works, what shape it makes as it moves, and with the cumulative effect of such shapes in the run of language, the discourse. (713).

Diction and syntax are introduced as useful terms to help us name "what it is possible to do with words in sentences" (713). While few students in the class were familiar with the technical terminology Fakundiny deployed, most felt that she was letting them in on something like a guild secret. They all had had someone mark "WC," or "word choice" on their papers at some time or another, often thinking (or being told) that the solution was to turn to a thesaurus to jazz up their writing; and they had all had teachers who told them as syntactical mandate to avoid passive construction; but thinking about "what it is possible to do with words in sentences" as a constructive matter, as a way to analyze what they read but also as a way of "shaping and polishing work-in-progress, rewriting until the think 'sounds right,' until it says what one wants it to say in the way necessary to say it"(p. 713)

—that had not been part of their experience.

To use diction and syntax as tools through which to read the first text, Jonathan Kozol's *Savage Inequalities,* however, could run the risk of turning a powerful critique of American education into a trivial language game. I did not want to have us lose sight of Kozol's purpose, at the same time that I wanted us to consider the extent to which how Kozol writes is not separable from his purpose. To prepare for class discussion, I asked class members not only to mark passages in the opening chapters of *Savage Inequalities* that they found interesting or problematic, but also that they make entries in a writer's notebook (akin to a commonplace book). For this first reading of Kozol, I asked the class to briefly discuss what they understood to be Kozol's stake in this discussion of American education: what is the nature of his commitment? what is his purpose in writing? and to whom is he addressing his concerns? are we as class members addressed here? or does he have someone else in mind? and how do we know? Having asked them first to attend to the larger rhetorical frame, I asked them next to take Fakundiny's questions about diction and syntax as their guide in describing what they thought to be a representative passage from Kozol. Fakundiny suggests that to help us think about diction, we might consider:

1) Which of the semantically most weighted words (the verbs, nouns, adjectives, adverbs) are general or abstract, which are specific and concrete? Are there, for instance, words that create images—evoke sensory experience?

2) At what levels of usage (sometimes called registers) do the significant words operate? Specifically, does the diction tend to be colloquial, or does it draw upon learned or technical vocabulary . . . ?

3) Do any of the words work non-literally, to create metaphors, similes, and other figures of speech? (1991, 715)

As she emphasizes, analyzing diction this way is not a matter of "the bare count of abstract and concrete, colloquial and learned, literal and figurative, but the . . . movement between and among these poles" (715). Similarly, she contends that to study syntax is to pay attention to words in motion, not only "what is happening within a given sentence" but "what is happening between and among consecutive sentences" (720). Thus one looks across sentences for the variety and range of syntax as well as for the patterns: do sentences tend to follow subject/verb/complement order? is the semantic work of the sentence performed primarily by the verbs? by nouns? What, Fakundiny asks, "is the architecture of the sentence like?" (721). Is it built periodically or cumulatively? In what ways are words, phrases, clauses and sentences connected not only grammatically, but also rhetorically?

This is a tall order. For students to work through even a paragraph of Kozol's text with this analytical specificity is difficult. What surprised me, however, was how seriously they took the assignment, and how generative it was for us in class conversation. Terms that were rather loosely a part of everyone's working vocabulary—general, abstract, specific, concrete, colloquial, and technical, along with the various figures of speech—were found to be not stable categories of language use with absolute valuations (as in "Never use colloquial diction in formal writing"), but rhetorically situated. We found that we needed to work through our differing understandings of such terms—with the recognition that what makes something specific or concrete, for example, depended in part on context and convention—and to think through when and how we would choose—say—the colloquial over the learned or the technical. What interested me about the class conversation was not that the class settled on either discursive absolutes or rhetorical relativism, but rather that they were interested in thinking strategically in terms of purpose about word choice and the architecture of sentences in relation to purpose. They were thinking as writers about craft.

The class paid particular attention to the way Kozol uses statistics, not as dry numbers but in tension with the stories told by the children, who are his most powerful witnesses. In Kozol's text, before we hear from the children, we are introduced to east St. Louis with its "eerily empty streets" that "suggest another world" (Kozol 1991, 7). To give us this sense of another world that is nonetheless a telling part of America, Kozol gives us sentence after sentence reporting facts: "The city, which is 98 percent black, has no obstetric services, no regular trash collection, and few jobs.

. . . Only three of the 13 buildings on Missouri Avenue, one of the city's major thoroughfares, are occupied. . . . The city, which by night and day is clouded by the fumes that pour from vents and smokestacks at the Pfizer and Monsanto chemical plants, has one of the highest rates of child asthma in America" (7). One could say that the work of these sentences is performed primarily through nouns—through acts of naming the parts of a city in deep distress. Initially, there are no human agents, except in the sense of the occasional eyewitness—a policeman, a governor, a professor at Knox College—someone in authority (not an insider who suffers the direct consequences of urban blight) who reports or notes or tells a visitor some fact about the city. The diction is precise but not technical, and only rarely overtly figurative—and then primarily as a way to boldface the significance of what is described, as when Kozol observes that while "metaphors of caste . . . are everywhere in the United States. Sadly, although dirt and water flow downhill, money and services do not" (10).

As we read further, however, we found that Kozol's prose becomes less and less the language of neutral reporting, but much closer to the tradition of American muckraking; that is, intent on exposing a hard truth. In our paperback version of the text, the first chapter begins with five pages of sentences whose architecture is "regular," subject/verb/ predicate with a fairly consistent use of descriptive clauses that add to the sense of piling on of details, and this regularity works to hammer home the reality of deplorable conditions. But then there is a break, a bit of white space that marks a shift in tone. If the first five pages describe the eerily empty streets with a largely agentless sentence structure, this next section peoples the page through sentences that work more slowly, with descriptive introductory clauses, verbs doing more of the work, and then three pages of children's dialogue. Significantly, Kozol lets the children speak only after he has set the stage so that we can hear their words reverberating against the backdrop created by the opening five pages of the chapter that bluntly describes fecal matter fouling playgrounds from the raw sewage that flows there from broken sewage mains, lead poisoning from smelters whose pollution means wealth only for those upwind, a city too poor to provide basic services, and so on and on. The children's "colloquial" diction takes on a power that it does not often have, to name the unconscionable space between idealized American childhood and the too-fast-grown (or snuffed out) lives these children lead. While some class members indicated that they would have preferred not to have to know about these children, they were nonetheless persuaded of the truth of

Kozol's account, in part because the discursive forms he chose were forms culturally and traditionally associated with truth telling. As we would find in the course of our collective inquiry, there was nothing in the style itself that certified the truth of what Kozol reported, but we trusted his account at least in part because his choice of diction and the architecture of his sentences made it more likely that we would understand what he was saying not as embroidered, or fabricated, but as based in fact. In this sense, he did not violate conventional expectations but counted on readers to share in the conventions.

Because the class had focused on Kozol's description of place in their analysis of his diction and syntax in relation to his aim to tell the truth, I asked them to take Kozol as a model for their next writer's notebook entry. I wanted them to think about his writerly choices from the inside, as writers. This is what I asked them to do:

> For this next notebook entry, take Kozol as a stylistic model and compose a vivid, detailed description of a setting you know well. It might be the place you work. It might be a house of worship, a store, a school, a Pittsburgh city bus, a park. Your task is to describe the setting—the surroundings, the physical structures, the people, the activities or actions—in order to suggest how this setting can represent or illustrate some larger question or concern. For example, you might choose to describe McDonald's in order to make clear the challenges one faces in working at a fast food restaurant. Or you might describe a church on a weekday in order to suggest the role the church plays in its community by serving food to the homeless. The purpose of your description may be to celebrate a place or the people who inhabit the place; or it could be to critique some aspect of the place or what occurs there.

Of course, there is nothing unusual about asking students to write descriptions. Description could be seen as the most basic of student writing assignments. But because we had been working to understand how description could be used rhetorically to build the ground for argument, the task took on more complex dimensions. Students came to class with descriptions of a variety of places. One writer described the preschool where he worked as a converted storefront, in the former steel mill town of Homestead, that represented for him both the loss of jobs and the irony of the nearby, largely unwelcoming upscale shopping center occupying the ground where the Homestead Works once stood. Drawing on his experience as a volunteer in the city morgue, another writer described his first crime scene where he learned how to step over a body as if it were just a piece of furniture. A writer who volunteered for a local religious charity that brought food to the homeless described the shelters men built under a highway overpass. Each student in the class had knowledge of some place that served as vantage from which to reflect on some question or concern that mattered to them. But, the class as a whole realized that "mattering" was not enough if they could not find ways of crafting a text to make the question or concern matter to others. Fakundiny's emphasis on style as choice took on greater importance.

In small groups, we worked on the descriptions as we had done with Kozol, and we found that identifying the writer's stake was inseparable from analyzing diction and syntax. How is the writer's stake marked textually? Must the "I" enter the scene? In what sense is the writer's stake marked in the very choice of diction and in the architecture of sentences? In whole class, we kept going back to Kozol's text, trying to figure out how he achieves a level of intensity and intimacy that makes what is at stake live for us as readers. In the process, we were honing our terminology, clarifying what we meant by such notions as "concrete language," weighing when "telling" is as necessary as "showing," and figuring out whether diction and syntax were enough to account for what we noticed as readers that we called "style." Based on this work, for the next writer's notebook entry, class members were asked to revise some portion of their descriptions. I have found that wholesale revision of a text does not always yield as much as asking the writer to focus on some part. Having in mind a visual artist who makes a dozen sketches of the human hand before going back to paint the particular placement of the right hand in a portrait of a particular person, I ask my students to pull out some piece of text to try out alternative approaches—and then to step back and consider what else would need to be revised if this piece were put back into the whole. Some students revised a portion of their description to see what they would need to do to address a different audience by shifting registers. One student who had described unsanitary conditions in a local restaurant where she waitressed considered how she might shift from a fairly straight reporting of the facts that did not seem to ask anything of anybody to an exposé of the sort appearing in one of the alternative newspapers in town. What would she gain rhetorically, but what would she lose? Who would listen? What would happen if she wrote this to her boss? Other students wanted to see whether they could convey a stronger sense of their larger concern or question indirectly through the description itself, rather than through overt statement, relying, as one student did, on an image of a homeless man who was always at the bus shelter, never getting on the bus, never going anywhere, as a way to register the student's concern about urban neglect.

As writers with something to say, trying out some of Kozol's strategies seemed to be more than an "exercise." Choosing and weighing the choices explicitly as matters of diction and syntax in the service of an argument, class members returned then to a reading of Kozol. In contrast to class conversations I sometimes experienced in the past, in which students would say that they did not like how a text was written because they did not agree with its ideas, in this discussion students seemed to respect Kozol's ideas the more they worked with his style. Several students said that at first they had no interest in his argument, that they did not want to read one more attack on their relative economic privilege, but because they could not simply skim over the text but had to attend to the ways Kozol's sentences were working, perhaps counterintuitively, they had to contend with his larger argument. In a sense, they trusted him first at the level of style before they trusted his larger argument, in the sense that they believed that what he chronicled was factually true, that he was honest, and that the problems he witnessed to were real. This is not to say that all students in class found the book fully successful. Most in fact were disappointed with what they called the absence of "solutions"—a failing, if you will, that Kozol himself addresses in his later books.[3] But it is to say that first attending to questions of form at the level of the sentence—not only as readers but as themselves writers struggling to say something that matters—seemed to give students the time and space to contend with his ideas.

Fakundiny's approach to diction and syntax as a matter of choice pointed us toward a larger consideration of rhetoric. Choice itself had to be complicated, to be broadened to include more than a matter of individual writerly choice. What is understood as a choice depended on the rhetorical context, and how one decided on what would be the appropriate diction and syntax depended in part on one's purpose, one's audience, and how one wanted to present oneself. Further, we found that writerly choice—a way to think, in fact, about intention—could not control what readers would do with a text. Readers come to texts with various investments, different levels of familiarity with rhetorical conventions, and various expectations about how certain kinds of words and certain kinds of sentence architecture work—how, that is, form itself signifies. To broaden our discussion of style, then, I introduced what Edward Corbett referred to as "modes of persuasion," using the Aristotelian terminology of ethos, pathos, and logos to see if that might add a useful level of complexity to our understanding. We could, for example, see the extent to which Kozol rested his appeal on evidence as well as on our human sympathies, but also how he cast himself as a character in his text, a character we could trust. He had been a teacher "in Boston in a segregated school so crowded and so poor that it could not provide [his] fourth grade with a classroom" (Kozol 1991, 1). When he attempted to "resuscitate" the students' interest in learning by teaching the poems of Langston Hughes and Robert Frost, he was fired because these poets were not on the "approved list" and were thought to be too "advanced," too "inflammatory" (2). Through such testimony, Kozol establishes credibility not as a well-meaning outsider, but as a heroic insider, as a variation on the familiar cultural figure of the rebel teacher. The power of the first person is not sufficient to persuade, of course, but the power of the first person goes to motive—this is why he seeks out the facts about a forgotten place like east St. Louis. He is thus disinterested in the best sense of the word—he is writing on behalf of others as a fellow human being, having nothing materially to gain from his argument other than the satisfaction of righting a wrong.

But, as the class recognized, the heroic insider is not a persona we can always adopt as writers, nor is the first person the most powerful or effective point of view from which to write. Having gotten some basic terms on the table, having tried those terms out as readers and writers, and raising further questions about what we mean by style, we turned to a series of "cases" through which to explore the question of style from other angles. The pivotal "case" for the course turned out to be James Agee and Walker Evans's *Let Us Now Praise Famous Men,* a sometimes maddening but also fascinating stylistic tour de force. Fakundiny's style of the sentence in relation to the traditional categories of argumentative appeal continued to inform our reading, but we also zoomed the lens out to larger structural questions, and in the process bumped up against the question of how or in what sense we read style as gendered. Because Agee worried quite a bit about the ethics of his undertaking, I had in mind that this text would be particularly useful in complicating our conversation about how stylistic choices contribute to our sense of a text's reliability or believability. I expected, in other words, that the text would focus attention on ethos, complicating our sense of how the first person can be said to work. Agee and Evans set out to study "North American cotton tenantry . . . in the daily living of three representative white tenant families" (Agee and Evans

1988, xlvi). How, Agee asked, were they to "contrive techniques proper to [the] recording, communication, analysis and defense" of a "portion of unimagined existence"? (xlvi). They spent only a fortnight with the families, with Evans taking photographs and Agee taking notes. What might appear to have been a straightforward task of reporting turned out to be not straightforward at all. Agee struggled to render the experience of entering, however briefly, into the lives of the families, but the text itself testifies to his lack of faith in the journalist's language of "fact": "It seems to me curious, not to say obscene and thoroughly terrifying, . . . to pry intimately into the lives of an undefended and appallingly damaged group of human beings" (7). And yet, he desires to "speak as carefully and as near truly as I am able," even though he contends that "nothing I might write could make any difference whatever" (10, 13). If the class valued Kozol's text because it seemed to offer a trustworthy account—and some degree of faith that writing about the deplorable conditions of American schools would in fact make a difference—Agee and Evans's extended photographic essay complicates our conventional reliance on the value of reporting.

We began our exploration with Walker Evans's photographs, which serve as preamble to the written text. The photographs precede the conventional apparatus of the book, they appear without captions or explanation, and nowhere in the book itself does one get a "key." While photography, as John Berger has argued, has been used as if it were a mere recording of the facts of the world, Evans's photographs work to disorient such use (Berger & Mohr 1982, 86–89). They do not "illustrate" the text that follows, but operate as another way of telling the story. I asked class members to choose one photograph that interested them and then, depending only on the photograph itself, to compose a story to accompany it. If description is treated as a basic writing assignment, story might appear to be a more basic still. And yet, just as the class found description to be a rhetorically complex operation, they found story similarly challenging.

The notebook entry assignment set up the task this way:

> Spend some time looking through the series of photographs at the beginning of *Let Us Now Praise Famous Men.* You have no other reading to do for this assignment, so take the time to really look at the details and to let your imagination work together with your knowledge of the world to help you make sense of these images. Clearly you don't know much about the photographs

other than what you see and what you can guess about the interrelationships among the pictures. So you will have to use your imagination. What story can you tell based on the photograph, one that would not do an injustice to the picture or the people depicted? You will need to draw on what you have already learned about the power of the concrete, specific description, and the importance of using description to illuminate a larger question or concern. We have seen how Kozol tells a story through the description of place, but also what he achieves through dialogue. He "peoples the setting," as the class decided. As you "make up" a story to accompany one of Evans's photographs, work on bringing people into the scene. How can you tell your story in such a way that the reader will experience the people as vividly real?

Writers in class experienced the photographs as simultaneously providing too much and too little information—as full of detail but without providing a sure sense of how (or if) the details were meant to signify. They could not rely on straight reporting because they did not have either a sure sense of the photographer's intentions or the historical guy wires that would tether the elements to a particular place and time. They thus wrote with a degree of respectful caution that is not always valued in approaches to teaching argument that privilege the affected certainty of thesis-driven prose, but was necessary here. They had to situate themselves somehow in the story as the tellers-of-the-tale, and as such they had to make evident what they could or could not know about this other human being. Almost to a person, they were loathe to presume. When we read the stories in class, we were struck by how many sentences were structured around qualifying clauses, and how much of the persuasiveness of a given story hinged on the writer making visible his or her grounds for interpreting detail in this way rather than that. Few writers presumed to write as if they were the person in the photograph, and almost all adopted some version of what one student described as an F. Scott Fitzgerald persona—thinking of the *Great Gatsby* narrator who is not the central character but a kind of curious, largely sympathetic bystander. In many of the stories, the class identified a tone of respectful distance, marked by inverted word order, clausal complexity, and words that had more to do with how one feels than a description of the material world. The least persuasive stories, in fact, seemed to be those that presumed to know more than what one could say about another human being based only on a snapshot of that physical world.

Having confronted the difficulty of making sense in writing of other people's lives based only on what we could see in a series of photographs, we turned to John Berger and Jean Mohr's *Another Way of Telling* to get some critical purchase on our interpretive practice. The history of photography as Berger constructs it, in particular photography's emergence in the nineteenth century alongside the social sciences and hence the positivist burden it bears to speak a kind of unmediated truth, provided a useful vantage point for considering conventional expectations about truth telling. We had to ask what cultural and historical presumptions do we bring to a reading of photograph or written text? What conventions do we count on, knowingly or unknowingly, to make sense of image or written word? Berger's argument is not easy, nor was it entirely useful for everyone in class, but it provided for some students in class an especially powerful way back into Agee's text and enabled one of those class discussions that marks a turning point for the whole semester.

For the next notebook entry, I asked the class to return to their photographs and this time to write a description based only on what Agee tells us, citing passages to support the interpretation. Because there is no numbered chart that connects sections of the book to particular photographs, class members once again had to write with qualifications: "[I]f I take this child to be one of the Gudgers, then I could say . . .," or "This porch, like the one Agee describes, is an important place for the family," and so on. Having on a small scale experienced the difficulty of writing about another person, they were particularly sensitive to how—or on what basis—Agee made his claims. Even though Agee expresses doubts—even agonizes—about what he is doing as a writer and observer, the class for the most part was unmoved, especially when they felt Agee was presuming to describe what one of the young women in the host family was thinking and feeling.

One of the men in class first raised the question of gender. He was made uneasy—it "creeped him out"—when he read Agee's supposition that the young woman had sexual feelings for Agee. The student apologized for what he thought was his "derailing" of the class discussion, but he needed to say that Agee's writing registered an egotism that was akin to male locker-room talk. His "derailing" was in fact a pivotal moment in the class. His comment set off a long debate about how egotism might be signaled stylistically and whether or not one can say that style is gendered in terms of diction or syntax. Egotism, as the class understood it, was not simply a matter of using the first person. They did not find Kozol, for example, egotistical. Few in class would agree that there were some set of exclusive "girl" words or "boy" words. Few would agree that men were more likely to choose some kinds of sentence structures than women.

But they all agreed that there were "ways of talking" that were associated more with men than with women, and visa versa. While few would argue that genderless prose was necessarily a good thing because they believed that "voice" was in part a matter of gender, they were concerned in reading Agee that he forgot the limitations of what he could know when he presumed that his male "eye/I" was somehow omniscient.

This was not the final word on Agee. His writing is too various to sum up this way and then discard. In subsequent notebook entries, the class worked on the different argumentative appeals—where and how he appeals to reason and logic, how he establishes credibility as an observer, how he calls on our fellow feelings. But, perhaps more importantly, Agee asks us to judge his work as art, rather than journalism. It would be difficult to say that Agee employs only one style of writing. Rather, *Let Us Now Praise Famous Men* is something like a stylistic sampler: there are bits of personal essay and of nature writing, bits that mimic musical composition, bits of philosophy and sociopolitical analysis, and there are bits that defy any attempt at an easy label. As much as Agee feels an ethical obligation to render the "real" on behalf of the tenant families, he believes that to do so he must turn to what he calls the language of imagination. In asking the class to consider where they see the "language of imagination" and how or in what ways it can be said to be distinguishable from any other kind of language, we had to confront in yet another way how diction and syntax alone cannot distinguish between fact and fiction, much less an ethical or unethical intent.

This discussion anticipated our reading of Patricia Williams's text later in the semester, but it is of course one thing to come to an understanding of style as never just a neutral matter nor simply there on the page, and something else for such an understanding to enable writing. We needed to work on a longer piece of writing to do the work of synthesizing understandings they had been developing. With Berger/Mohr and Agee/Evans as their guides, I asked them to compose a photographic essay that makes visible to the reader something that may not be so apparent about an issue or question that the writer takes to be important or in need of attention. The writers were to choose an issue or question about which they had some expertise or knowledge but about which they still had more to learn. The writers needed to take their own photographs, understanding that they should not simply illustrate the written text but have a degree of independence on the model of Evans's photographs' relationship to Agee's text. The challenge was not only to think of a question or concern, but also how best to compose the essay given the stylistic choices and challenges we had been exploring thus far. The stance of the essay might be to critique, to celebrate, to poke fun, to try to make sense of . . . and to do so in such a way as to engage the reader in what the writer is seeing, noticing, and thinking. Members of the class submitted a proposal for the essay with a set of five photographs and a preliminary sense of what stance they wanted to take. I expected that the assignment would be challenging because it was open-ended and because it depended on each student having a strong enough stake in a question or problem to propel a sustained piece of writing.

Most striking about the class response to the assignment was the students surprise that their commitments, investments, or expertise might actually serve as the basis for intellectual work in the classroom. Mostly juniors and seniors in a large university, they had experienced primarily large classes in which the delivery of information was the primary form of teaching. Such an education did not prevent them from having their own private views or from putting what they learned in one class together with what they learned in another, but rarely did they feel that their own views and their own ways of synthesizing knowledge found a way into course work. If anything, the excitement most of them expressed about the assignment added to the anxiety, because they wanted to do this well. The range of proposed topics was the first sign that this assignment might just work. Some members of the class proposed topics close to their vocational interests, while others took the opportunity to reflect on aspects of the urban environment that troubled or intrigued them. Still others wanted to explore some part of their family history, or the history of their hometowns, or a relationship with a friend, a parent, a teacher. The photographic essays far exceeded in sophistication, strength of research, and sheer interest any papers I had read before.

A premed student, Allan Wong, the student who wrote about the morgue for an earlier notebook assignment, decided to reflect on his father's medical practice.[4] Born in Taiwan, his father had spent his career working to merge Eastern and Western approaches to medicine, and Wong wanted to think through how his own anticipated practice as a physician would be strengthened if he could effect a similar synthesis. Wong wanted to compose his essay in such a way that the writing itself would embody the different approaches, but also the possibility of synthesis. He wanted, in other words, to put in conversation the language of his organic chemistry textbook with the language of his father's practice, his father's wisdom. Agee's text, in particular, gave Wong permission to mix registers, mix styles of writing. The result is a quite beautiful reflection on Western culture's expectation that science should engineer the perfect body, as if the flawless body would ensure a life without flaw, without pain.

John Douglas, who is now a high school teacher, chose to write about the Montour Trail, part of the rails-to-trails network that will eventually link Pittsburgh to Washington, D.C. Walking the Montour Trail gave Douglas the opportunity to reestablish a relationship with his father, and he renders luminous key places along his stretch of the trail. Standing on an old railroad trestle bridge, leaning against the rusting railing, Douglas and his father are startled into feeling their tethered mortality when the railing gives way; they pull back just in time, while flakes of rust drift down to the water below, resting on the surface for only a second before settling to the river bottom along with the other detritus of industrial America. Like the best of nature writers, Douglas lets the description of place get us to an understanding of these two men and their relationship.

Jennie Welter chose to write about her hometown, downriver from Pittsburgh, one of a number of towns that in losing the steel mill seemed to lose its reason for being. A mother of two children, planning to be a teacher, Welter writes about rehabbing a once-derelict building that had been a crack house. In her photographic essay, she did not want to dwell on the past, but wanted to write a "history for the future" as a kind of gift for her children. Her tone is maternal, protective of both her children and her hometown, as she describes the dedicated hand labor that rebuilds the house.

Another photographic essay explores, through a reading of the graffiti that decorates their walls, the abandoned factories in Pittsburgh's Strip District, a bustling section of wholesale and retail produce markets and trendy nightclubs that are shadowed by the multistoried brick hulls of abandoned industry; another celebrates the quirky "neighborhood" patched together by transients living in substandard student housing through the recounting of an odd barbecue ritual; still another proposes how Frick Park, one of the largest parks in the city, could be improved to better meet the health and environmental needs of the city. Whether about alcoholism in the dorms, anorexia, a brother who nearly dies of a heroin overdose, male bonding in a frat house, the "club scene" and the star D.J.'s that help to define that scene, or the necessary tranquility of a university fountain—almost all of the photographic essays hinged on the particular knowledge and vision of the writer. For the most part, the challenge for writers was not in finding something to say, but in making the right writerly choices that would allow the writer to stay true to his or her vision. Re-vision then was particularly productive because it was a collaborative effort, with the peer readers and me "lending ourselves to the other's project" as fellow writers, often by giving the writer "permission" to try something from our readings or discussion that he or she had not thought permissible in school writing before.

Kozol served as a necessary model not only because he has a clear commitment to righting a wrong but because he had researched his facts. Kozol teaches us the power of the declarative sentence and the power of testimonial, of giving those most directly affected the space to be heard. Agee too was necessary because he showed how it was possible to switch registers, mix genres, extend understanding of the inevitably inadequate facts through the intervention of the imagination, because he exposed the limitations and blindnesses of the first person—and because he makes most evident the writer's ethical responsibility to others, not only the subject one writes about but the readers one is addressing. The expectation that writers take their own photographs that should have some degree of independence from the words also proved especially powerful, in part because the photographs were a reminder that simply stating "facts" was not going to be enough. But perhaps most important was the recognition that almost all the writers in the class had a stake in what they were writing, so that crafting their writing was not externally imposed burden but writerly necessity.

These were not essays rooted in the social text of neutrality, but strongly situated writing. As they negotiated the context of class readings and conversations, as well as the expectations of readers (what would a reader need to know to understand the importance of the writer's project, they had to ask), and as they tested the limits of what had appeared to them as the monolithic style of conventional academic writing, they performed a complex understanding of style as a multiphonic set of choices. Thus, no photographic essay was "just a matter of style"; or, put differently, each essay enacted style as necessarily ideologically charged, as powerful because not neutral, as live because persuasively invested. "Lending oneself to another's project" is my colleague Paul Kameen's resonant phrase.

PART II: BELLES LETTRES AND COMPOSITION
Introduction

T. R. Johnson

Composition has long been defined as a service course—a fairly tedious set of drills to polish the skills that will enable students to proceed to the real intellectual work of the university. The five-paragraph theme, the thesis sentence, the summary, the proper citation of sources, and so on. And, above all, the ideal of "clear," error-free prose. But as long ago as 1974, Richard Lanham in *Style: An Anti-textbook* began to delineate a rather more adventurous way of approaching prose, one that had much to do with creativity and beauty. As we saw in the last section, Lanham's ideas didn't find especially fertile ground within the growing field of composition studies, and, today, any discussion of "the beautiful" would seem utterly against the grain of the central interests of the academic humanities. As Elaine Scarry has noted (1999), all discussion of beauty has been banished from the academic humanities, for beauty would seem to distract from the task of righting injustices in the world and, moreover, any engagement with beauty is always a form of exploitation. Scarry deftly argues, however, that the sorts of symmetries undergirding our delight in beautiful things is itself an indispensable aid to our attention to justice.

While teachers of composition have long celebrated critical thinking and the need to enable our students to become active citizens, we've had little to say about creativity, about writing as an "art," and about the experience of beauty. We assume such stuff belongs only to MFA programs. But part of what happens when composition teachers attend to style is precisely such an opening onto the beautiful. Students can become truly excited about their writing and cultivate an intense commitment to it. They can begin to understand craft in ways that, otherwise, most would assume is exclusively and mysteriously the province of the artist.

The first essay in this section, Tina Kelleher's "The Uses of Literature," considers the disciplinary and social dynamics of the eighteenth century, how they drove the valorization of "clarity," and how a very similar set of dynamics has reappeared today in the drive toward multicultural, content-based courses in composition. Next, Allison Alsup, in "Persuasion, More Than Argument: Moving Toward a Literary Sensitivity in the Classroom," describes from the perspective of a fiction writer who teaches composition how she seeks to instill in her students the sorts of awareness cultivated by literary artists—in particular, awareness about issues of authorial point of view and identity. The third essay in this section, Gabriel Gomez's "An Arts-Centric Composition Classroom," describes a curriculum for teaching art in an underprivileged school in the San Francisco Bay area and how it shapes his teaching of first-year composition today. Next, Melissa Goldthwaite, in "Playing with Echo: Strategies for Teaching Repetition in the Writing Classroom," explores ways of enabling students to discover repetition—repetition of sound, of image, of phrase—as a means to experiences of rhythm, which in turn can lead to increasingly powerful writing. Then Keith Rhodes, in "The 'Weird Al' Style Method: Playful Imitation as Serious Pedagogy," argues that we can ask students to imitate other writers in ways that will drastically improve their ability to craft sentences. Finally, J. Scott Farrin, in "When Their Voice Is Their Problem: Using Imitation to Teach the Classroom Dialect," delineates the way he addresses the issue of personal voice, academic discourse, and even grammar by assigning his students imitation exercises.

5

THE USES OF LITERATURE

Tina Kelleher

Writing suspends all the familiar ways of organizing thought and experience: the genres of discourse, the distinctions between disciplinary and disciplining modes of thinking, such as that between literature and philosophy. . . . [Writing] does not have a pole and does not proceed from truth. As an operator of destabilization, it liberates a space within which the separation between the sensible and the intelligible which has been mapped upon the distinction and the association of language to thought can no longer function. It breaks up closure by producing signs and effects. It produces an immanence of its own, which excludes that of a meaning prior or exterior to the process of writing itself. It is a form of autonomy, to be sure, but one that protests against the concept, for it both represents and is difference.

—Wlad Godzich, *The Culture of Literacy*

Elizabeth Rankin (2000) has identified two primary positions in contemporary style debates: neoclassicists contend style can be cultivated and learned through mimetic and practical exercises, to dress ideas and polish prose; neoromantics, on the other hand, construe style as a manifestation of a distinct voice, and the pedagogue serves to facilitate its realization and performance. Rankin contends that while neoclassicists ignore the extent to which anxieties about style interfere with an ability to formulate cogent arguments, neoromanticists imagine that "style is the man," that achieving a distinct style somehow exemplifies the ineluctable character of a person. Both positions potentially leave students mystified about how language (as a techne) works: how syntactical arrangements pace prose and reinforce meaning; how figurative language shapes thought and produces varied effects; how factors such as audience, context, and genre inform the deployment of stylistic tactics. Rankin thereby calls for a "new theory of style," supple enough to encompass the broad-ranging heuristic, psychological, and social factors that make style-based pedagogy challenging to negotiate.

My essay situates Rankin's pedagogical objectives within a broader matrix of disciplinary and social dynamics by examining how an "old theory of style," Adam Smith's *Lectures on Rhetoric and Belles Lettres* (1985; delivered in 1748),[1] postulated a series of contradictory oppositions, among and between ideas and expression, prose and poetry, work and leisure—all of which inform in varying degrees assumptions and dispositions that vex contemporary debates about relations among and between language and thought, process and product, composition and literary studies. Smith (better known for his work in moral philosophy and political economy) debunked classical rhetoricians by claiming among other things that language held the most currency when shorn of artifice, when it enabled clear, direct communication. He valued the stylistic ideal of "perspicuity" and lamented how the English language was becoming mongrelized by "foreign" and "vulgar" elements. This conservative conception of style—resistant to both linguistic and social change and intolerant of diversity, literal and figurative—assumes language bears a transparent relation to the object world, serving simply as a medium of communication (a static technology, rather than a dynamic techne).[2]

I cite Smith's interest in style as homogenized social commerce as an illustrative backdrop to a more recent trend, in which composition and expository writing courses have adopted content and principles generally associated with the field of cultural studies.[3] In an effort to make the practice of writing more accessible to students from a diverse range of disciplinary and sociocultural backgrounds, courses often draw upon reading material thought to be more relevant to students' lives: noncanonical literature, contemporary fiction and prose, as well as popular and mass culture. This preference for course content that figures issues of language style as transparent (a tendency coinciding with an ostensible turn away from certain genres and forms of literature and rhetoric deemed too remote in language usage) potentially occludes the complex ways style intensifies and motivates reading experiences and practices, and in turn, facilitates the realization of goals and objectives specific to writing pedagogy.

In the following discussion, I examine the consequences of disentangling ideas from the complexities of means and methods of written communication and oral expression, and how this obscures the relevance of style in students' development as writers. I first outline how Smith's *Lectures* conflated issues of logic and expression, by imagining style as a manifestation of individual temperament, a construal that remained in fundamental tension with the broader nationalistic and normative aims of the "new rhetoric." I then weigh the extent to which cultural studies has revivified style debates in writing pedagogy by prioritizing experience and identity, championing expressive pluralism, and retaining a preference for accessible subject matter, that is, mass and popular cultural artifacts—a predilection that in some ways mirrors Adam Smith's reductive contention that "[n]o one ever made a bargain in verse" (1985, 137), that figurative language and poetic ornament obstruct the plain dealings of popular forms of discourse and representation. By examining these stances, I wish to come to terms with how writing pedagogy can confront style impasses and honor the difficulties and frustrations students in fact experience when working to cultivate and refine their writing.[4]

* * *

The eighteenth-century Scottish belles lettres movement distinguished itself from antecedent neoclassical principles of disputation, invention, and imitation. Adam Smith's *Lectures* emphasized perspicuity of style, correct language usage, and diversity of emotional effect, largely bracketing questions of logic and persuasion to prioritize authorial character, audience reception, and dispositional taste.[5] Drawing upon existing disciplines such as moral and natural philosophy, as well as political economy, Smith postulated a "new rhetoric," which took as its object of study the vernacular and took as its social mission civil exchange, rather than political oratory.[6] The discipline from which he largely derived the basis for his theory of style—moral philosophy—later splintered into various humanistic and social scientific fields, such as aesthetics and ethnology. Smith's *Lectures* contemplated writing styles of ancient and contemporaneous sources in drama, history, law, philosophy, and politics. It provided detailed character analyses of authors (dead and living) and the style of their works and recommended methods for depicting characters in a variety of contexts. The *Lectures* range widely across genres and disciplines, surveying how emotions, such as awe, grief, modesty, and surprise, are experienced and expressed through writing; it deemed capturing "the spirit" of an author, an action, or an occasion as paramount, not only when translating a work from one language to another, but also when determining a style's effectiveness.

Smith's conception of style as temperament—as a mercurial rhetorical barometer—highlighted the expressive and social dimensions of language in unprecedented ways. At the individual level, its execution devolved from the passions and lived experience, rather than moral precepts. Swift's propensity for ridicule garners praise, for example, because his "harsh and unpleasant . . . compositions" distill a style "suit[ed] well enough with [his] morose humour" (1985, 23), while Lord Shaftsbury's "polite dignity" (59) comes under fire for breeding halfhearted expositions, imitative of the ancients. At the national level, Smith's stylistic tenet of perspicuity spoke to large-scale efforts to personify a normative moral character and to standardize the English language, to promote cultural hegemony and social assimilation in the colonies, the provinces, and the mainland.[7] His more thoroughgoing emphasis upon emotional phenomena and resonance mystified, however, some of the actual basis upon which stylistic effects were achieved—that is, through a knowledge and application of grammar and a socialized awareness of conventions of language usage. In short, the cause or means of producing a style mattered less than the end result: prose bristling with passionate conviction or the spirit of an age.

Smith's *Lectures* vividly register incongruities between the practical enactment of and theoretical justification for an ethos, and this tension has left its trace upon how style variously figures in contemporary writing pedagogy within the humanities and across the disciplines. Writing-intensive courses, for example, often prioritize academic argument, valorizing a "plain style" to create knowledge and to convey research findings. Indeed, Smith in "Lecture 7" notably differentiated the characters and styles of the "plain" and "simple" man, regarding the former as one who, among other things, clings to a "self-sufficient imperious temper" (1985, 37) and the latter as one who was "open to conviction" and "more given to admiration and pity . . . and compassion than the contrary affections" (38). While in the *Lectures,* a plain style does not necessarily correspond to or rest upon the same exclusionary premises of perspicuity, it does presuppose a known standard; and while such style discourse continues to saturate commentary about and descriptions of writing, it's not necessarily accompanied by reflection upon the ways in which language produces its plain effects.

Smith equated a plain style with a certain detached cognitive self-satisfaction (exemplified for him by Swift's critical forte, ridicule), and this epistemological orientation potentially resonates with contemporary calls for a "plain style," to the extent that it assumes one can channel ideas and logic through language, without explicitly addressing how the medium of language realizes the expression of ideas in written form. It uncritically perpetuates the *belles lettres* conflation of style of language

usage with the character and disposition of authors, as if writing unprob-
lematically reflected such diverse and varied human attributes as intelligence and personality. It discounts how the complexities of interpersonal
dynamics and social expectations can inhibit self-expression, or indeed,
determine whether one in fact practices the skill of writing in various
disciplinary and social contexts. David Russell, for example, trenchantly
traces the evolution of these conflicting understandings of writing, noting how in late-nineteenth-century America "the mass education system
tenaciously clung to the outmoded conception of writing as transcribed
speech and to the vanishing ideal of a single academic community, united by common values, goals, and standards of discourse," which resulted
in "a conceptual split between 'content' and 'expression,' learning and
writing" (1991, 5).[8]

Critics and teachers within the contemporary humanities have regarded ad hominem style talk circumspectly, in part for the evident way it casts
specious judgments upon means and methods of self-expression. The
invocation of a plain style particularly stirs serious misgivings and conten-
tious questioning: what social norms belie "straight talk"? what emotional
sterility does it impossibly require? what political naïveté underscores
this rhetorical populism? While well warranted, such skepticism forestalls
discussions of how these issues can be used to pedagogical advantage;
further, preemptively scorning style has had far-reaching consequences
for teachers of writing: causing some to disavow their specific disciplinary expertise or to efface the intellectual and social value of their labor
by dismissing stylistic considerations as finessed lessons in grammatical
instruction. Such responses impact how students experience and value
our pedagogical ministrations. Cultural studies has in recent years posed
a compelling challenge to style talk, and I now wish to examine briefly the
extent to which some of its methods and procedures in the writing classroom have at once enabled valuable interrogation, while also replicating
in key ways some of the signature logistical and methodological impasses
of its belle-lettristic predecessor.[9]

Cultural studies approaches commonly interrogate the ethical and
social assumptions underlying service-oriented writing courses that aim
primarily to prepare students to truck, barter, and trade in academic
discourse. But just as *belles lettres* reoriented scholastic interest away from
Greek and Latin texts toward contemporaneous vernacular literature,
cultural studies shifts academic focus from literature and rhetoric toward
mass culture and other popular forms of representation. The historical

circumstances and justifications underscoring these respective methods of inquiry obviously differ. Cultural studies performs its maneuvers
presuming in part that privileging categories such as experience, personal expression, and identity democratizes access to higher education,
encouraging students to participate in their learning by reflecting upon
issues relevant to, and capable of transforming, their individual lives and
the social world. *Belles lettres,* on the other hand, appealed to perspicuity,
claiming it promoted the kind of discursive homogeneity and social harmony that yielded productive commercial and managerial exchanges.

These contrasting humanistic initiatives nonetheless bear striking
resemblances when juxtaposed. *Belles lettres* glossed style's particularity as a
phenomenon of written language by collapsing it into individual temperament; cultural studies likewise eclipsed the specificity of style with respect
to matters of writing by casting it as a product of social and political effects.
Both models consequently emphasize the role of consumers: while *belles
lettres* addressed the emotional reactions of audiences and readers, cultural
studies focused upon the construction and formation of individual and
group identities within the context of, and in relation to, mass and popular culture. As a result, each approach rests upon its own set of normative
assumptions about how individuals identify with or relate to dominant and
marginalized social identities: for example, *belles lettres* assumed that sympathetic identifications among persons yielded productive civil and social
exchanges, while cultural studies often explores frictive relations among
classes of persons with competing interests and values.

In spite of such disparate premises, these respective humanistic
agendas purport to promote social inclusion, inside and outside the
classroom. *Belles lettres* imagined that establishing standards by which to
judge means and methods of expression made the sphere of commercial
and social commerce more inclusive, even while it required participants
to conform to conventions and ideals designed to shore up the cultural
hegemony and social manners of an emergent mercantile class. Cultural
studies largely assumed that academic inquiry into the constructed nature
of identities, as well as the function and purpose of quotidian cultural
artifacts and popular discourse, would level the playing field for students
with limited access to the kind of cultural and social capital of more privileged peers.

While cultural studies pitches its vision of the humanities as being
more politically and practically oriented than the field of literature, *belles
lettres* postulated that effective language communication promoted social

awareness and sympathy in everyday life, in ways that an anachronistic and politically motivated classical rhetoric could not. Each account consequently regards the political as somehow instrumental, without explicitly weighing the extent to which politically motivated disciplinary justifications compromise knowledge claims and pedagogical goals or the extent to which one's actions or practices do in fact achieve "political" consequences in a sphere (at best) auxiliary or tangential to the actual workings of the political domain. If Smith distilled style in part to temperament, cultural studies largely displaced it onto political and social effects; both models as a result dismiss ESL issues, tacitly assigning, for antithetical reasons, a polemic and stigma to meeting the specific language difficulties and needs of nonnative speakers. A conscientiously deployed style-based pedagogy could more openly address social inclusion in the classroom by not presupposing students already recognize linguistic and social conventions of the so-called high or low cultural kind.

Kathryn Flannery alternatively suggests, for example, that style-based pedagogy promotes civic and social virtues by equipping students with the rhetorical resources to participate actively in democratic practices, to critique and understand various kinds of rhetoric inside and outside the academy. While by and large consistent with the politics of a cultural studies approach, Flannery emphasizes the necessity for understanding style in ways that connect form to content and in terms of individual choices and effects, which manifest within preexisting disciplinary, ethical, literate, and social contexts. She perceptively notes, for example, the prevalence in composition studies of an "odd conjuncture of a liberatory (but not therefore revolutionary) rhetoric and the privileging of a normative hygienic prose (clear, concise, forceful and sincere)." (1995, 4).[10] Her historical materialist study fruitfully examines how various style agendas overlook the role of rhetoric within practices of writing, though she's less relentless about pursuing the normative flipside of counterrhetorics: that is, the so-called revolutionary rhetoric, which might lead her to places where language substantively falls short (i.e., pain, violence, the material world).

Certain kinds of agonized and aggressive language, such as cussing and swearing, commonly fall off the humanist rhetorical radar; these often figure instead as spontaneous rages of speech, beyond the more reflective pale of writing. In addition to recuperating rhetoric as an object of study, speech needs to be factored as a phenomenon that leaves an indelible impression upon the ways in which one relates to and practices writing.[11] Barthes paradoxically noted:

[I]t is ephemeral speech that is indelible, not monumental writing. . . . The correcting and improving movement of speech is the wavering of a flow of words, a weave which wears itself out catching itself up, a chain of augmentative corrections. . . . context is a structural given not of language but of speech and it is the very status of context to be reductive of meaning. The spoken word is "clear"; the banishment of polysemy (such banishment being the definition of "clarity") serves the Law—all speech is on the side of the Law. (1977b, 190–91; emphasis in original)

While acknowledging that speech transactions routinely result in misunderstandings, Barthes equates speech with "clarity," assuming that a situated context allows for clarification, which ignores the obvious fact that individuals (by definition) cannot inhabit the exact lived context of an interlocutor, regardless of whether they share a proximate social context. Barthes's series of negations in relation to speech—that is, not writing, not language, not polysemy—in short does not factor the ways in which it comes to bear upon language acquisition and writing proficiency.

My brief exegesis of cultural studies' absorption into composition and writing curricula suggested this recent development has in effect reproduced dilemmas registered long ago within *belles lettres* and other "clear, concise, forceful and sincere" style movements. Flannery, too, grasps this point at some level when she caps off her introduction, "Style as Cultural Capital," by noting:

I see this book contributing to a growing conversation concerning postmodern democratic institutions. It is neither possible nor desirable to simply recuperate John Dewey's progressive vision [of democratic education], but it does seem to be the moment—in the midst of, on the one hand, a sometimes alienating critical discourse that too often leads to nothing other than its reproduction, and on the other hand, a nostalgic return to a humanism that never was . . . [to reconsider] the paradoxical possibilities of a postmodern democracy. (1995, 32)

Following Flannery's lead, I focus less upon the real or imagined political consequences of these methodologies than on the bearing they have upon institutional and professional responsibilities, to value commensurately and proportionately the teaching of reading and writing, alongside other forms of research, scholarship, and knowledge production. As questions of style have obsessed rhetoricians from antiquity to the modern world, I wish to consider the extent to which an enduring interest in and suspicion of style informs present-day professional convictions. This essay thereby focuses less upon the particular ways style achieves sundry intellectual skills and virtues (i.e., specific exercises or lessons exceed the scope of this discussion),[12] than on making the versatility of style an evident cognitive and experiential feature that touches upon and weaves through so many dimensions of our reading and writing practices.

***

In recent years, writing programs have increasingly deemed literary texts (especially poetry and pre-nineteenth-century novels and prose works) as too remote in their language, syntax, and subject matter to help students develop the techniques of effective writers. James Slevin (2001) productively challenges this assumption by suggesting composition and expository writing programs strategically adopt canonical parents that cut across various genres, to expose students to language's rich array of expressive possibilities.[13] Stylistic analyses of literary works abet such reflection, precisely because these artifacts often consist of intensified uses of language, different from most conventional disciplinary and everyday discourse. Poetry may in fact, for example, best illustrate these issues, as it at once emphasizes and problematizes the notion of "self-expression," casting interpretive focus onto the ways in which diction, rhythm. and syntax structure lines of verse and convey a menagerie of emotions that may or may not be conducive to economic or social commerce. Poetry, of course, existed prior to writing and, generally speaking, flourished in communal-based and oral cultures. Smith, for example, begins "Lecture 23" marveling at the fact that "a species of writing [i.e., poetry] so vastly more difficult [than prose] should be in all countries prior to that in which men naturally express themselves" (1985, 136). He then conveniently dichotomized the function and purpose of these respective discursive "species": for Smith, poetry aligns with "barbarous nations," with pleasure and amusement, with unnatural expressive constructs, fettered by numbers; prose, by contrast, aligns with commerce and modernity, with conducting business and the refinement of social manners, with spontaneous expressive exchanges—that is, conversation. Smith thereby concluded:

> In the first ages of Society, when men have their necessities on their hands, they keep their business and their pleasure altogether distinct; they neither mix pleasure with their business, nor business with their pleasure; Prose is not ornamental nor is verse applied to subjects of Business. It is only when

pleasure is the only thing sought after that Prose comes to be studied. People who are rich and at their ease cannot give themselves the trouble of anything where they do not expect some pleasure. The common transactions of life, as Deliberation and Consultation on what they are to do, are of themselves too dry and unpleasant for them, without the ornaments of language and elegance of expression. 'Tis then Deliberative and Judicial eloquence are studied and every ornament is sought out for them. (1985, 137–38)

Smith superimposed a mutually exclusive relation among the spheres of business and pleasure, work and leisure, casting classical rhetoricians' interest in elegance and ornament in prose as a kind of baleful quest for luxurious goods, which required a new rhetoric capable of regulating the profligate tendencies of poetic ornament within the arena of prose.

I originally titled this essay Adam Smith's "Rhetorical Hand" to render visible a critical historical juncture when practices of writing and elements of style were reconceived in terms I believe have had far-reaching consequences for modern-day pedagogical contexts and professional convictions. For with Smith, generic distinctions among kinds and styles of writing become complexly imbricated with various forms of social distinction, associated with the sphere of political economy as well as moral philosophy. The composition of poetry became anathema to prose writing, and figurative language was cast as a potential obstacle to efficient communication. Smith in effect naturalized prose as an expressive enterprise that improved with, and in fact helped optimize, commerce. In his rigid bifurcation of work and pleasure, prose and poetry, he glossed how writing entails a kind of alienation of speech, how prose flows from neither conversation nor commerce, but from writers grappling with the cognitive and experiential challenges posed when navigating the complexities of language and written forms of communication. By the same token, the cultural studies movement has amply demonstrated that stylistic considerations extend to nonliterary as well as nonlinguistic artifacts, which suggests that reading practices play a pivotal role in determining how and whether students apprehend and reflect upon issues of style within the context of their own writing.

While I therefore largely agree with Slevin's call to include literature and a diverse array of cultural artifacts in writing curricula and syllabi, I am also proposing something more skeptical of language's relation to experience, of its freewheeling expressive possibilities: that is, perhaps we have overlooked the obvious—the immeasurable virtues of depersonalizing the stakes of style. I raise this point acknowledging the need to encourage students to care about their writing, without taking critical feedback personally (a central paradox of effective writing pedagogy). During workshops, for instance, students often censor themselves, perhaps because they have so thoroughly internalized at various stages of their educational instruction the spurious notion that "writing is a form of self-expression," a conviction that makes it difficult to reflect upon writing as a techne that requires ongoing practice and reflection.[14] I hence propose that a style-based pedagogy emphasizing how language and sign systems produce various effects, which cannot necessarily be controlled or fully foreseen, would foster frank and respectful engagement with peers' written work. Some basic principles of literary interpretation—that is, not confusing the narrative perspective or voice with the author and understanding how stylistic considerations factor in determining explicit and implied meaning—do, I think, apply to generating constructive workshop dynamics, particularly if the historically situated values of students can be challenged and made relevant to the effects and mechanics of writing in various disciplinary, generic, and social contexts. Further, conceiving writing and its attendant stylistic matters as an expressive enterprise potentially inhibits students needing the most help when working to build writing proficiency, because difficulties and setbacks become experienced—by logical extension—as a kind of personal failure.

I therefore contend that curriculum content at once matters more and less than imagined: it matters more because unhelpful assumptions continue to be made about the relevance of style to the development of strategies and techniques of writers, and it matters less because the care and facilitative efforts of the pedagogue models for students how to pursue and to realize independent thinking, how to labor at and relish the beauty of a craft. Two prominent figures serve as instructive examples of how personal voice frequently figures in style debates and writing pedagogy; they also register the extent to which contradictory disciplinary and professional anxieties about style lie at the heart of conflicts among, between, and within composition, literary, and cultural studies. Peter Elbow's career and work eloquently attests to how a passion for medieval literature and metrics can translate into a belief in and commitment to style as the realization of authorial voice in composition classrooms; likewise, Richard Rodriguez poignantly relates in his popular essay "The Achievement of Desire" the rewards and struggles of reconciling a bilingual upbringing with a fascination for the otherness of the Renaissance (see Elbow 2002; Rodriguez 2002). Each ambivalently attests to the virtues of studying subjects far removed from their personal experiences and social circumstances, how a turn away from the self potentially enabled a more authentic authorial voice to flourish.

Rodriguez's meditation, inspired in part by his deep identification with Richard Hoggart's description of the "scholarship boy" in *The Uses of Literacy,* commences with a pedagogical scene in which he tries to interest students in the sounds of words, while later in the essay, he contemplates occasions when he imitated teachers' ways of speaking, a form of emulation that coincided with a pall of silence that socially detached him from his parents. A breaking point of sorts eventually occurs as he completes his doctoral studies in Renaissance literature; "drawn by professionalism to the edge of sterility [he can produce only] pedantic, lifeless, unassailable prose" (p. 669) and he takes solace in a nostalgia for the past and a journey to unearth his own unadulterated voice. Elbow also registers professional anxieties around the topic of style as he contemplates the respective "cultures" of literature and composition studies:

> The culture of literary studies puts a high value on style and on not being like everyone else. I think I see more mannerism, artifice, and self-consciousness in bearing (sometimes even slightly self-conscious speech production) among literary folk than composition folk. Occasionally I resist, yet I value style and artifice. What could be more wonderful than the pleasure of creating or appreciating forms that are different, amazing, outlandish, useless—the opposite of ordinary, everyday, pragmatic? Every child is blessed with an effortless ability to do this: it's called play (p. 540).

Elbow strikingly personifies style in terms of professional demeanors: just like Smith's "simple" man prone to modesty and sympathy, composition "folk" emerge as down-to-earth foils to their more fashionable cousins in literature, who more or less pose in this account as dandified versions of Smith's "plain" man: indulgently lecturing about literary texts, imperiously ignoring what students and others feel and think, and unabashedly relishing "not being like everyone else." Elbow ends by reveling in the prospect of "style play," paradoxically admitting that it's something he simultaneously "resist[s]" and "value[s]," yet something any unschooled "child" can perform. His fixation upon the palaver of "literary folk"—the "self-conscious speech production"—also curiously deflects (in a manner similar to Rodriguez) questions of reading and writing to matters of sound and speech, a maneuver that reveals the extreme to which Elbow equates style with self-expression and voice.

For my purposes, these testimonies—engaging and remarkable as they are as autobiographic sketches—are of interest for the ways in which they figure issues of speech and voice in relation to practices of writing and how they reference process in the development of readers and writers. As both Elbow and Rodriguez confess, writing can be a real pain; yet both precipitously jump to the palliative punch line: it's in the end a pleasurable experience, because it helps cultivate and realize authentic voices. Repressing the tribulations of process deprives us of a means to describe and to manage pain, which makes a significant psychological difference from the student's perspective, when persevering through those all-too-familiar moments when writing feels like strenuous effort, rather than a hedonic orgy with the Muses atop Mt. Helicon. Connecting style to process exposes possibilities for sentence-level and global revisions and provides working vocabularies to explain how writing communicates meaning—whether it be in creative or disciplinary contexts or in workaday lives. I also believe emphasizing style as a volatile yet integral part of understanding cultural artifacts, as well as the writing process itself, could assist in reevaluating the pedagogical virtues of process as praxis. Many have dismissed process theory for its alleged scientific pretensions, though the primary bone of contention has perhaps always in fact been the notion that any process could be definitively theorized, independent of context-specific writing occasions. As stylistic considerations can be fraught with matters of choice and contingency, it holds out the possibility of addressing issues of process in ways that neither fetishize nor reify matters particular to practices of writing.

Additionally, when teaching writing from sources, the category of style productively straddles a variety of interrelated concerns and objectives: drawing attention to factors that illuminate how and on what terms any given source derives its authority; highlighting how issues of tone factor in the articulation and reception of claims; prompting critical reflection when selecting and interrogating passages representing, or indeed contradicting, an author's ostensible meaning; inspiring students to create knowledge and to place ideas into a meaningful dialogue with thinkers past and present.

Cultural studies' preference for popular subject matter and reading material poses special challenges when using stylistic considerations to negotiate the teaching of writing from sources, to the extent that it often requires students to investigate and research topics for which only recent journalistic sources exist. In this case, the assumption that students feel more engaged by, or can more readily access, current events and mass and popular cultural artifacts confronts the stresses and trials of a lived experiment. Students sometimes discover during the research process that a library's academic resources can and should be bypassed by whatever a Google search regurgitates, as often academic articles and books about contemporary subjects and popular culture have not yet made their way into library collections.[15] This introduces problems specific to evaluating and negotiating online sources, and even the hippest cultural studies practitioner can find him- or herself staring down a yawning generational chasm, as rapid technological developments transform the ways a new generation conducts research and writing. Such changes acutely register around Internet plagiarism crises that have recently beleaguered the academy in unprecedented ways and that have extended to and troubled the ways in which we regard the credibility of journalistic sources. I can here only gesture toward some of the broader ramifications of these trends—for example, how blogging, e-mail, and chat rooms contribute to understanding writing as speech, as spontaneous, unreflective exchange,[16] and how news venues and Web sites use stylistic flourishes as a substitute for substantive content—but the bottom line remains that it's now more than ever important to stage a counteroffensive by equipping students with the means to evaluate stylistic matters with critical acumen and verve.

***

The comparisons I have drawn among some general tenets of the eighteenth-century Scottish *belles lettres* movement, as articulated by Adam Smith, and the contemporary, heterogeneous field of cultural studies, suggest that conventional wisdom concerning how individuals interact with and relate to practices of reading and writing can be productively challenged. Nowhere does this state of affairs become more obvious than when examining the complexities of style debates in writing pedagogy. Smith may have imagined business and pleasure, prose and poetry, as if in colloidal suspension, but as I have tried to demonstrate, this fallacious reasoning belied the porous disciplinary foundations of the new rhetoric. Effective writing pedagogy should explore ways in which business and pleasure coalesce and intermingle with each other, and a style-based pedagogy can serve as a potent vehicle, synthesizing the various strengths of composition, literature, and cultural studies[17]—in the service of effective writing pedagogy across the curriculum, and most importantly, in the service of promoting the intellectual and personal growth of students. By exposing the limitations and virtues of linguistic choice, style highlights the synergistic cognitive and experiential components of reading and writing and provides a provisional means to traverse vast disciplinary terrains.

The OED indicates that a synonym of style, glamour (i.e., a charm, spell, or personal effect), in fact manifested as a corrupt version of the Scottish term grammar (i.e., linguistic conventions, principles, and rules), and I conclude this essay emphasizing how these phonetic cousins, though ostensibly not etymologically related, in fact have always, in some degree, provoked interconnecting anxieties and desires relating to cultural prestige and social status. Some may regard these as immiscible terms—the remedial and thankless work of grammar (i.e., composition) versus the sophisticated and wondrous phenomenon of glamour (i.e., literature)—and I have suggested throughout this essay that the pedagogical and professional consequences of this narrow conception of complex and diverse language effects begs continued scrutiny. Far from being a transient academic fashion craze, style discourse continues to incite debate and provoke interest in ways that attest to its vitality in promoting an engaged and reflective writing pedagogy.

6

PERSUASION, MORE THAN ARGUMENT: MOVING TOWARD A LITERARY SENSITIVITY IN THE CLASSROOM

Allison Alsup

As an aspiring author of fiction, I know that style is critical, and for those of us who consider ourselves literary fiction writers, style is often paramount. For the most part, we do not write about elves or vampires, bodies found in bathtubs or mutineered nuclear subs. This is not to make a snobbish distinction or to imply that writers such as C. S. Lewis or J. R. R. Tolkien have not produced work worthy of being called literature. The term literary fiction does not usually designate a qualitative distinction but rather functions as the jargon of book promoters to let retailers know in which section of the store a book should be shelved. However, it is safe to say that most creative writing MFA programs focus on literary fiction, filling their students' heads with hopes of book critic circle and university press awards, for these prizes are almost always given to works of literary fiction rather than to exercises in genre.

However, producing such work can be a burden. For in the absence of ripped bodices and space-borne viruses, what most of us choose to work with is relatively mundane: everyday people and their often pedestrian problems: growing bellies, shrinking love lives, distant fathers, inexplicable apathy. Somehow we have to make such characters fresh, their ennui compelling, their crises sympathetic. Given that most of us eschew real plots almost to the point of pride, style remains our primary resource. Indeed, one of the highest praises that can be given to an author of literary fiction is that he or she writes of ordinary people in extraordinary detail. We want to see rough woolen lives combed until they gently brush our senses like a cashmere blanket.

The importance of style becomes obvious when one reads a critically acclaimed piece of fiction. While book flaps are dedicated to trying to explain often paltry plots or the tenuous connections between a collection of stories, the back covers and inside pages are often dedicated to praising the author's style. Scanning my bookshelves for some recent favorites yields two quick examples. Author Charles Baxter notes of Tony Earley's *Here We Are in Paradise:* "You can open this book almost anywhere at random and find a beautifully written and compelling paragraph. Tony Earley writes his stories with care, word by word, and sentence by sentence, and they are distinguished by their feeling for the specifics of lives lived in one place, and for their intelligence and for their humor." *New York Times* critic Michiko Kakutani has this to say about Jhumpa Lahiri's Pulitzer Prize–winning debut: "A wonderfully distinctive new voice. . . . Ms. Lahiri's prose is so eloquent and assured that the reader forgets that *Interpreter of Maladies* is a young writer's first book." Critics and reviewers expound not on what possible readers can expect to read, but how they will feel while reading it.

"Crafting fiction" is an expression constantly uttered in creative writing workshops, a phrase that calls to mind a fine cabinetmaker whose work is distinguished by precision: measuring, trimming, planing, sanding, polishing. So, too, are we writers to approach our fiction, to smooth the rough edges of our work through meticulous editing. Charles Baxter's praise of Earley's work—word by word, sentence by sentence—follows the same metaphor. What emerges from such diligent efforts is really our style, the most important distinction between literary writers. In fact, one could argue that literary fiction, more than anything else, is an exercise in style. About half the writers I've met seem to think everything worth saying has already been said and by someone more intelligent. If this is indeed true, then what is literary fiction but an exercise in style? Of course, there are those writers with whom we identify certain themes or settings: Ernest Hemingway's Spain, John Updike and Richard Ford's perennial adulterers, Alice Munro's historical inconoclasts. But certainly their styles are equally identifiable, and I would suggest it is their stylistic mastery rather than their subjects that attracts a loyal audience. Writing is art, and art without style is simply not art.

Readers often ask writers how it is that they begin stories. One would guess that stories begin with a character, an event, or perhaps a specific setting. Sometimes this is true in my own writing. However, what is just as often an impetus is the particular mood I want to evoke. Do I want my readers to confront a hard-hitting first-person narrator, to be lulled by an elegant omniscience, or to savor a small-town chaw? Do I want the hard-boiled immediacy of the present tense or the mandarin voice of the past, seducing its readers with antiquated words? Evoking a particular style or feeling is not only my starting point, but often my goal.

Several years ago, I read Ethan Canin's novel, *For Kings and Planets.* Though ultimately disappointed in the plot (and again, this now seems a minor flaw), I was positively smitten by its opening paragraph:

> Years later, Orno Thatcher would think of his days in New York as a seduction. A seduction and a near miss, a time when his memory of the world around him—the shining stone stairwells, the taxicabs, the sea of nighttime lights— was glinting and of heroic proportion. Like a dream. He had almost been taken away from himself. That was the feeling he had, looking back. Smells and sounds: the roll and thunder of the number 1 train; the wind like a flute through the deck rafters of the Empire State Building; the waft of dope in the halls. Different girls and their lives coming back to him: hallways and slants of light. Daphne and Anne-Marie and Sofia. He remembered meeting Marshall Emerson on his second day at college, at dawn on the curb of 116th Street and Broadway, the air touched with the memory of heat that lingered in the barest rain. It had reminded him of home.

I stopped reading after this passage, put the book down. I reread the passage again, noting all the hallmarks of fine prose: his crisp word choice—shining stone stairwells, the curb of 116th Street and Broadway— then his rhythm, built by several series of details linked by commas or semicolons. There is a lovely cadence to this passage, beginning with a simply stated yet enticing sentence: "Years later, Orno Thatcher would think of his days in New York as a seduction." Following the rhythmic repetition of the "er" sound, Canin lulls the reader with details, occasionally reminding us again of the scope of the passage with phrases such as "Like a dream," stroking our imaginations with additional details before packing the final punch, a return to the simple: "It had reminded him of home." There is both surprise and cohesion in Canin's juxtaposed imagery: the hypnotic music of the wind like a flute through the deck rafters of the Empire State Building and the hypnotic smell of the waft of dope in the halls. Canin is writing about the seduction of New York City, yet it is his own prose that is the seduction, a whispered promise to the reader of intimacy to follow.

I vowed that someday I would write a passage as finely crafted as this. I yearned to imitate Canin's sweep and sentiment, and as I struggle to edit my first collection of fiction, I keep in mind how I felt when I read this passage. More than anything else, it is the attempt (at times, I admit, a far cry) to re-create something akin to Canin that has anchored my own efforts. A while back, I hit on the phrase "urban fairytale" and for months on end, repeated it like a mantra. This summer, while exchanging manu-scripts with another writer, I found myself evoking the phrase once again. My main concern for one of the stories was that it feel "beautiful. Like an urban fairytale," I told him. He nodded and scribbled down a note to himself, and indeed when we met next to discuss our thoughts on the pieces, he pointed out several places where there's additional room for ethereal possibilities.

Then summer ends. I would like to say that come fall I continually apply the same literary sensitivity in my classroom as I have to my own work in the months before. But I must make a confession. I am often guilty of sidelining style, relegating it to a quick cameo appearance in the classroom. So often as an instructor, I downplay issues of style as if matters of point of view, for example, were a concern only for the more technically adept, as if my students just wouldn't understand or appreci-ate such discussions. I assign beautifully tailored pieces only to assume that my students lack the ability to re-create such quality. I tell them that in the best works, content and structure and style are not distinct elements but rather an integrated whole. Yet I rarely ask them to aim for this synthesis in their own work. I think we have to get down to the basics—grammar, paragraph organization, the almighty thesis. By the third week of August, issues of style seem to inhabit a distant universe. I become the ultimate hypocrite.

But I fear I am not alone. I fear many of my fellow teachers do the same. If they could just produce a competent argument, we bemoan over beers, then complain how we have to read seventy-five papers that could be titled "Why Women Need Equal Rights but Not Feminism." As one teacher friend recently said, "Style? Who has time for style? My students can't write a complete sentence." Our litanies intone the same words over and over again: competency, argument, logic, fallacy, evidence, Evidence, EVIDENCE. The same words we would hope to see applied to our own work—lyrical, dramatic, suspenseful—disappear from our vocabulary. It's as if style has become an extra feature like power windows rather than part of the basic model. The problem? Absolute hypocrisy. We leave stu-dents to grasp instinctually what we have painstakingly honed since we left our graduate programs: a style worthy of notice.

One can chalk such attitudes up to snubbing or poor teaching. But one cannot just point fingers at burned-out instructors. Avoiding teaching style is not just a matter of a bad attitude. Some of us, I know, are ach-ing to devote more time to rhythm, metaphor, and detail but question whether such intense focus on style is in keeping with the aims of our course. Despite numerous discussions at faculty meetings, I continue to find myself asking just what kind of writing am I supposed to be teaching in freshman comp? And particularly for those programs with exit exams: can we take the chance that the evocative, detailed narrative will not be considered in keeping with departmental standards ? Or that, as I have heard some say, it is not even an essay at all? If the operating words are argumentation and logic, then we should not be surprised when stylistic considerations become afterthoughts. On the other hand, if the operating words are persuasion and suggestion, then style matters. I suspect that my department is not alone in having somewhat ambiguous objectives. One could argue that it is precisely such ambiguity that allows teachers a certain freedom. However, when it is not evident that such latitude is acceptable, we should not be surprised when newer, untenured faculty fail to devote time to explore style. Not only do the students miss out, but so do the instructors. MFA's like myself, who are increasingly teaching university composition courses to make a living, are trained in style. Should we be teaching without capitalizing on our expertise? Promotion and tenure committees themselves may also send a message that style is not as important as other factors. Among faculty publications, most university promotion committees tend to weigh research and argumentative papers more heavily than creative or reflective pieces. Though unintentional, slighting style is endemic to the way most colleges operate.

I've begun to address this problem in my classroom. During the third segment of the semester, we take a break from studying the formal features of argument to examine what are essentially narratives. It is not that the texts are not essays. They contain a thesis, evidence, development. It is that they, as I tell my students, persuade rather than argue. Thematically, the series of readings focuses on outsiders or ethnic and socioeconomic difference. We read several essays by minority writers, writers who are marginalized not only within the dominant Anglo culture, but often within their own communities as well. Joan Nestle's "A Restricted Country," for instance, recounts her family's first trip together. Joan, a teenage Jew from the Bronx and longtime dreamer of the Wild West, joins her older brother and single, working-class mother on a trip to a western dude ranch in Arizona only to discover anti-Semitism from gentiles and class snobbery among wealthy Jews. In "Complexion," Richard Rodriguez, a native of California's Central Valley, examines his childhood anxieties. Rodriguez describes the double bind he faced growing up as a Mexican

American male: the dark skin that his female relatives found unattractive and the interest in literature that his male relatives found unmacho. The third essay, Brent Staples's "Black Men and Public Space," describes how Staples, as a large African American male, has met with suspicion, fear, and even physical threats when he walks on city streets.

However, after teaching these particular essays my discussions tend to be less about politics than about poetics. These essays are ripe with compelling stylistic choices. They provide ample context for addressing rhythm, detail sequencing, metaphor, and point of view, the same kinds of issues that short story writers and novelists routinely face when producing their own work.

At the end of the segment, students are given a choice to write either an analytical paper about the author's stylistic choices or a creative narrative based on the structures provided by Brent Staples or Joan Nestle. Not surprisingly, almost all of the students choose the latter. Staples's organization is fairly straightforward: hook, thesis, examples, background, more examples, stakes and consequences, solution. Nestle, in contrast, divides her essays into a set of scenes, each with its own minithesis or epiphany. Staples's essay offers a macroview in describing incidents that span his life; Nestle delivers a microview, instead focusing on one week of her adolescence. Though both essays are about identity, Staples's work aims to prove a social phenomenon exists, Nestle's to trace one case of personal development. Once the students have selected the format they think will best explain their experience, the usually tough tasks of structure and content are largely resolved and the students are freer to devote themselves to stylistic considerations.

The students seem to respond to these essays more than most. Perhaps this is because we as readers tend to respond in kind when writers expose their vulnerabilities. Perhaps it is because so many of my students have just narrowly escaped the pit of adolescence and are still raw with memories of social ostracism. Or it could also be that students, although not necessarily able to articulate their reasons, recognize powerful prose when they read it.

Flannery O'Connor once noted that she strove to distill the essence of the story in its opening sentence. Nestle, Rodriguez, and Staples have followed suit. Here is Joan Nestle's: "When the plane landed on the blazing tar strip, I knew Arizona was a new world." Rodriguez begins like this: "Complexion. My first conscious experience of sexual excitement concerns my complexion." Staples chooses to play with his reader, masquerading as a criminal: "My first victim was a woman—white, well dressed, probably in her early twenties." In doing so, he underscored the essay's major theme: the stereotyping of black men. These first lines serve as a segue into discussing how content and style can mesh, how the strongest of hooks not only pique the reader's attention but also underscore an essay's major point.

My students tend to call these pieces stories and though I am quick to point out that they are in fact essays, my students are right in that these texts employ the same literary sensitivities as fiction. It is interesting that all three authors chose to begin in-scene—that is, with an action set in a particular time and place. All fiction writers know that the first few lines of a story should not only ground the reader but also set the tone for what follows. Given the importance of synthesizing description and mood, the ordering of details can be tricky territory. If given six critical details, how do we, as writers, decide what should go first or second or third?

Sometimes sequencing is a matter of logic. Others would argue that this is largely an issue of content. It is content but only to a certain degree, especially when one is dealing with the first paragraphs of a paper. Fiction writers agonize over their opening paragraphs, and agents and editors often suggest cutting the author's original paragraphs, integrating that information later and starting the work a few paragraphs down. So it's not just a matter of content. It's a matter of style, of establishing mood and pacing. What are the details that will introduce not only the subject or plot, but the author's tone? What are the observations that will, as Ethan Canin does, seduce the reader? I would argue that any ordering calculated to create a certain effect on the reader is more a question of style than content or structure.

Nestle, for instance, chooses to end her opening paragraph like this: "The desert air hit us with its startling clarity: this was not the intimate heat of New York, the heat that penetrated our flesh and transformed itself into our sweat and earned our curses." When questioned why Nestle might choose to begin her piece with an observation about the air, my students are quick to respond. As veterans of the narcotic heat of New Orleans summers, they understand why Nestle quickly moves to describing the Arizona air. Nestle's choice also makes sense logically: air is immediate, our most fundamental environment. Novelists are prone to beginning with stunning visual images that suggest the central theme of the book. And this image, my students point out, is also symbolic. Air is life. The classroom discussion then turns to what Nestle's observation portends for the rest of the essay, specifically the fate of this family, how different air suggests foreignness, even a sense of danger.

Nestle is following the old fiction adage "show, don't tell." Of course, all fiction occasionally does tell, but not without having earned the right through description that resonates with meaning and metaphor that foreshadows larger themes. Typical first-year student compositions that have argument as their sole purpose tend to do a lot of telling. Suggesting is a considerably more difficult task. Again, Nestle's essay offers another metaphor for classroom discussion. After Nestle's mother publicly embarrasses herself by trying to ride a horse, the teenage Nestle finds her mother on the outskirts of the dude ranch: "She was sitting on a child's swing, trailing one leg in the dust. A small round woman whose belly bulged in her too-tight, too-cheap pants." Several sentences later, Nestle does tell us that "Arizona was not for Regina Nestle," but only after letting her reader chew on the metaphor of powerlessness suggested by the swing, the role reversal of mother and daughter that portends Nestle's coming-of-age. Classroom discussion can also address the word choice of "too" and how this small word suggests the daughter's judgment in a way that "very" tight and "very" cheap cannot. Nestle's final line suggests a growing distance between the mother and daughter: "While I scrambled over this new brown earth, my mother sat in the desert, a silent exile."

Of course, there is always the question of what the students actually retain and even beyond that, what they will apply to their own writing. Fortunately, the students' papers have yielded some pleasant surprises. The image of Nestle's mother on the swing and all its unempowering implications of powerlessness stuck with one student as she wrote her narrative. This student explored the same helplessness and exile in her own narrative about being the only single young mother at her daughter's preschool holiday show. Here Nestle's metaphorical swing is replaced by a small plastic chair:

> I take a seat next to Haylee in one of the miniature chairs. It is cold and I am the only adult sitting down; the rest stand joined in conversation. We wait for the teacher to arrive to give us the program. As we wait, the school director comes in and suggests that we each say our name. I begin to think of a way to get out of saying my name. No such luck! It is now my turn and all eyes are on me. Their stares burn like hot lasers. In my eyes, I am just like any other parent, but to them I am merely a child myself. When I speak my head is hung low and I am nearly whispering. The rest of the parents continue their conversations.

I want nothing more than for them to include me, but instead I sit there all alone in the miniature chair.

A paragraph later, Nestle's essay once again provides an opportunity for students to analyze ordering of detail as she describes the individual motivations for her family's trip out west:

I had dreamed horses all my sixteen years, played wild stallion in the Bronx vacant lots that were my childhood fields, had read every book about wild horses, mustangs, rangy colts that I could find, and through all the splintering agonies of my family I galloped on plains that were smooth and never ending. For my brother, who had seldom been with my mother and me, this trip was both a reunion and an offering. After years of turmoil, mistakes and rage, he was giving us the spoils of his manhood. He lay this vacation at the feet of our fatherless family as if it were a long awaited homecoming gift. For my mother, it was a simple thing: her week's vacation from the office, her first trip in over twenty years.

In fiction, we might call this backstory. Nestle is supremely efficient, sketching three characters in five sentences. But Nestle's description also sets forth stakes and consequences, letting readers know from the onset all that is riding on this family trip: style and structure merge. In terms of its structure or ordering of detail, students are able to witness the progression from the least intense to the most dramatic. As we move from Nestle's fantasy to her brother's regret to her mother's subjugation, we understand there is an increasing set of stakes. Reading this passage out loud, students can also hear how rhythm itself packs the final punch. Joan's sketch of herself is like a wild horse, unbridled and roaming. With her brother, she begins to pull in the reins, paying more attention to the conventional constraints of length and grammar. And her mother's portrait, with its ironic use of "simple" juxtaposed with her own romanticized description, makes Nestle's last line—the plainest and shortest of all—the most devastating.

An ESL student, originally from Cyprus, chose to model his essay structure on Nestle. He saw similarities with his story, an analysis of his postapartheid return to South Africa where he had spent most of his childhood. This student wanted to set his first scene, as Nestle had done, with his airplane touching down. He also had considerable backstory to incorporate, which, like Nestle, would offer his readers a set of stakes for the trip. We went through multiple drafts, rearranging and tightening.

The primary challenge was how to establish a tone that felt true to his experience. After several tries, he managed to order the details so as to build intensity. Lyrical descriptions and metaphors were for the most part cut in order to mimic the blunt, rapid-fire tension of South Africa's civil strife. Here is the first paragraph of his final draft:

> I could not believe that I was on the plane returning to South Africa. We had left the country like criminals on the run after all our efforts to stay failed. The South Africans had demanded to take their role as a majority in their country. Immigrants, like us, were to be thrown out with the minority and the monarchs. Natives robbed our new house, right after my mother had finished redecorating. They not only robbed our store twice, but threatened to take the life of my father and his employees. Nothing was impossible at that time, especially after all the punishment that native Africans had suffered for so many years. When my uncle was killed in front of my sister's eyes, the glass overflowed; my parents took us and left.

Note how this student mimicked Nestle's final punch, a simple statement of the paragraph's most dramatic details: his uncle's murder and his family's fleeing.

Nestle, Rodriguez, and Staples have all written first-person essays. The "I" narrative indeed becomes the camera "eye" panning around the setting, grounding the reader in time and place. Staples and Nestle and to some degree Rodriguez's piece provide forays into classroom discussions of point of view and how this seemingly small stylistic choice has huge repercussions for the meaning and mood of the text. In my own writing and in previous writing groups, one of the most frequently asked questions is "Should this story be in the third or in the first person?" One does not have to be a fiction writer to know that a story in which every thought or action is personalized with an "I" creates a more personal, immediate effect than one filled with he's or she's. "I" narratives can be tricky, even manipulative. At least since *Catcher in the Rye,* no first-person narrator can ever be trusted completely again. In my own work, I rarely use "I" narrators. This is because first-person narrators are hard to contain. When I do employ the first person it is to portray characters who cannot articulate their aspirations, their fears, their needs with the clarity that a third-person narrator could. For me, the "I" protagonist, like Holden Caulfield, is the mark of confusion. Likewise, Rodriguez, Nestle, and Staples's first-person narrators are appropriate not only because they write of personal experiences but also because they cast themselves as developing characters: dynamic, unfixed, at times confused. Each of the pieces ends with a bittersweet moment that reveals that none of these authors has completely come to clear-cut resolution about his or her experiences as an outsider. In this way, point of view is a stylistic device; it also suggests meaning. Once again, a stylistic choice reinforces content. "I" narrators are almost always illogical, often the antithesis of the voice of argumentative essay.

However, students have not necessarily been trained to understand point of view as a choice they make as writers. Most students see the pronoun "I" as an indicator only—in other words, the pronoun that indicates not "you," not "they," not "he." They have not been trained to see it as a designation that holds considerable interpretative value. Some of my students have even been taught that the "I" is inappropriate for classroom essays. Nestle, Rodriguez, and Staples offer evidence that the first person can be appropriate. In these pieces, as in all pieces that examine identity, this single letter is a loaded word. "I" can signify positive connotations of agency, autonomy, or self-realization. It can also suggest negative connotations: alienation, separation, rejection, as in Nestle's epiphany at a "gentile only" dude ranch: "Finally, I found what I knew had to be there: a finely bound volume of *Mein Kampf.* For one moment, it wasn't 1956, but another time, a time of flaming torches and forced marches. It wasn't just my Jewishness that I learned at that moment: it was also the stunning reality of exclusion unto death." The value of the first person can shift within a piece—at times indicating a clear sense of self-definition, other times self-loathing or frustration.

The first person plural, "we," can likewise demonstrate unity and belonging. However, its absence can be even more telling. Though Staples titles his essay "Black Men and Public Space," and though he suggests that all African American males face similar stereotyping, he never refers to himself as part of a larger "we." Staples refers to himself only in the first person singular. When students are pressed to explain what could be seen as a discrepancy, they conclude that Staples wants to be recognized an as individual, not just as a black male, and that to use the plural instead of the singular would go against the spirit of his thesis. Likewise, though "Complexion" focuses on Rodriguez's family, normally a very "we" type of unit, Rodriguez never refers to his family in the first person plural. In this case, the "I" resonates strongly, for even in the presence of his parents, Rodriguez is alone: too dark for his mother's tastes, too soft for his father's. The only time Rodriguez uses "we" is in reference to his circle of awkward comrades at school, whose bodies, he notes, were "too short or too tall, all graceless and all—except mine—pale." I think many of my students understand what it feels like to fall short of parental expectation, and given our discussion about "I," they quickly deduce the significance of Rodriguez's omitted "we."

In an analytical paper about point of view and identity, one student explained what he saw as the links between Rodriguez's self-appraisals and his choice of pronouns:

> In "Complexion" Rodriguez also writes his essay in the first person singular, but unlike Nestle, he does not refer to his family as "we." This shows how much his family has affected him because he does not even view himself as part of his family. Rodriguez gives many examples of how he views himself. All of them were negative feelings due to his complexion and personality differences. Rodriguez explains why he feels separated, such as his interest in literature, his lack of socialization, and his inability to be "man" enough. Rodriguez does identify with a group of outsiders, his friends. This is when he switches to the "we" perspective . . . because they seem to go through the same experiences he is going through. They all have felt the loneliness and shame they have brought to the world.

Another student also chose to write an analytical paper on point of view and identity. In rereading "A Restricted Country," Ronielle focused on each pronoun reference and discovered that there was an almost exact correlation between Nestle's pronoun choice and her evolution as a character. At the beginning of the section, this student admitted she didn't know what point of view even meant. Yet the final version of her paper reveals a close, expert reading of Nestle's shifting pronouns and how each change signals a new step in the development of the author's identity. She notes not only Nestle's pronoun choices, but what Nestle chose not to include:

> Nestle begins her story by using the word "I" to describe the scenery. She uses the "I" to describe her thoughts but uses "we" to describe her family. Nestle remarks, "We were Jewish, but we were different" after she notices class differences between the Jewish people on the ranch and her mother. Nestle's mother "dressed wrong" and she could not keep up with the rich Jewish people. At this point Nestle claims to be part of the difference, but she changes her pov [point of view] again when she is embarrassed by her mother's differences. The other guests laugh at her mother as she tries to ride a horse in a "checked polyester suit." Nestle distances herself from her mother by referring to her as a "she" rather than a "we" and removes her from the story by never bringing her name

up again nor by ever using "we" to describe her own family again. She is also an adolescent daughter trying to form an independent identity from her family. This breaks up her family unit and Nestle is alone.

The word "I" returns the night she makes out in a car with an older worker on the ranch named Bill. Nestle does not use "we" to refer to herself and Bill, thus showing that this is not a serious relationship. She uses "I" to express that she is identifying only with herself and is no longer part of a group. Nestle matures throughout the story and we find her changing her pov again in the last few paragraphs. A relationship is discovered between Elizabeth, another guest at the ranch, and Bill. In the end, Nestle is riding through the pastures with her brother Elliot, Elizabeth and Bill. They are enjoying the afternoon together and the land in which they are riding. She no longer refers to herself as "I" and says, "We had come down from the mountain on a different path." Nestle is part of a new family and is no longer on her own.

An awareness of the connection between point of view and identity also found its way into several creative pieces in which students examined their own struggles with difference. For instance, one student chose to end her narrative with a play on point of view. In this case, the switch from the first person singular "I" to the plural "we" suggested a positive development. For this student, who traced her experiences as a young boot camp trainee. The loss of her "I," which until this point had been synonymous with selfishness and lack of direction, was replaced by the "we" of solidarity and discipline. On graduation day, the student suggests that part of her honor is in being promoted to a "we," a contributing member of her battalion and new family: "The battalion walks onto the field, heads held high, shoulders squared. The many "I"'s that arrived eight weeks earlier have become one. Members of a family that spans gender, religion and color, we are brothers and sisters. We bleed Army green."

In my own education, the significance of pronoun choice was never discussed until upper-level literature classes. Yet, if we ask our students to include themselves in their work, which most of my colleagues seem to find rewarding, then perhaps discussions like these are very much to the point in basic composition classes. When students go to write their own narrative essays, they should be conscious of what their "I" signifies at any given point in the work. Nor should we as faculty create oceans between the studying of great works of literature and encouraging the writing of works that demonstrate various forms of literary sensitivity.

Composition is not simply about winning arguments or understanding logic. The term is used in music and in painting, the expressive result of an artist's study. Likewise, as instructors of written composition, we must also find a place for the more ambitious goal of evoking experience and suggesting meaning, not through some unguided student exploration but from rigorous attention to literary devices. As readers and graders, it may prove difficult to break our molds and to acknowledge that some issues have no clear resolution and to recognize the inability to come to a conclusion as not necessarily the mark of incompetent argument but, in some cases, the only possible result of honest intellectual pursuit. We, who are teachers and have often lived longer than our students, know that truth does not stem from firmness of opinion but from the exploration of subtle differences. Literature has long navigated such grey waters. Unfortunately, many of us continue to point to it as if it were a distant ship on the horizon rather than an immediate means of conveyance. Meanwhile, many of our students tread water in its wake.

7

AN ARTS-CENTRIC COMPOSITION CLASSROOM

Gabriel Gomez

The Spanish poet Federico Garcia Lorca wrote about a Dionysian spirit of inspiration called *duende,* a cornerstone of his poetics: "The *duende* is a momentary burst of inspiration, the blush all that is truly alive." He adds, "[B]efore reading poems aloud before many creatures, the first thing to do is evoke *duende.* That is the only way that everybody will immediately succeed at the hard task of understanding metaphor" (p. viii). Lorca argued that *duende* captivated the poet, musician, and dancer into an enlightened trance beyond the limitations of ordinary intelligence. Despite his unorthodox theory, Lorca understood the importance of engaging in a creative act such as a musical performance or writing in order to understand its connection and relevance to the outside world. As an English instructor, I have yet to encounter a similar theory of inspiration for students to write an effective argument, complete with a thought-provoking thesis, seamless transitions, and comprehensive conclusion.

Judging from the fact that U.S. federal support for all arts education in 1995, including music, was less than $21 million annually for K-12, while $193 million of taxpayer money was spent on ceremonial military bands, $25 million more than the entire budget of the National Endowments for the Arts (Gannon 1995), art—its creation, instruction, and relevance—has largely been consigned to the kiddy table. Ceremonial posturing exemplifies our cultural priorities for the arts. They are a symbolic and patronizing afterthought, like wearing commencement regalia during graduation.

Moreover, art's intrinsic benefits in the classroom have been decidedly ignored, if not vanquished from academic discussions. As an undergraduate creative writing student, I read a passage in Richard Hugo's book *The Triggering Town* that echoes in my teaching style: "Every moment, I am without wanting or trying to, telling you to write like me. But I hope you learn to write like you. In a sense, I hope I don't teach you how to write but how to teach yourself how to write" (1979, 3). My methods for teaching English composition have been founded on principles anchored to Hugo's idea of self-guided pedagogy. Additionally, my interests in poetry, music, and ceramics have contributed to ideas on nurturing creativity and style in writing. I have found that by exposing students to visual and musical genres of art, I can supplement their understanding of the writing process in very productive ways.

I have designed lessons based on an arts-integrated curriculum established by the California Alliance of Art Education (CAAE), and my experience working as an arts and education coordinator for the East Bay Center for the Performing Arts (EBCPA) in Richmond, California. These art-oriented approaches to teaching are rooted in K-12 art and education programs, but they are designed with enough flexibility to apply to curricula. In fact, I have customized and currently use the CAAE framework as a component for teaching college-level English composition.

More specifically, a handbook of arts-integrated teaching methodologies entitled *Creative Collaboration: Teachers and Artists in the Classroom* (Lind and Lindsey 2003), recently published by the CAAE and the San Bernardino City Unified School District (SBUSD), has proven to be a useful resource in planning my arts-centric classroom strategies. The handbook, designed in consideration of the skill and knowledge standards for visual and performing arts set by the California State Board of Education, is geared for artist and teacher collaborations in the classroom and centers around five content strands: (1) artistic perception; (2) creative expression; (3) historical and cultural context; (4) aesthetic valuing; and (5) connections, relationships, and applications. The strands function as guidelines that are meant to be implemented as a group to ensure successful K-12 arts-integrated programming. I adapted the artistic perception, creative expression, and historical and cultural context strands into my lessons by concentrating on their fundamental artistic principles and using them to meet my curricular goals of developing students' prose style and teaching them to examine ideas holistically. Meanwhile, aesthetic valuing, or the aesthetic critique of art, fits naturally into the majority of my integrated teaching methods, while connections, relationships, and applications outlines how a specific art form can supplement other areas of the curriculum; these fourth and fifth strands are entwined throughout the first three strands and inherently capture the spirit and value of my arts-integrated methodologies.

The lessons are designed as informal and supplemental writing exercises and are not meant to replace formal argumentative and persuasive essays. I typically use these arts-integrated methods with fairly advanced English composition students who are familiar with the process of constructing essays but are not yet experienced or comfortable in formulating persuasive arguments. My reason for targeting advanced students is to focus primarily on ideas of style and content development. I focus more on the mechanics of writing with students in introductory levels of composition. The ultimate goals of my lessons are not to teach students to be creative or to measure their artistic ability. On the contrary, my goals are to teach students to be stylistically flexible and engaged in their writing and to prepare them for future academic courses by examining ideas in an artistic, cultural, and political context. In the spirit of Lorca's theory of *duende,* I am trying to realize a connection between arts expression and writing by having my students analyze, critique, and create works of art. The following is a breakdown of the artistic perception, creative expression, and historical and cultural context strands with examples of my customized lessons.

Artistic perception engages students in perceiving and responding using the language specific to the respective arts discipline. Instruction is designed to develop the basic building blocks of the arts, including specific language, technical skills, and perceptual skills (Lind and Lindsey 2003, 13). The artistic perception strand has helped me to focus my lessons on language and how it is used to express particular ideas about specific subjects. It helps students build context around their subjects by analyzing multifaceted ideas.

During the first week of class, I introduce students to the writing process by using a replica of Alexander Calder's mobile entitled *Horizontal Black and Red Sieve.* I have them observe the movable sculpture as its arched limbs of wire and colored shapes of angular metal change positions and overall character as the piece drifts seamlessly on its own kinetic energy. The mobile introduces infinite interpretations of itself as it subtly contorts into new shapes. I have each student write two ten-minute assessments of what the sculpture could possibly represent when not moving and what it could possibly represent in relation to their first assessment when it begins to move. Students, who do not know the name of the piece, cannot use the words sculpture, wire, color, shape, space, movement, line, or art in their assessment of the piece. I limit their vocabulary to encourage students to think independently and not depend on or be limited by technical terminology. This liberates the students to examine the sculpture from a variety of angles and encourages them to exchange vague and abstract language for descriptive and concrete diction. The exercise allows the students to examine the sculpture from a variety of different perspectives while referring to its original shape. After the two assessments are composed, I have students read them aloud and compare their observations with the class.

Their assessments are usually influenced by their immediate environment and major current events. It's interesting to note that students usually write brief, choppy sentences for their first ten-minute interpretations and then shift to longer narrative descriptions once the sculpture begins to move. Their longer descriptions have a tendency to assume more human or lifelike characteristics, while their primary assessments allude to concepts and abstract ideas. I've asked them why they feel compelled to write their interpretations in one particular way as opposed to any other way. The answers are typically, "How else are we supposed to talk about it without calling it what it is?" or "I don't get it, so I wrote down what it reminded me of." The exercise encourages them not to "get it" or not to feel zealously committed to one idea about a particular thing because the result will always limit their response and ultimate understanding of the topic.

I explain to them that similar to the sculpture itself, writing an argumentative essay should be a collection of ideas that occupy all aspects of a subject while remaining focused on the thesis. What's more, an argument must evolve and shift to account for changes and movements that rise in the writer's thinking while he or she works on the argument. Ultimately, the exercise sharpens their analytical skills and allows them to explore an idea from various points of view.

Another lesson that evolved from the artistic perception strand is an exercise I call the "Shape of Music." The exercise targets the development of introductory paragraphs and background information. I begin the exercise with a somewhat breezy analogy. An introductory paragraph functions in the same way a boat slip functions on a riverbank. If one where to simply drop a boat into the water from a steep embankment it would probably damage if not capsize the vessel, but if the boat were gently slipped into the water it would be stable enough to float. I expand my example by playing Miles Davis's composition "So What" from his album *Kind of Blue.* "So What" begins with a sinewy melody that slowly evolves around a bass and drum rhythm and a two-note trumpet and saxophone riff. I describe how each particular instrument, trumpet, drums, bass, saxophone, and piano, plays an integral and equal part in the composition while supporting a lead instrument that plays above the others. Miles's trumpet has its own personality, with room for structured and improvised playing.

Developing background information in the introductory paragraph works the same way. Examples, quotes, narratives, and personal observations introduce the theme of the essay. Each note that the musicians play adds texture and dimension to the entire piece. I ask them, "What part of this tune could be interpreted as the thesis statement?" The unanimous answer is usually the moment when the melody reaches a slight crescendo that's punctuated with a cymbal crash and Davis's trumpet begins to play above the other instruments. Ironically, "So What" helps students visualize an effective introductory paragraph through music.

Creative expression involves students in the creative process within an arts discipline, building upon the processes and skills learned within that art form (Lind and Lindsey 2003). In a lesson entitled "Lost in Translation," I have my students imitate a selected piece of writing by Andrei Codrescu. Codrescu's piece is entitled "San Francisco Noir" and is part of his monthly column in a local weekly newspaper devoted to arts and culture. The lesson allows students to write through the style of another writer while using their own words. The brief essay describes a trip to San Francisco and the old memories particular parts of the city evoke. Codrescu uses cultural references, "long ago when the hippies came here to find paradise"; location references, "Sutro Baths, Fulton Street, Golden Gate Park"; and heightened diction, "lugubrious," "ephemera," "taciturn" (Codrescu 2003). The objective of this lesson is to "translate" this essay into the student's own words and closely examine a piece of prose with a very distinctive voice and style. They must paraphrase and imitate the content and syntax patterns.

We begin by analyzing the essay in class. We discuss the style and tone of the piece. I ask them about audience expectation. What kind of reader would read this and understand all of the references? As a nonnative English speaker himself, do you suppose Codrescu was targeting a specific audience? I ask them about content. Does this essay try to convince you of something? If so, can all of this information be stated in a different way without losing all the concrete details? I ask them about his writing style. What is it about his language that seems to make his ideas connect effortlessly? After our discussion, the students take the essay home and invariably spend time researching the city of San Francisco, names, dates, and authors that Codrescu writes about in order to make an informed paraphrase. The students instinctively do one of two things: They replace details with vague references or use long-winded analogies. San Francisco becomes the "city" or the "northern California city throttled in fog," the Sutro Baths become a "spa" or the "site for ritualistic bathing," and the hippies become "unemployed drug users" or "trust-afarians," (Codrescu 2003). We can then discuss their choices and in doing so students develop an increasingly subtle sensitivity to the dynamics between meaning and style.

Historical and cultural context allows the students to analyze the role of the arts in the past and present. This strand builds understanding of the contributions and cultural dimensions of each art discipline (Lind and Lindsey 2003). The basis of my lessons on historical and cultural context are founded on my experience as the art and public education coordinator for the East Bay Center for the Performing Arts, where I worked with professional artists and school teachers in K-12 classrooms. My job was to facilitate the integration of performing and visual arts into the standard elementary and middle school curriculum. The art forms that were represented were not typically Western art forms but rather folk and indigenous art such as Mexican music and dance, African drumming and dance, and Brazilian capoeira. Our target populations were public school students who were recent immigrants and refugees from Southeast Asia, Mexico, Central and South America and disenfranchised by educational, social, and emotional neglect. We recognized the importance of keeping their traditions alive by teaching and promoting art forms that represented their cultural backgrounds. The ultimate goal was to empower people by becoming active in the educational, economic, social, and political systems of their new communities.

This same sense of cultural relevance and community has influenced me greatly in my own transition from an administrator to an educator. At the EBCPA, I realized that artists and art forms normally associated with the traditional Western canon were forced upon students. Shakespeare, Picasso, and Mozart, although undoubtedly relevant, were alien to their immediate environments and experiences. I sensed that my students lacked a sense of urgency when it came to creating and understanding art. Their lives are filled with vapid television shows, sophomoric movies, and candy cane pop songs, and as a result their curiosity and observation of the world is often unproductive. I decided to design a lesson that incorporates language, form, and culture in an attempt to reinvigorate and perhaps ignite their interest in writing.

The final step is a twenty-minute freewriting exercise that analyzes the photograph's meaning. We begin this step by interpreting the intricacies of the photograph. I have them consider the significance of the cathedral and the boulevard independently and as part of the photomontage when the two images are spliced together. The writing prompt for the writing exercise is "How does the meaning of these two images change once they have been combined and why?" Here are two brief excerpts of student writing that attempt to answer this question.

> The vitality suggested by the coupling of these two images (cathedral and city) is one of emergence—social emergence, which ultimately leads to spiritual emergence. I believe the superimposition that the artist manipulates stems from his/her own convictions of art/life/spirituality and their symbiotic implications.

> The photograph shows two contrasts between bustling city life with chaotic inclinations and the peaceful ambiance of the cathedral. It compares the difference between technological progressions of the world of man to the absence of religion in contemporary societies.

These two examples are fairly sophisticated yet indicative of the typical responses to Mutter's photomontage. This exercise helps the students analyze contrasting and multidimensional images by anchoring their attention on two things: the recognition of familiar images and the renegotiation of their meanings once they have been paired with unlikely partners. The familiarity of the spliced images in Mutter's photomontage provides an accessible introduction for students to begin a successful analysis of meaning.

This lesson could be easily adapted and developed into longer reading or writing assignments. Students could explore the relationships between opposing ideas in argumentative essays by using the same steps I used to discuss the photomontage. For example, the concrete and abstract lists could be replaced with a pro and con list for essays that propose solutions; essays with extensive supporting material could be organized one supporting example at a time; refutation material could be developed and implemented into calculated steps throughout entire essays.

Instructors who use fiction as a tool for teaching composition can adapt this lesson to discuss the probability of meaning when analyzing short stories or novels. As part of a lesson on the components of fiction such as plot, characterization, point of view, setting, and so forth, students can use the list or twenty-minute writing techniques to summarize the work of fiction into their own words. Furthermore, response papers that identify abstract themes in works of fiction such as struggle, identity, and freedom can be based on the concrete and abstract list steps of the lesson and help students explore the differences between literal and figurative language.

Connections, relationships, and applications content standards outline student expectations focused on what the students have learned in a specific art form and are then able to apply to other areas of the curriculum (Lind and Lindsey 2003). The final strand provides students with the opportunity to apply the skills they've developed through the arts-centric writing discussions and assignments in their first formal out-of-class essay. I usually assign an essay for students to read and respond to that is tangential to our discussions of arts-centric themes and concepts; it is usually an essay written by an artist that discusses the artist's methodologies and ideologies of creating art and its connection to the world. However, I recently used Thomas Frank's essay "Down and Out in the Red Zone" (2003), a commentary on his experience at Super Bowl XXXVI in New Orleans. His observations of the ravenous media, decadent pageantry, and gluttonous consumerism that surround the Super Bowl proved to be a meaningful backdrop for students to exercise their analyzing skills. I also wanted my students to translate their skills of analyzing art into analyzing argumentative essays.

I chose this particular essay because of its own criticism and exploration of meaning in a spectacle that is heroically complex, emotionally encumbered, and brazenly ceremonial. Frank's search for meaning is built upon his observations of the frenzy that accompanies the Super Bowl in week-long pre-game rituals that surround the actual game. I felt that this essay would create a solid transition between engaging in arts-centric lessons and writing formal essays.

The challenge of this assignment was composing a direct and effective prompt that would guide students through the essay rather than prescribe a specific component to search for and reflect our previous arts-centric writing assignments and discussions. I decided to use the five strands as a framework for the question, but first I pared and altered the wording and description of each strand. The result was this question:

In his essay "Down and out in the Red Zone," Thomas Frank describes the pre–Super Bowl events in his introductory paragraph:

Super Bowl XXXVI was to be played only five months after the catastrophic attacks on the World Trade Center and the Pentagon, four months after powdered anthrax appeared in the mail of prominent US senators, and mere weeks after the Enron bankruptcy. . . . The warm, safe old world was coming apart, but the greatest TV spectacle of them all would stand like Gibraltar, replenish our faith in our nation's ability to sell itself beer, cars, chips, and all manner of online services. (2003, 3)

This excerpt exemplifies the tone of the essay. It's a premeditation of ideas and thoughts to come. In many ways, the essay resembles a site-specific work of art in that the moment, location, and materials are central to the art's meaning. The "zeitgeist" in the U.S. after the September 11th attacks embodied unity, patriotism, and strength. Super Bowl XXXVI, at least according to Thomas Frank, exemplified this spirit of the time.

Use the following topics as guide for a 500–700–word analytical paper on "Down and Out in the Red Zone."

Perception: What is the author's thesis? How does the author address particular ideas about specific subjects? Is there relevance to the order of examples?

Expression: Discuss the author's use of style and overall structure in the essay.

Context: Elaborate on the historical context of this event. Does the author suggest particular importance to this yearly event?

Theme: What are the themes in this essay? Consumerism? Power? Patriotism? How does the author build and support these themes?

Connections: How are these themes relevant to the essay's audience? Does the essay have a didactic purpose?

Conclusion: What is your overall assessment on the essay? Are the ideas presented in a clear and concise manner? Is the author overzealous? Misinformed?

The reaction to such a specific writing prompt is generally one of horror and anxiety. Nevertheless, the prompt is flexible. It's important to remember that the arts-centric lessons are somewhat informal exercises that demand as much from the imagination as analytical skill. Their application and connection to writing formal essays, if done effectively, exercises both of these components simultaneously. For example, one student wrote, "In the sea of players, journalists, Hawaiian Tropics models and beauty queens, Frank met only one genuine human being. The Super Bowl was injected with patriotic vigor and pride, but even they could not exist in today's vain, consumerist world." Here the student comments on the contrast of illusion and reality by pairing concrete and abstract examples from the essay. Her style is vibrant; her tone is ironic and direct. Another student identified one major theme in the essay and listed examples to substantiate his point: "Themes of consumerism ran rampant throughout the essay, including the Cadillac SUV's and the gigantic yacht owned by Paul Allen." A third student poignantly observes an almost existential stance of the essay: "Frank learns that nothing has changed about our society after September 11th despite the newfound unity in Americans; everything will always be centered on money."

The original framers of the content strands meant for them to be "circular," not "linear." The strands, when implemented together, should overlap and supplement each other. I have been conscientious about this while adapting them to my classes. Again, the purpose of these exercises is not to train aspiring artists. The purpose of these lessons is to teach students how to write more effectively and clearly through an arts-centric rubric. These strands have helped me to guide students through the writing process in an open yet structured context. As a result, their formal argumentative and persuasive papers have assumed a richer texture of language and purposeful development of ideas.

8

PLAYING WITH ECHO: STRATEGIES FOR TEACHING REPETITION IN THE WRITING CLASSROOM

Melissa A. Goldthwaite

I remember the day in college when my advanced writing teacher introduced the class to "resumptive modifiers," a term culled from Joseph M. Williams's *Style: Ten Lessons in Clarity and Grace* (2002, 196). Besides my introduction to the dash—which quickly became my favorite form of punctuation—I remember no lesson so clearly. I loved the way a resumptive modifier, which repeats a key word or phrase, could help me lengthen a sentence, the way it moved the sentence forward with such, well, clarity and grace.

I quickly found, though, that not all of my teachers had been introduced to the resumptive modifer—and not all of them liked it once they were introduced. I remember the little red circles around repeated words and no further explanation; the circles spoke for themselves: repetition equals redundancy.

Often, writing teachers try to move students away from repetition and toward concision, asking them to state their claims as succinctly as possible, seeing repetition as unnecessary, as wordy, as lacking variety. While concision is, indeed, an important element of powerful prose, so is repetition—repetition of sound, of image, and of phrase.

Teaching college writing classes myself a decade after my introduction to various forms of repetition, I learned that I couldn't simply tell students to pay attention to sentence rhythm or that repetition is okay. Early in my teaching career, I read passages from published essays aloud, praising the attention to rhythm. I did this naïvely until a student handed in a draft of an essay in which every two sentences rhymed. The essay itself was greeting-card shallow, forced, short on specifics and depth, but the student had worked hard on "rhythm" and was loathe to change anything since it would ruin his prose couplets. His failed experiment was my failure as a teacher. It forced me to think hard about what I meant by sentence rhythm, about how it's achieved. His experiment forced me to look more carefully at the passages I praised, to understand how and why those passages worked when the rhyming couplets did not.

As with other elements of style, students need to be taught to recognize uses of repetition in published writing, to analyze their effects, and to understand when and how repetition can be used in their own writing. In order to use it effectively, students must be introduced to traditional rhetorical schemes of repetition, those associated with both poetry and prose—repetition of sounds (alliteration, assonance, consonance, and even rhyme), repetition of single words in a particular order, and repetition of groups of words. In addition, students should understand the formal importance of other kinds of repetition—such as the repetition of key images and ways of marrying style and content. The work of contemporary nonfiction writers, essays often taught in composition courses, provides a rich source of examples for analyzing the effects of differing schemes and how such schemes reinforce the meaning or theme of particular texts.

Echoing Williams: The Cyclical Text

In her essay "Yellowstone: The Erotics of Place," Terry Tempest Williams writes of echoes:

> Echoes are real—not imaginary.
>   We call out—and the land calls back. It is our interaction with the ecosystem; the Echo System.
>   We understand it intellectually.
>   We respond to it emotionally—joyously.
>   When was the last time we played with Echo? (1994, 82)

Stylistically, Williams plays with Echo throughout her essay. In places, she repeats phrases and sentence structures; she also includes refrains. When discussing the ways the Greek god Pan played with the nymph Echo (and tying this mythology to her topic, Yellowstone), Williams uses word play, almost identical phrasings, and similar sentence structure in three successive paragraphs. She writes that "the Greater Yellowstone Ecosystem/Echo System is a Pansexual landscape. Of Pan. A landscape that loves bison, bear, elk, deer" (83–84). After this initial alliteration (the b of bison and bear) and near rhyme (bear/deer), the list continues, including the names of twenty-one animals and birds.

In her next paragraph, Williams repeats a central phrase—"Pansexual. Of Pan"—and introduces another list: "A landscape that loves white pine, limber pine, lodgepole" (84). Like the preceding list, this one continues, including the names of twenty trees and plants. As the short section I've quoted illustrates (with its repetition of l and p sounds), Williams makes use of alliteration again, echoing sounds. She opens her next paragraph with the refrain "Pansexual. Of Pan" and provides another list, this one of mountain and river names. Through refrain and sentence structure, Williams connects the lists, yet by categorizing her lists differently, she moves the essay forward.

Williams also moves the essay forward through a changing refrain. Three times in the essay, she uses a similar phrase, but one she changes slightly each time. Early in the essay, she writes, "We call its name—and the land calls back" (81). Later, the first part of the refrain changes: "We call out—and the land calls back" (82). And at the end of the essay, the first part changes again: "We call to the land—and the land calls back" (87). The subjects ("we" and "the land"), the verbs, and the sentence structure remain the same; this changing refrain is part of the "echo system" Williams creates in the entire piece.

In terms of structure, Williams begins and ends the piece with essentially the same paragraph, a paragraph made up of imagistic nouns followed by gerunds: "Steam rising. Water boiling. Geysers surging. Mud pots gurgling. Herds breathing. Hooves stampeding. Wings flocking. Sky darkening. Clouds gathering. Rain falling. Rivers raging" (81). By repeating the paragraph at the end of her essay, Williams makes her form echo her content, creating an intellectually and emotionally satisfying piece.

This strategy, creating a cyclical text, is one Williams uses often, bringing her readers full circle through powerful resonance. She opens her essay "Winter Solstice at the Moab Slough" with an echo of her title, saying she is spending winter solstice at the Moab Slough "as an act of faith, believing the sun has completed the southern end of its journey and is now contemplating its return toward light" (1994, 61). The essay is about hope, about a place of renewal, about daring to love. And it ends as it begins, with Williams standing at the slough: "I stand at the edge of these wetlands, a place of renewal, an oasis in the desert, as an act of faith, believing the sun has completed the southern end of its journey and is now contemplating its return toward light" (65). In the beginning of the essay, Williams sets her reflection in a particular time and place, announcing her presence at the slough on the shortest, darkest day of the year "as an act of faith." In the end, she reaffirms her commitment to place as an act of faith, creating a text that follows the cyclical pattern of the year.

She's able to have faith in the return toward light because it happens in the natural, yearly cycle. Likewise, she makes her use of repetition, of a cyclical form, seem natural.

Definition and Contrast: Finding a Focus, Building an Argument

In using a cyclical form for some of her essays, Williams achieves a kind of balance, a balance that in most essays is more common in smaller, syntactical units. Repetition through parallelism creates cohesion and balance. Particularly effective in texts that will be delivered orally, this kind of repetition helps reinforce the author/speaker's point. Testifying before a subcommittee concerning the Pacific Yew Act of 1991, Williams told lawmakers: "It is not a story about us versus them. That is too easy. It is not a story to pit conservationists against cancer patients. That is too easy also. Nor is it a story about corporate greed against a free-market economy. It is a story about healing and how we might live with hope" (1991, 130). Here, Williams uses anaphora (repeating both "It is not a story" and "That is too easy") as she defines her position and counters possible objections to that position, focusing and building an argument through repetition and contrasts.

Similarly, environmental writer David James Duncan uses parallel structure in the following two sentences, repeating the phrases that begin (anaphora) and end (epistrophe) each sentence to create balance and to reinforce his point: "The belief that one can safely pump thousands of gallons of water a minute, or safely spray thousands of gallons of cyanide, round the clock in sub-zero weather is not credible. The belief that one can create cyanide reservoirs, toxic heaps, and toxic mountains, line them with plastics that crack in the cold, and declare the adjacent river safe in perpetuity is not credible" (2001, 141). Duncan reinforces his concerns about safety and toxicity by repeating key words and phrases in a patterned way. Through this structure, he orders his argument, strengthening the force of his claims.

Like Williams, Duncan also uses repetition as a way of focusing and building his topic. He makes a claim—"I believe corporate transformation is the crucial (in)human topic of our time" (2001, 172)—and then shifts his focus, writing, "But it's not my topic." Duncan then devotes the rest of the paragraph to explaining what his topic will be:

> My topic is the five-people-at-once whom Bob Pyle and I feel we have to be in order to earn a living while also decrying the havoc that corporate power is wreaking upon the butterflies and salmonids to which we've sworn our allegiance.

My topic is the hash that fleshless, bloodless "independent existences" are making of the contemplative and artistic lives of the fleshed and blooded. My topic is the grief and frenzy that daily invade every sincere human's attempts to simply pursue a vocation that expresses gratitude and respect for life.

Anaphora allows Duncan to define and extend his topic, moving from the personal (the pressures he and another writer feel) to the more universal (pressures on all artists, even all sincere humans). The repetition allows Duncan to make this move in just three sentences.

In another essay, Duncan uses a similar pattern—making a claim and then creating a contrast through anaphora, showing why fishers do not need guides. He writes:

Fly fishing at its best is an unmediated, one-on-one music played by a body of flesh and blood upon a body of water: it is a satisfying duet, till a fish makes it an even more satisfying trio. The average guide renders duet and trio inaudible. The average guide is a Top Forty disc jockey who dictates the day's music. The average guide mediates so relentlessly between you and your fishing that it feels as if you and the river are divorcing and trying to split up the property. The average guide plants an invisible ego-flag on every fish you catch, as if he were a mountaineer, the fish were a summit, and your stupidity were Mount Everest. (2001, 233–34)

Through a range of metaphors and similes, Duncan paints a humorous portrait of a controlling guide and unsuspecting fisher who pays for a disrupted experience. Duncan could have stopped with his second sentence, which extends the music metaphor and makes the corrective. He decides, however, to keep going, piling simile upon simile, increasing the comical effect. Through this use of anaphora and metaphor/simile, he makes "the average guide" and the person who might hire a guide seem ridiculous.

WHAT IT LOOKS LIKE, WHAT IT IS: REPETITION AND SIMILE

While Duncan allows his similes to pile up, Annie Dillard uses repetition and simile for a different purpose in her essay "Total Eclipse." Through description, reflection, and her use of style, she shows that moments of awakening, powerful as they are, tend to be fleeting, and language can't easily capture the power of such moments. Still, Dillard uses simile and repetition to capture what she can. She opens with a series of similes:

It had been like dying, that sliding down the mountain pass. It had been like the death of someone, irrational, that sliding down the mountain pass and into the region of dread. It was like slipping into a fever, or falling down that hole in sleep from which you wake yourself whimpering. (1982, 9)

In this passage, Dillard uses anaphora to introduce her similes (repeating the phrase "It had been like") and reinforces the comparison by repeating "that sliding down the mountain pass." Her use of polyptoton, repeating words derived from the same root, creates further cohesion between the sentences and the images she presents; it is no mistake that Dillard uses "dying" and "death" in successive sentences or "slipping," "sliding," and "falling" in close proximity. The effect of this repetition reinforces a theme in the essay: the difficulty of finding the right words to describe particular experiences. Each phrase, each sentence in this quotation, seems to build on the one preceding it as she tries to create a more specific word picture of her experience through simile.

Through simile, Dillard also creates subtle connections among those gathered to view the eclipse. Describing the crowd, she writes, "All of us rugged individualists were wearing knit caps and blue nylon parkas" (13). She then emphasizes the irony of a bunch of "rugged individualists" dressed exactly alike, including the color and material of their parkas, through anaphora and a series of similes:

It looked as though we had all gathered on hilltops to pray for the world on its last day. It looked as though we had all crawled out of spaceships and were preparing to assault the valley below. It looked as though we were scattered on hilltops at dawn to sacrifice virgins, make rain, set stone stelae in a ring. (14)

This group, ordinary people in blue parkas, gathered for an extraordinary event, could have been from another time, another culture; this group could even be aliens.

Later in the essay, the difficulty of finding the right words is evident again as Dillard describes the eclipse using metaphors: "In the sky was something that should not be there. In the black sky was a ring of light. It was a thin ring, an old, thin silver wedding band, an old, worn ring. It was an old wedding band in the sky, or a morsel of bone" (18). Through repetition and the articulation of these metaphors, Dillard expands the reader's knowledge of what the eclipse was like without providing a set picture. Like a Polaroid developing before the reader's eyes, the picture grows more clear yet remains incomplete. In the first sentence I've quoted, we don't know what is in the sky, just that it "should not be there." In the second sentence, we learn that the sky is black and that what should not be there is a "ring of light." Each of the next two sentences provides a little more information. In just four sentences, "sky," "ring," and "old" are each repeated three times; "wedding band" and "thin" are each repeated twice, but we're not left with a clear image of an old, silver wedding band; it could have been more like "a morsel of bone."

Dillard's attempts at simile and metaphor seem to fail her; she can't find the right words to describe the eclipse until she overhears a college student describing the sight: "Did you see that little white ring? It looked like a Life Saver. It looked like a Life Saver up in the sky" (23). In considering his simile, Dillard agrees: "And so it did. The boy spoke well. . . . I myself had at that time no access to such a word. He could write a sentence, and I could not." Through her own sentences—her many attempts to describe the eclipse—Dillard shows the importance of finding the right words. She argues that all "those things for which we have no words are lost" (24), yet she finds the experience again through finding a fitting expression in words.

THE COLOR OF PASSION, SHADES OF EMOTION

In *Classical Rhetoric for the Modern Student,* Edward Corbett and Robert Connors argue that anaphora is always deliberate and "usually reserved for those passages where the author wants to produce a strong emotional effect" (2000, 391). David James Duncan uses anaphora and other rhetorical schemes in just this way—often writing about his own emotions in a way that enhances the emotional effect of his prose. He writes, for example, with considerable passion about a grebe:

> I am haunted by a grebe. A grebe encountered, in the mid-1980s, at the height of the Reagan-Watt-Crowell-Bush-Luhan-Hodell-Hatfield-Packwood rape and pillage of my homeland, the Oregon Cascades and coast range; height of the destruction of the world I had grown up in and loved and given my writing life to; height of an eight-year spate of Pacific Northwest deforestation that outpaced the rate in Brazil; height of the war on rivers, birds, wildlife, small towns, biological diversity, tolerance, mercy, beauty; height of my personal rage; depth of my despair; height of my need for light. (2001, 40)

It's not just the repetition that conveys emotion in this passage. Duncan uses several emotion-laden words: "haunted," "rape," "pillage," "destruction," "war," "rage," "despair." The many repetitions he uses, though, create cohesion and enhance the emotional effect. Early in the quotation, he uses anadiplosis, repetition of "a grebe" in the final part of the first sentence and at the beginning of the following clause. This use of repetition is similar to Joseph Williams's resumptive modifier, though such modifiers usually occur in the same sentence. Duncan's repetition of "a grebe," however, functions as a resumptive modifier, creating cohesion and allowing readers to pause before taking in his lengthy list.

Another form of repetition evident in this quotation is rhyme, the repetition of the stressed vowel sound and the sound that follows the vowel: he uses "eight," "spate," and "rate" in one clause and "height" and "light" in another. Although rhyme is more often a feature of poetry, when done well and sparingly, it can also be an effective element of prose.

The most obvious repetition, though, in this quotation is anaphora; "height" is repeated six times at the beginning of successive clauses, creating a rhythm that is interrupted only once by "depth." Through that repetition, Duncan guides the reader, emphasizing the height and depth of his feelings not only for the grebe but also about the environmental destruction he's witnessed.

In a later passage, he links the grebe and his feelings again through anaphora: "just shy of the first dune—its eyes as red as fury, as red as my feelings, as red as the fast sinking sun—sat a solitary male western grebe" (2001, 42). This series of similes describes not only the color of the grebe's eyes but also the rage-red "color" of Duncan's emotions. Following this quotation, Duncan uses the same strategy, a list set off as an appositive, for a similar purpose, writing: "But—sick of humans, sick of my own impotence, sick with the knowledge of how much had been destroyed—I gazed out at the grebe through my sickness" (42). In this use of anaphora, Duncan emphasizes his emotion, a feeling stressed by the inclusion of "sickness" at the end of the sentence.

Though he often writes of rage, sickness, and loss, Duncan also uses repetition to highlight another powerful emotion—love. In discussing a gift he once gave to his then future wife, Adrian, Duncan lists several reasons why he loved giving her a clay bowl he formed and fired for her:

I loved giving her a bowl because bowls are beautiful but also as humble, utilitarian, handmade, and breakable as a marriage. I loved giving her a bowl because now both of us, our two daughters, and even our dog eat out of it, as if out of the marriage. I loved giving her a bowl because my mind seems at times about the size of a bowl, if not smaller. I loved giving her a bowl because, once you've wandered your house looking for reading glasses or car keys only to find the latter in your pocket, or even in your hand, the former atop your head, or even on your nose, you can't help but wonder in what sense they're "your" glasses or keys even after you find them—which in turn makes you wonder whether it's really "your" house, "your" life, "your" marriage, and whether even you are "yours." I loved giving Adrian a bowl because my life, home, marriage, and self are gifts I must beg daily—must place in the moment as if in a bowl, and bend down over as if over a mound of begged rice—lest I forget to consider them, forget to be grateful for them, and so lose them, though they rest on my very head, in my hand, on my nose. (74–75)

In this passage, Duncan uses some variation of the phrase "I loved giving her a bowl" (once modifying the phrase to include his wife's name) five times; he uses "bowl" or "bowls" eight times, creating satisfying coherence rather than annoying redundancy. "I loved giving her a bowl" becomes a refrain in this poetic passage. Through metaphor, simile, and repetition, Duncan develops the bowl as a symbol of marriage.

Other repetitions—the repetition of "your" and the repeated suggestion of places you might "lose" glasses or keys—allow Duncan to reflect on the related concepts of ownership and gifts, especially as they relate to marriage. In the quotation, Duncan reveals his passion for the bowl, for his marriage, for gifts and giving through repeating these interconnected words, images, concepts, and symbols. His writing shows that no matter what shade or color a writer's passions and emotions are, various forms of repetition can help convey those feelings.

PLAYING WITH ECHO IN THE WRITING CLASSROOM

One way to introduce students to rhetorical schemes of repetition is to point to such schemes and how they function in the texts you're reading for class (as I've done in this essay with texts I often teach). If the books or essays your class is reading do not include effective examples, presidential State of the Union addresses always include multiple forms of repetition and so provide a fruitful starting place. Spending time on stylistic analysis in class allows students to move beyond summary (what a text says) and to consider how a writer does what he or she does. Without reinforcement and practice, though, students likely won't remember the terms nor will they learn how to incorporate effective uses of repetition in their own writing.

To reinforce what they see in published sources, I often put students in small groups and provide them with a list of rhetorical schemes of repetition and their definitions (such lists are available in Corbett and

Connors's *Classical Rhetoric for the Modern Student* [2000] and Richard A. Lanham's *A Handlist of Rhetorical Terms* [1991]) as well as passages that illustrate several forms of repetition. I ask groups to identify the kinds of repetition and their effects. I've used, for example, the following passage from Duncan's *My Story as Told by Water:*

> I fell into a daze, kept fishing, kept catching and releasing big, gasping browns. Every trout I touched was an emissary of death—river death; food-chain death; our death. Yet every trout I touched filled me with weird bursts of empathy for a man who'd abandoned my father at age four. (2001, 132)

Many students recognize how in "kept fishing, kept catching and releasing," the repetition of "kept" (anaphora) signals the repetitive physical action Duncan describes. Others recognize, in the repetition of "death," Duncan's use of epistrophe (or what Richard Lanham terms "antistrophe" [190]) and also a climatic order, through which he suggests that death of the river, by affecting the food chain, is related to the death of humans. And through further analysis, students understand that Duncan's repetition of the phrase "every trout I touched" reveals a contrast. In the midst of death, he highlights hope: "every trout [he] touched" was both "an emissary of death" and a source of empathy.

Though I've included just one example for illustrative purposes, in a classroom setting, it's helpful to provide many examples, for in being offered several passages from different writers, students can also compare and contrast how different writers use repetition, recognizing both patterns and differing options.

To reinforce what they've done in class, I ask students to take their list of rhetorical schemes of repetition home with them and to go on a scavenger hunt, finding at least one example of each term. Such examples can become a basis for class discussion. In addition, copying examples from other sources—by hand or word processing—tends to help students internalize the rhythms used by other writers.

After they learn to recognize and understand effective uses of repetition, I encourage students to practice such schemes in their own prose (or poetry, depending on the course), using such strategies for a few important sentences or to structure an entire piece. In a course on the form of the essay, for example, we read Annie Dillard's "Total Eclipse." As an assignment, I asked students to begin one of their own essays by repeating a series of metaphors that describe something they've experienced, just as Dillard does in the opening of her essay. Kate Finley, a poet and essayist, began a short essay about her baby sister this way:

> In the little tub she is an impressionist painting. A bad impressionist painting that we bought at a yard sale for $2.99. A splotchy painting—splotches of dark red and jaundice yellow and purple bruised black. A swollen canvas with smooth and rough strokes, and bumpy acne spots where dirt got caught in the brush's bristles.
>
> In the little tub she is a peach. A too ripened, bruised peach with hollowed soft spots threatening to rip, exposing liquidy flesh. Fuzzy. Fuzzy all over the imperfect roundness. The imperfect peach. Spoiling fruit in the center of the bowl.

Kate carries these metaphors and her powerful, fragmented, imagistic style throughout the essay, using alliteration, anadiplosis, polyptoton, anaphora, and other schemes of repetition throughout. Though based on an assignment that encouraged imitation, her work is quite original, showcasing her own voice and style.

Kate's example is a good one: full of color, texture, sensory images. While not all initial attempts are as strong, most show potential, giving both teachers and students something to work on and with. In the midst of my own bumpy and spoiled attempts at using and teaching repetition, I've learned that through stylistic analysis and practice in their own writing, students can learn the ways repetition not only helps writers to create rhythm, cohesion, and coherence but also helps to reinforce theme and meaning. Further, students themselves can become writers who play with Echo, experimenting with form and creating opportunities for readers to understand intellectually even as they respond emotionally.

9

THE "WEIRD AL" STYLE METHOD: PLAYFUL IMITATION AS SERIOUS PEDAGOGY

Keith Rhodes

I am going to argue that creative uses of imitation are the most promising approaches to teaching better style to first-year college students—and probably most college students. Like everyone else who wants to argue about teaching style by any means other than sentence combining, I do not have direct empirical support. Still, I hope to show that if we place creative imitation in the context of what else we know about teaching style, its prospects are the best available.

Of course, we have to start with that great negative finding, that black hole whose gravitational field defines the territory of all composition pedagogy. Currently, our best hypothesis is that teaching grammar is one of the worst ways to produce better writers (Hillocks 1986, 1995; Daniels 1983; Hartwell 1985). The main knock against grammar teaching is not that it hurts self-esteem or limits creativity or takes away students' own language; the main knock is that it can't work, it doesn't help, and it probably hurts most writers. Thus, if writing teachers hold ourselves accountable not only for the state of knowledge in our field but also for producing the best possible writers, we should not teach grammar. Apparently, the art of grammar, far from being "basic," is highly advanced, and follows the development of other abilities. That grammar teaching is a theoretical and practical failure shouldn't surprise anyone who has looked into the history of the theories behind grammar instruction. The psychological theories out of which grammar instruction developed were the fruit of a long-abandoned mechanistic paradigm (Connors 1985; Daniels 1983). As a result, grammar instruction has never worked. As Daniels explains, the consistently negative findings have been rolling in since 1906. There is no record of preexisting, effective teaching "basics" to "get back to." Indeed, no one has yet shown that ignoring grammar entirely hurts the quality of student writing. Anyone can tell horror stories, but those who love to make this claim have never shouldered the burden of providing serious evidence. Quite to the contrary, Hillocks finds that even when grammar is taught thoroughly and well enough to raise scores of grammatical quality, the overall impression of the quality of the writing does not improve (1995). More recent studies continue to affirm this finding (see especially Holden 1994). Indeed, the most likely interpretation of the record is that grammar study uniquely retards the development of more highly valued writing.

Yet we still must do something. I will start to turn toward the positive by means of one last critique, one that eventually I will need to distinguish closely. One common argument for grammar teaching, and particularly for having students do grammar exercises, suggests that we build a sort of "muscle memory" of the mind by doing such practice. The most common analogies are to shooting basketballs or playing scales on a musical instrument. I will pass over lightly the rather large leap we make when we compare training muscle, which is fundamentally binary (contract/relax), and training thought, which is fundamentally complex (always the product of multiple neural connections and multiple neurotransmitters). The more easily attacked presumption here is the implicit claim that forming grammar along lines of drilled habit is a significant part of what the mind does when it writes. The analogies fail the test of correspondence. When players shoot basketballs in games, they use motions similar to the practice shots; most music is written in some relationship to scales (though here we should note that few if any expert musicians limit their practice of repetitive motion to repetition of scales). When writers write, they think mostly about what they mean, and the words come out—overwhelmingly, even for weak stylists, in close relationship to correct form. We learn the habitual "moves" of syntax early and well. Young children have rather more trouble handling the exceptions than the rules ("We eated pizza!"). It simply would not be possible to drill into place the amazingly complex variations of correct language that even very poor writers execute correctly most of the time. If we needed drill to write properly, none of us could do it. Exactly how humans manage this trick of syntax is still an open question, even if one to which we have some insight (see Terrence Deacon's *The Symbolic Species* [1997] for the best recent treatment approaching lay terms); but we've long known that drill and correction cannot account for it.

Instead, we need to match practice with performance. Musicians who play music already written for them benefit most from practicing the "rules" of scales. That is a common and valuable kind of musicianship, but it forms a poor analogy for writing. Musicians who have to create on the spot more often tend to spend more time practicing fresh combinations of canonical riffs that they learned originally from their idols and from models of what they want to achieve. Similarly, much less than a set of simplistic grammatical "scales," an effective writer needs to come up with a steady stream of "riffs"—novel connections and judgments. That is, writers mainly need to learn to create fresh material using variations on standard moves; and so that's mainly what they need to practice. Writers need to practice more of the things that actually happen in the minds of good writers when they write. A limited range of grammar moves isn't even on the top ten list. Whether it is actually on the bottom ten list is a more serious question in light of the data.

This brings us at last to the one method that has demonstrated robust and strong gains in both usage and overall writing quality: sentence combining. It's dull at times, but it's something a grammarian can do well and that probably can satisfy the grammarian soul to some degree. Books by leading figures like Don Daiker, Max Morenberg, and William Strong guide teachers through reliable, proven exercises that really work; and the research is fairly clear that it all works just as well without grammar instruction as with it. As Robert Connors pointed out in his landmark article, "The Erasure of the Sentence," there is no truth to the common perception that sentence-combining research eventually turned against the practice. Sentence combining, so far as we know, worked and still works, and the worst that can be said about it is that other students who persist in college might eventually catch up with those who experience its immediate gains. As Connors writes, "[I]f people believe that research has shown that [sentence combining, imitation, and Christensen rhetoric] don't work, their belief exists not because the record bears it out but because it is what people want to believe" (2000, 120).

If we are to get any further with the teaching of style in composition, we need to learn as much from these contrasting facts as we can. Grammar study hurts; sentence combining helps. There are no sturdier findings in all of the research into how students learn to improve their writing. We literally have just about nothing else that is concrete on which to proceed. The NAEP tests of writing in secondary schools found that socioeconomic status was by far the most powerful determiner of writing ability, and that only two pedagogical interventions had even weakly significant effects: keeping portfolios and writing multiple drafts (National Center for Education Statistics 2000). Hillocks was able to identify the success of a complex classroom approach, one he dubbed "environmental" (1995); but for the most part this simply seems to mean that good teaching is better than bad teaching. The success of sentence combining is literally the only strong, dependable, robust, and straightforward clue we have about how students learn to improve their writing.

At this point, I'll pause for what will seem an aside at first, but that I hope to connect up eventually. Ann Berthoff has demonstrated about as well as one can why it should be true that writing is best approached as a process of "forming." In her explanations, writing becomes an intellectual art, best improved by practice at looking and looking again, training the eye and hand to work with ever-increasing imaginative power. Her central insistence is on the "allatonceness" of such arts, the fact that they must be practiced whole, always, rather than being subject to a breaking analysis that seeks to build one "subskill" at a time (see especially *The Sense of Learning* [1990]). Berthoff, we should note, is one of the few composition scholars who is also accepted as a major figure in the intellectual arts from which she "borrows," having published successful semiotics scholarship (see especially *The Mysterious Barricades* [1999]). A genuinely great philosopher of language who also happens to take an interest in composition, Berthoff has argued consistently, extensively, and well for her positions. If there is another truth that we know about learning to write, it is that writing is a whole thing that grows organically, not a set of steps moving from "basic" to "expert." I absolutely do not mean to raise hope that sentence combining can be the beginning of a new "skill set" approach to writing. Rather, I hope that we can learn from sentence combining more about how "allatonceness" can still be approached in manageable pedagogical units that require perhaps a bit less of us than the brilliance of Berthoff and the exemplary teachers to whom she so often refers us.

To do that, we need to know just a bit more about how that organic wholeness works. I will note here only condensed highlights from the main things we know about how the mind manages language. At the level of physiology, language use is perhaps the most widely distributed activity in the brain. While local centers manage things like syntax and vocabulary, in fact language fires up the whole organ (see Deacon 1997). There is no "right/left" side for language; it's both/and. This is not because there are not some distinctions, often associated with hemispheres, in the kinds of mental processing. Roughly, acts of brain do divide into serial and holistic processes, and there is yet much to support a view that these are distinct operations, even if their association with brain hemispheres has always been a severe oversimplification. Yet in any operation, and especially managing language, we need both. Language is distinct and whole at once—allatonceness. Further, the syntactic operations of language particularly make strong use of the hippocampus, an organ mostly used by other animals to map terrain. The hippocampus specializes in reducing complex information into habitual responses keyed to complex mental shapes, while also constantly comparing and bringing to consciousness novel variations to the expected forms (Wallace 1989). The hippocampus, a part of the "old brain," is not designed to work in ways that become "visible" to higher processing, so that to the extent that it manages its complex forms along expected lines, it seems to our minds to operate like a "black box." It is thus only problematically available to conscious control. When we add to the brain's burdens monitoring the motor skills of writing, we have possibly the most complete use of the entire brain that most people are asked to do successfully.

At the level of use, language is inevitably social and contextualized, not so much "meaning things" as generating both possible boundaries for meaning and possible new escapes from those boundaries. As Berthoff (1999) explains well with her title metaphor, language forms "mysterious barricades" of definition that melt as soon as we come too close to them. As Bakhtin and others demonstrate, we use old habitual forms of language, often barely conscious of what meanings we pass on, but then re-create and interanimate these "monologic" language acts with new forms of words generated within evolving speech genres. Everything is constantly negotiated and shifting. And yet as Berthoff also points out, in the coming closer to definitions, histories, and explanations of terms, the "seeing and seeing again," we constantly deepen our sense of exactly what they might mean. We manage to act appropriately in response to language to a very high degree. As Peirce (see especially "How to Make Our Ideas Clear" [1878]), Davidson, and a few others propose, we form what Davidson calls passing theories of the meanings we construct out of each other's words, interpreting them closely enough that, in the context of our actions in response to them, we can largely see agreement about what we intend. Add in the obvious social dynamism of language, with its dialects and slang, its cross-cultural borrowings from among these, its art of the occasion, and we can see that language is enormously complex and unruly.

On the whole, the ways in which language is managed, both biologically and socially, is by a means of artful forming and reforming, as Berthoff has been trying to tell us all along. Our practices need to work within that reality. That brings us back again to sentence combining. The findings about sentence combining make great sense in this light, even if its limitations are also clearer. In sentence combining, students work with forming at the level of whole ideas, at least, using and using again the main tactics favored by the most broadly shared "passing theories" of English usage. We could call these tactics by their grammatical names: in general, modification, subordination, and parallelism; in specifics, verbal phrases, appositives, absolute phrases, and relative and subordinate clauses. But that description generalizes the form of the moves poorly. We can get farther by identifying the "moves": redescribing, listing, extending, and limiting. Appositives redescribe; parallel forms list; verbal and absolute phrases redescribe too, but also often extend; and clauses either limit (or condition) results or extend the logic of a statement. The terms redescribing, listing, extending, and limiting can account not only for "grammatical" performances, but also "nongrammatical" slang and even hybrids of language and other forms of communication, like images. I would theorize, in light of information about language use only glossed lightly above, that it is the extent to which students catch on to these "moves" while sentence combining that determines their writing performance, including their ability to write more grammatically.

Linguist Sharon A. Myers has described an even more particularized set of "moves" that students need to learn. In "ReMembering the Sentence" (2003), she writes of the "grammar of words," the ways in which specific words tend to create unique grammars around them, and the ways in which "templates," or particular patterns of terms, serve as generative frames for students who are learning to express new ideas in the language of newly explored kinds of expertise. This idea, similar to Berthoff's concept of "workhorse sentences" (1982, 87–95), explains part of the power of sentence combining as a way to learn not only (or perhaps not mainly) generalized moves, but rather ones that relate to specific contexts. Myers sees these more particular patterns as possibly more the point of sentence combining than any generalized syntactical goals. Instead, she offers the hope that we can find and ask students to repeat specific sets of valuable templates, finding examples in linguistic materials. That is, there turns out to be something analogous to the "muscle memory" of musical scale exercise after all; but the repetition that helps turns out to be analogous to "riffs" rather than scales—to passages rather than grammar.

Like Myers, I propose that we can do better than sentence combining; but I propose further that imitation, handled effectively, is the key practice for doing so. Imitation is a broad term, and I don't mean to encourage everything it might suggest, but if we can imagine what Berthoff calls "persona paraphrase" (1982, 211) and kindred practices as the core of imitative practice, it remains a handy short term. That is, in thoughtful imitation there need be no mere scrivening; students may, for instance, put personally relevant thought into more distant patterns, "paraphrasing" the "persona" but not the content of their models.

The key advantage of a thoughtful imitation is that it works at the level of whole and parts at once—what my colleague Greg Roper has been calling "macrostructure and microstructure" as we have developed materials to support thoughtful imitation. When students take on the voice of, say, Aquinas's arguments for purposes such as arguing that one's father should watch his diet, their attention is at once on structures of both passages and sentences, on the structures of their own arguments and those of an argumentative craftsman, on the "moves" that add up to a supported and rhetorically deft claim. It is a practice of "allatonceness" that is not just a revel in one's own mind, but instead a subjecting of one's voice to the gravitational pull of some great "chops." As Myers discusses, students become familiar with how specific new terms affect the language around them and how set phrases contain and position new knowledge. But going beyond Myers's proposals, imitated "natural" texts will have a greater variety of templates and—because found in clearly successful writing—templates with more credibility as exactly the kind students should be learning. Myers partially repeats the mistake of grammar teaching by hoping that a limited set of exact information can be conveyed, even though her own arguments also make the point that language is much more varied than any grammar can capture.

Seeking a more rich process that builds both specific and generalized "moves," Dr. Roper and I have, over the last six years, developed and applied imitations toward general purposes, finding models less of aesthetic completeness and more of standard "chops" that real "players" know—the essayistic flight of Virginia Woolf, the layered call and response of Sojourner Truth, the structured "Rogerian" argumentation of Aquinas, and the tightly modified descriptions of Loren Eiseley, for instance. This work is not always easy. Students cycle through a regular pattern of self-doubt, growing interest, epiphany, and expert practice, a pattern that they often repeat anew as we start again with a new author. But what they retain is more interesting. From Aquinas's pattern of setting out opponents' arguments first, they pick up and use again the practices of rebuttal and cautious unfolding of unpopular views; from Eiseley's chaining of causes and effects, they pick up and use again the practice of narrative as drama, the sense that telling a story of what happened can also work as a powerful analysis of why it happened. And as with sentence combining, students develop an easier ear for things like trailing free modifiers that enhance the maturity of their style. In any area, they pick up set patterns of words that they directly practice applying to new material.

Yet there is a limitation to such "generalist" approaches to imitation. It is likely that our approach, like sentence combining, can produce gains only up to a point. It could well be that the more successful venue for thoughtful imitation would be within disciplinary inquiry. While Myers does not adequately explain away the advantages of sentence combining as a way of learning general syntactic moves, she certainly does explain well the role of sentence-level work in learning context-specific set phrases. In imitation, as in sentence combining, students imitate their way toward specific kinds of language.

Imitation is not necessarily a popular approach to composition, particularly caught as it is among a "current-traditional" kind of simplistic modeling, an "expressivist" quest for originality, and a "social epistemic" resistance to tradition. Yet in truth it borrows the best of all three. Students enjoy their work and write about their own experiences; they model more profoundly; and they come to understand (with some external assistance) a great deal about the social constructions of knowledge that generate genre conventions. Of all practices, it seems to connect most directly with what little we know about how students improve their ability to form better sentences. Indeed, while the findings were not as robust as those for sentence combining, Connors found in 2000 that the empirical research pointed to, if anything, even stronger gains from imitation than from sentence combining. Thus, while its durability in the annals of rhetoric is not alone proof of its value, certainly the intersection of experience, explanation, and empirical findings adds strength to all three parts of this rhetorical tripod. At the very least, there seems to be no principled ground upon which the practice of imitation should be disdained. Writing teachers should instead aim to refine its uses and study the results. There does not appear, at least, to be a better path toward improving the evaluation of students' sentences even while improving the evaluation of their work as a whole.

That is why, at last, we should not ignore the one great reason why "grammar hope" persists: that's why, after all, there even are college composition courses, which in turn is why there even is a field of rhetoric and composition. After all is said and done, no matter how much there is to be said and done, we have work because there is an enormous demand for better sentences. We do have to do something. According to the current state of evidence, thoughtful use of imitation offers the most promise for the least pain. It deserves to be one of the hottest topics of composition research, theory, and practice.

10

WHEN THEIR VOICE IS THEIR PROBLEM: USING IMITATION TO TEACH THE CLASSROOM DIALECT

J. Scott Farrin

A colleague once told me that she learned grammar in order to teach it. "I never knew the rules," she said. Did she mean she learned them so well that she was able to forget them? Maybe. But if she was like me, she gained her facility with language through conversation and reading. She learned how to use language by using it, by reading and speaking and being spoken to, her vocabulary and diction increasingly more sophisticated as the language she encountered was added to her own repertoire. That's how I learned to write, if it's not the method I teach my students. An inattentive student before college, I had read over four hundred novels prior to graduating high school. Five large boxes still gather dust in my parents' garage. Those boxes of books were my teachers.

In high school I read novels, pulp works, science fiction, and the like to the exclusion of everything else. I read through the night, until my room brightened with sunlight and I could hear my parents awaken downstairs. At that time, I would kill my lights and pretend to be asleep—night after night of this, getting what sleep I could during my classes, which was a surprising amount. I remember more than once being awoken by a classmate who was handing out tests to the desks in the rear of the classroom. I didn't know we were having a test, and looking down at it, the material was totally unfamiliar to me. I had checked out of academics.

Earlier, in middle school, I recall getting grammar instruction through self-paced "modules." Over the course of the year, you checked out these modules, read them and worked the exercises, and your grade was determined by how many of these you completed. There was a module on the semicolon, on conjunctions, on irregular verbs. It was mostly unsupervised activity, and cheating was rampant. Kids sold the answers to the exercises along with bubble gum (25 cents a piece) during recess and after school. But even cheating was not enough for me. By the end of seventh grade, I had failed to finish the minimum number of modules.

The only reason I remember this at all is because of the terrible time I had with the school and with my parents during the last month of that year. I can vaguely remember the covers of these things, in colored construction paper, each piece of punctuation given legs, arms, and a smiling face in hand-drawn illustrations, and nothing else, not a single thing they might have taught me.

The one class in which I did well was literature. I scored exceedingly well in reading comprehension on the California Achievement Tests, and so I knew what I was reading, and if I wasn't reading the texts, if I wasn't asleep, I understood the lectures enough to fake it on the tests. Like many con artists, I learned that a glib tongue and a glib pen could substitute for effort. My teacher Mrs. Harvey once wrote on the bottom of one of my typically short and pointed essays that I ought to give others classes in writing. It wasn't the first time this "gift" of mine had been identified. Like most people, I was quick to claim it as an innate quality, as if all the reading I'd done might not have been the distinguishing variable between my peers and myself.

At the University of Texas, I read and reread my favorite authors. By then I'd upgraded to more "literary" works. And I made a name for myself as a writer, turning out editorials for the campus newspaper and taking a sequence of intensive expository writing courses. Flannery O'Connor said that she became a writer because she wrote well, and I was steered along in much the same way. Eventually, I entered a graduate creative writing program, where I began to take seriously the idea that my writing skills originated in the texts I read. I developed a systematic method of hastening the process.

I transcribed passages from authors who I believed could teach me something, and I improvised my own passages in the rhythms of those transcriptions. I did it until I could mimic the rhythms of their prose even in speech. I gave myself exercises, transcribing a page of Barry Hannah's unique prose and segueing into a freewriting exercise in which I continued the passage with my own material, with his rhythms, diction, and vocabulary. Here is an exercise I did back then based on two passages taken from two different stories by Raymond Carver. The first two passages are his. The third is mine.

> It seemed to me everything took a bad turn for my father after that. Just like Dummy, he wasn't the same man anymore. That arm coming up and going back down in the water, it was like so long to good times and hello to bad.

Because it was nothing but that all the years after Dummy drowned himself in that dark water. (Carver 1988b, 159)

Later, after things had changed for us, and the kid had come along, all of that, Fran would look back on that evening at Bud's place as the beginning of the change. But she's wrong. The change came later—and when it came, it was like something that happened to other people, not something that could have happened to us. (264)

When everybody finished painting, they came over around the front of the house. They came over to where I was. At the curb was where I had situated myself, where I could get a good look. The house looked different. It wasn't the place it was yesterday. It looked like someplace another family lived. From where I stood, the sun hit the windows and the windows blinked, as if to let me in on the joke. I'm still yours, it seemed to say. And I wanted to believe that. But it was hard somehow. That things could change really. One day looks nothing like the one before it and your thinking you'll turn over a new leaf. I've left all that behind me. But it's a trick. Because that day's just like the one before it and the one before that, and all the others strung together so tightly it doesn't matter that one may not look like another. What I'm saying is that it's all closely related, whether you see it or not.

One of the first things I learned was that prose styles invite particular stories. In the passages above, the language lends itself to the expression of how our lives can be irrevocably changed in ways we only partly understand or can articulate. The prose of these passages is perfect for such a revelation, the short sentence that leaps into and is redefined by the sentence that follows. It simulates a mind at work, dramatizing more than describing.

Doing these exercises, I learned that I couldn't write a Raymond Carveresque story in T. Coraghessan Boyle's vivid, hyperactive prose. I couldn't write a story of a young man's first romantic disappointment in the cynical prose of Flannery O'Connor. Of course, a writer must borrow and alter and merge styles to write the story she wants to write.

I've written stories in the prose rhythms of some of my most admired authors, and I've published a few of them. Like me, writers as disparate as Joan Didion, Hunter S. Thompson, Malcolm X, Somerset Maugham, Winston Churchill, and Benjamin Franklin have all credited their development as writers to the practice of imitation. Much recent scholarship has deciphered how the most "original" art is the product of earlier art, and the idea of an "original voice" has been reconstructed. It exists not in the mythic, whole-cloth manner we once supposed but as a unique blend of influences. The practice of imitation can take this process, raise it to the surface, and accelerate it.

Of course, as Paul Butler has noted in his essay advocating imitation and writing immersion, composition scholars who privilege an expressionist pedagogy, one that has as its goal the finding and expression of "voice," have been suspicious of imitation (2001, 108). They may even blame poor student writing on imitation. They note the not uncommon incidents when a student attempts to "put on" a language over which he or she has no control. Essays written in this way are often mockeries of formal, academic prose, clumsily patched together, riddled with grammatical errors. Like every teacher of writing, I'm familiar with these phenomena. Here's a sample from an essay I recently received:

> Were the women of minority left in the gutter of society? Well the answer to that is yes this advancement that has happen was equal to all women of all ethical races and class. These women were all treated as one because they were well educated to be a candidate for a position, the more independent, and their responsibility was at a minimum.

You can see the student grasping at a level of discourse he doesn't understand. Ethical races and classes? What position? Their responsibility was at a minimum? David Bartholomae described a similar essay as "more a matter if imitation or parody than a matter of invention and discovery"(1986, 11). He says such writing seems to "come through the writer, and not from the writer" (8). But the question really is not whether the writing comes "through" the writer. Of course it does. The important question is: from where is it coming?

And it is true that some students are greatly helped by the simple advice: speak as yourself, without overreaching, in your best language. Usually such students have a foundation of Standard American English, broadly defined. Their writing breaks down when they try to sound like masters of academic discourse, but clears up when they relax and tune in to the language of MTV news jockey Tabitha Soren, or any other member of that student's speech community, including not only individuals to whom the students speak, but those individuals the students value and listen to regularly.

There are other students that have it harder, however. Their speech community doesn't include anyone who could write "correctly," and even if they were to find their voice, they could not use it to write a passing essay. And I have students like this, who write naturally, in their recognizable speech rhythms, and when I read their essays, I can hear them speak. Once, while part of a committee of college writing teachers who were grading student essays, a colleague said of such a student: "This writer has a voice. And that's his problem." I knew immediately what he meant, because as well as those students who try to "put on" language, students I find relatively easy to coach and whose writing reliably improves, I have such students whose "voice" is their problem, at least in the classroom.

Such students aren't less intelligent. In his essay "Tense Present," David Foster Wallace contrasts the bully who flunks English but rules the playground with the "brain" who gets good marks but whose so-proper speech earns him beatings outside the classroom door; both have failed in exactly the same way. They have failed to master the language of more than one context, in this case, the dialect of the playground as well as that of the classroom (2001, 52). Students who are strangers to the language of the classroom are often my most insightful; they are usually my most worldly. They have mastered the language of the street corner or the language of the vocations open to someone who begins to work at age fourteen. Sometimes these students are truly ESL students, but more often they are students who have only one dialect at their command and thus their problems in the classroom only resemble those of ESL students. It is a difference of degree and not of kind. I have speakers and writers of Black English, with its more sophisticated use of aspect, verb use that indicates the duration, completion, or repetition of action. For example, "he be swimming" means not that "he is swimming," but that he has been swimming for a while, not just now, and not just once (Kurland 2000). I have speakers and writers of creolized dialects such as that used by some second-generation Vietnamese immigrants. Other students are harder to pin down. I teach in New Orleans, a place of extraordinary linguistic diversity that is protected by centuries-old divisions of race, class, occupation, and sometimes even neighborhood. It's a polyglot city. The differences between the English they speak and Standard American English are as difficult to address as the differences between Spanish and English, and when they are addressed, they should probably be addressed the same way.

The superficial similarities between the English dialects and the English demanded by the classroom lures us into half measures. When my students' prose shows systemic grammar errors (not grammar slips), I point them out, offer rules, demand they track and correct their errors in proofreading journals, but those errors still beleaguer their writing at the end of the semester. Understandably, the students become frustrated with proofreading in order to correct language use that isn't incorrect, but rather only being employed in a context where it isn't appropriate. They too are confused by the superficial similarities between their English and my English. They are being told their use of language is wrong when they know the truth: it is not wrong. It is not only appropriate, but necessary in other contexts, at home, at certain jobs, among their friends, and so on. Instead of trying to correct a dialect that needs no correction, they should be learning an entirely new dialect, that employed by the classroom. Intuitively, they know this, and in trying to "put on" a new dialect, they create the feared "imitations." The problem is not that they are trying to imitate, but that they have no sources to imitate, and the rhetoric of an "individual voice" discourages them from finding and studying such sources. A student won't become truly fluent in Standard American English until she has moved to where the language is lived, the prose of proficient writers.

The truth is that students who fall into imitations that read as parodies of academic discourse are working largely from models that are unknown— and, I'd argue, nonexistent. In front of a room of English faculty, I heard a job applicant, when asked about the readings she assigned her writing classes, respond that she didn't assign readings, that her students already had enough texts. I watched heads swivel, eyebrows lift, a gasp was almost audible. If it were the movies, a newsman would have dashed for a payphone. I ask my students sometimes how many of them have read a single book, really, cover to cover, and I respect their candor when in a class of twenty-five freshmen, I see four or five raised hands. The truth is, many of my students could hardly be said to imitate anything. They have no models. What they produce could more accurately be labeled simulations, in the way Baudrillard defined that term: copies without originals. The problem isn't that they are trying to sound like someone else, but that through a lack of resources, their efforts meet with failure. They are trying to invent or discover within themselves an appropriate language to address the assignment, but no matter how long they look or how deeply they go, they cannot find that language inside them.

How to help such a student? Self-expression, an authentic voice, fails to meet the class's goal. Constructing the student as one with a transcendent, monolithic self leaves the teacher with no effective pedagogy. It becomes readily clear that the student must express something other than the self, and we can help that student by following a theoretical model that dismisses the old idea of the self. Instead of characterizing a failing text as coming "through" a writer, and not "from" him, we must acknowledge that our best writing does, in fact, move through us.

In "The Death of the Author," Roland Barthes says, "[T]ext is a tissue of quotations drawn from innumerable centers of culture"(1988, 170). An act of writing is a dance of sources, or appropriated language and concepts, expressing themselves in their combinations and conflicts. And the reader, as Barthes says, "ought at least to know that the inner thing he thinks to translate is itself only a ready-formed dictionary" (170). Thus conceived, the author has multiple selves. He is a unique confluence of other voices, none his own. "It is the language which speaks, not the author" (168). The writer does not invent; he can, as Barthes states, "only imitate a gesture that is always anterior, never original" (170). Foucault also asserted what he called the "plurality of self" that an author contains, or which contains him or her (1988, 205). When one refers to an author, one "does not refer purely and simply to a real individual, since [writing] can give rise simultaneously to several selves" (205). As a result, Foucault says, "writing has freed itself from the dimension of expression" (197).

How freeing this line of thought can be! When one's writing fails its subject and purpose, it is not a failure of the writer or of a process that looks no further than the writer, that holds the writer morally accountable for its sentences as well as its ideas. The student will not be constructed with an Emersonian model, a god in ruins, one whose potential she betrays with each failed piece of writing. A failure in writing is a failure in appropriation. Barthes states that "language knows a subject, not a person"(1988, 169). Students are often unacquainted with the language that knows the subject upon which they must write. They must absorb that language before they can write on that subject. Let's understand what we mean by appropriation, since, as writing teachers, we are wary of a pedagogy that might seem to celebrate plagiarism. By appropriation, I am not talking about the short-term borrowing of ideas but the intuitive use of the language that addresses a subject. The goal of a student writer is the absorption or channeling of language that transforms the self and thus the writer from who he might be in the workplace, who he might be on Friday nights, to who he must be in the classroom, one who navigates the language of the academy because he has become a locus for its expression.

If one looks at writing in this way, one understands why it proves so difficult to help a student through grammar instruction. Beyond the

fundamental universals, people acquire language through appropriation, not the memorization and practice of grammar rules. Grammar,
the linguist Julia S. Falk writes, "describes the knowledge that speakers
have about their language, but it does not describe the ways in which
people actually produce sentences or determine the meaning of the sentences they encounter" (1973, 195). In other words, she says, "it is not an
imitative model of the faculty itself." We must give students an imitative
model.

Looking at the process of how language is acquired can help. The
linguists Elizabeth Stine and John Bohannon state that language acquisition "is clearly some form of observational learning, broadly construed"
(1983, 590). Although innate faculties set the stage for language acquisition, Skinner's assertion that "echoic behavior [imitation] is useful in
the process of language acquisition because it allows the 'short-circuiting
of the process of progressive approximations" remains valid (Stine and
Bohannon 1983, 591). Whitehurst and Vasta also argue for the necessity
of imitation, and describe the acquisition of syntax with "the comprehen-
sion-imitation-production hypothesis" (Stine and Bohannon 1983 591).
Basically, it asserts that first one understands an utterance, then one may
faithfully and appropriately imitate that utterance; finally one is able to
use that language, lexicon, and syntax spontaneously. Research has shown
that grammatical forms appear in imitated speech prior to their appearance in spontaneous speech.

To use imitation effectively in the classroom, one must employ all its
forms: (1) topographical, which is an exact point-to-point copy of the
modeled text; (2) partial, in which the copy is partially improvised, or
rearranged; and (3) selective, in which the imitation is controlled by the
grammatical structure. The selective imitation has the same grammatical
structure, but may describe completely new events or objects. Students
should be given an appropriate model and assigned transcriptions and
improvisations off that model, first as a class, then individually.

That was exactly what I was doing when I created for myself those
exercises in graduate school. I took exemplary passages from admired
authors and transcribed them, word by word, either on the page or the
computer screen. Often, I built grammar trees over the sentences that
broke down the ways the various elements interacted with one another.
(Winston Churchill attributed the success of his writing to the practice of
diagramming sentences when he was younger.) I asked myself, were the
sentences cumulative or periodic? How did the parallelism work? Then

I would edit their prose, turning their sentences around, turning them back. I combined sentences and separated them. Lastly, I wrote my own passages in the rhythms of their prose. I might start literally substituting my own words into their sentence structures, and as I grew more confident, changing those structures a bit while remaining faithful to that particular author's "voice."

Remember the student who asserted that women were "left in the gutter of society?" In the same essay, he wrote: "With women being focus on their career and out of the kitchen send messages to their mate, which is, help out or I am gone." He was one of my seemingly hopeless cases. In order to pass out of Freshman Composition, he had to pass the university's exit examination, an in-class essay of at least four hundred words that would be graded blindly by other members of the English faculty. He'd either gotten discouraged and dropped out of previous courses, or seen them through only to fail the final essay. My class made his fourth attempt, and he was a senior and hoping to graduate. I felt as desperate as he did. In my office one afternoon, I asked if he'd be willing to try something different. He was vaguely familiar with the parts of speech; he didn't know how to break down sentences, and it seemed a little late to learn. We had only a couple of months until the end of the semester. So he agreed to some transcription exercises, outside the classroom, to be brought in to me only as a guarantee it would be done. I began with Hemingway, not as an ethical model but because of the simplicity of his style and because he had been used as a model for so many other successful writers. The first passage he transcribed was the first paragraph of *The Sun Also Rises*. The first paragraph reads like this:

> Robert Cohn was once middleweight boxing champion of Princeton. Do not think that I am very much impressed by that as a boxing title, but it meant a lot to Cohn. He cared nothing for boxing, in fact he disliked it, but he learned it painfully and thoroughly to counteract the feeling of inferiority and shyness he had felt on being treated as a Jew at Princeton. There was a certain inner comfort in knowing he could knock down anybody who was snooty to him, although, being very shy and a thoroughly nice boy, he never fought except in the gym. He was Spider Kelly's star pupil. Spider Kelly taught all his young gentlemen to box like featherweights, no matter whether they weighed one hundred and five or two hundred and five pounds. But it seemed to fit Cohn. He was really very fast. He was so good that Spider promptly overmatched him and got his nose permanently flattened. This increased Cohn's distaste for boxing, but it gave him a certain satisfaction of some strange sort, and it certainly

improved his nose. In his last year at Princeton he read too much and took to wearing spectacles. I never met any one of his class who remembered him. They did not even remember that he was middleweight boxing champion. (1926, 3–4)

My student wrote his own passage modeled on his transcription.

Joshua Anderson was once a rally car champion of the U.S. Do not think I was impressed with his ability to win races, but his ability to race the races. He cared nothing for being a top racer. In fact, he hated it, but rather be on the track then running circles on victory lane. There was a certain inner comfort in knowing he could race anybody at any given moment and not worry about the end results. He was Mike Miller star pupil. Mike Miller taught all his apprentice to race for the race, no matter what size engine that one may have. But it seemed to fit Anderson. He was really very fast. He was so good that Miller promptly overmatched him and got his car totaled. This increased Anderson's distance from racing, but it gave him a certain satisfaction for some strange reason, and it certainly improved his attitude. In his last year in the circuit, he races so much that the bottom of his foot was shaped like a pedal. I don't think anyone on the circuit now remembered him. They don't even remember that he was the best rally car champion of his time.

Although his imitation seems parodic, it's mostly correct, concrete and understandable—a tremendous improvement from the often incoherent prose he previously produced. But who gets the credit for the improvement? Although transcription is a shortcut for the process of language acquisition through reading, it's no immediate fix. After several such exercises, I moved him on to other sources. Part of my idea was that language dictates content, and Hemingway's prose was mostly the prose of a fiction writer. George Orwell is more of an essayist, and we focused next on his article "A Hanging." It opens with this paragraph:

It was in Burma, a sodden morning of the rains. A sickly light, like yellow tinfoil, was slanting over the high walls into the jail yard. We were waiting outside the condemned cells, a row of sheds fronted with double bars, like small animal cages. Each cell measured about ten feet by ten and was quite bare within except for a plank bed and a pot of drinking water. In some of them brown silent men were squatting at the inner bars, with their blankets draped round them. These were the condemned men, due to be hanged within the next week or two. (1950, 142)

And here is my student's exercise:

It was in New Orleans, a humid afternoon of sunshine. A bright light, like leaves was touching the buildings, hiding the evil in the shadows. We were waiting outside the Superdome, a row of people flooded the streets, like Times Square in New York. Each float was dressed with glitter, beads, and excited costume wearing riders. Some consisted of face painted children, who were dressed in super hero costumes, with their capes draped over them. These were Mardi Gras participants, due to have the time of their life in New Orleans.

When the time came for the exit examination, my student felt confident. I had been giving him positive, though qualified, feedback on his work. And he passed the examination, writing an essay that was flawed but demonstrated tremendous improvement. Here is a passage from his exit examination. The prompt asked whether the news media should show its audience graphic images from our latest war in Iraq.

> If the media started showing it's viewers pictures of dead soldiers from the aftermath of a battle, then people would see the truth about what goes on during war. The media is not supposed to be sympathetic towards its viewers, and debate if the viewers can handle seeing dead bodies on their TV sets. The media's job is to report the news on what happens in the world, good or bad. They should not twist the facts to the public in fear the countries morale may go down or speak against their nation.

There is a striking parallelism error in that last sentence, but if you compare it to the paragraph I excerpted earlier in this essay, you will see that he is expressing his ideas much more coherently. This is anecdotal evidence, I admit, but combined with my own experiences and the testimony of professional writers, it certainly encourages more experimentation. If my students could write as well as Orwell, even if they wrote slavishly in the manner of Orwell, they would make an A in my class. And then they would study someone else, and someone else, until these integrated sources had been absorbed and had changed them, making them like no one else, and the prose that came through them, channeled through a complex web of appropriated voices, those anterior sources, would be their own. Having mastered so many dialects, they could play the language in any idiom, improvising as they did so.

I've often wished I could tell certain students, go home, take a year, consume ten to fifteen books, reading pages out loud, then come back to class. I believe their writing ability would vastly improve. Such an action, though, either isn't practical or within the authority of most composition instructors. Imitation, therefore, may provide an abbreviated way of immersing those students in an effective classroom dialect, to make that language part of them, or maybe more accurately, make them part of that language, and thus improve their writing.

PART III: TEACHING PROSE STYLE
Introduction

Tom Pace

When the field of rhetoric and composition moved away from an interest in prose style in the early 1980s, part of what drove this removal was the widespread sense that an interest in prose style simply meant requiring students to do a lot of exercises—and these exercises had no particular justification in the realm of high theory, which was then coming into vogue. In short, the problem with style-based pedagogy was that its value was exclusively practical. Now that the great boom of high theory has largely subsided, such a critique of style-based pedagogies looks awfully quaint and, ironically, rather naïve. Nonetheless, the essays that follow in this section base their interest in daily classroom practice in rich theoretical warrants. Of course, these aren't the only essays in the book that explicitly offer particular classroom practices, but we group these together because they do so in ways that go to the very heart of today's standard writing curricula.

In her essay "Style: The New Grammar in Composition Studies?" Nicole Amare argues for a more overt instruction in style that leads students to a better working knowledge of grammar. Next, Lisa Baird, in "Balancing Thought and Expression: A Short Course in Style," continues the thread that emerged in the preceding essay by showing how a focus on prose style can actually help minimize the grammatical errors that can otherwise diminish the writer's impact on their audience. William J. Carpenter, in his essay "Rethinking Stylistic Analysis in the Writing Class," describes the way he teaches students to perform stylistic analysis and how it enables them to reflect on their own writing in ways that dramatically improve it. Next, Peter Clements in "Re-Placing the Sentence: Approaching Style through Genre," explains how he organizes his composition course around three interrelated notions of context, style, and genre. Finally, this section ends with Jesse Kavadlo's "Tutoring Taboo: A Reconsideration of Style in the Writing Center," in which he describes how questions of prose style can be addressed in ways wholly integrated with a draft's content and meaning, an approach that also moves us beyond the process/product binary that has perhaps cast too long a shadow on writing center practice.

11

STYLE: THE NEW GRAMMAR IN COMPOSITION STUDIES?

Nicole Amare

Grammar is a set of rules; style is a matter of choice. One of my high school English teachers gave me these two definitions, and I believed them as truths until I took my first introduction to literature course at a large midwestern university. During my first college English class, it didn't take long for me to realize that style had its boundaries—for example, a student was dismissed from class one time for using the idiom "kick the bucket" and the diction "unnecessary abortion" in the same sentence—and that grammar had its preferences. Like most first-year students, I didn't fully understand grammatical conventions, so I developed my writing style by imitating the "grammar" of the model essays that the instructor gave to us as sample A's. If the sample essay had a lot of dashes, so did mine; I often employed similar diction as was found in the A authored paper; I copied the same syntactical structures; I even tried to use humor in the same places or a similar catchy title. To my astonishment, I scored poorly on my first poetry analysis, which contained the following end comment: "While I'm intrigued by your comparison of these two poets [sic] personas, I find it disturbing that you refer to William Wordsworth in your essay as Wordsworth and Emily Dickinson as Emily. Also, please watch those coma [sic] splices! Grade: C."

Although the red marks on my essay convinced me that my low grade was due to errors of grammatical conventions, a brief meeting with the instructor during office hours revealed that it was my use of "Emily" that had deeply offended my feminist instructor. In short, I had fallen short of the desired A because I had a sexist style, not because I couldn't write well. On subsequent assignments, I referred to all authors by their last names only and eventually scored an A in the course.

I didn't know it then, but what I took from my instructor was a small piece of what Kathryn Flannery and others have called cultural capital. In *The Emperor's New Clothes: Literature, Literacy, and the Ideology of Style*, Flannery argues: "What counts as style, what counts as valued written form, is part of and derives its meaning from a matrix of elements that comprise a given culture" (1995, 3). Therefore, in order to succeed in academe, I had to learn to write not only what was grammatically correct but also what was considered stylistically correct by the given culture, namely my professors. The conventions for style and grammar depended upon the type of class, writing assignment, and text, but mostly on my professors' whims. They were my primary audience, and once I figured out their stylistic conventions, I did well. It was discovering these hidden taxonomies that was difficult, though, because most professors didn't and still don't overtly explain their writing style preferences because to do so would be contrary to the democratic and humanistic cultural capital of our profession's ideology. We let our students uncover what we want from a piece of writing—and/or what the given culture wants—under the guise of critical thinking and original thought (see Berlin 1991; Harris and Rosen 1991; Spellmeyer 1991). Unfortunately, demonstrating what makes a text an example of great writing in our culture via innuendo only—if we choose to address writing style at all in our classrooms—leaves our students on the losing end of a very complex guessing game. Thus, my purpose in this essay is to encourage more overt style instruction in our composition courses so that our students can be empowered not only through receiving the cultural capital that is inherently linked to appropriate academic writing styles but also so that they can have a better working knowledge of grammar through this effective style instruction.

GRAMMAR REMAINS A FOUR-LETTER WORD

For the past forty years, many of us have believed we have justifiable reasons for erasing formal grammar instruction from our composition classrooms. The Braddock Report of 1963—*Research in Written Composition* (Braddock, Lloyd-Jones, and Schoer 1963)—and similar studies since then have told us that formal grammar instruction not only does not improve our students' writing but in fact may have an adverse affect on their compositions. Such studies, combined with the push for process pedagogy since the early 1980s, have placed audience, purpose, and politics in the writing classroom well above grammar. Our reasons for snubbing style, however, are less clear. Edward Corbett reassures us that we ignore style because "all the requirements—and time constraints—of a composition course" make addressing style "more than [we] can handle" (1996, 222). Or we don't teach it because we think our students first need a better understanding of grammar (Harris and Rowan 1996, 258).

I think both of these excuses are suspect, and the recent bemoaning of our discipline's abject treatment of style and grammar, as evidenced in Sharon Myers's "ReMembering the Sentence" (2003), Robert Connors's "The Erasure of the Sentence" (2000), and Peter Elbow's "The Cultures of Literature and Composition: What Could Each Learn from the Other?" (2002), among others, illustrates a need to reconsider grammar and style instruction in the composition classroom. I contend that we owe it to our students and ourselves to teach style in the composition classroom to help our students become better writers and to reveal that good writing style is essentially linked to cultural capital. I base this assertion partially on style advocates' scholarly attention to the traditions of classical rhetoricians and the practices of imitation and sentence combining, but the greater part of my motivation for treating style as an approach to effective student writing in composition studies stems from the disciplines of business and technical communication. In both of these fields, students are taught style as an effective means of improving their own writing. Unlike composition studies, most authors of business and technical communication textbooks address style overtly, often devoting an entire chapter or more to the subject. In addition, business and technical communication textbooks routinely and successfully treat grammar as style issues, an approach that I argue might solve the "grammar wars" in composition studies during the last four decades.

Grammar scholars like Martha Kolln (1999) and Rei Noguchi (1991) and anthologies such as Susan Hunter and Ray Wallace's *The Place of Grammar in Writing Instruction: Past, Present, and Future* (1995) have tried to rescue grammar through advocacy scholarship and development of new approaches to teaching grammar. We remain in the shadow of Braddock's study. Style, on the other hand, has recently experienced a resurgence in scholarly and pedagogical interest as we continually return to classical rhetoricians for guidance in writing instruction practices. Aristotle's concept of ethos still underlies how we teach argument to our composition students. According to Aristotle, "the technical study of rhetoric" (1984, 2153) is necessary to understand the modes of persuasion, and this technical study involves the analysis and learning of effective stylistic conventions in order to achieve a successful rhetoric. For example, students today may consider a speaker's appeals to reason as more effective than appeals to emotion (Flannery 1995, 201), and we as instructors may teach our students types of logical fallacies, such as ad hominem, post hoc, overgeneralization, and so on, so that they can identify these fallacies in others' arguments as well as avoid them in their own writing. Like Aristotle, Quintilian also believed in analyzing oratory to understand and create rhetoric that is more effective. Quintilian is best known for his conceptualizing rhetoric around the ideal of *vir bonus dicendi peritus* from the *Institutio Oratoria,* which is most commonly translated as "good man speaking well." Both Cicero and Quintilian believed one of the most important precepts of learning good rhetoric was imitation, or using the models of excellent rhetoricians in order to learn how they effectively employ language (Quintilian 1987, 125). In sum, these classical rhetoricians often employed analyzing or copying the grammatical structure of language to achieve a successful style, one that is appropriate to the cultural conventions of the time.

Although the imitation of language content is considered taboo today (plagiarism), the copying of syntactical structure—or the "form" of writing—is still accepted by some compositionists as a constructive means of teaching style. Robert Connors, Sharon Myers, and William Gruber are just a few supporters; however, imitation as a pedagogical approach remains largely out of favor because it is "perceived as 'mere servile copying,' destructive of student individuality and contributory to a mechanized, dehumanizing Skinnerian view of writing" (Connors 2000, 114). Because sentence-level instruction suggests "demeaning" grammar drills to many compositionists, we avoid it, unless we teach or do research in basic writing, remedial composition, or ESL classes. This is unfortunate, considering the success that classical rhetoricians and modern-day compositionists have had with imitation exercises. Says Corbett, "In my own rhetoric texts, I have suggested a number of imitative exercises that have proven fruitful for me and my students" (1996, 222). However, rhetoric and composition texts like Corbett's are in the minority today because of the process pedagogy push of the 1980s. Most post-1980 composition textbooks contain no grammar instruction, save an occasional brief editing checklist. Nonetheless, we saturate our basic writing and ESL textbooks with word-, sentence-, and paragraph-level exercises and examples. It is important to note the striking differences between the treatment of style issues in Rise Axelrod and Charles Cooper's enduring composition textbook, *The St. Martin's Guide to Writing* (2004), and a basic writing textbook such as Barbara Clouse's *Progressions with Readings* (2005). Seventy-five percent of Clouse's textbook is on style, with entire sections devoted to "The Paragraph"; "Effective Sentences"; and "Grammar and Usage." Conversely, *The St. Martin's Guide to Writing* contains only brief editing checklists at the end of certain assignments, which is the norm for composition textbooks.

If we continually deny that grammar instruction improves student writing, why do we still teach it in textbooks that are aimed at (mostly) marginalized students? Perhaps it is because, as Lynn Bloom notes, we tend to "punish lower-class students for not being, well, more middle class" (1996, 655) by giving them grammar instruction instead of the "cultural capital" of critical thinking that we save for our "mainstream" composition students. The loss is twofold: our composition students miss out on valuable style instruction, whereas our basic writing and ESL students are denied access to what we view as valuable cultural capital until—if and when, that is—they pass the remedial course and take a "higher-level" writing class. Thus, grammar remains in exile for composition studies, and we are scolded for talking about it; in "Grammar, Grammars, and the Teaching of Grammar," Patrick Hartwell instructs us to "move on to more interesting areas of inquiry" (1985, 252).

Like imitation exercises, sentence combining has a mixed past in the field of composition. While research by Rosemary Hake and Joseph Williams (1985) and other similar studies have demonstrated sentence-combining instruction to be beneficial to student writing, many teachers of composition devalue sentence combining. Moreover, many compositionists believe that sentence combining and other word-, sentence-, and even paragraph-level exercises are designed for either basic writers, ESL students, or for teachers invested in product-oriented pedagogy. But articles like Richard Gebhardt's "Sentence Combining in the Teaching of the Writing Process" clearly defend sentence combining as a necessary and helpful component of process pedagogy. According to Gebhardt, sentence-combining instruction "can help students develop the ability to combine many facts and details into fewer generalizations, with a resultant reduction in the cognitive overload" (Gebhardt 1985, 232). If we continue to avoid style instruction via sentence-level instruction, such as sentence combining and imitation exercises, we are potentially missing out on an opportunity to enhance our students' composing process as well as the quality of their finished work.

WHY ADDRESS GRAMMAR AS STYLE?

The position that grammar instruction is boring and even disempowering has persisted for decades in composition studies. In his 1964 *English Journal* article "Grammar and Linguistics: A Contrast in Realities," Don

Wolfe describes why English teachers and students hate grammar: "The more grammar, the less self-expression; it was grammar that defined the student's [negative] attitude toward English, not themes which opened the deep streams of life and let them flow into burning images" (73). Grammar was perceived then as it often is now as contrary to creative and critical thinking, although no studies have supported this conviction. Wolfe also makes that point that grammar is separate from style and that "[m]any critics felt, indeed, that no great amount of grammar teaching could be applied to style" (73). For Wolfe, grammar is a set of rules, whereas style is based on language usage. Today in composition studies, scholars and teachers still make a case about defining style and grammar as separate categories with distinct conventions, definitions, and functions. For example, Joseph Williams's influential *Style: Ten Lessons in Clarity and Grace* (2002) mentions grammar only twice in passing and once in detail, and his twenty pages on grammar in detail is entirely about punctuation.

When Peter Elbow says in "The Cultures of Literature and Composition" that he misses "sophistication" in writing, namely "elegance and irony and indirection—qualities that composition has sometimes reacted against" (2002, 540), he is talking about his pining for style, and for Elbow, it is a literary style. However, because many of our composition students tend to shut down when they hear grammar terms, combined with our belief that grammar instruction impedes creative thought and good writing, we as composition researchers, instructors, and textbook writers avoid grammar when possible. Our interest in style, as indicated by Elbow, Flannery, and others, is on the rise; however, it is difficult (if not impossible) to discuss style without including grammar. Richard Weaver's *The Ethics of Rhetoric* explains the interdependence between grammar and style:

> The verb is regularly ranked with the nouns in force, and it seems that these two parts of speech express the two aspects under which we habitually see phenomena, that of determinate things and that of actions or states of being. Between them the two divide up the world at a pretty fundamental depth; and it is a commonplace of rhetorical instruction that a style made up predominantly of nouns and verbs will be a vigorous style. (1953, 135)

I believe that our longing for more style discourse in composition studies stems from a desire to inform our students about grammar issues in a more meaningful and useful way. I advocate teaching grammar as a style issue because our students can and will benefit from it.

At first glance, it would appear that teaching grammar as style would be limiting; for instance, in "Grammar, Grammars, and the Teaching of Grammar," Patrick Hartwell glosses over his "grammar 3" as a matter of "linguistic etiquette." However, he does refer to "grammar 5" as stylistic grammar, and he includes Joseph Williams's style classifications as well as Martha Kolln's definition: "grammatical terms used in the interest of teaching prose style" (Kolln, 1981, 140). In teaching grammar to composition students, style works: students care about writing style and discuss it willingly, without the fear and loathing they traditionally have toward grammar. The "Postscript: Classroom Dialogue" to Flannery's *The Emperor's New Clothes* illustrates how students are open to talking about rhetorical style, even if they do not yet have the terms available to describe why they prefer one style over another (1995, 199–202). We as teachers can more freely talk about grammar issues with our students as elements of style; our students will, for example, see their diction and syntax choices not as grammar rules but instead as a critical means of reaching and impressing their target audience.

Although Peter Elbow and others have turned to the field of literature to rejuvenate the teaching of style in the composition classroom, my motivation for treating style as an approach to effective student writing in composition studies stems mainly from the field of business and technical communication. For instance, research in business communication supports the teaching of style as an effective means to improving student writing. In "Exploring How Instruction in Style Affects Writing Quality," Kim Sydow Campbell and associates argue that formal style instruction, via classroom exercises and textbook instruction, noticeably improves student writing. Through studying the student writing samples of pre- and post-style classroom instruction over the course of a single semester, Campbell et al. discovered that students improved in the areas of appropriate active/passive voice usage, parallelism, conciseness, directness, and diction. These are all areas of style, but grammar instruction was inherently linked to each area: for example, appropriate active/passive voice usage involved instructions and exercises about the syntactical roles of the agent vs. the patient; instruction on parallelism involved identification of verb consistency; and so on. Campbell et al. conclude that their study "supports a commonsense yet controversial notion among business communication instructors that word- and sentence-level instruction must be taught" (1999, 85). Moreover, Kathryn Riley and associates' *Revising Professional Writing in Science and Technology, Business, and the Social Sciences* (1999), one of the texts used in

Campbell et al.'s study, teaches grammar as style in order to help students see their writing as based on word and sentence choices about audience and genre suitability, not language conventions. Business communication students "learn grammar" in the context that changing a word, choosing punctuation, or rearranging syntactical structures in their writing is done with respect to audience needs and expectations rather than from obedience to abstract grammar rules.

Other business and technical communication textbooks routinely and successfully treat grammar as style issues. Most devote at least one detailed chapter to the subject; others include elements of style instruction throughout the text. Mike Markel's *Technical Communication* (2001) includes a chapter on "Drafting and Revising Effective Sentences" and another chapter on "Designing the Document," which includes instruction on formatting as well as appropriate style issues for an intended audience. John Thill and Courtland Bovée's *Excellence in Business Communication* (2001) approaches style instruction recurrently in each chapter. As with Riley et al.'s text, grammar is treated as a style issue, and students reading Thill and Bovée's textbook are consistently encouraged to stylistically compose, adapt, and revise their documents based on rhetorical situations. A. C. Krizan et al.'s *Business Communication* (2002), Mary Ellen Guffey's *Essentials of Business Communication* (2001), and John Lannon's *Technical Communication* (2002) all take a similar approach to the necessary relationship between style instruction, audience, and document appropriateness. Finally, Rebecca Burnett's *Technical Communication* (2001) devotes the first four chapters to style issues as related to the rhetorical situation (reader, writer, text) and then later gives a chapter on revision and editing entitled "Ensuring Usability: Testing, Revising, and Editing," which links writing high-quality documents to pleasing the target audience. In addition, Burnett includes a "Usage Handbook" at the end of her text. No mention is made of the word "grammar" in the index, table of contents, or headers, yet "grammar lessons" per se clearly exist throughout all of the above textbooks in the form of style instruction.

What most business and technical communication textbooks have in common is that they address grammar as a choice, as an issue of style. Recently, some composition textbooks have begun addressing grammar as a style issue. Former *College English* editor James C. Raymond wrote his first-year composition textbook, *Moves Writers Make* (1999), almost completely as a writing style guide. Raymond shows through his discussion and analysis of writers' "moves" that good writing is merely a matter of writer agency: writers, including student writers, must choose the appropriate subject, words, and arrangement of words in sentences. Students are then encouraged to make their own "moves" and to change these moves or use new style moves, depending on the genre of writing, the discipline, and the audience. Raymond also supports localized imitation of sentence structure and style as a means of improving student writing. In *Moves Writers Make*, composition students are instructed to copy the "moves" or syntactical forms that authors make in writing, but not the diction. In chapter 12, entitled "Sentence Exercises," Raymond tells students to read sentences from famous authors and then "write sentences of your own, imitating the moves you like best" (289) in the section of this chapter called "Additional Sentences for Analysis and Imitation." Raymond encourages students to look at grammatical structures, such as an author's effective use of present participles to avoid overuse of the "to be" verb, and copy those syntactical structures in an attempt to master some elements of good writing.

Similarly, Joseph Williams's *The Craft of Argument* (2003) is one of the few composition textbooks that includes extended style instruction. All of "Part 4: The Languages of Argument," which includes chapters on "Clear Language" and "The Overt and Covert Force of Language," provides specific instructions and examples on how students can revise their writing through specific style instruction. As in his influential *Style: Ten Lesson in Clarity and Grace,* Williams's use of style in *The Craft of Argument,* like the treatment of style in technical and business communication textbooks, is symbiotic with grammar: Williams mentions phrases and clauses, subject and verb agreement, and the like. Grammar as a term or concept, however, is not formally addressed or mentioned.

Neither my proposal to teach grammar as style nor my desire to broaden the definition of style is new. The clearest example of grammar addressed as style is Virginia Tufte's *Grammar as Style* (1971), a book-length study of professional writing that "presumes that grammar and style can be thought of in some way as a single subject" (1971, 1). Tufte's text offers excellent examples of grammatical constructions and formations that can be most easily understood and even mastered when they are interpreted as elements of a stylistic discourse. Although most of Tufte's sentences and paragraphs are taken from technical and business writers, some familiar literary names are present as well: Ernest Hemingway, Thomas Wolfe, E. M. Forster, and Aldous Huxley, to name a few. Readers of *Grammar as Style* learn the parts of speech, modifiers, cohesion, and so on only in the context of how certain elements create effective style in specific rhetorical contexts. The popularity of William Strunk, Jr. and E. B. White's *The Elements of Style* (1999) is further evidence that treating grammar as a style issue is a desirable approach not only to become a better writer but also to learn grammar.

In 1974, Tim Shopen argued in "Some Contributions from Grammar to the Theory of Style" that style was about ideas, whereas grammar was more about meaning (775). Although Shopen does clarify his difference between ideas and meaning later in his article, for me his article serves as support as to why we might not want to split hairs over the differences in a composition classroom context. Not surprisingly, Shopen also defines grammar as rules and style as language use, and his figure 1 on page 777 of this piece illustrates how he views grammar almost like a bank from which elements may be plucked in order to create an effective style. For first-year composition pedagogy, I would propose a reversal of this figure, where style is more the catchall term, and features like "punctuation" and "capitalization" and "spelling" are addressed in our classrooms as elements of writing style. This approach would loosen the grammar albatross that has been choking our profession for four decades, and at the same it would allow our students to learn effective writing strategies that would improve both their cognitive processes and their final written products.

HOW SHOULD WE TEACH GRAMMAR AS STYLE?

In order to teach grammar as style, we must first adjust our curriculum and research to include, more readily, style discourse. According to Edward Corbett, unless composition teachers "devote at least two weeks to the study of style, either in a concentrated period or in scattered session throughout the semester," we might as well not teach style at all (1996, 216). Corbett bases this time frame on the diligence of the classical rhetoricians and the Renaissance teachers who spent countless hours each week on style instruction. Campbell addressed style in her business communication classes in "6 of 28 class meetings during the semester (around 20 percent)" (Campbell et al. 1999, 80), and I also teach style to my composition, business, and technical communication students for at least one-fifth of the semester if not more. Unlike Corbett, I do not break my style instruction into two-week blocks but rather incorporate discussions of style throughout the entire semester. However, I agree with Corbett that "[m]any students learn their grammar while studying style" (1996, 216). Students in my classes see style discourse as empowering and fun, and given the opportunity to learn style, most write better papers and are more confident writers at the end of the semester. Style instruction has a purpose beyond rote memorization of rules or being scolded for writing something incorrectly; students compose, revise, and shape their writing to suit the assignment and their target audience. Moreover, they learn about grammar in a fun, nonthreatening atmosphere; they explore appositives, participles, and other "grammatical conventions" under the guise of effective writing for their target audience. A misplaced modifier, instead of serving as an example of the student's failed knowledge of grammar, under style instruction becomes an element that the student can choose to move elsewhere in the sentence in order to improve the style quality of his or her writing.

There are a number of ways we as composition teachers can approach style with our students. Sentence combining is just one of many exercises our students can do. The assignment below, adapted from James C. Raymond's "Trick the Teacher" assignment in *Writing Is an Unnatural Act* (1986), employs the imitation methods of Cicero and Quintilian, with a specific focus on writing style.

> Find a passage of published, credible, and professional writing that is a work of literature or that analyzes or discusses a work of literature. Then, create your own "forgery" that you hope will "trick the teacher." Pick a paragraph about the size of the example below or longer (at least ninety words). Make sure you cite the author and title of your passage. Type your passage and bring twenty-five copies to Friday's class. If you "trick the teacher," you will get an extra credit of five points. For doing this assignment, you will receive a homework credit of fifteen points.
>
> Note: Do not indicate on the copies which passage is the forgery. Instead, bring in a copy of the original piece of literature, stapled to your forgery. Please note that your entry will be disqualified if (1) the original is not provided at the end of the trick session; (2) there are any typographical or grammar errors on the copies; (3) the example is too short; (4) your version is too much like the original; (5) there are not twenty-five copies; (6) the example is not from a credible source.

Here is an example from one of my classes. Read the following passages closely and decide which one is the forgery.

> 1. His life had begun in sacrifice, in enthusiasm for generous ideas; he had traveled very far, on various ways, on strange paths, and whatever he followed it had been without faltering, and therefore without shame and without regret.

In so far he was right. That was the way, no doubt. Yet for all that the great plain on which men wander amongst graves and pitfalls remained very desolate under the impalpable poesy of crepuscular light, overshadowed in the center, circled with a bright edge as if surrounded by an abyss full of flames. (Joseph Conrad, *Lord Jim*)

2. From the multitude, then, he effectively concealed the agonizing stamp of humanity with which he was branded. But to a precious few—those who, by looking at his face, caught a glimpse of the conflagration in the man's soul— the mythic power of Tuan Jim was overshadowed by the horror that enveloped his very existence. They knew he had come to their country not to escape the outside world but to wrest himself free from his own self, his own shadow of shame and iniquity that tortured him to the core. He had come to escape his own fate. (Joseph Conrad, *Lord Jim*)

(In case you're curious, the second passage is the student forgery.)

Because this assignment is based on the imitative methods developed by classical rhetoricians, the danger of this assignment for today's composition student is obvious in terms of plagiarism: for example, I have had a student copy some of the diction (three words or more in a row) from the original source, and the entry was disqualified.[1] But the goal of this assignment is to show students that they can successfully write syntactical structures and use tone similar to that of published writers. This assignment also opens the door for discussions of plagiarism as well as style use. Using the style repertoire we have been compiling all semester, we as a class discuss why we think one of the paragraphs is or is not the forgery. Are there incidences of ineffective repetition? Is there enough sentence length and syntactical variety? Is the diction inflated or too general? I usually do this activity toward the end of the course in order to reinforce the style concepts we have been working on all semester. In those cases where the student successfully "tricks the teacher" into thinking that the student's paragraph is the original and the published work is the student forgery, the student[2] sees him- or herself as similar to a published author. The students not only learn improved style and voice through this assignment, but they also discover that they are authors, just as good as and sometimes better than published ones.

Not only should we use style instruction to teach our students how to write more effectively, but we should also tell them why we are advocating a certain style. For example, if we advocate a nonsexist style with our students, we could use this style instruction to explore issues about why sexist language is not effective and is usually harmful. In addition, many of us teach visual rhetoric to our students; we have them analyze visual cues in magazine advertisements, commercials, and now Web pages so that they will understand the cultural capital of visual rhetoric features in hopes that they won't become victimized consumers. Therefore, the transition for us to talk about stylistic elements in prose texts should be an easy one. If our students already analyze texts for purpose and organization, they should be able to break down the whole of a text into the sum of its stylistic parts. However, I encourage that grammar as style instruction be implemented only in the context of the students' own writing. I agree with Patrick Hartwell's assertion that "one learns to control the language of print by manipulating language in meaningful contexts, not by learning about language in isolation" (1996, 250). We can accomplish this contextual goal by using examples from our students' own work for instruction. Sentence-combining exercises could be developed from the student essays. Examples of excellent elements of writing style, whether word-, sentence-, paragraph-, or essay-level, could be taken from one student's work and shown to the rest of the class.[3] Imitation exercises, like the "Trick the Teacher" assignment, have also proven effective. Another approach to addressing style in the composition classroom is through textual analysis. As mentioned earlier, Flannery's rhetorical analysis in "Postscript: Classroom Dialogue" demonstrates how style discourse liberates us from formal grammar instruction while still allowing our students to openly discuss grammar as style issues in their writing.

Style instruction has been advocated by classical rhetoricians and is recently thriving as a successful means of improving student writing in business and technical communication. Instead of demarcating style and grammar as related but still very distinct elements of language, I have suggested that addressing grammar in the research and teaching of composition as a feature of style will open doors for new means of improving students' writing and increasing their confidence with their knowledge of language and writing style. This type of pedagogy can be done as formal instruction and/or classroom discourse, provided it is performed within the context of the students' rhetorical situation(s). In addition to improving the finished writing product, style instruction has also shown, as in the case of Gebhardt and others' use of sentence combining, to be an effective means of enhancing and encouraging a more successful writing process. Finally, grammar as style instruction will expose our students more readily to the cultural capital of creative and critical thinking as well as the politics of writing style, subjects we already promote in our research articles as being the most worthwhile use of our and our students' time in the composition classroom.

12

BALANCING THOUGHT AND EXPRESSION: A SHORT COURSE IN STYLE

Lisa Baird

Recently, a colleague and I were discussing my project on style. I said I thought students could write better prose if they were taught more explicitly about how nuances of language play an important, if indirect, role in argument. *"Au contraire,"* said my colleague, "what students need to learn is more rigorous argument."

Our conversation raised several issues, not the least of which is the perception writing instructors have of style. Style, it is assumed, is separate from the reasoning that goes into written argument. Such an assumption is easy to make since the field tends to portray style as ornament to thought. The notion is difficult to correct when handbooks of the day offer sections on style that turn out to be tips on revision. A reader of these handbooks might gather from these tips that style is something mustered into a text after the reasoning process is complete.

My colleague's statement implied that writing instruction ought to teach students to create "logically valid arguments," what I take "rigorous argument" to mean. This rigor arises from logic but not, so it would seem, from expression. These are separate concerns, so the assumption goes.

I understand my colleague's point, because too many student papers are thinly veiled opinions supported only to the degree to which students glom onto expert authorities. The papers tend to be variations of the five-paragraph themes taught throughout the nation's high schools. We want students to stop writing these kinds of papers, yet we do not furnish alternatives or models to help them see how their writing can be different.

The solution does not seem to be to teach more "rigorous argument." Such teaching seems to cast writing as an academic exercise, a skill to be learned rather than an intellectual engagement with the discourse that surrounds students. Saying "we need more rigorous argument" is like saying what artists need is more crimson. Even the master logician himself, Aristotle, recognized the art of rhetoric relied on more than reason alone. The strength of Aristotle's treatise *On Rhetoric* (1991), what some would call the most influential work on how people make decisions about values and preferences, is its attention to the many ways arguments are made compelling: through appeals to the appetites, through the credibility of the writer or speaker, through the use of appropriate expression. Writers must pay attention to expression if they are to secure the goodwill of their readers.

If the aims of discourse are not just to exercise a skill but also to invite readers to listen, then the requirements of writing are even more rigorous than simply achieving validity. When reason and expression act in concert, the rigor of thought is even more arduous because writers are not simply laying down propositions with the attendant evidence. They are preparing words meant for the consideration of others.

Teaching students to write "more rigorous" arguments suggests to me that the act of writing responds to one kind of situation alone: the needs of academic discourse. These needs are often artificial (Thomas and Turner 1994, 83). Writing instruction, however, is about training students to respond to a variety of writing situations, not just academic ones. I prefer to think of writing as a balance of wisdom and eloquence, something like Isocrates' vision for his students.

To enact my belief about this balance, I have taken a stylistic approach to writing instruction. Taking such an approach not only corrects what I see as an imbalance in the field—the emphasis upon demonstration over style—but also engenders in students a means to write responsively to a number of writing situations. These were the goals I set for my writing students in a short course I taught on style.

My optimism about style stems, in part, from the writing of Francis-Noël Thomas and Mark Turner. Their book, *Clear and Simple as the Truth: Writing Classic Prose,* traces the development and use of classic style. In doing so, they argue for a new definition of style. Where style is typically seen as a sign of correctness based on surface features, Thomas and Turner challenge this view (1994, 72–74). Style, they write, is a "conceptual stand" a writer makes when confronted with different needs and purposes in a writing situation. That is, style is not a standard of clear prose (Lanham 1974, 32) but is, instead, the result of certain decisions a writer makes at the outset of writing. Because writers may respond to a number of different purposes and needs, many conceptual stances are possible and thus many styles are possible, not just one.

By explaining style as a conceptual stance, Thomas and Turner restore to style its status as part of invention. That is, as writers decide how to approach a writing situation, stylistic concerns give way to a variety of discursive patterns, to differences in sentence constructions, and to differences in the selection and presentation of evidence. In other words, rigorous argument is but one consideration of the writing act. Stylistic considerations help the writer determine to what extent personal experience will play in the argument, or which of the rhetorical appeals ought to be prominent.

Thomas and Turner are not the first to consider the act of writing as a conceptual undertaking. James Berlin's *Rhetoric and Reality: Writing Instruction in American Colleges, 1900–1985* argues that writing taught in American colleges arises from three very discrete epistemological views about language and reality: "The nature of truth," Berlin writes, "will determine the roles of the interlocutor (the writer or speaker) and the audience in discovering and communicating it" (1987, 4). The three views, in brief, are objective, subjective, and transactional views of reality (7–19), each differing in where they locate truth. The objective view asserts: "Truth, located first in nature and then in the response of the faculties to nature, exists prior to language" (8). The subjective view locates "truth either within the individual or within a realm that is accessible only through the individual's internal apprehension, apart from the empirically verifiable sensory world" (11). The transactional view "sees truth as arising out of the interaction of the elements of the rhetorical situation: an interaction of subject and object, or of subject and audience or even of all the elements" (15).

These three views, in turn, lead to different approaches to writing instruction. The objective view, for instance, leads to the so-called current-traditional model of writing, which emphasizes "patterns of arrangement and superficial correctness" (Berlin 1987, 9). The subjective view leads students to use writing as a means of discovering the truth within themselves. Such is the appeal of expressivist writing. The transactional view sees writing as epistemic, wherein "the material, the social, and the personal" interact through language "as the agent of mediation" (17).

Some of the features of writing described by Berlin are echoed by the Thomas-Turner approach outlined below. But there are important differences. In Berlin's epistemological configuration, truth is the primary force shaping all the other writing relationships. As such, truth seems to be invisible to the writer, a given that arises from the writer's ideological background and thus cannot be modified. If assumptions about truth remain invisible to the writer, then truth is outside the inventional process. In the Thomas-Turner configuration, truth is but one consideration of many. By acknowledging that different writing situations can prompt different locations of truth, the Thomas-Turner approach does not privilege any one style over another. Further, when a writer responds to a writing task, considerations about the nature of truth assist the invention process. Thus, all stylistic stances are rhetorical in nature.

I based a minicourse on Thomas and Turner's depiction of style. The approach I outline below can be taught within the context of almost any writing course. In the following discussion, I explain how my stylistic approach played out in the institution where I teach. The course covered three styles: contemplative, classic, and reflexive. I discuss each style in more detail below. Along with a description of the three styles, I offer a model of the style and a discussion of how my students learned to use the style effectively.

CONTEMPLATIVE STYLE

As Thomas and Turner describe the process, styles can be generated through this rubric: "truth, presentation, scene, cast, and thought and language" (1994, 27).[1] Contemplative style, for example, begins with the premise that knowledge can be discovered, especially through the act of writing. Truth, intrinsic to the writer, can be discovered through language. Consequently, the "model scene" in the contemplative style is a writer talking to himself or herself as he or she weighs the merits of competing claims. A bit like classical rhetoric's *dissoi logoi*—the practice of placing competing arguments side by side—or a bit like Peter Elbow's believing/doubting game, wherein writers take up two opposite positions in order to expand their insights, contemplative style reveals a writer's "inner monologue" as he considers the consequences of various positions. The writer writes to interpret an experience or an issue (Thomas and Turner 1994, 88). In other words, she does not know what position to take on an issue but writes to clarify her thinking in order to reach a new understanding of an experience or to reach a tentative position.

The relationship between reader and writer is established through identification because the writer is so candid about his own thoughts. He lays out his thought process, thus inviting the reader to join him in the journey toward insight. Contemplative style often relies upon personal experience and upon metaphorical associations. Through these references, the reader is drawn to the writer's argument by following the writer's mental journey.

In some respects, the contemplative style shares features of "expressivist" discourse (Berlin 1987, 145–55). Expressivist rhetoric, like contemplative style, presents a very personal view of a topic or experience. In both cases, language serves as a heuristic, helping writers to discover what they understand or believe about a topic. On the other hand, however, where expressivist rhetoric "authenticates and affirms the self" (147), contemplative style is a type of language use adopted by a writer for a particular writing situation, namely a situation that is too complex for the writer's limited experience or when there are no real solutions to a problem. A writer may contemplate the issue, nonetheless, by using language to probe the warrants behind official positions on the issue. Contemplative style, then, does not follow Berlin's out-there/in-here dichotomy but is, rather, an effective means for individuals to engage with public issues.

This is exactly what E. B. White does in his essay "Sootfall and Fallout." White, a good example of a contemplative stylistic, considers the consequences of nuclear testing against the need for national security. He quotes Eisenhower's position on nuclear armament: "Strong we shall remain free." Sensing the perils of taking this position, White reasons that our nuclear armor will paralyze us and metaphorically connects the situation of the United States with a medieval knight. "No knight," he writes, "could fight with armor that turns out to be a coffin" (1979, 94). White contemplates an issue larger than any one person, any one nation, yet his essay responds to this magnitude through the voice of one person who sees the issue in a very private way.

Using White's essay as a model, students wrote their first paper assignment on a public issue. Students were required to find several official statements arguing for a particular point of view about a public issue. This collection of statements generated competing claims that students "contemplated" by weighing the merits of each. Using contemplative style, students addressed a public issue and interpreted that issue—its consequences, its complexity—from a private standpoint.

This writing situation asks students to respond to an issue they may have limited experience with or firsthand knowledge of. In spite of the limitations a student has regarding a public issue, students may still address these complex topics in writing. In fact, contemplative style lends itself to such complex issues because the writer takes a conceptual attitude toward writing, namely, that she does not know all the facts, but uses writing to consider the implications of various positions, relying on personal reflection as a way to think through the complexities.

Generally, students responded well to the contemplative style. For the first time in my experience as a writing teacher, I found my students complicating their positions on issues, allowing the possibilities of competing positions to weave through their writing. For example, one of my students wrote about the aftermath of September 11, about the invasion of privacy he felt when pulled aside at an airport security check. Kevin struggled with the invasion of personal liberties on one hand and the obvious need for heightened safety measures on the other. He tried to balance his love of freedom against the need for tougher security in airports.

In his paper, Kevin reported how he was pulled aside at a security checkpoint, taken to a room by two "rent-a-cops," and subjected to a search of his belongings. He wrote, "I felt as if my privacy had been invaded and was an inmate at the state penitentiary. . . . The way this man was probing through my carry-on bags (as if there was nothing valuable in them) made me feel as if I, as well as my bags, belonged to the state." Later, he considered another side of the issue. "Methods such as this seem so intrusive and in opposition to what our Constitution states. But if it keeps 3,000 individuals alive and safe from a future attack I could possibly justify it to myself." He ended by thinking perhaps security measures need time to catch up with the problem posed by terrorism.

Reflecting on the paper, Kevin reported, "As I wrote, I was still unsure which side to take. I truly believed in my rights as well as others and that heightening security often times intruded on my civil liberties and invaded my privacy. I also felt that the security measures taken were sending out false senses of security." Kevin's paper reflected this struggle with conflicting interests of protecting personal rights on one hand and maintaining civil order on the other. Blending bewilderment and outrage, Kevin re-created the lived experience of this "invasion of privacy." The resulting paper was a compelling interpretation of the public issue regarding heightened security. Kevin's writing came across as mature and balanced, a welcome change from the one-sided papers I normally read.

CLASSIC STYLE

Where contemplative style works to discover an intrinsic truth about a topic, classic style begins with the assumption that truth exists extrinsically and can be communicated to the reader through the "window" of language. "The first fundamental distinction between classic style and contemplative style," write Thomas and Turner, "is thus that classic style presents something but contemplative style presents an interpretation of something. This entails many different decisions concerning truth, presentation, cast, and scene" (1994, 89). A writer begins to write only after she knows clearly what she wants to communicate to the reader. The model scene, then, is one person speaking to another (41). The cast is a speaker and an audience of one, the objective of which is to bring the reader to the same perspective on a topic the writer has.

Classic style works like a close-up photograph, by isolating a subject from its background. Thus, language use takes shape around a number of sentence patterns that serve to compare, distinguish, and intensify the subject under scrutiny. Where the contemplative style seems warm and companionable, the classic style can seem a bit detached. Where the organization of contemplative style often concludes with a tentative resolution about its subject, the classic style begins with precise knowledge of a subject and proceeds, point by point, to offer "refinements" upon a topic, the aim of which is to depict a subject from a very specific point of view (Thomas and Turner 1994, 19). Unlike most academic writing, classic style does not argue overtly (102). In other words, the work of classic style proceeds from the assumption that truth can be understood by anyone who can see clearly and distinctly. Thus, classic style seeks to clear away misconceptions, seeks to present its subject in such clear terms that the reader cannot fail to share the same view of the topic as the writer.

In some respects, the classic style can be cataloged under Berlin's "objective rhetorics." Like objective approaches to writing, classic style assumes truth exists externally and language acts as a window to display that truth. As with current-traditional writing, classic style pays attention to surface features of writing. That is, "It is a convention of classic style that every thought has a perfect expression" (Thomas and Turner 1994, 66). The writer's job, then, is to match expression with thought.

Where objective rhetorics such as the so-called current-traditional approach settle upon surface features exclusively as a matter of correctness, however, classic style relies on the structure of language to provide nuance and meaning. An example of a classic stylist is John Berger. In his *Ways of Seeing*, chapter 7, Berger refines upon the influence of the publicity image. He uses certain classic moves to isolate why these images are so seductive. He writes, "Publicity is not merely an assembly of competing images: it is a language in itself which is always being used to make the same general proposal. . . . It proposes to each of us that we transform ourselves, or our lives, by buying something more" (1972, 131). The structure of Berger's writing sets up a "series of refinements": the publicity image does not merely communicate, but more explicitly, it lures the viewer. In other words, the structure suggests that the subject is this way, but to an even greater degree than one might think.

Comparison is also a method of refinement in the classic style. The classic writer compares a subject with other like subjects and contrasts it with those that are dissimilar, thus making distinctions regarding the subject in question. By means of refinements such as comparison and contrast and the not-only-but-also patterns, the classic style foregrounds its subject, conveying information through formal structures as much as through words themselves.

To demonstrate an understanding of the classic style, students in my writing class had to grasp classic methods of developing a topic. Students were to employ these strategies to write paper 2, which required them to portray themselves as a member of a community. One student wrote about himself as a member of a band. As a percussionist, his expertise in certain techniques set him apart as a musician. Shaun wrote:

> Many drummers just cannot resist putting the latest, fastest drum fill (an accented "lick" in a certain part of a song, typically every 4 bars) they have learned into whatever song they are playing. I love learning fast or complex fills, but unlike the drummer who throws them into whatever song he or she is playing, I play tastefully, depending on what the song requires. The song might not need a huge drum solo. I follow the rule "less is best." Songs that get too busy (instrumentally) sometimes lose the feel of the song, or the lyrics become obscured by overplaying. I always focus on what complements the song and never on what I want to play.

This passage reflects Shaun's technique in comparing and contrasting his skill against other drummers of his community. He is like other drummers in some respects—he uses fills to augment a song—but unlike other drummers his playing follows aesthetic rules. His writing helps us, the readers, see not only his ability in relief from other drummers, but also the community of drummers to which he belongs. He has isolated details by showing his artistry against the background of the percussionist community. This "isolating" move is the essence of classic style.

In a reflection on his writing, Shaun reported, "I tend to think of writing styles as mathematical equations, each with their own rules of operation and exceptions. Within these equations I exercise my own personal creativity in writing, but the structure of similarities and differences [in classic style] is what guided my strategy." Interestingly, Shaun sees style as a kind of method or structure, but a flexible one that allows for creative interpretation.

REFLEXIVE STYLE

Reflexive style is a self-conscious style adopted by writers when they wish to critique social norms. One method of producing the reflexive style is to parody a dominant style in order to emphasize its shortcomings or its assumptions. Its model scene can mimic the model scene of another style, yet do so through exaggeration that often stings with satire. The reflexivity of the style arises from the fact that the stylist recognizes the inability to be completely free of the constraints of discourse. Thus, the reflexive style questions the ability of language to deliver truth. The reflexive stylist, remark Thomas and Turner, "is careful to gesture periodically toward the contingent frame of his own discourse, to disclaim any belief that his writing can treat any subject directly" (1994, 79),

Reflexive style may seem, in some respects, to exemplify one of Berlin's "transactional rhetorics." Like other transactional rhetorics, reflexive style recognizes "knowledge is always knowledge for someone standing in relation to others in a linguistically circumscribed situation" (1987, 166). That is, knowledge is created by cultures through language so that discourse is always contingent.

While it is true that stylistic stances are all rhetorical in nature—sensitive to the relationships inherent in the writing act—the reflexive style responds to particular situations in which the act of writing itself comes into question. In other words, in Berlin's configuration, because truth assumptions are often invisible, epistemic rhetoricians may or may not refer to their own positionality or the style may or may not call attention to itself. With reflexive style, however, the question of truth is part of the rhetorical mix. As Thomas and Turner observe: "In such styles, the writer's chief, if unstated, concern is to escape being convicted of philosophical naïveté about his own enterprise. . . . The style stays in the foreground, inextricably mingled with its announced subject. It is marked with formulaic hedges concerning the possibility of knowledge, the contingency of knowledge, and the ability of language to express knowledge" (1994, 79). As a result of this awareness about language, reflexive style often results in parody of dominant styles in order to foreground the problematic nature of discourse.

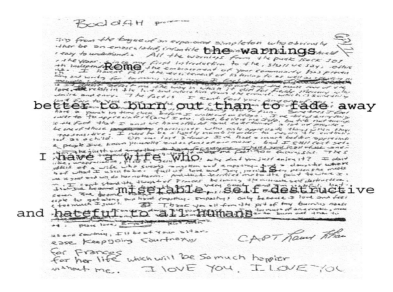

Figure 1. The letter is Kurt Cobain's suicide note; my students emphasized and high-lighted certain lines from the letter to demonstrate how creators of discourse select what to show to the public.

Hélène Cixous is an example of a reflexive stylist—actually an interesting variation on the style. Instead of being constrained by the "contingent frame of her own discourse," Cixous's "Laugh of the Medusa" (1975) turns on its head the male view of women's writing and uses that view as the basis for celebrating the very contingency of the female body as a power to inscribe itself in feminine discourse. The very contingency of woman's being gives impetus to her writing.

To demonstrate reflexive style, students in my writing class came up with their own style, either a parody or some other type of wordplay. The paper on reflexive style required students to make a rhetorical case analysis of an issue that was highly influenced by public discourse. Their goal was to analyze the discourse for ways in which it furthered the interests of stakeholders. My student writers were then to create a parody of the discourse under investigation in order to show how the discourse revealed certain aspects of an issue while obscuring others.

A team of two young men looked at the story about Nirvana's former lead singer, Kurt Cobain—at rumors circulating that Cobain's suicide was actually a murder. Their final project identified stakeholders such as Cobain's wife, the record company, Virgin, that reaped great profits following Cobain's death, and the private investigator who handled the case. In presenting the project as a parody, the team used some lyrics from Cobain's songs to reveal how discourse can make salient certain aspects of any issue. The following is a sample of what this team put together:

In their reflection, Jeff wrote:

> In the process of research for salient facts [about Cobain] we have found many things that are pertinent to the situation. Due to limited time and resources we can only show a limited amount of the truth. . . . I point out this fact not because we have intentionally hidden things from the viewers, but I think it is interesting to look at our own methods transparently and objectively. To clarify the statement, "we can only show a limited amount of truth," I mean that we have found the most interesting and most "salient" facts and have presented them in a concise manner for the convenience of the viewer.

This young man explained how he and his partner selected details to include in the final project. Since they could not include all the materials, they had to be selective.

Selection of what should be prominent or salient in the Cobain case was particularly demonstrated by this team in their discussion of Cobain's so-called suicide note. In their visual project, the team exaggerated Cobain's words "I have a wife who is miserable, self-destructive and hateful to all humans." By exaggerating this aspect of the note, the team tried to show Cobain's attitude toward his wife as less than positive. On the other hand, Cobain wrote in the same note that he loved his wife very much. The team showed that by emphasizing the negative attitude toward his wife rather than the positive, they painted Courtney Love as a possible murderess. In another example, the students superimposed Cobain's lyrics over his suicide note: "Better to burn out than to fade away," suggesting Cobain wanted to go out with a bang. Therefore suicide seems more probable than murder.

The process of selecting is what makes discourse so problematic. These young men showed awareness of this dilemma in a visual/verbal text. The text revealed how they made salient certain facts and obscured others, thus shaping how their audience perceived their work.

In the student paper just described, stylistic concerns reveal the complex nature of discourse. Through style, writers control what gets emphasized in texts and what remains in the background. By practicing the features of saliency, students learn to be more discerning about stakeholders and special interests when they pick up newspapers or watch television news reporting. Through practicing stylistic devices, they have become more savvy consumers of media discourse.

CONCLUSIONS

From a teaching practicum I had with Gary Tate, I took with me his advice about student writing. First, students need to "internalize the sound of a good English sentence." Second, writing instruction ought to make a clear connection between students and their lives. Tate's counsel is embodied in my course on style. In one sense, the course focused on expression so that students could hear how their writing changed from paper to paper. In another sense, the assignments helped students use writing as a means to engage with the issues that surround them. What I found most gratifying about the course was that my students were more engaged with their topics than have been students of previous classes I have taught. While I cannot credit a stylistic approach exclusively, I am convinced that attention to expression changes the way students approach writing assignments. I believe this because attention to style acknowledges that writerly authority can arise through a variety of means, not just through appeals to expert authority. In other words, students can establish their authority through figuring out answers to competing claims, through needling dominant styles with parody, or by seeing an object or experience in a particular way. Writing in different styles gives students practice in using language to establish their authority in new and refreshing ways. I think students were more engaged by a stylistic approach because style enabled them to use language with more confidence.

Another benefit I see in taking a stylistic approach has to do with the nature of writing. Different methods of presenting evidence, different modes of development, different appeals—these decisions are based on the needs of a variety of writing situations. By taking a stylistic approach, especially from the standpoint of style as a conceptual stance, a writer learns not just how to marshal evidence but why he or she does so in this way—using metaphors in the contemplative style, for instance. The notion of style as a conceptual stance helps writers decide how to organize material at the same time they think about sentence patterns, how to establish a certain relationship with a reader at the same time they deal with the construction of paragraphs. In short, style as a conceptual stance requires students to work at the holistic level and at the sentence level at once. The results are student papers that naturally appeal through ethos, logos, and pathos because students are learning to respond to a situation rather than merely practicing a skill.

My intention in taking a stylistic approach—to overset formulaic writing and to balance the thought/style split—echoes some responses by other critics of writing instruction. Notably, Albert Kitzhaber, writing several decades ago, responded to the influence of the modes of discourse upon writing instruction, commenting that such instruction tends to decontextualize writing. By divorcing the act of writing from real purpose, he said, the modes of discourse drilled students in academic exercise rather than in a "meaningful act of communication in a social context" (quoted in Connors 1981, 453-54). Further, the modes tended to emphasize the product of writing without regard for the purposes (454). In many ways, formulaic models like the modes of discourse are still promoted in writing classes (the five-paragraph theme, for example, the categorization of writing into persuasion, exploration, and analysis for another). By taking a stylistic approach, I am helping my students see writing as a response to a particular situation.

Naturally, there are weaknesses to my approach. Many students have a difficult time breaking away from the traditional mode of academic writing which, as Paul Heilker (1996) describes it, consists of presenting a thesis followed by support. Students feel safe using the thesis-support type of writing because it is most familiar to them. It is the style that has allowed them some measure of success in high school and college. Dependence upon the tried-and-trusted is especially true of international students who struggle not only with presenting a sophisticated idea but also with the very language itself. I spent a great deal of time helping international students work through the three assignments. For the most part, though, when the final assessments came in, these nonnative speakers often performed better than did native speakers of English.

Students who have difficulty in creating a variety of styles tend also to have difficulty with analyzing texts in terms of language use. Often these students resort to an analysis of content rather than to an analysis of how language works in a text. For example, when comparing two writing styles, students who were better at handling stylistic differences were able to talk more specifically about language without referring to content. When comparing the contemplative and classic styles, one student wrote, "[The contemplative piece] is mainly written in the past tense and reflects on a certain event while [the classic piece] focuses on an ongoing subject (images), and is written in present tense for the most part." This student's answer shows he is much more aware of the part language plays in writing than is the student who says of the two styles, "[The] points they [the writers] make relate to society." This second student is unable to separate content from language use. The difficulty some students have talking systematically about language use suggests that writing instruction needs to foster more sensitivity to language. The stylistic approach I have outlined here can help foster that sensitivity without resorting to lessons on grammar or mechanics.

Despite drawbacks, I am pleased with the results of my stylistic approach. I am pleased mostly because this approach allows me to enact my most cherished belief about writing, that thought and expression are a balanced pair. They entail each other. To teach one without the other is to strip writing of its natural vitality. I have been able to give more balanced instruction on writing because of the notion of style as a conceptual stance. In this sense, I am in agreement with Ron Fortune, who remarks, "There is a powerful intuition among many scholars and teachers in the field that style is at the heart of what we do in composition; it is just a matter of developing a new understanding of it in relation to other aspects of composing and the process principles that govern our thinking about texts and writing" (1989, 527). I trust I have mapped out here a possible new future for style in the writing classroom.

13

RETHINKING STYLISTIC ANALYSIS IN THE WRITING CLASS

William J. Carpenter

My title suggests two complementary ideas: that stylistic analysis can have a useful role in writing instruction, but that it needs retheorizing for it to do so. The purposes of this essay are to explain just what that role could be and to describe a theoretical basis for stylistic analysis that correlates with what we know about composing processes and textual functions. Stylistic analysis is a type of research, a study of trends and irregularities in the linguistic and organizational structures of texts. It is meant to elucidate, to explain how authors manipulate language to achieve particular effects and coherent texts. In the field of literature, analysis became an interpreting tool in the area of stylistics, used to unearth meanings from texts. In composition, analysis was used to introduce students to the wide range of rhetorical options at their disposal and to demonstrate how different their texts were from those of professionals.[1] Both uses of analysis share a larger goal: the greater awareness on the part of students of the uses and functions of language. It is this purpose that I think still defines the role of stylistic analysis in the writing class.

But the traditional methods of analysis describe written products and ignore writing processes, thus separating writers from their experiences creating texts. There is little room in traditional methods for relating the results of authors' composing decisions to their understanding of writing situations and the roles of their texts—to their rhetorical awareness and to what Carol Berkenkotter and Thomas Huckin call "genre knowledge" (1995, 3). One reason for this is that stylistic analysis has depended on arhetorical models of grammar, such as formalist or transformational-generative (TG), for amassing data about writers' uses of language to communicate. Linguist Geoff Thompson argues that formal grammars such as these focus on the propositional meaning of clauses rather than the semantic and social meanings (1996, 5). For example, in TG grammar, a declarative sentence (John is handsome.) can have the same propositional meaning as an interrogative (Is John handsome?). Both examples prove that a sentence requires a noun phrase (NP) and a verb phrase (VP). It doesn't matter that the sentences normally serve two different purposes in communication. As Thompson notes, "The aim [of TG and other formal grammars] is to discover the rules which govern how constituents can be put together to form grammatically correct sentences . . .; therefore each sentence is analyzed in complete isolation, both from other sentences and from the situations in which it might be used" (5). Formal grammars simply do not consider meanings and contexts when describing clause structures or rules.[2]

So if a writer writes,

John kicked the ball and it hurt Jenny

she could label those clauses

subject—verb—object (conjunction) subject—verb—object

or perhaps

NP VP (and) NP VP

but neither labeling system would offer much information as to how the sentence means something different from, say,

John ignored the greeting and it hurt Jenny.

"Kicked" and "ignored" are two different verbs, both in terms of meaning and type. The first is a physical action, the second mental. Likewise, "the ball" and "the greeting" are different types of objects. One a physical thing, the other a completed process. When we recognize the difference between objects, we then recognize different possible meanings for the verb "hurt" in the second clause. The first use entails physical damage, the second emotional. Labeling the structures using formalist or TG grammar demonstrates that the writer understands the rules for creating compound sentences, but says nothing about her exploiting the possibility of "hurt" representing an emotional response. Nor does it draw attention to the appropriate relationship between the mental action of ignoring something and the mental response to being ignored. The labels tell the writer nothing about how her language enabled her to create a layered, cohesive meaning with the two clauses. In short, the labels say nothing about how grammar makes meaning.

None of this is news, of course, but it does drive home the point that familiar models of grammar provide no information about how language is used by people in social situations—like writing to an audience.[3] If stylistic analysis is to enhance students' awareness of how they use language in their writing, it needs to be grounded in a theory that explains language use according to how it realizes meaning. Functional grammar, a model first developed by M. A. K. Halliday and based on his theories of systemic-functional linguistics, does just this by describing how language structures create semantic value and textual coherence. Functional grammar assumes the rhetorical nature of language use—the fact that language is meant to be used by living, thinking people—and it incorporates a system of labels that draw attention to the multiple purposes words can fulfill in clauses and the interdependent relationships that exist among words, clauses, and texts.

Let me offer a brief example to show how functional grammar differs from other formal grammars (I offer a more detailed explanation later in the chapter). In the sample sentences above—

John kicked the ball and it hurt Jenny

John ignored the greeting and it hurt Jenny

—"kicked" and "ignored" are labeled material and mental actions, respectively. The constituents traditionally labeled objects—"the ball" and "the greeting"—are labeled goal and phenomenon. "The ball" received an action from John; it was the focus, or goal, of the action. "The greeting," however, was something John acted in response to, a phenomenon that spurred an action. These labels explain the semantic relationships among the constituents in the opening clauses of each sentence, giving us a way of explaining in grammatical terms how the clauses mean different things.

We should be able to do the same with the second clause of each sentence. To label these clauses requires determining what the pronoun "it" refers to. In the first sentence, we can interpret "it" to mean "the ball," and the clause communicates a material action, "hurt," and a human goal, "Jenny." In the second, "it" refers to the completed process of John ignoring the greeting. This process is restated in the second clause as a phenomenon, one that has a mental effect on a human sensor, "Jenny." The functional labels take note of the different uses of the word "hurt," demonstrating how it is used as a figure of speech in the second sentence. Interesting to note is how a change in interpretation would change the labeling. If the "it" in the first sentence is interpreted to mean the completed process of John kicking the ball, then the "hurt" in the accompanying clause would be a mental action and "Jenny" a sensor. (Perhaps Jenny really didn't want John to kick the ball.) The point here is that interpretation and grammatical structure inform one another.

The functional model assumes that language is open to interpretation at all times and that meaning occurs as a result of grammatical choices. This brief example demonstrates that a functional analysis requires two important skills that are already cornerstones of composition instruction: close reading and reflective thinking. To label clause constituents is to determine how they interact with each other and to articulate the relationships among them. Functional grammar provides a mechanism for helping students understand how their composing decisions create meaning. What all this means for stylistic analysis, is that writers can compare their composing decisions with their rhetorical purposes by employing a heuristic and vocabulary that identify just how constituents form meaningful clauses and, ultimately, how clauses form coherent texts.

In what follows, I briefly trace the role of style and stylistic analysis in composition, demonstrating that current thinking about style makes a functional approach the next logical step. Functional analyses of style can raise students' awareness of their language tendencies and of the possibilities the language affords them. To demonstrate, I turn to my own experiences using functional analysis in an upper-level composition theory course entitled Language, Writing, and Identity. Students in this course studied functional grammar and read scholarship on the social nature of language (such as Lev Vygotsky's *Thought and Language,* David Bleich's *Know and Tell* [1998], Karen Burke LeFevre's *Invention as a Social Act* [1987], and others). For their final projects, they devised systems for describing the structural components of their own texts. They then paired these descriptions with reflective pieces that explained the contexts surrounding their texts and created detailed analyses of their writing styles. I look to point out the usefulness of functional grammar in stylistic analysis and to make some suggestions for incorporating a new type of analysis into writing courses.

STYLE IN COMPOSITION

As this collection suggests, style is making something of a comeback in composition. Not that it ever went away entirely. Style has lurked in the back of handbooks and on the bottom of grading rubrics. It has popped in for visits during revision sessions and has stayed long enough for final drafts to be assessed. Style has existed in writing instruction for close to thirty years as an unwanted child, a reminder of past product-based pedagogies, brought out for exercise only when the real work of writing—the inventing, the organizing—had been done.

Style has suffered an image problem, especially in composition, a field determined to subvert any elitist strongholds. With its figures of speech and rhetorical tropes, style was easily seen as elitist territory compared to the work of helping students invent, organize, and revise. (This despite the usefulness of figures and tropes in raising students' awareness of the possibilities for layered meanings in language.) Also, as Elizabeth Rankin demonstrates, style in the process movement formed an unfortunate binary with invention, ultimately becoming the subordinate term in the pair (1985, 375). She also notes that the field never got around to theorizing style with the same vigor it theorized invention and process. Style became synonymous with so-called low-level textual concerns—mechanics, diction, tone—the things that could distract writers from creating coherent texts. Style always matters eventually, of course, usually during the late stages of revision when students try to clean up or fix their texts so that they flow.

With this conception of style dominant in the field, there was little for stylistic analysis to do. It might have helped students describe their grammatical tendencies, but such a skill would certainly come a distant second to constructing texts. Stylistic analysis usually served a diagnostic purpose, demonstrating to students how their writing differed from that of professional writers or better students. For example, Edward Corbett and Robert Connors's system for analyzing style creates numerical representations of students' and professional authors' composing choices. Corbett and Connors's intention is to impart to students an interest in "the various and acceptable ways in which we might say or write something" (1999, 1). Analysis of this type focused on the "what" of style: What did a writer put (or not put) on a page? It's clear that this focus ignored two equally important questions: Why did a writer compose what he had? And how did these choices affect the work of the text? The "why" and the "how" questions would place the writer and the process under examination, but they were never fully considered in style instruction. And finally, analysis required teaching grammar. Most analysis strategies call for students to recognize subjects, predicates, objects; nouns, verbs, adverbs; clauses, phrases. Teachers had to decide whether or not to dedicate class time to teaching these grammatical labels for an activity that would take time away from process concerns.

The largest knock against style and stylistic analysis is that they are product-centered concerns in a process world. In our post-process times, however, research and pedagogical interests have returned to texts, benefiting from advances in the areas of genre theory and discourse analysis. As the composition pendulum swings away from writers' internal processes and toward the work and functions of texts, style has benefited from a more complicated understanding of the relationships among writers, texts, and situations. When Rankin called for "a unified theory of style" back in 1985 (379), she saw in the field a coming convergence of psychology, philosophy, and linguistics—one that could potentially place style at the center of the writing process. It was during this period, for example, that John Gage demonstrated that styles emerge when writers "both undergo a process and hook into a taxonomy" (1980, 621). Process and taxonomy work together, and the writer generates ideas and forms that ultimately respond to and affect other ideas and forms. Style, in this sense, is a mental and textual phenomenon, in which ideas and forms shape each other.

Similarly, Louise Wetherbee Phelps recognized "the difficulty of handling textual issues—for example, matters of style or discourse form—within the process framework" (1985, 12). She responded by constructing an integrative theory of discourse analysis that "focuses on the interactions between readers and texts as the dynamic that defines coherence" (15). Phelps argued for contextualizing the choices writers and readers make in constructing and consuming texts. Later, Richard Coe made a complementary argument in "An Apology for Form; or, Who Took the Form out of the Process?" Coe, using Burke, establishes forms—the ways in which sentences, paragraphs, and texts are constructed—as "shaped emptinesses [that] motivate writers to generate appropriate information" (1987, 268). Writers construct forms based on their understanding of audience, context, and purpose, as well as their own past experiences reading texts.

Scholars' growing awareness of the important effects of socialization, identity, and language use on writers' composing processes has led to the retheorizing of style Rankin wanted. Min-Zhan Lu, for instance, politicizes style in her article "Professing Multiculturalism: The Politics of Style in the Contact Zone." She first explains the composing process as an act of establishing agency and position through the use of language. She then defines style as the site in which writers "consider their choice of position in the context of the socio-political power relationships within and among diverse discourses and in the context of their personal life, history, culture, and society" (1994, 448). Rebecca Moore Howard, in "Style, Race, Culture, Context," describes "a contextualist stylistics that attends to the mutual constitution of text and context and that celebrates the diversity of styles produced by cultural diversity and complexity" (2000, 14). I argue elsewhere that style is a three-part phenomenon formed through an intricate interdependence among a writer's cognitive processes, rhetorical interests, and written texts (2001). And in another article, Howard and coauthors (2002) establish style as a means of understanding, entering, and critiquing the various communities writers engage.

Style has become more than a textual trait; it has become more than a static personal trait; it has become more than an abstract notion of correctness or appropriateness. Like composing itself, style is dynamic, a fluid interchange among writers, texts, and contexts. Writers draw upon past experiences using language and writing in various situations. They recognize how language has worked for them and on them. This knowledge includes conscious and unconscious understandings of how language and texts realize meaning, define situations, and create relationships among people and communities. What writers know about their purposes, their language, and their situations informs the composing decisions they make. Their styles emerge through these decisions.

Recognizing the dynamism of style encourages asking the "why" and "how" questions left out in traditional style instruction. The "what" of writing—the phrases, sentences, paragraphs—reflects various interpretations of and negotiations within the writing situation. Every structure is explainable as a meaning-making act, one influenced by the writer's purposes and previous decisions. The new turn toward style in composition credits the writer with constructing a political persona, balancing text and context, negotiating between perceptions and intentions, and recognizing community traits. The writer, in this view of style, is celebrated as an agent in her own composing process. Such an empowering approach to style calls out for a pedagogical tool that enables students to realize their potential for being conscious actors in the exchange of discourse.

FUNCTIONAL GRAMMAR AS A TOOL FOR ANALYSIS

In the dynamic view of style, writers continually negotiate their own intentions in relation to the texts and contexts they experience. Their own texts are the results of these negotiations. Such is also the line of reasoning behind systemic-functional linguistics, which presents language use as a behavior, an acting out in language. As a behavior, language use can be interpreted for how it represents writers' decisions to make certain meanings in certain ways. Systemic-functional linguistics gives us a rationale for stylistic analysis by relating language structures to the users' rhetorical decisions. In this section, I want to move toward an analytical method by first describing the systemic-functional theory of language and then explaining how its grammatical model, functional grammar, can work as a heuristic for coding and explaining textual features.

According to systemic-functional linguistics, a reciprocal relationship exists between culture and language. The culture shapes the language to serve various purposes, establishing a system of grammatical forms capable of responding to all types of situations and contexts. At the same time, the language shapes the culture, teaching users through its forms and structures cultural relationships, values, and expectations. Halliday argues that the lexicogrammatical components of a language have "been determined by the functions [the language] has evolved to serve" (1973, vii). That is to say that language both responds to and determines the purposes for which people use language, as well as the meanings they wish to communicate to each other. A child internalizes the cultural characteristics while he internalizes the language, creating a link between the cultural beliefs and expectations and his own uses of language. Every linguistic communication he attempts has its roots in this link, and his understanding of this link affects what he does with language.

People within a culture learn the lexicon and grammar of their language. They also learn how to manipulate those things to make useable meanings, which are realized when people construct linguistic forms for the purpose of acting on and within a situation. To construct these forms, users make a series of decisions within the grammatical and rhetorical systems of the language. These systems of options allow for what Halliday calls the "sets of alternative meanings which collectively account for the total meaning potential [of the language]" (1973, 47). What people say or write is understood in relation to what they could have said or written, given the constraints established by the language, the culture, and the context. The act of selecting options is neither random nor rote. Rather, it is gleaned from experiencing language in use.

Systemic-functional linguistics informs the dynamic view of style by providing a theory of language that corresponds with current concerns for the sociopolitical nature of text production. The theory connects a person's knowledge of language to his socialization processes, cultural values, and perceptions of language roles. Language use is always rhetorical, always affected by how users' interpret situations, their own intentions, and their knowledge of language. People use language in ways that broadly match how others in the culture use it. Yet because people learn language through individual experiences, it stands to reason that they use and respond to it in individual ways. People want to be understood; they want their meanings to affect other people. A person's unique knowledge of language must somehow conform to cultural expectations if that person wants to participate in conversations. If we accept this premise, then we can examine language use for how it meets cultural expectations for communication.

According to Halliday, uses of language represent "the selection of options within the linguistic system in the context of actual situation types" (1978, 46). In this sense, uses of the language are great in number, too great to be catalogued. Situations never repeat themselves exactly, and so uses of language in response to these situations are never repeated exactly either. However, while the uses of language may not be completely similar, they do perform basic communicatory functions that enable discourse to be created and continued. All uses of language enable the writer to communicate her perception of the situation; this is the experiential function. They also establish a relationship between the speaker and the hearer, the interpersonal function. And they allow for extended discourse between users, the textual function. The three functions taken together constitute what systemic-functional linguistics calls the macrofunctions. Every use of language fulfills these functions in a way particular to the forms that are created.

Distinguishing between uses and functions of language enables a practical and systematic approach to analyzing texts. The three macrofunctions provide distinct lenses through which to view every use of language. Put together, these three views can tell us a great deal about how a particular use of language comes to have all the semantic and social meaning it does. More importantly for our purposes here, macrofunctions provide writers with methods for describing the ways in which their surface forms, the most outward signs of their styles, correspond to the inner components of their style, their perceptions of and intentions within situations. For example, describing how the language achieves the experiential function encourages a writer to consider how she perceived various actions or understood ideas. Descriptions of the interpersonal function can demonstrate how the writer chose to present herself and to exchange information with the audience. And describing the textual function can shed light on how the writer understands the relationships among clauses and texts.

To facilitate such descriptions, systemic-functional linguistics employs functional grammar, a system for describing language that employs different sets of labels for each of the three macrofunctions. Functional analysis of language begins at the level of the clause, what linguist John Collerson calls "a structure in which several components are brought together to form a message" (1994, 13). The clause organizes its constituents in relation to one another, and it is this organizing that establishes the meaning of the clause. Consider a pair of sentences, one active, one passive:

John kicked the ball.

The ball was kicked by John.

We understand that the sentences describe the same event: John performed the action of kicking a ball. But we also understand that the sentences communicate two different intentions on the part of the writer. In the first, to emphasize John as the kicker. In the second, to emphasize the ball as the thing being kicked. There is a difference in the rhetorical effects of the sentences, which also creates a difference in the overall meaning of the sentences. In terms of functional grammar, we could say that the sentences achieve the experiential function in similar ways, but differ in how they achieve the interpersonal and textual functions.

To explain, let me introduce some terms from functional grammar, some of which I used in the first section.[4] From the experiential perspective, the action of the clause serves as the dominant constituent since it establishes the roles of the other constituents. Functional grammar uses the term processes to describe the action of the clause, a term that denotes change from one state to another. In our example above, the process is "kicked." Processes require something or someone to perform them. "John" is the actor in both sentences. Some processes allow for something to be acted upon, to be the focus of the action. Above, "the ball" is the goal, the thing being acted upon. Notice that the change in syntax does not affect the labeling. Both sentences communicate the same experience.

It's important to note that functional grammar distinguishes between a number of process types. In the above example, "kicked" and "was kicked" are material processes. Action verbs like "kick" require an actor and a goal. Mental processes, however, don't necessarily entail an actor. In "I heard a rumor," the mental process "heard" requires a sensor ("I") and a phenomenon ("a rumor"). A sentence such as "Janet is tired" has a relational process ("is"), a carrier ("Janet"), and an attribute ("tired"). My point here is that functional grammar recognizes the action of the clause as the defining trait of the experiential function. The different labels allow for important distinctions among clause types.

The sentences achieve the interpersonal function in different ways, though, which affects the interaction between the writer and the reader. The interpersonal function communicates the writer's intentions for how the reader should interpret the clause. In the active sentence, the subject, "John," is paired with the predicate "kicked." "The ball" functions as the complement. In the passive sentence, "the ball" is the subject, "was kicked" the predicate, and "by John" an adjunct. Here, the term subject is not meant in the traditional way. Rather, it "expresses the entity that the speaker wants to make responsible for the validity of the proposition being advanced in the clause" (Thompson 1996, 45). The active sentence urges the reader to accept a fact about John's action, while the passive urges the reader to accept a fact about the ball's condition. To demonstrate just how these sentences act on the reader, consider what questions a reader could reasonably ask after each sentence. To the active sentence, a reader could ask "Did he?" but not "Was it?" And the opposite is true for the passive. So in structuring the sentence in one way or the other, the writer has affected the reader's range of possible responses.

Finally, the sentences complete the textual function in different ways, too. In functional grammar, the first constituent of a clause is considered the theme of the sentence. The rest of the clause is the theme. The active sentence presents "John" as the theme, the passive, "the ball." Themes play an important role in the coherence among clauses, in that they either establish new information, repeat old information, or create transitions. When clauses "flow" for us, when they seem to inform each other in meaningful ways, often the pattern of themes is responsible. Themes produce a meaning beyond the individual clause by creating the often nonarticulated relationships among clauses. They give a text meaning that is more than the sum of the lexical parts.

Functional grammar entails much more than I've presented here, but the examples prove the main point of this section thus far. By labeling clauses in terms of the three macrofunctions, writers can pinpoint where the choices they made while composing create the meanings in their texts. Doing so does not by itself provide a stylistic analysis. The writers must collate the data and reflect on how and why they chose to write what they did. In other words, writers can bring their knowledge of their processes to bear on the data produced by functional analysis. Performing the analysis requires writers to read their own works closely and to interpret such things as process types, clause participants, adjunct information, and themes. This grammatical data provides them with a three-dimensional model of what they have produced and enables them to examine how their communicative intentions were or were not met. Examining the relationship between texts and processes encourages an awareness of linguistic choice and personal tendencies, one that could help students understand how their texts represent them as writers and act upon readers.

A STYLISTIC ANALYSIS ASSIGNMENT

In the fall of 2002, the students in my Language, Writing, and Identity course completed extensive stylistic analyses of their own writing using functional grammar and a series of reflective writing assignments. They familiarized themselves with systemic-functional linguistics and became quite fluent in the methods and vocabulary of functional analysis. All of this took time, the better half of a semester, really. So I want to recognize at the outset of this section that my use of stylistic analysis occurred under very special circumstances, certainly not the kind that can be easily duplicated in a first-year writing course. But I do think that the spirit and general approach of the assignment make it malleable enough to be reworked for various types and levels of writing courses. I end this chapter with some ideas for doing just that.

The analysis assignment (see appendix) was designed around the three central questions of the course:

1. How do individuals' intentions, perceptions, and expectations within the act of composing affect their constructions of written language?
2. What can textual analyses tell us about how language functions in different settings and through different genres?
3. What can we learn about ourselves as language users by studying the texts we create?

To answer these questions, students analyzed texts they created for school or other public settings. The texts were not to be poetry or fiction, but rather some type of academic or nonfiction essay. They produced full functional analyses of three-hundred- to four-hundred-word passages from their texts. These analyses required them to describe each clause in the passage according to how it fulfilled the three macrofunctions. Every clause, then, had three descriptions. The students became quite inventive in their diagramming, often employing colored pencils, various fonts, and intricate coding systems.

To assist the students in reflecting on their writing situations, I assigned a five-page "context paper," in which they articulated their purposes and goals for the paper. The students considered why they chose their topics, what expectations they had for the paper, what experiences affected their writing, and what processes they went through to compose the paper. The context papers were a new type of writing for most of the students, and many of them had a difficult time starting the assignment. Many students had never thought critically about their writing goals or about how those goals compared to what was being asked of them in the assignments. Though the papers proved torturous to some, they did provide students the kind of personal information that could help them explain some of their tendencies in their writing.

Lastly, the students completed ten-page summaries/explanations of their functional analyses. I asked students to avoid listing their findings in quantitative forms. I wanted them instead to construct intellectual discussions of their more interesting results. In other words, they were not simply to list the different numbers of process types, adjunct phrases, and actorless clauses. Rather, they were to consider those numbers in light of the contexts they defined for their texts and their own understanding of what and why they were writing. I never asked them to define their styles—such a question seems unfair given our awareness of the shifting nature of style. Instead, they were asked to describe what they thought their texts said about them as writers. Many of the students found themselves able to relate certain tendencies and repeated structures to context-specific impetuses and personal reactions.

For example, James Homsey, a student in the class, offered an interesting discussion of the politics surrounding his writing of a history paper on the Vietnam War. In his context paper, Homsey explains that he chose his topic, the U.S. bombings of Cambodia, because it seemed eerily connected to present-day events.

> The September 11 terrorist attacks occurred during the semester I was taking this Vietnam War class, and discussions about what response the U.S. should take were all over the news. . . . It was while reading about the terror

in Cambodia with such thoughts on my mind that I began thinking about how careless the United States often is with the well being of other nations. Reading about the horrors that we inadvertently let loose in Cambodia, and thinking about the polarization of the world that we were now striving for, I finally came upon the topic I would choose to write my paper on.

Homsey's purposes in his original paper are "to discuss a tragic event that . . . does not get discussed enough, . . . to form opinions on why the massacre happened, and to decide . . . what this meant as far as who was at fault." He argues that America deserves "the brunt of the paper's criticism," and demonstrates how his decisions to organize the paper support this stance.

In the discussion of his functional analysis, Homsey makes an interesting political observation concerning his own presentation of the Cambodian people. He notes that actors in many of his clauses are "large scale political groups," meaning whole nations or governments. Placing these groups in the actors' slots achieves Homsey's goal of placing responsibility on the United States, but he recognizes how these selections marginalize further the victims of the events. He observes:

> Although the paper is about a series of tragedies that befell the Cambodian people, the general population is never the actor in a clause. . . . This pattern makes the Cambodian people into non-participants, with certain political forces acting in ways that affect them. This passiveness of the Cambodian population is not entirely false, for there was little the relatively small and non-militaristic population could do . . , but the fact that so many Cambodians died in these events makes their complete absence as actors alarming.

Homsey's own analysis from the experiential perspective brought him to a better understanding of how language can erase the human presence, can mask the cruelty of war. "It is easy to just consider political groups and political events when typing a historical paper," he writes, "and to ignore the cultural and societal effects on what happened, for there are more records about political occurrences." He seems to recognize that his language use in this situation is affected by his understanding of the genre he is writing and by the types of sources he finds.

I offer these glimpses of Homsey's project to demonstrate just how thoughtful a writer can be about his perceptions, intentions, and composing processes. The data Homsey collected from his analysis, coupled with the reflective writing assignments, changed his understanding of his paper and his style within it. He recognized how he attempts to meet genre expectations and how those expectations at times conflict with his personal views and emotions. Perhaps more importantly, the process of analyzing his text made him aware of his own position as a political being, as a person who must continually place himself at the nexus of language, culture, and texts. He realized the power of his language to erase whole populations, to infer meanings without stating them, and to support or subvert popular opinion. This is the kind of awareness stylistic analysis can bring to the writing class.

For composition courses, this type of stylistic analysis can be modified to fit time constraints and to match other course goals. The grammatical analysis should always be accompanied by a reflective assignment, something that grounds the linguistic data in the personal and the rhetorical. Without such grounding, the analytical exercise becomes a rote placement of labels and descriptors. And nothing about style is rote. Textual forms represent the result of a series of decisions, choices that were influenced by a host of factors, many of which were unique to their time and place. Remember that the goal of analysis is simply to raise students' awareness of their language use; what aspect of it they become more aware of is up to them and their instructors. Teachers can use analysis to pinpoint certain textual features they think students should consider. For example, students can read their texts for the type of processes they use in their sentences. They could then reflect on the rhetorical effects of these processes or on how they relate to their own perceptions of events. If teachers want to discuss coherence, they could ask students to identify the themes of their clauses and to articulate the relationships among them and their other clauses. The possibilities are many. This type of analysis offers students a way of reclaiming agency in their writing by gaining a method for describing how and why they create meaning.

Appendix

**ENGLISH 350: STUDIES IN WRITING AND RHETORIC
LANGUAGE, WRITING, AND IDENTITY
FALL 2002
FINAL PROJECT**

Description: The final project is designed to help us answer the three central questions of the course:

1. How do individuals' intentions, perceptions, and expectations within the act of composing affect their constructions of written language?
2. What can textual analyses tell us about how language functions in different settings and through different genres?
3. What can we learn about ourselves as language users by studying the texts we create?

The project asks you to analyze a text you created for school or another public setting as a way of answering these questions. You are expected to create a full functional analysis of the text, drawing on the concepts and vocabulary of functional grammar. You are also asked to articulate and explain the context surrounding the text, your purposes in writing, your writing process, and your own understanding of the coherence of the text.

The final project should demonstrate your understanding of the concepts and skills learned in this course, as well as your ability to put this understanding into practice in useful and intelligent ways. This is not a project that can be done in a short amount of time. It requires you to keep up with the course readings and to employ what you learn from those readings. It requires you to produce full functional analyses of every clause in your text and to articulate clearly the findings of those analyses. Do not underestimate the amount of time this project will take to complete.

Requirements: The various requirements are listed below. Note that many of them are interdependent.

1. Locate a 300–400 word passage of your own writing. This passage should come from a text created for school or for some other public audience. Fiction and poetry are not allowed. Nonfiction essays written for class or

    publication are acceptable. The passage should include at least two full paragraphs.

2. Produce a full functional analysis of every clause in the text. Your analyses should include descriptions from the three metafunctions. The system for describing clauses is yours to create, but it should be easily understood and followed by an outside reader. Neatness and readability will be considered in the final grade. You might want to experiment with several ways of presenting the analyses.

3. On a full copy of the text, identify all cohesive ties and grammatical metaphors.

4. In a separate document, articulate and discuss the context surrounding your text, as well as the purposes and goals you defined for yourself within this context. Explain how your perception of the context, the subject matter, and your purposes affected what you wrote and how you wrote it. This document should be at least 5 pages in length.

5. In a separate document, summarize the findings from your functional analysis. Some items to consider are subject types, transitivity, themes, grammatical metaphors, moods, clause complexes, etc. Rather than listing your findings, weave them into a coherent discussion of the relevant traits of your text. You should consider the multifunctionality of clauses and the determining role of context. Also, consider these questions: What does the text and your analysis say about the genre? What do they say about your own writing style and your perceptions of the writing situation? What do they say about you? This document should be at least 10 pages in length.

Assessment: The final project will be assessed according to three criteria:

1. Correct, consistent, and understandable use of labels, terms, and concepts.
2. Depth, clarity, and preciseness of analysis.
3. Level of intellectual engagement, especially in regards to the three main questions of the assignment.

Understand that the further you take your analysis of clauses, the more data you produce for your discussion. You also demonstrate a greater understanding of the systemic nature of functional grammar and of the importance of nuance and subtlety in the interpretation of meaning. I fully expect you to discuss your system of analysis with me and to share your ideas with me and the class.

The final project is due in its complete form on Friday, December 6. Late projects will lose one letter grade for each missed day.

14

RE-PLACING THE SENTENCE: APPROACHING STYLE THROUGH GENRE

Peter Clements

The last decade or so has seen a critical reappraisal of the place of style in composition theory and pedagogy. For some, this reappraisal takes the form of a "what-if" story that questions the field's wholesale rejection of style as a valid concern of writing classrooms in the late 1970s and early 1980s. In "The Erasure of the Sentence," for example, Robert Connors (2000) examines the sentence-based pedagogies of the 1960s and 1970s, as well as the "counterforces" that led to their devaluation at the beginning of the 1980s. He ties this devaluation to the antiformalist and antiempiricist attitudes that accompanied the field's attainment of disciplinary status as a subfield of English studies. Connors looks askance at this situation, which he likens to a tornado leaving a trail of destruction (121–22). In a similar vein, Lester Faigley, in the third chapter of *Fragments of Rationality* (1992), offers a tantalizing glimpse of the direction composition studies might have taken if it had not effectively dismissed linguistics as a major disciplinary influence by the end of the 1980s. Faigley speculates on the ways in which composition scholarship might benefit from the insights of critical linguistics—that is, analyses of how specific features of language help to consolidate and reflect sociohistorical relations of power and dominance.

Connors (2000) provides a useful reminder that, despite all the criticism, sentence-based pedagogies were never really proved ineffective; however, his focus on the antiscientism of English departments neglects a more incisive critique that was leveled against the teaching of style in general. One example is Richard Ohmann's 1979 article "Use Definite, Specific, Concrete Language," which takes on the maxims of clarity that were a regular feature of composition textbooks of the time from an ideological standpoint. Such maxims, he argues, push students "toward the language that most nearly reproduces immediate experience and away from the language that might be used to understand it, transform it, and relate it to everything else," thus obscuring social relations, reducing conflict, and maintaining the status quo (396).

Connors himself makes a similar point in his early essay "The Rise and Fall of the Modes of Discourse" (1981), which traces the history of instruction based on rhetorical patterns: the modes of discourse (narration, description, exposition, argument) and their modern counterparts, the methods of exposition (definition, comparison/contrast, cause/effect, and so forth). Connors contends that the modes became a popular focus of writing instruction during the late nineteenth and early twentieth centuries "because they fit into the abstract, mechanical nature of writing instruction at the time" (453), in which writing had become an academic exercise cut off from any meaningful relation with social context. What this has led to in many textbook approaches to composition (particularly those designed for the teaching of academic writing for ESL students; see Spack 1988) is a privileging of form over content, in which students are expected to come up with topics to fit the given mode—in short, an obsession with the how of writing to the almost complete neglect of the why.

These arguments point the way toward a more critical conceptualization of style: one that looks at style as historically situated and ideologically motivated. The question arises, however, as to how to incorporate such a conceptualization usefully into pedagogy. Specifically, how can composition instruction engage student writers with stylistic features and formal patterns while at the same time inspiring them to reflect on and articulate their own positioning? In answering this question, I turn to rhetorical genre theory to flesh out a critical approach to style that reenvisions its relevance as a tool for interrogating discourse and defining writerly choices. My purpose here, following Richard Coe (2002), is not just to present readers with ideas that they can adapt and use in their own classrooms (although I will certainly be pleased if I am able to do so), but to suggest that approaching style through genre urges us "to reexamine certain basic assumptions that have long underpinned how we teach writing and what sorts of writing abilities we encourage our students to develop" (197).

THE PROCESSING OF STYLE

In his doctoral dissertation, William Carpenter (2000) offers a historical sketch of style from ancient to modern times. Carpenter notes that style was originally closely interrelated with the other elements of classical rhetoric, including invention, arrangement, memorization, and delivery. Basic to this formulation was the view that knowledge is communally constructed. Style in this sense was the means by which rhetors both composed and arranged their ideas according to audience, message, and purpose (3–5). Modern formulations of rhetoric, on the other hand, have been based in a view of knowledge, rooted in Enlightenment philosophy, as originating in the mind of the individual, thus creating a division between thought and language (7). Writing in this view becomes a process of first organizing one's thoughts and then choosing the most effective language to represent those thoughts, making style a pursuit in and of itself. Hence, the emphasis on forms and products that characterized current-traditional rhetoric was part of a tendency to see style as the most directly accessible and measurable aspect of writing (9–10). One can teach good style, but one cannot (necessarily) teach good thinking.

Interestingly, as Carpenter (2000) points out, this division between thought and language not only formed the basis for current-traditional ideas about how writing is produced ("clear writing is preceded by clear thinking"), but was also foundational to the early process movement, which militated against current-traditional pedagogy by emphasizing strategies for invention and revision. In order to validate these concepts, the idea had to be maintained that the writer's thoughts existed prior to their expression in linguistic form, so that invention and revision strategies became the primary techniques for making the written words match the writer's ideas more closely. As a result, concern for style came to be seen as something that could get in the way of the writer's inner process of self-discovery, and was therefore best left to the final editing stages of writing (10–11). This view of style was also symptomatic of the process movement's tendency to dichotomize: product vs. process, style vs. invention, form vs. content. It was not that we shouldn't teach style, but that style became a strictly surface-level phenomenon that was secondary to and separate from issues of voice, audience, and purpose (15). The sort of critique offered by Carpenter is perhaps given its most forceful voice in Sharon Crowley, whose essay "Around 1971" (1998) historicizes the process movement as a reactionary effort that eventually became part of the very establishment that its exponents protested. Current-traditionalism and process, Crowley argues, are the yin and yang of a more general historical phenomenon.

We have to keep in mind, however, that the process movement was not so much a unitary concept as a diverse group of people coming together under the same banner. Besides the expressivism and cognitivism that were its hallmarks in the early 1980s, the process movement also brought with it an interest in the socially constructed nature of reality and the ways in which writers function within discourse communities. Often considered a later development of process, the social-constructionist turn in composition, which began to be articulated in the mid-1980s by writers such as James Berlin (1987), Patricia Bizzell (1982) and Lester Faigley (1986), was in fact part of a more general epistemological shift toward a view of knowledge as transactional, created in interactions among individuals. It is in critiques such as those of Ohmann (1979) and Connors (1981), I think, that we can hear early indications of the influence that this shift was to have on composition.

As social constructionism gained currency, inspiring in turn its own lines of inquiry, professional and scholarly attitudes toward style within the field began to shift as well. For many compositionists, the separation of form and content was no longer necessary to process pedagogy; and for some it even became problematic. One example is Min-Zhan Lu (1999), who argues that such a separation depoliticizes assumptions about which forms are most appropriate to express a writer's ideas. In "Professing Multiculturalism" (1994), Lu elaborates the place of style within what she calls "border pedagogy." Through examples from classroom handouts and teacher-student conferences, Lu describes an inductive and collaborative interrogation of students' choices of linguistic features that foregrounds the ways in which their voices conflict with the discourses of academia (173). Language and thought are reunited in that style is no longer a unitary construct, but rather an integral part of the discourses by which communities, disciplines, and institutions create knowledge.

Aside from this questioning of the apparent disappearance of style from composition, several writers have recently called for bringing explicit attention to style back to the center of the writing classroom. In *The Emperor's New Clothes,* Kathryn Flannery (1995) takes up, in a sense, where Ohmann's essay leaves off by examining different kinds of "style talk"—generalized assumptions about what constitutes "good style"—for the particular interests that they support and help maintain (7). The brief pedagogical example with which she ends her book, although it shies away from making specific statements about how style talk might inform teaching, underscores her point that such an examination is crucially important for what compositionists do as practitioners (199–202). Carpenter (2000), on the other hand, takes a somewhat different approach, arguing for a reintegration of style with the other more venerated elements of the writing process, so that style becomes one of the central components of a fully realized pedagogy.

STYLE AT THE MARGINS

In spite of the vehemence of the process movement's denunciations of style, the fact remains that it has continued to be written about and discussed (see, for example, Noguchi 1991). More importantly, however, it has continued to be taught, as can be readily observed from the plethora of textbooks, handbooks, and style guides that are published annually—and that continue to be included on course syllabi as required or recommended texts. Faigley (1992) cites numerous examples of textbooks whose continuing popularity would seem to indicate that even relatively traditional approaches to style retain their adherents. For example, Sheridan Baker's *The Practical Stylist,* first published in 1962, is currently in its eighth edition (1997), while Joseph Williams's *Style,* first published in 1986, is in its seventh (2003). More recently, books such as Kolln's *Rhetorical Grammar* (1999) have offered an updated approach to style that focuses on the effects of specific linguistic choices.

Besides maintaining a presence, however subordinated, within mainstream composition, the teaching of style has continued to be a critical concern in specialized areas of theory and pedagogy residing at the boundaries of composition studies. One of these areas is second language (or L2) writing, which has paid a great deal of attention to the development of techniques for responding to formal errors in student writing (for a review, see Ferris 2002). Indeed, the study of contrastive rhetoric, which was initiated by Robert Kaplan's seminal article in 1966, represents a systematic effort to understand the forms of L2 text as realizations of cross-cultural modes of expression and argumentation. Over the past decade or so, second language writing has asserted itself as a field of inquiry separate from composition in large part through the advocacy of scholars such as Tony Silva, Ilona Leki, and Joy Reid, as well as the founding of the *Journal of Second Language Writing.* A primary aspect of this separation has been a recognition that style and form are simply inescapable for second language writers, and that many of composition's most favored practices are inadequate for L2 writers' needs. Leki (1992) makes this point quite powerfully in *Understanding ESL Writers* when she asks readers to imagine having to freewrite in a second language. Suddenly, the notion that writers can forget about form and let their thoughts flow onto the page becomes absurd.

Similarly, the idea that style cannot be ignored has been a defining point in the history of the basic writing movement. In "The 'Birth' of 'Basic Writing,'" James Horner (1999) critically analyzes the discourse of Basic Writing (note the capital letters) as a response to the wider public debates on higher education surrounding the start of City University of New York's open admissions policy in 1969. He describes a catch-22 situation, in which basic writing teachers have to expend all of their efforts on teaching students grammar and mechanics in order to prove that those students can be taught to write—thus leaving little room for the actual teaching of writing (16). These discourses reified the historical moment in which Basic Writing was born, defining basic writing as perpetually behind mainstream composition.

In the late 1980s, however, the necessity of teaching style came to be seen less as emblematic of the problems of Basic Writing, and more as a recognition of students' right of access to institutionally validated discourses. In a now-famous article, Lisa Delpit (1988) accuses process adherents of hypocrisy, contending that focusing instruction on helping students to find a writerly voice expects them to use forms and conventions that they haven't been explicitly taught, thereby denying those forms to students of color. Min-Zhan Lu (1999) frames the issue more specifically in terms of the relationship between thought and language, arguing that Basic Writing has theorized writing as the formal expression of preexisting meanings. The problem with this assumption is that it ignores the fact that changes in form often result in changes in meaning, however subtle. Lu catalogues a range of examples from *Errors and Expectations* (Shaughnessy 1977) that demonstrate how writers' stylistic "improvements" also minimize the conflicts and tensions between home and academic discourses. In this sense, teachers are never just instructing writers in the means and methods for realizing their thoughts more effectively on paper, but rather are coercing students into specific political choices about how to align themselves within various discourses.

As universities in the United States have begun, however reluctantly, to acknowledge conditions of diversity on their campuses, second language writing and basic writing have garnered a certain amount of institutional support. However, scholars in both areas continue to highlight the institutional dilemmas that their students face—for example, that "nonmainstream" student populations (students of color, international students, "generation 1.5"[1] students, underprepared students—the list goes on) are here to stay; that their needs are not adequately addressed by "quick-fix"

measures such as intensive programs and remedial courses; and that the
issues involved in teaching them are not peripheral to composition. From
this standpoint, style's compartmentalization within process is analogous
to the marginalization of those whose education is deemed nonessential
to the main business of the academy. The issue of style thus becomes a
crucial one because it forces us to confront as writing teachers the institutional divisions that underlie and inform our classroom practices—divisions that construct student populations according to "special" needs
requiring separation and containment.

RHETORICAL GENRE THEORY: FROM APPLIED LINGUISTICS TO COMPOSITION

As a theoretical construct, genre provides a point around which have
converged many of the issues at stake in the teaching of academic literacy.
For over two decades, genre researchers and theorists have developed a
diverse range of approaches to the study of genre, as well as applications
to pedagogical issues. Once viewed primarily as a classification system for
literary texts, genres have come to be understood as complex discursive
structures that instantiate social actions (Freedman and Medway 1994b).
An essential aim of much of this work has been to demystify particular
genres so as to make them accessible to students. An example of this is
the Sydney School, a group of researchers in Australia who developed
genre-based pedagogies for the teaching of writing in secondary schools,
partly as a reaction to the whole language and process pedagogies that
became prevalent there in the early 1980s. As with Delpit (1988) in the
North American context, these researchers held that process pedagogies unwittingly favored monolingual middle-class students (Richardson
1994). Although the Sydney School eventually drew criticism for focusing too narrowly on a static conception of genres as text types, its theoretical basis was located in the systemic-functional linguistics of Michael
Halliday: a fundamentally social theory of language as a complex relationship between form and function.

In North America, the work of John Swales as well combines a linguist's
perspective with practical aims. His *Genre Analysis* (1990), which is an
extended study of the research article for second language writers, oper-
ates from a sociolinguistically grounded definition of genre as expressing
the communicative purposes of particular discourse communities. As with
the Sydney School, however, his application of genre is also largely textual, concentrating on close readings and comparisons of genre exemplars

for "move structure"—a taxonomy of the typified moves, or rhetorical gestures, that occur within the genre, often in a fairly fixed order. Swales's work has defined the English for Specific Purposes (ESP) movement, in which discourse conventions are seen as primarily instrumental in that they provide access to specific communities for business or professional purposes. The typical ESP student, who is already established in a field of study or profession, is assumed to possess the background knowledge (the "content"), and simply requires the means to express that content in an unfamiliar form.

While linguistic approaches to genre have taken an increasingly contextual viewpoint, researchers and theorists operating within a new rhetorical framework have further problematized notions of genres as static, stable texts that can be studied apart from the social contexts in which they are embedded. A good deal of this work stems from Carolyn Miller's influential article, "Genre as Social Action" (1984), which defines genres as "typified rhetorical actions based in recurrent situations" (159). That is, genres arise as speakers respond in socially acceptable and recognizable ways to situational exigencies that recur over time. According to Miller, these recurring situations are intersubjective phenomena, encompassing both the context of the genre and the social relations of the speakers who use it. Subsequent work has built on Miller's thesis by examining the ways in which genres not only respond to situations but also constitute them (Bawarshi 2003; Devitt 1993), as well as their dialogic nature (Freadman 1994). That is, genres help shape reality even as they are shaped by it, and they respond to other genres within larger intertextual systems.

These theoretical developments, useful though they may be for genre research, also raise serious questions about the potential for genre to inform composition pedagogy in any useful way. Genres, the new rhetoricians argue, represent highly abstract and largely subliminal forms of social knowledge, or "situated cognition" (Berkenkotter and Huckin 1993, 477), which users acquire through repeated exposure within meaningful contexts of actual usage. Moreover, genres are dynamic and evolving; hence, any theory of how a given genre is produced and understood can never be more than a working model (or, in Thomas Kent's terms, a "passing theory") that has to be continually adjusted with each new communicative event. Not surprisingly, therefore, some scholars (for example, Freedman 1994) have contended that explicit teaching of genres and genre features is not only not useful, it may in some cases be harmful in that it can give students a reductive and uncritical view of the socially constructed power relationships that are realized through communicative events.

Rhetorical genre theory thus poses an interesting challenge for the teaching of style: how can explicit discussions of genre features contribute to students' awareness of style as a site of social and institutional struggle? And how can style address the dynamic nature of genres in ways that will be valuable for students as they engage this struggle both within and beyond the writing classroom? Ann Johns provides a point of departure in suggesting that teachers' responsibility is to help students become genre theorists: "to destabilize their often simplistic and sterile theories of texts and enrich their views of the complexity of text processing, negotiation, and production within communities of practice" (2002a, 240). In other words, genres provide rich contexts for getting students to think about how specific stylistic choices position them within competing discourses and communicative situations.

STYLE WITHIN A GENRE-BASED PEDAGOGY

In the first-year composition courses that I currently teach, I conceptualize the use of genre in three general stages: a textual stage, involving close reading and comparison of genre exemplars; a contextual stage, which focuses on the rhetorical purposes of texts as they are realized in specific features and patterns; and, finally, a critical stage, which further extends the discussion to include the typified reading and writing practices, as well as the social roles that genres instantiate. These stages are recursive, usually cycling through several times during the term as the students complete major writing assignments. For the first one or two of these assignments, I have students analyze public genres that are usually familiar and easily accessible to them. News reports and movie reviews have proven particularly useful here because they provide fertile material for application of the ideas in course readings: news reports as a place to examine Jane Tompkins's (2000) claims about the perspectival nature of factual accounts, and movie reviews for John Berger's (2000) exploration of how art is consumed in modern society. More importantly, though, public genres are a good way to start because their very familiarity makes them a challenge for close reading and analysis. During the final part of the course, students complete a research project in which they choose a genre, gather data (for example, textual samples, interviews with and observations of users of the genre), and then write an analysis of their findings.

As we are examining and talking about the styles and contexts of these genres, I also try to focus students' attention on the genres of the writing classroom as well. I introduce the concept of genre simply by asking students a series of questions to explore their experiences of the term itself: what they think "genre" means, what constitutes a genre, how genres are distinguished from one another, and so forth. I also ask students about the genres that they are familiar with as readers and writers: what genres they come into contact with at home, and what genres they have previously used in school. Later, we read and discuss essays written by former participants in the course, first for textual features and then for rhetorical context. Finally, we discuss the social roles that are constructed through not only the essays themselves, but the other genres of the writing class: the assignment sheets, the essays in the reader, peer review forms, and so forth. As we continue through this analytical cycle (from text to context to social positioning), my underlying aim is to involve students in closely reading and manipulating texts, and this is where style becomes important.

EXAMINING TEXTS

There are several activities that I have found particularly helpful in getting students to look carefully at textual features. I often start discussions of the course readings by asking students to identify the features in the text that they consider unusual for "formal" academic writing. Observations that typically come up in this regard are things that students are often told not to do in their high school writing classes. Students notice, for example, that the opening of Jane Tompkins's essay is peppered with the first-person singular pronoun, which in turn provides the opportunity to talk about her use of personal narrative in the introduction to her argument. Students also notice that John Berger tends to put coordinating conjunctions at the beginnings of sentences, and also to use single-sentence paragraphs as a means of emphasizing specific points. This is usually a good time to introduce Swalesean move structure by having students divide the text into sections. After we compare the sections that they have identified and reach a consensus on the divisions, I have small groups each take one section and list its most noticeable characteristics, focusing particularly on sentence structure, vocabulary, and transition signals. In this way, we start to talk about stylistic features in terms of their purpose within the structure of the essay. We notice, for example, that Tompkins's essay shifts from past to present tense—a shift that signals her rhetorical use of narrative (in the past tense) to frame her analyses of historians' texts (in the present tense).

Another useful point of entry into a discussion of textual features is to present students with texts that have been altered or manipulated in some way. For example, I have presented students with a parody "workplace" article from the *Onion*, which begins as follows:

> SANTA FE, NM—When Santa Fe–area marketing and sales professionals are looking for an office-management consultant with a nose for improving productivity and cost-effectiveness, they turn to Jim Smuda. For the past six years, this pitiful little man has served as senior field consultant at VisTech, one of Santa Fe's leading service-support companies.
>
> "I provide office solutions," the sniveling, detestable Smuda said. "Whether you need help with digital networking, facilities management, outsourcing, systems integration or document services, I have the experience and know-how to guide you through today's business maze."
>
> "If you've got questions," the 41-year-old worm added, "the team of experts at VisTech has got the answers." ("'I Provide Office Solutions'" 1998)

The story, which looks in every way like a normal article, is accompanied by a photograph that further juxtaposes the almost vacuous normality and self-presentation of the business consultant with a sardonic caption that begins, "Spineless nonentity Jim Smuda . . .". I give this article to students with the publication information removed, as if it were an actual news article. Then, once they realize that it is a parody, I ask them to figure out which features tell them so. This helps to make a simple point about the close relationship between form and content, as students can see that the grammatical function of modifying phrases such as "the sniveling, detestable Smuda" and "the 41-year-old worm" are completely appropriate to an actual news article, while the content is just the opposite.

In the unit on movie reviews, I often present students with a review of a popular movie that has been scrambled so that the paragraphs are in random order. Working together, students unscramble the paragraphs, and then we discuss the specific words and phrases that indicate the order of the paragraphs, paying attention as well to paragraphs that appear to fit in more than one place. This discussion helps to connect grammatical and lexical elements with the move structure of the review, and also to get students to talk about possible variations in the order of moves.

Students can also be asked to manipulate texts themselves, either within or across genres. One way to do this is to have the class suggest a recent event that many of them might have attended (for example, a party), then have everyone write two "letters home"—one to an older relative (such as a parent or grandparent) and the other to a best friend, but without naming the person in the letter. After they have done this, students exchange letters and try to guess, based on the style of each letter, which person it was written to.[2] The following discussion can focus on the decisions that students made as they wrote their own letters, as well as the clues that helped them to determine the addressees of other letters. Activities like these are, of course, nothing new to composition; however, by focusing on genre, issues of audience, purpose and voice can be explicitly connected to stylistic features. (See Caudery 1998; Kroll 2001 for further examples of activities.)

INTERROGATING CONTEXTS

Once students have gained some facility with picking apart specific texts, the next stage is to facilitate what Terence Pang calls "contextual awareness building," which "highlights speaker intent and encourages learners to analyze the speech event and the situational variables underlying genres" (2002, 146). I have found it useful at this point to use a series of genre analysis questions formulated by Devitt, Bawarshi, and Reiff (2004; also included in Bawarshi 2003, 159–60), which are divided into the following steps:

1. Study the situation of the genre.
2. Identify and describe patterns in the genre's features.
3. Analyze what these patterns reveal about the situation.

These questions ask students to first gather information about the context (participants, setting, topic) of a genre, and then study its specific formal features (typical sentence structures, vocabulary, format). The final step is to make connections between features and context. Although we use these questions to a certain extent for all of the genres we discuss in class, I tend to wait until students have spent some time talking and writing about the stylistic features of at least one public genre before asking them to concentrate on the connections between genre patterns and scene. I want students to spend plenty of time working with the details of style before they start to articulate inferences about how those details realize rhetorical situations, because I find that this will encourage them to avoid reaching overly simplistic conclusions about the genre.

The following example serves to illustrate some of the directions discussion can take. During one course, I had students read a newspaper report of the 1993 FBI raid on the Branch Davidian compound in Waco, Texas. The report begins as follows:

The compound where cult leader David Koresh and 95 followers holed up for 51 days burned to the ground today after FBI agents in an armored vehicle smashed the buildings and pumped in tear gas. The Justice Department said cult members set the fire. A White House official said FBI agents were doing everything possible to rescue the 95 cult followers from the compound, and at least 20 people had left it. (Brown 1993)

Two things that students pointed out right away were the use of the past tense and the long, densely packed first sentence. These were fairly quickly connected with the genre's purpose of relating an event that is assumed to have already occurred, as well as the expectation that the report communicate the most relevant information about the event within the first paragraph. Students also noted that an important aspect of this genre is to maintain an "objective" tone. To follow up on this, I focused attention on clause structure and agency by asking students to enumerate the verbs, who was performing them, and whether each subject-verb construction occurred in a main or subordinate clause. This started a discussion of how reported speech is often the most concrete and verifiable kind of fact in a news story; thus, most of the main clause actions attributed to people are statements. Actions other than speaking are embedded within subordinate clauses, usually following a verb like "say." I then asked students to read the passage again, and, according to the information presented there, state who they think started the fire. With few exceptions, students answered Koresh or his "followers" or the cult. This allowed us to explore the ways in which news reports like this one "spin" events so that specific causal connections are easier to make. Not only is the reader given "just the facts," but also a simple choice for who or what caused the event to occur.

Contextual awareness can make for some particularly revealing discussions of student writing as well. About two-thirds of the way through the term, I have students apply the genre analysis questions to the argumentative essays that they have to write for the course. By this point, students have usually completed at least one major writing assignment, involving multiple drafts, peer review, and teacher commentary, and have seen samples of previously submitted papers. Thus, they have plenty of direct experience with the demands of the genre, as well as my expectations, and they can quickly produce a list of "typical" features and moves (usually based on instructions in my assignment sheets). In discussing the context of the genre, students usually note, understandably enough, its largely instrumental purpose—that one of its functions is to display an understanding of and engagement with the course readings, as well as to demonstrate the use of conventionalized aspects of language in the construction of an academic argument, to receive a grade, and pass a writing requirement. It often takes some careful questioning, however, to get students to make connections between the features of style and the situation of the genre.

A good example of this has to do with what is commonly referred to as the "road map"—that part of the essay that signals the structure of the argument. I encourage my students to include a road map—indeed, assignment sheets and peer review forms often mention road maps; moreover, I try to provide students with varying examples of how to construct a road map. In a recent discussion, however, several of my students reacted negatively to a former student's essay in which the road map was explicitly stated in a form similar to "In this essay, I will argue that . . .". This led to a discussion of the stylistic shift of the student's road map, which, they argued, sounded overly formal and pedestrian in comparison with the rest of the essay up to that point. Students pointed particularly to the writer referring to himself and the argument that his essay was making ("I will . . ."). I asked the class to consider the issue in terms of the context of the assignment—for example, what would happen if the road map were simply omitted. In this sense, I suggested, the road map is a kind of contract between student and teacher in that it represents the writer's meta-discursive claim as to what the argument of the essay is, so that the instructor can evaluate that claim, provide guidance for revision, and eventually assign a grade. Thus, we were able to consider how the multiple purposes of the genre can conflict with one another so that, as in this instance, the need to be explicit can lead to what was perceived as an awkward-sounding style. We concluded by talking about other ways in which the writer could have handled the road map—by, for example, integrating the road map sentences with other sections of the essay, rather than presenting it as a bald statement of purpose, or alternatively by restructuring the "I will . . ." sentence so that there would be less emphasis on the writer.

ANALYZING SCENES

The final stage involves investigating social roles as they are constituted through genres. For the research project, in which students select a genre to study and analyze on their own, I encourage students to choose genres related to their academic or career goals, although I allow them to choose any specific genre that interests them.[3] Students' choices of professional and academic genres have included law reviews, medical research reviews, floral arrangement articles, chemistry lab reports, and psychological research reports. Other choices have included newspaper editorials, sports columns, album reviews, and job application forms. While students are choosing a genre, I have them read a methodological text such as Anthony Paré and Graham Smart's "Observing Genres in Action" (1994) or Susan Peck MacDonald's "The Analysis of Academic Discourse(s)" (2002). Then I have them brainstorm some of the ways that they can research the genres that they are thinking of analyzing—how to obtain samples, other types of data that might be relevant, and so forth. Although many students, for various reasons, choose to focus their final paper on a textual analysis of their exemplars, several have gone a step further by interviewing readers and writers of the genre. One student I worked with, for example, looked at floral arrangement articles because she had her own floral business. She contacted an older, more established florist and interviewed her about how she used the articles to get ideas for her own arrangements.

As with the previous assignments in the course, I have students apply Devitt, Bawarshi, and Reiff's (2004) steps for genre analysis to their samples, again focusing on connections between features and situation. Here, however, I try to draw attention specifically to the roles of reader and writer as they are constructed by the genre. Questions pertinent to this goal include:

1. How is the subject of the genre treated? What content is considered most important? What content (topics or details) is ignored?
2. What values, beliefs, goals, and assumptions are revealed through the genre's patterns?
3. What actions does the genre help make possible? What actions does the genre make difficult? What roles do its users perform?
4. Who is included in the genre, and who is excluded? (from Devitt, Bawarshi, and Reiff 1994, 93–94).

Style is crucial here because it gives students concrete ways of drawing conclusions about the how well the texts that they are looking at fit into a genre, as well as how readers and writers are constituted through the genre: how texts fulfill readers' expectations, how they assert specific forms of authority, and how they signal affiliation with discourse communities.

One student, for example, analyzed the lesson columns that appear in magazines such as *Guitar* and *Guitar Player* offering readers tips on playing techniques. He identified two specific features: the relatively simple syntax of the articles (employing, for example, a conversational style that refers directly to "you" the reader) and their use of music theory terms, which he then connected to the genre's positioning of the writer as a kind of specialist. Writers of the genre have to show that they are professional musicians, that they possess knowledge and skill far beyond the amateur players who are assumed to read the column; at the same time, they have to be able to take musical techniques and present them in lay terms—so that it sounds like virtually anyone could learn them with a little practice. In other words, the genre posits a gap between lay knowledge about guitar playing and professional knowledge, and it is in the style of the article that that gap can most clearly be seen.

As students are completing their projects, we revisit our discussion of classroom genres and extend it to the other genres of the course, as well as to reader/writer roles. A stylistic issue that we usually talk about at this point, because it is one that arises consistently in drafts, is how to refer to course readings and other sources in support of a written argument. As with the road map issue mentioned earlier, students seem to grapple with a tension between, on the one hand, pedagogical and ethical requirements that they cite their sources correctly and distinguish their own ideas from those of, say, Jane Tompkins; and, on the other, the need to maintain an orderly and cohesive progression of ideas (a notion that many students refer to with the elusive term "flow"). Once again, style becomes the tangible material around which this tension is addressed: how to restate a writer's argument with specific action verbs ("Tompkins argues"; "Berger asserts"); how to make quoted material fit grammatically with the sentence structure of the draft; how to paraphrase.

I have found it fruitful to frame this issue by having students consider how the various documents of the course—assignment sheets, essay drafts, comments, and so forth—construct the teacher as reader of student writing. Students note from assignment sheets, as well as my comments on their drafts, that they are expected to "introduce" sources to their reader "as if the reader has never read them before." I ask students what this suggests about how I read their texts, which leads us into a discussion of the institutional functions that student writing performs, and the ways in which it constitutes a social relationship between teacher (or reader) and student (writer). The requirement to clearly explicate sources can be seen, on the one hand, as a means for the teacher to check that the student has done the reading and has understood how it relates to the argument of the paper. On the other hand, it can be seen as part of the expectation that the teacher read student writing from the standpoint of a generalized academic audience. In this way, specific stylistic concerns can be discussed and clearly related to the ways in which they position students within the writing course and within the university.

As I hope the above examples show, genre can be used to talk about style in a range of different ways: to get students to look closely at style in the texts that they read and write, to draw out into the open their assumptions and questions about specific aspects of style, and, perhaps most importantly, to help them see writing styles and conventions as the realization of what Carolyn Miller describes as "the abstract yet distinctive influence of a culture, a society, or an institution" (1994, 70). By encouraging students to reflect on the particular forms that this influence takes, we can, I would suggest, increase students' awareness of how writing positions them within the discourses of the academy, and guide them toward informed choices in their own uses of language, thereby re-placing style within the structures that give it meaning.

15

TUTORING TABOO: A RECONSIDERATION OF STYLE IN THE WRITING CENTER

Jesse Kavadlo

Writing center tutors are often advised to disregard style in their students' essays, and for good reason: the earliest writing centers of the 1950s and 1960s, far from centers, were often remedial fix-it shops, designed as marginal facilities accommodating marginalized students (for writing center history, see Carino 1995). These centers, then more commonly called "labs," and later "clinics," frequently lived up to their medical metaphors, diagnosing and treating any number of grammatical maladies and functioning like emergency rooms more than providing preventative medicine. With the changes in ideology and pedagogy of the 1970s and 1980s, however, writing centers changed their names and frequently their locations, with the hopes of moving from margin to, indeed, center; as Jim Addison and Henry Wilson suggest, the "surface shift in terminology represents dramatic alterations in the underlying philosophy, role, and function of a writing center in the academic community" (1991, 56). With these changes in identification, then, came changes in mission. Rather than focusing on error, as it did in its lab and clinic manifestations, the writing center represented a safe and centralized location whose axiom, for Stephen North in his landmark essay "The Idea of a Writing Center," would be "better writers, not necessarily—or immediately—better texts" (1984, 73).

Writing center theory thus emphasizes writers more than writing, so writing center practice frequently focuses on students' writing process, relationship with writing, or conceptual progress, especially by means of oral development, freewriting, outlining, brainstorming, or clustering. Tutors are frequently trained to emphasize structural, global, and higher order concerns over specific language; in post-structuralist terms, they follow the langue of the system called "essay writing" over the parole, the specific utterances of the paper at hand. Consequently, style is seldom addressed, or it is assigned a low priority during the session. (Some manuals, such as *The Bedford Guide for Writing Tutors* [Ryan 1998], for example, focus almost entirely on issues of professionalism, writing process, and global revision strategies without mentioning style or the writer's language at all.) Echoing North, Jeff Brooks espouses "minimalist tutoring," sessions characterized by writing "to learn, not to make perfect papers" (1991, 221).

Given the writing center's decades-long struggle to embrace the needs of mainstream students and university missions—and to dismiss misgivings that it is a mere proofreading service—such emphases make sound theory and practical policy. They also, crucially, preclude the possibility of undue tutorial influence or unethical advantage, since tutors seldom comment directly on diction and syntax themselves, and "departments of literature are particularly concerned with the issue of plagiarism in terms of style and text structure" (Clark and Healy 1996, 244–45; my emphasis). Unfortunately, they frequently also preclude discussions of style, which can be treated very differently from the rote mechanical exercises and sometimes mandated remediation that the writing center strives to relegate to a bemoaned past. As Robert J. Connors, Winston Weathers, and Elizabeth D. Rankin have argued of composition theory—elaborated upon more recently by Sharon A. Myers—perhaps writing centers may strive to include discussions of style in conjunction with, rather than in addition, or opposition, to the creation of better writers.

STYLE AND WRITING CENTERS: A BRIEF HISTORY

The history of the writing center is the history of its contested relationship with grammar, and its changing names, senses of identification, and function reflect this dynamic. While the "lab," the earliest term, suggests the experimental, the hypothetical with unknowable results, the "clinic" suggests something more predictable, if similarly medical. Unfortunately, "clinic," though an improvement, nonetheless implies remedy, that is, remedial, with its associations of short-term, last-minute medical assistance and urgent measures after the patient is already sick, over the preventative care of the regular consultation. In keeping, Ralph E. Lowe's *The Writing Clinic* titles its introduction "The Diagnosis" and its final section "Check Out of the Clinic" (1973). In between, the book is an anatomy of sentence structures and parts of speech, its focus a grammatical taxonomy with no mention of process—or writers, for that matter—at all.

Not surprisingly, theory and pedagogy shifted from the margins of remediation to "center," the word representative of a midpoint, heart, hub, focal point, and gathering place. The move is from remedial to restorative: as Christina Murphy suggests, students who enter the writing center are often "hurt" psychologically, even as this metaphor conjures images of the clinic (1989, 297). The difference, then, is that "the tutoring process, like the therapeutic process, partakes in the power of language to reshape and empower consciousness" (300). Yet the language of the writing center, like the language of therapy, is frequently oral, rather than written. Grammar—frequently in the form of what are now derided as "drill and kill" exercises—was all that the clinics of old addressed; they neglected the writer him- or herself. At the other end of the spectrum, the contemporary writing center has given itself over completely to the writer, perhaps at the expense of his or her language, the actual words that appear on the page as concrete collections of the writer's thoughts, the palpable result imprinted after the ephemeral spoken word or intangible (and, crucially, ungradable) cerebral process is finished.

The clinics were all mechanics without consideration of style; the centers are primarily process, but again at the expense of style, which in writing center orthodoxy veers dangerously close to anachronistic revivals of remediation. But as Elizabeth Rankin has suggested of composition pedagogy, and as I am suggesting of writing center theory and practice now, new, student-centered approaches to teaching—and tutoring—have led to "a noticeable decline in the status of style as a pedagogical concept. By this I mean that the teaching of style no longer enjoys a prominent place in our discipline" (1985, 374). While the past's exclusively grammatical approach to tutoring (evident in Lowe's *Writing Clinic)* seems stiflingly antiquated, North's "better writers" maxim seems, as Rankin says of writing pedagogy in general, an "overcorrection of sorts. Style hasn't just stepped back to take a less dominant role in our teaching"—or, I would add, our tutoring. "Style," Rankin concludes, "is out of style" (374).

Robert Moore, in "The Writing Clinic and the Writing Laboratory," writes that "writing practice, with emphasis on specific diction, concise phrasing and the necessity of revisional rereading of what was actually written, not what was merely intended, can be of . . . assistance to the student who, in the haste of writing examinations or belated papers, produces vague, telescoped, or garbled sentences. It must, however, be pointed out that such writing often accompanies garbled information or habitually confused thinking (1950, 7). What is striking about this assertion is that it was written in 1950, before the emergence of writing center theory or practice (indeed, before the name had been coined). While

Moore focuses on the student's writing as opposed to the writer, a return to language—not just what students are trying to say, but the syntax and diction that they use to say it, and the relationship between what they say and how they say it—seems just the sort of balanced approach that one-on-one tutoring and collaboration can foster. And so the relationship between what students say and how they say it, after more than fifty years and multiple paradigm shifts, again seems the appropriate avenue for writing center debate.

Among others, Peter Elbow—an original and primary proponent of the expressivist school of pedagogy—now writes that composition must learn the merit of "style . . . artifice, [and] mannerism. . . . I value style and artifice" (2002, 542). Similarly, Clark and Healy's "new ethics for the writing center" include specific sensitivity "to other people's writing, assignments, and goals" through "individualized writing instruction" that eschews "rigid policy statements—e.g. 'Refuse to proofread,' or 'Don't even hold a pencil while you're tutoring'" (1996, 255). Linda K. Shamoon and Deborah H. Burns balance Jeff Brooks's espousal of "minimalist tutoring"—which never delves into style—with their "Critique of Pure Tutoring." Although they remain theoretical, offering little suggestion for what the analogy of "master classes in music" would look like in writing center practice, their essay lays the theoretical groundwork for a movement away from the invisible thoughts of the writer and into the indelible craft of their writing (1995, 231). At the same time, however, "style"—in composition or in the writing center—should not suggest a reflexive lurch into traditionalist grammatical prescriptivism, a return to the lamentable rote assignments of the recent past. And while I have analyzed the "center" half of the "writing center," I would add that the "writing" of the writing center must be understood as a gerund—acting as a noun, a thing, a subject or object—as much as a present participle—a process or unending action. The "writing" center must serve students' writing process as it advances toward a product: the act of writing, certainly, but the words on the page as well.

CONCERNS

While composition theory has moved beyond the binary opposition of process and product, in many ways writing center theory has not; because tutors hear ethereal ideas or see exploratory drafts (or, perhaps more frequently, hear exploratory drafts, since many guidebooks encourage tutors to have their students read aloud), it is difficult to call what they do anything other than process. Ultimately, though, it may be politically naïve, if romantic, to adhere blindly to North's "better writers, not better texts" dictum, to imagine that, as North continues, "writing centers [can be] the centers of consciousness about writing on campuses" (1984, 73). North himself, of course, in his later essay "Revisiting 'The Idea of a Writing Center,'" calls this idea "the most accurate [passage] and, at the same time, the most genuinely laughable" (1994, 86). But the "better writers, not better texts" pronouncement is also, in a sense, epistemologically impossible, as the current breakdown between the process/product dichotomy exemplifies: students, lamentably but realistically, are judged—graded—primarily on "product," frequently a final draft, sometimes collected absent earlier drafts and revisions. Composition programs continue to experiment with portfolio approaches to accumulated student works—for example, "the National Council of Teachers of English supports the use of portfolios" (Reynolds 2000, 1)—and universities have largely embraced the idea of writing across the curriculum and writing in the disciplines. Yet, too often, this "support" still means a single writing assignment, tacked on at the end of the semester, without discussion of the writing process, research methodologies, and documentation systems of the particular discipline; the need for—let alone strategies of—revision; or opportunities for instructor or peer feedback before the final version (and there is always a final version) is due.[1]

The writing center's frequent fallback position, then, is to provide those crucial discussions of process, revision, citation, and, one hopes, language, that instructors expect their students to employ but do not necessarily work into their classrooms or curriculums personally. This dynamic, however, complicates the writing center's emphasis on process, for process, as students understand too well, eventually must be demonstrated as product. The only way that many—perhaps most—instructors will gauge whether or not the writing center has indeed produced better writers is whether these better writers themselves produce better writing. In "Revisiting 'The Idea of a Writing Center,'" North does not advocate "taking upon [the writing center's] shoulders the whole institution's (real or imagined) sins of illiteracy . . .: to serve as conscience, savior, or sacrificial victim" (1994, 89). The writing center, then, must serve a pragmatic—not idealistic—function, especially in the regional and state colleges, branch campuses of universities, and various satellite campuses where working-class, immigrant, first-generation, and rural students need to learn the conventions of college writing in which their instructors will hold them accountable, even if they, the instructors, themselves don't teach students those conventions. The writing center must not sacrifice these students upon the altar of its theoretical ideals, and a tutorial focused on style may be just the midpoint between writing-the-participle and writing-the-gerund that will allow the writing center's sometimes subversive politics to meet its ultimately conventional and frequently conservative practice.

But first, I must clarify those elements of style that the writing center, given its past predicaments and current position, must strive to avoid. In the writing center:

Style should not feel remedial. Labs and clinics provided remedies, but centers must not. There is no cure for an essay, because an ineffective essay is not sick or ailing. Such personification evokes Foucault's arguments (to which North alludes, tongue in cheek [1994, 87]) that the function of the hospital, the prison, and the madhouse is to create a clear division between the sick and the healthy, an unmistakably physical and subject-positional sense of Otherness. If universities truly want to remove the stigma of the writing center, faculty members must stop using it to punish their students. Mandatory tutorials turn the writing center into a prison, creating an unfortunate additional pun on Robert J. Connor's title "The Erasure of the Sentence": when the writing class avoids (erases) the sentence, it is the student who will be sentenced. Similarly, the writing center is not a cure-all (writing center as hospital; the implication of "clinic") or a place to remand students that instructors simply do not know what to do with (Foucault's madhouse, which seems the dark pre-Freudian converse of Christina Murphy's tutorial psychoanalytics). No paper, or student, should be seen as sick, physically or mentally. The writing center's mission, then, merges self-improvement with institutional assistance, a combination of American ideals that are sometimes presented as contradictory or mutually excusive. They don't have to be.

Style should not be prescriptive, mechanical, or arbitrary. Like "remedial," the word "prescriptive" again is rooted in dated medical metaphor ("prescription"), and telling students the way they are supposed to write turns the tutor, who is frequently a peer, into a pale reflection of the teacher and institution. Tutors should not be placed in the awkward position of telling students what they "should" do. Instead, they can remind them of rhetorical considerations, possibilities, and consequences concomitant with various and variable modes of expression. Further, style, unlike prescriptive grammar, involves a series of choices that demonstrate many layers of meaning simultaneously: the writer's style demonstrates what he or she thinks, but also the relationships between those ideas, the relative importance of weighed ideas, the writer's attitude toward those ideas, and the writer's ability to present those ideas effectively and persuasively. The tutor, then, must use questions to make the writer aware that what he or she says is a series of rational and discrete options, not blind adherence to a set of rules. While rhetoric feels logical, some rules of the English language are merely mutually accepted conventions that are frequently irrational. Linguist Steven Pinker provocatively argues that "many prescriptive rules of grammar are just plain dumb," but he grants that "the aspect of language use that is most worth changing is the clarity and style of written prose" (1995, 400, 401).

How, then, can tutors improve "clarity and style"?

INTEGRATING STYLE WITH CONTENT: POSSIBLE STRATEGIES

In their guidebook, *Training Tutors for Writing Conferences,* Thomas Reigstad and Donald McAndrew break down tutoring priorities according to higher order concerns (HOCs) and lower order concerns (LOCs) (1984, 11–19). Moving away from discussion of grammar and toward discussion of the paper's main point, purpose, or development, this model (sometimes referred to in composition contexts as global vs. local concerns) allows tutors to prioritize the session's time. As Reigstad and McAndrew state, "Some types of problems are more responsible for the low quality of a piece than others. Since the tutoring session is geared to improving the piece within reasonable time limits, these more serious problems [HOCs] must be given priority" (11).

The approach makes sense: a writer whose paper merely summarizes when the assignment calls for argument, or a paper that does not have what most instructors would see as a (viable) main point, may not benefit from a discussion of, say, pronoun/antecedent agreement, even if such errors also appear in the essay. (Indeed, the "one/they" error is even still a matter of contention, as Dunn and Pinker separately describe in detail.) Certain errors certainly feel less important than an overall lack of point or purpose.

However, the terminology—HOC vs. LOC; global vs. local—may be misleading. The concerns are not necessarily hierarchical but gridlike; the paper's difficulties are frequently (although not always) related to each other (as Moore noted in 1950), so that HOCs and LOCs are frequently correlations, not chains of being. The table below correlates certain HOCs with their common grammatical and rhetorical manifestations. While I'm providing possibilities and—in keeping with my own recommendations above—certainly not rules, the chart may demonstrate the possibility that HOCs and LOCs tend to be integrated or connected.

Higher order concerns	*Lower order concerns*	*Rhetorical concerns*
Importance, focus	Sentence variety, coordination and subordination, comma splices, articles—the thing (Aristotelian, material, concrete) or a thing (Platonic, ideal, abstract)	Thesis, claim, premise, and support; can the writer distinguish between his or her main and supporting points?
Details, development and support	Repetition (often creates, or attempts to mask, lack of specificity), overuse of vague words, such as "thing," "you," "person," "this" or "that" with no clear referent, articles (as above)	Identification, description
Causes and consequences	Overuse of passive voice, "you," modifiers and subordination (both often demonstrate a sentence's agency)	Causality, cause and effect
Order and unity	Parallelism (must use like or unified parts of speech), prepositions, modifiers (must be correctly placed), pronoun agreement (probably necessitating sexist language discussion, below)	Classification
Transitions	See Importance and focus; also introductory clauses, conjunctive adverbs, conjunctions, metadiscourse	Comparison, sometimes causality or classification
Audience consideration and appropriateness	Cliché, slang, jargon, sexist language and gender-specific pronouns (probably necessitating pronoun agreement), inflated or inflammatory language	Tone, bias

A weak thesis, or a lack of thesis, is one of the more frequent problems that students need help with. And talking the writer through what he or she is trying to say may strengthen (or help create) a main point. But then, once the writer arrives at this point, how will he or she express it? How will this expression differ from the one already on the page? One way to address these concerns is to focus on style, language, and syntax. An essay with little sentence variety and limited vocabulary will not just bore the reader, which is the usual injunction toward "style"; the paper composed almost entirely of simple sentences or repetitive constructions, more importantly, will not alert the reader to the degree in which the writer believes in those ideas, the respective importance of the various ideas presented, or the sometimes contested relationships between those ideas. Actual errors, such as comma splices, obscure the relationships between ideas and their respective importance even more.

Reigstad and McAndrew suggest that tutors focus on HOCs, leaving LOCs to the end of the session. But such an approach can lead to tacking grammar on, bringing in unrelated or inappropriate grammatical concerns, or—my main concern here—ignoring language entirely when it seems crucial to the paper's argument, agency, and clarity. Take the following opening paragraphs from a student essay:

> There are many different forms of communication out there for people to use to get information. Some ways of communication are fast and some take a bit longer, but all get the job done. Telephones, cell phones, pagers, fax, e-mail, instant messenger, internet, postcards, letters (snail mail), newspaper, and television are all ways to get messages delivered to people from around the world.
>
> People, these days, tend to be more fast-paced so, e-mail use, internet and telephone are the most common ways to communicate. Hand-written letters, postcards and other similar things take time, although they are more personal and exciting to receive, they are not as commonly used.[2]

The writer has a topic (already a plus in terms of HOCs) and many examples (another HOC, even if upon closer inspection these "examples" are more of a list). But the style—the sense of voice and variety—is flat, disinterested, and uninteresting. A tutor, of course, would not say such a thing; the session would focus on what the student believed to be her main point, and ways in which she could support that main point more clearly. But what is her main point? Certainly it is not that "there are many different forms of communication"—that's obvious and unargumentative. Similarly, the idea that some forms of communication are faster than other does not lend itself to argument. Emphasis on "thesis," "focus," or "detail" may not help to emphasize that much of this setup is inadequate.

On the other hand, we can look at the repeated constructions and the run-on sentence (the last sentence), not as lower order concerns or grammatical maladies, but as ways to help the writer shape her HOCs: the focus, sense of cause, and need for contrast. In some ways, the tutor can begin, not end, with the error and the repetitive use of "communication," the fact the several examples are listed twice in a short space, and that most of the verbs are linking rather than transitive. The student could read the passage out loud in order to talk more about which forms of communication appeal to her the most, and why those forms are, for her, the most appealing. Such discussion, in fact, revealed the writer's fondness, even nostalgia, for the handwritten letter, even though she herself seldom sent them. The last sentence, the run-on, was, then, in many ways the most instructive. Far from mere error in need of correction, run-ons and comma splices frequently show a student who is struggling to weigh and measure contrasting or contradictory—yet sophisticated and significant—ideas.

The solution is not to flatten out the contrast, but, to paraphrase Peter Elbow's title, to embrace contraries. This student had trouble deciding whether the "although they are more personal and exciting to receive" clause of the final sentence is subordinate to the idea that "hand-written letters, postcards and other similar things take time" or the fact that that "they are not as commonly used." The student, in this sentence, the only one attempting to juggle three ideas simultaneously, begins to embrace the possibility of genuine argument. Like Sharon Myers, Irvin Hashimoto recommends templates in order to help students write; he wants "students to write thesis statements—not just to tell [him] what they're going to say, but to begin to make those commitments, to risk their ideas and opinions" (1991, 124). The only remotely risky statement of this student's essay is the last one; the rest are simply, dully undeniable. One of Hashimoto's thesis templates, although admittedly "mechanical-looking" is: "Although . . . X is . . . I think X is . . . because . . ." (124). The structure works here: it allows the student to use her own language to fill in the ellipses, but the structure organizes the relationships between the material and crucially forces her to recast her originally passive construction ("are not as commonly used") into some version of the active voice, most likely the transitive subject-verb-object clause, "I don't send letters." The student ended up writing this sentence: "Although handwritten letters are more exciting and personal, I don't send them because they take time." This sentence may not stay exactly this way in the revision. But its syntax, its balance between three uneasy ideas, poises the writer to explain herself in ways that the original oversimplification, reflected by the simple sentences, would not allow.

The error forces the writer to reevaluate her focus: what condition constitutes the "although"?; the attention to repetition shows that the writing is not as detailed as she may have thought (examples are not always the same as details and certainly not the same as description); the shift from "not commonly used" to "I don't send" allows her to contemplate cause and consequence; and the discussion of the word "although" may allow her to reconsider the uses of importance and transition. By correcting, then elaborating upon, and then personalizing the run-on, the student may leave the session not just with a better idea of what her main point is, but how she may be able to write that main point clearly and effectively. The sentence also, importantly, sets her up to say, explain, and describe much more. Such a tutorial discussion, in practice, may take an entire half hour or more. But the student will not only talk about her paper: she will write it, and she is poised to continue.

This grid of correspondences suggests a descriptive, not prescriptive, understanding of style, one that avoids the clinic's elevation of correctness and convention over all other concerns, such as the writer's point and personality. Although "grammar" and "style" are frequently conflated, tutoring grammar in isolation of the paper's particulars is antithetical to tutoring style, which by definition involves, for Lea Masiello (in the only published essay that specifically addresses style in the writing center), "choice and voice" (2000, 55). As Masiello continues, in a way that seems perfectly applicable to the student writing I've provided here, "It pays to remind writers that in college they're expected to try out new ideas and styles" (60)—and the two, as she implies, are linked. Once the student began to let go of the rote conventions that dragged down her introduction, the paper—in style and substance—became more interesting. Moreover, neither "choice" nor "voice" is necessarily a part of mechanical correctness; if anything, great stylists frequently flout convention. The grid also, I hope, shows the way in which words like "style" vs. "content," as my heading suggests, are another set of binaries, like "higher order" and "lower order" concerns, "global and local" questions, or "process and product," that ultimately break down, since any discussion of the paper's actual language must always, at some level, involve both style and content.

Style, as Connors's discussion of sentence combining and Myers's stress upon diction suggest, shapes and generates meaning. Or as William Zinsser, in his famous book *On Writing Well*, suggests, the writer "will be impatient to find a 'style.'. . . You will reach for gaudy similes and tinseled adjectives, as if 'style' were something you could buy in a style store and drape onto your words in bright decorator colors. . . . Resist this shopping expenditure: there is no style store" (1980, 20). Style, then, is intrinsic to meaning, in that the way we state and shape our argument affects the content, nature, and reception of that argument itself. Stylistic, syntactical, and sentence-level strategies, then, may nonetheless adhere to the writing center's mission: better writers, and, as a result, better texts.

PART IV: NEW DEFINITIONS OF STYLE
Introduction

T. R. Johnson

At the outset of this book, we suggested that perhaps part of what makes style such a difficult issue to discuss is that the topic is potentially too rich—that is, it can mean so many different things to so many different people that, at last, the possibility arises that it means nothing at all. We hope, however, that by carefully surveying the recent history of the discussion of prose style in the field of composition studies, by exploring ways it invites a certain overlap and cross-fertilization with the literary-aesthetic curricula, and by showing how it can focus practical issues of the writing classroom, we've mapped enough solid ground upon which to base more speculative discussions. In this section, four essays explore the range of possibilities for extending our definitions of what, in the writing classroom, prose style can mean.

First, Dion Cautrell, in "Rhetor-Fitting: Defining Ethics through Style," shows us how the entire field of rhetoric can be understood in terms of ethics, how the moment-to-moment decisions we make about sentences and paragraphs can be understood in terms of the contemporary philosophical discussion of ethics. Next, Drew Loewe, in "Style as a System: Toward a Cybernetic Model of Composition Style," delineates the shortcomings in traditional understandings of style and points the way to a new branch of systems theory (cybernetics) as a means to describing what prose style is. The third essay, M. Todd Harper's "Teaching the Tropics of Inquiry in the Composition Classroom," shows how a variety of academic fields can be presented to students in a composition course as elaborate flowerings of a particular trope, and, in so doing, he implicitly focuses the far-flung possibilities of programs in writing across the curriculum very firmly in matters of prose style. Finally, T. R. Johnson concludes the book by exploring what "Writing with the Ear" might mean in terms of recent studies of bodily movement, affect, and sensation, as well as literary and mystical traditions of listening.

16

RHETOR-FITTING: DEFINING ETHICS THROUGH STYLE

Dion C. Cautrell

Style is indeed, as Buffon most famously said, the man himself—but the man sometimes as he is, sometimes as he wants to be, sometimes as he is palpably pretending to be, sometimes, as in comedy, both as he pretends to be and as he is. Stylistic pedagogy ought to cover the whole range. Only by doing so can it perform its authentic social duty: to enhance both clear communication between citizens and the selfhood of the citizens who are communicating.

—Richard Lanham, *Style: An Anti-textbook*

No comprehensive treatment of rhetorical style (Greek lexis, Latin elocutio) rightfully avoids the ethical criticism that has plagued the third canon since at least the time of Gorgias (483–378 BCE). Plato censured rhetoric for its potentially damaging social and moral effects, deeming it a "knack" for mass manipulation rather than a discipline proper to achieving Truth, Beauty, and Goodness (Plato 2003, 463b; see also 465c). During the Renaissance, Peter Ramus limited rhetoric primarily to style, which he considered less rational because of its supposed imprudence. Ramus's decision left stylistics with little more than a catalogue of verbal niceties (schemes and tropes) and underlies the charges of "empty" or "mere" rhetoric that still populate contemporary public discourse. Because such criticisms are not universally accepted, these and other disputes have proven impossible to settle, and stylistic theories that seek consistency or closure often skirt ethics to do so. Style's ongoing troubles derive partly from the long-standing friction between philosophy and rhetoric.[1] Because ethics stands within philosophy's traditional purview, rhetorical treatments of ethics are often seen as inadequate, if not wrongheaded. Scholars and teachers of rhetoric are thus left appealing to philosophical principles in order to satisfy criticism, criticism at times engendered by skepticism about the very idea of rhetoric.

Yet beyond philosophical disagreements stand additional challenges springing from the character of human communication. Stylistics treats the elementary patterns of language and of language use that drive discourse—words put to work in the world—but those patterns vary according to context and, as patterns, may be assigned ethical value only through disregard or distortion. That is, no stylistic strategy may be judged "good" or "bad" apart from actual writers and readers, the thinking, feeling human beings who create and interpret discourse. Moreover, and even in context, what "good" or "bad" might mean remains open to debate precisely because different interlocutors value different (kinds of) outcomes. That is, rhetorical value necessarily remains in flux—even if due simply to differing expectations of how discourse should function. The question any ethics of style must answer, then, is How does one define ethics in the dynamic context of stylistic enactment, rhetorical give-and-take?

In actuality, a robust stylistics carries certain advantages in grappling with rhetoric's ethical conundrums because the third canon is directly caught up in discourse's 'values dynamic': "A style is a response to a situation. When you call a style bad, or exaggerated, much less mad, you ought to make sure you understand the situation it responds to. You may be objecting to the situation, not to the style invented to cope with it" (Lanham 1974, 58). The sort of judgment Richard Lanham describes may come without conscious, much less formalized, criteria, but it carries the traces of valuation all the same. Indeed, Lanham counsels readers to read self-reflectively to ensure their (e)valuations do not spring from faulty assumptions about style's relationship to communicative context. Readers ought knowingly to affirm/confirm their responses, ethical and aesthetic, by accepting that they (those responses) are inevitably the confusion of a style and its attendant situation.

That a style is ever confused with a situation, however, does not come solely from missing or misunderstanding the relationship among styles, situations, and values. Because styles are pragmatically inseparable from their rhetorical situations, stylistics bears not only on the underlying language choices that writers and readers make but also—because the choices come in response to a particular situation—on how contexts enable or constrain styles. A given judgment may not rightly apply to this or that style, but this or that style surely entails a value judgment, at times an entire ethical system. Styles potentially reveal how the values behind a judgment encourage or discourage rhetorical action; the pragmatic confluence of style with judgment discloses the obligations and opportunities that rhetorical contexts carry. Lanham extends the idea to its ultimate state, placing style at the center of human socialization: "By a sense of style we socialize ourselves. Style finally becomes, as Burke works it out, social custom. . . . Style defines situations, tells us how to act in them. . . . We return to the self-consciousness shared by writer and reader. In society, it is called manners, in literature, decorum" (1974, 132–33).

Of particular note is the third canon's reversal of roles, "defin[ing] situations" along with being (as on page 58) a reaction or response to them. Style thereby becomes so thoroughly implicated in socialization that it is both a kind of social (inter)(re)action and a commentary on it. Thus, for Lanham, stylistics' primary ethical dilemma comes in practitioners' unreflective enactment of social obligation and responsibility. Especially for this reason, scholarship and teaching are most effective when they equip writers and readers to understand how ethical (inter)(re)actions come about—as well as how any one of us might create those opportunities—rather than what judgments ought finally to be made. In the classroom, for example, Lanham's model encourages teachers and student writers to focus on enacting the situational habit of mind that style embodies, not on a specific set of ethical injunctions or precepts. Classrooms that privilege the latter are likely, in Susan Miller's estimation, to produce student writers who "only compose exercises in order to reflect on or display their grasp of democratic consciousness. In these . . . classrooms, their writing is not positioned to enact that consciousness because they, as writers, are not taught that they have the power to do so" (1997, 498).

In addition, the overlapping of writing-reading and theorizing-teaching enables Lanham's "self-consciousness," the capacity to envision the third canon as itself an ethics of rhetorical (inter)(re)action: "Prose style exercises . . . our range of possible behavior. By allowing the luxury of imaginative rehearsal, it confers real ethical choice, and to this extent frees us from necessity. Ethics at this point touches taste, indeed becomes it" (1974, 133). Taste is no more stable a concept than ethics, though, and scholars and teachers of writing must determine whether switching terms produces more than a pleasing if only momentary flourish. Lanham casts the values dynamic in terms of style, but he leaves largely unchallenged style's position within rhetoric—which he formulates in the sophistic and Ciceronian tradition.[2] By contrast, Friedrich Nietzsche draws on rhetorical prudence to reconfigure ethics and taste rather than simply equate one with the other: "The real secret of the rhetorical art is now the prudent relation of both aspects, of the sincere and the artistic. . . .

It is a playing at the boundary of the aesthetic and the moral: any one-sidedness destroys the outcome. The aesthetic fascination must join the moral confidence; but they should not cancel one another out" (1989, 37, 39). Prudence centers Nietzsche's rhetoric, defines the habit of mind that allows rhetorical action to have/take effect in the world. Without the prudent pairing of "the sincere and the artistic," style's potential for defining ethical (inter)(re)action—for acknowledging its opportunities and obligations—is "destroy[ed]."[3]

According to Stephen Halliwell, Aristotle held a complementary view of rhetoric and morality: "[T]he Rhetoric remains open to the possibility that the orator's engagement with popular morality will sometimes, and non-accidentally, succeed in contributing to the realization of the human good and will do so in ways that embrace legitimate appeal to the criteria both of phronesis and of to sumpheron" (1994, 228). Phronesis (practical wisdom, prudence) and sumpheron (expediency, advantage, benefit) coincide in ways that violate neither rhetoric's efficacy nor the principles underlying public morality or advantage. A "practically realizable sumpheron" indeed "represents . . . an evaluative mode of bringing conceptions of 'good' to bear on the situation" (226).[4] It is, thus, the socioethical equivalent of phronesis, and though the two need not always coincide, they may operate simultaneously without inherent contradiction or conflict.

To make this equivalency more tangible, we might liken the relationship between prudence and benefit to the tension ready-built into pedagogy. Teaching is, of course, a rhetorical performance, and through that performance instructors seek to achieve certain curricular goals while also meeting the needs of students. Effective teachers are effective precisely because they manage to define their own goals in terms of others' needs, to fulfill the promise of the former by accepting the reality of the latter. Prudence-benefit, the whole complex of competing demands placed on teachers, circumscribes the range of choices available within a classroom. For example, in helping student writers to understand stylistic strategies, do I ask them to memorize those strategies acontextually, or do I ask them to recognize how specific writers deploy strategies in individual situations? Do I demand that student writers accept those strategies' importance a priori, or do I create opportunities for them to judge for themselves when/how/why the strategies most effectively engage readers? Although the prudence-benefit dynamic does not predetermine what choices teachers make, it does make certain choices (im)possible in the first place. Prudence—what I find most effective or "best"—must be brought into productive tension with benefit—what students gain from my (and their own) choices. Effective teachers strive for this kind of mutual challenge and discovery, and in doing so they embody the prudence-benefit dynamic. Likewise, an ethics of style is defined by the questions that prudence-benefit poses to writers and readers, not the answers on which they eventually settle.

The complex interaction of phronesis and sumpheron does not easily suffer formulation, at least not as Aristotle describes it, but that interaction seems fairly well to describe what Nietzsche terms "playing at the boundary" (1989, 39) between taste and ethics—the same zone within which Lanham's style supposedly functions. More importantly, Aristotle's treatment renders each mode as a habit of mind, a distinctive way of evaluating rhetorical contexts, thereby ensuring that stylistics and rhetoric in general retain the self-consciousness (prudence) and social connection (benefit) that Lanham accentuates. In this way scholars, teachers, and writers-readers stand a good chance of understanding the range of ethical judgments invited by rhetorical choices as well those choices most likely to affect the world outside their own heads. To understand, however, they must envision phronesis and sumpheron as an internally linked binary, as neither a pure synthesis nor a pure disjunction, for a truly stylistic ethics is not a single action but rather a way of looking at things through my own prudence as well as others' benefit or self-interest.

Kenneth Burke, in *A Rhetoric of Motives* (1962), posits internally linked binaries as "transformanda," pairings that simultaneously suspend neither and both of their constituents.[5] Like "terms for transformation in general," then, prudence and benefit must not "be placed statically against each other, but in given poetic contexts usually represent a development from one order of motives to another" (Burke 1962, 11). Indeed, Burke's emphasis on "order[s] of motives" implies that prudence-benefit properly defines stylistic ethics. Ethics is nothing, after all, if not a judgment about motives and their consequences.[6] Furthermore, because this motival development occurs "in given poetic contexts"—that is, within/through language-in-use—Burke leaves open the possibility that rhetorical action produces (or causes to be produced) the linking of and negotiation between one order of motives and another, between phronesis and sumpheron. As my pedagogy illustration suggests, it is the identification of my goals with the needs of others that activates the prudence-benefit binary and that, consequently, makes possible an assessment of ethical rhetoric. Both teacher and student writers come to recognize the other's investment in a particular course of action—the rote memorization of stylistic strategies, for example—and thereby leave the other (and themselves) with some opportunity for (inter)(re)acting in rhetorically ethical ways.

We might schematize style's transformandum, then, through the (pairs of) terms proposed by the authors I cite, remembering that the pairs are both internally linked and bound to other (internally linked) pairs. Rhetoric-philosophy, for instance, represents one aspect of the tranformandum but should not be isolated from decorum-manners or exposure-discipline.

phronesis	sumpheron
prudence, practical wisdom	benefit, advantage
rhetoric	philosophy
aesthetics and taste	ethics and morality
decorum	manners
literature	society
exposure (non resistance)	discipline (resistance)
self	other

Assuming stylistic practices do enact the prudence-benefit dynamic, the third canon should lay bare the discursive means adequate and appropriate to ethical (inter)(re)action. And yet, even if an ethics of style might be so identified, scholars and teachers of writing—as well as writers of all stripes—should still return to my epigraph and Lanham's definition of style. Does it or can it conform to the dynamic I outline? Or more directly, how do we address the questions begged by the definition, and come to embody the "authentic social duty" that Lanham ascribes to the third canon and its pedagogy (1974, 124)? This duty is fulfilled only if it "enhances clear communication" as well as the "selfhood" of citizen-communicators. While Lanham takes up these two principles, it is not self-evident how/why they necessarily define stylistic ethics, especially if style embodies ethics through taste. The principles seem to have little or nothing to do with the sort of aesthetic Nietzsche, and Lanham himself, describes. Furthermore, the singularities within the definition—"authentic," "clear," "selfhood"—(seem to) work against the multiplicity of roles and contexts that Lanham establishes as style's distinctive demesne. Perhaps he attempts, as many stylisticians before him, to have his cake and eat it, too, or perhaps his reliance on these terms challenges the belief that singularity is the core characteristic of clarity, authenticity, and selfhood. Is there a compelling reason for defining these concepts as unities, as tolerating no multiplicity of meaning or function?

Rather than situate this question within the traditional debates surrounding style, Lanham would have us accept that the canon's own multiple character necessarily demands multiple notions of clarity and authenticity. Of what use is rhetorical judgment, after all, if it cannot be enacted? How could rhetorical judgment exist outside the possibility of, and means for, stylistic enactment? Lanham champions multiplicity throughout *Style*, and he attaches both stylistic and pedagogical importance to the interplay that Nietzsche describes: "Style as visible, selfconscious, opaque, forms part of a curriculum whose center will be self-consciousness, whose rock-bottom is an awareness of boundary conditions" (1974, 132; emphasis added). It is on the rhetorical margins, where prudence-benefit and taste-ethics challenge and interpenetrate, that style is most potent. The reason that until recently writing scholars and (especially) teachers have generally been reticent to accept this proposition lies in long-standing attitudes about what discourse, particularly writing, is and represents.[7]

Post-process theories of writing have gained acceptance within rhetoric and composition only in the last decade or so, and it is only through the changes they have wrought that my questions seem appropriate, even commonsensical. While differences exist among these theories, few adherents would dispute that "(1) writing is public; (2) writing is interpretive; and (3) writing is situated" (Kent 1999, 1). Because, however, so much yet needs to be done to bring writing pedagogy and treatments of style into full accord with these principles, Lanham's assumption of them (the principles) represents a defining choice, literally and figuratively.

Without claiming any superiority for this or that post-process theory, we can apply Thomas Kent's three criteria directly to the ethics developed in *Style*. Three interlinked forces in flux, the criteria shift attention from the unity-multiplicity debate to a world inhabited by necessary difference and discrepancy, the realm of the contingent and the rightly rhetorical. Whatever truths or realities exist in the world, rhetorical action cannot grant unmediated access to them; the best that discourse may provide is the means for understanding the world and oneself. Understanding—knowledge at work in new contexts—comes for Lanham in the form of taste, situated and public interpretation, the social custom on which Burke and others rely so heavily and which the Sophists favored over Plato's dialectical rhetoric.[8] The ethics of stylistic rhetoric could, therefore, never be defined as an absolute way of thinking or acting without violating the fundamental character of writing itself, whether taken as a phenomenon or as a habit of mind.

Let us return to Lanham's 1974 definition, then, through the lens of Kent's 1999 criteria, a stylistic subversion of chronology that proves revealing. Stubbornly unitary on their face, the trio of terms I cite still seems unchanged. Drawing on a tradition that has been largely abandoned, they appear to have little to do with a postmodern—some would say "posthuman"—understanding of the world. Yet what if, at least for a moment, Lanham's terms are considered, not simply through the lens of post-process writing theories but as being the rhetorical consequences of those theories? In other words, what if we envision the terms as indices for what style makes possible and, consequently, what the third canon brings to any explanation of rhetorical ethics? Style might, according this view, be the means by which clarity, authenticity, and selfhood are created and maintained in a world that would otherwise leave interlocutors radically destabilized, perhaps too imbalanced even to (presume to) act. These social(izing) qualities would be the result of, and the primary benefit accruing to, stylistic action, not merely archaic fictions with which contemporary scholars have been able to dispense—and perhaps too easily at that.

The philosopher Donald Davidson has long been known for suggesting that, as often as not, what seems the case is the case—at least for those not caught up in theoretical intricacies, for ordinary people living ordinary lives. One of his most incisive illustrations of that principle involves how someone might come to believe a pot of water is boiling: "My view . . . is that if someone perceives that the pot is on the boil, then the boiling pot causes him or her, through the medium of the senses, to believe the pot is on the boil. It may be that sensations, perturbations of the visual field, sense data and the like, are also always present, but this is of no epistemological significance" (1999b, 135).[9] Those investigating style might likewise wonder if, while writing, I perceive that I am a certain someone (self) and I perceive the meaningfulness and accuracy of what I say (authenticity and clarity), why are those perceptions not necessary and useful beliefs? That they do not, or cannot, exist outside the rhetorical moment matters less than whether their existence might be understood through and embodied by stylistics, whether they are the rhetorical consequence of a situation's style. Philosophers and theorists will continue to investigate the nature of the self and what could or should be meant by the term authenticity, but within the realm of stylistic ethics, Lanham's treatment seems the most viable precisely because it does not dispense with the attitudes that style engenders in writers and readers alike.

Bolstered by the prudence-benefit dynamic, Lanham's concept of taste stands as an index of how effectively language users assume—take onto themselves as well as fulfill—the stylistic demands of clarity, authenticity, and selfhood in a given context. In short, Lanham supplies the means by which an ethics of style might be judged, tested, or reconsidered. What he does not, cannot manage is a sense of what might replace stable criteria/ values for judgment in the world of stylistic rhetoric. The answer instead lies in my earlier pedagogy illustration, in what teachers and student writers do in their classrooms every day. To teach effectively, I must (re)cast my goals in the form of my students' needs. That principle does not ensure ethical action, for how could I predict beforehand what would/n't be ethical on any given day, in any given classroom? But it does ensure that my students and I are able to work toward an ethics that accounts for everyone's needs while also demanding more from us than simply what we might wish or want for our individual selves. For example, if I believe that my goals can benefit students most directly through the memorization of stylistic strategies, the issue will not be settled until we understand, together and alone, that foreclosing other opportunities—which is what rote memorization often does when taken alone—is unethical. Similarly, a stylistic ethics is created the moment a writer puts words to paper or a reader engages a text. It is created in the moment of communication and cannot be taught as one teaches names or dates or geographic features. It is created by/through the interchange between prudence and benefit, between one self and another, between worlds that would otherwise orbit different suns.

* * *

The continual revision of patterns and potentials that drives style occurs only with feedback, both other and self-produced, for its (style's) effects and judgments about them are what constitute perspective over time and across contexts. Stylistic feedback allows interlocutors to understand language situations through what Kent calls "hermeneutic guessing," a contextual revision of our thoughts about which patterns fit which potentials (1993, 14). Presuming that hermeneutics (a theory of interpretation) stands at the center of rhetorical patterning, Kent contends that discourse cannot be theorized without also being distorted, that the only viable means for gauging writing or speech is a description, however tentative, of what occurs as interlocutors interact in an individual context. Narratives of this sort are necessarily incomplete, involving as they do the analyst's own stylistic (read: interpretative) choices, but Kent's paralogic theory accepts its own provisionalism as a necessary precursor to meaning making. That is, the theory posits that meaning is generated through the disjunctions and consequent tensions between or among words.

In this way Kent does for meaning what Lanham does for ethics, leveraging the ready-built multiplicity of the rhetorical situation. Although Kent's approach precludes meaning from being stored within words, I suggest that the meaning (making) he describes is accessed through style, which determines what gets written, in what ways, and for what reasons. When I encounter Kent's repeated use of "guessing" and "guesswork," for example, I do not construct meaning only from individual words in isolation. Every use after the first reinforces a pattern of polyptoton (repetition of forms or cases) that invites me to (re)consider (1) whether and why the root guess- might be more significant than others used less frequently in his book; and (2) whether, according to context, guess- in its ordinary meaning is all that Kent in fact expresses through the strategy. In short, to make sense of Kent's text, I must ask why he might have used this specific set of words in these specific ways. While the self-conscious enactment of style provides decided advantages, Kent's polyptoton need not be purposeful or exist for precisely the reasons that readers imagine. The asking of the question is the immediate goal of stylistic awareness because it (the asking) sensitizes the questioner to the likelihood that X or Y be the case. Words' individual uses are always potentially meaningful, of course, but the complex they form when taken as a group reveals even more about Kent's (making of) meaning, the situation those words both create and respond to.

Assuming Lanham's theory of taste works as promised, something like I describe should occur not only with semantic judgments but also with ethical ones. The confluence of phronesis and sumpheron, however, does not automatically follow from the pair's potential for integration through judgment or ethical action. Moreover, their transformandum undermines assumptions about the ways in which judgments get made. How do I judge what remains in flux? Which rhetorical or ethical criteria could possibly generate and organize my response to an ever-changing stylistic performance? Lyotard maintains that ethical evaluations of this kind must be made "without criteria": "[Aristotle] recognizes—and he does so explicitly in the *Rhetoric,* as well as in the *Nicomachean Ethics,* that a judge worthy of the name has no true model to guide his judgments, and that the true nature of the judge is to pronounce judgments, and therefore prescriptions, just so, without criteria. This is, after all, what Aristotle calls prudence. It consists in dispensing justice without models" (Lyotard and Thébaud 1985, 25–26).

Judgment comes without guidelines, in the rhetorical moment, because those things that might lead to predictable judgment are occluded or shut out. The dynamism of rhetorical (inter)(re)action stands apart because "[o]ne does not know whom one is speaking to; one must be very prudent; one must negotiate; one must ruse; and one must be on the lookout when one has won" (43). Because style puts everything into play—selfhood, authenticity, and so forth—stability comes only in the necessity for judging. Writers-readers must judge styles, motives, consequences, and as Lanham reveals, this process of evaluation teaches us what it means to, in Lyotard's words, "negotiate . . . on the boundaries" (43).

Lester Faigley, building on these and other principles, concludes that what remains for prudence and, therefore, rhetorical ethics is "a matter of recognizing the responsibility of linking phrases" (1992, 237). In this way, Faigley suggests, "Lyotard relocates ethics in the material practices of reading and writing." The pragmatic actions of writers-readers are an ethics, serve contextually to define that which is just or unjust. Lyotard (and presumably others) "would not have writers look to an external theory of ethics but would encourage them to consider the implications of their linkages" (238). Lyotard's theorizing thereby "points to a missing ethics through the activities of composing, for all are involved in linkage" (239). In *Just Gaming* (Au Juste), Lyotard admits what Faigley calls "the contradictoriness of his position" (233):

> [I]f one remains within these [language] games (the narrative, the denotative, or any other) that are not prescriptive, the idea of justice does not have to intrude. It intervenes inasmuch as these games are impure. By which I mean something very specific: inasmuch as these games are infiltrated by prescriptions. . . . To the extent that these language games are accompanied by prescriptions . . ., then the idea of justice must regulate these obligations. (Lyotard and Thébaud 1985, 96–97)

Lyotard moves beyond Faigley's characterization, however, suggesting that while "there is first a multiplicity of justices, each one of them defined in relation to the rules specific to each game . . ., [j]ustice here does not consist merely in the observance of the rules; as in all games, it consists in working at the limits of what the rules permit, in order to invent new moves, perhaps new rules and therefore new games" (100).

The obligation produced by linkages is not only to oneself or other thinking, feeling human beings but also to the linkages themselves. By mobilizing the elementary patterns of discourse that drive composition, style provides the means by which the implications and probable outcomes of linkages are both accessible and malleable. Such an ethics of style opens the possibility that those who speak might find a way to be heard and makes the third canon the generative engine for communication in a postmodern world.

Charles Paine agitates for precisely this approach in the classroom, what he calls a "responsible pedagogy" based on individuals' "permeability" and openness to the dissonance inherent in postmodern culture (1999, xiv, xiii). Living with chaos and conflict—the discourses and power relations that create them—is best managed through stylistic self-awareness, the acceptance that style implicates not only selfhood but also society because, in Lanham's words, rhetoric "allocates emphasis and attention," underlies "the construction and allocation of attention-structures" (1993, 61, 227). Paine underwrites and extends this conclusion: "It would be far more valuable to allow our students to, as Lanham puts it, 'mix motives,' oscillating between the critical distance of the intellectual and 'the getting things done' motive—or even the profit motive—of the everyday world" (Paine 1999, 201). As with the world it intersects, stylistics must accept the variability of human motives, of unknowable (or at least inexpressible) feelings and attitudes, and focus on that which it does, and can do, effectively: remind each of us that her capacity to act through rhetoric depends on how her (inter)(re)action affects others' capacity to do likewise. Above all else, her obligation is not only to speak, not only to be heard, but also to enable in good faith and with goodwill others' speaking and being heard, however various the motives or potential outcomes.

As rhetoric-composition has matured, it has become increasingly common for its practitioners to refer to rhetorics (in the plural) as a gesture toward the presence of divergent attitudes about and formulations of rhetorical theory. One popular textbook, for example, bears the title *Everything's an Argument,* privileging argumentation as the informing principle behind rhetorical action, whereas the title of the rhetorical reader *A World of Ideas* implicitly argues that discursive action is driven not by the world per se but rather by the world of intellectual inquiry and discovery.

The vantage points offered by various rhetorical theories are complementary even in their conflicts, however, precisely because they (re)inscribe the multithreaded history of rhetoric from its birth in the ancient Greece of 2,500 years ago. In that helter-skelter world of burgeoning literacy and rational inquiry, ars rhetorike was far from monolithic, much less unitary. It is only right, then, that rhetoric-composition, the contemporary discipline that has sprung from those roots, should begin to reexamine the multiple character of its history and tradition.

Likewise, the ethical dimension of style need not be expressed as a unitary precept or principle. The exigencies of context intermingle with the values that may (or may not) be shared by author and audience, intermingle in ways that thwart formalized inquiry. What remains is not to accede to a radical relativism that allows any discursive action providing it might somehow be excused by tenuous arguments or rationalizations. On the contrary, the intermingling of exigency and value is precisely what rhetoric controls through language, Lanham's "'economics' of human attention-structures," and nothing short of willful blindness could produce a stylistics that is not, at heart, built on that principle (1993, 227). Stylistic rhetoric draws on that intermingling to provide both writers and readers with bottom-up opportunities for making prudent discursive choices. Ethics, in this view, becomes the direct consequence of rhetorical action, the language choices interlocutors make/enact through stylistic strategies. The obligation I assume to my readers comes, therefore, as a result of my making discursive choices, and it is the character of that obligation that determines the ethics of our discursive interaction, the consequences of my working through words in the world: "[E]thics is also the obligation of rhetoric. It is accepting the responsibility for judgment. It is a pausing to reflect on the limits of understanding. It is respect for diversity and unassimilated otherness. It is finding the spaces to listen" (Faigley 1992, 239).

17

STYLE AS A SYSTEM: TOWARD A CYBERNETIC MODEL OF COMPOSITION STYLE

Drew Loewe

As a writer and composition teacher, I have always been intrigued—and nearly as often bedeviled—by style. In trying to conceptualize and explain style, I've often felt like Potter Stewart trying to define obscenity; I can't quite say what style is, yet I feel confident I know it when I see it. Using present theoretical models of style, I have found myself clinging to atomized descriptions that tend to focus on the writer's choices, on speculations about the writer's personality, or on the marriage of form and content. Too often, I have been left with the feeling that something was missing, that present theoretical models of style fail to fully describe style's dynamic nature or account for how it works. We need a new model.

What should a new theoretical model of style look like? In my view, it should have three characteristics. First, a new theoretical model of style should be dynamic. It should conceptualize style as a system of processes and relationships, not as a set of static properties belonging to the individual members of what I will call "the triad"—the writer, the audience, and the text. To do justice to style's complexity, a new model should avoid privileging any one member of the triad over the other members. A new model of style should also help to demystify the ineffable sense that, in style, the whole of writing is more than the sum of its parts. Finally, by grounding the typical impressionistic terms used to describe style in a well-developed body of theory, it should better explain how style works.

In mapping what a new theoretical model of style might look like, I will draw from an interdisciplinary body of theory on processes and relationships, namely, systems theory and cybernetics. This body of theory provides both a framework and a vocabulary for describing how, through exchanges of information, members of a system interact with and affect each other dynamically. As a result, this body of theory could point the way toward the recursive and holistic conversation our discipline should be having about composition style. This essay is a first step toward mapping the outline of a cybernetic model of style. Drawing on general systems theory, second-order cybernetics, and the three related concepts of emergent properties, reflexivity, and autopoiesis, I theorize about how a cybernetic model of style could move beyond existing models and enhance our understanding and teaching of style.

SYSTEMS THEORY AND STYLE

So what exactly is a system? Systems theorist Gerald Weinberg contends that, "as any poet knows, a system is a way of looking at the world" (1975, 51). For Weinberg, a system is a "point of view of one or several observers" (62). For Stafford Beer, founder of management cybernetics, "a system is not something presented to the observer, it is something recognized by him [or her]" (1980, 67). The constructivist epistemology underlying systems theory can help us to develop a better theoretical model of prose style because it can help us to account for the reciprocal interrelationships among writers, texts, and audiences that we describe when we talk about style. For example, as Weinberg notes, we often talk about systems "having" purposes, but "purpose" really describes sets of dynamic relationships between observers and systems, not fixed qualities that systems possess (57). That is, instead of understanding a system's purpose as a discrete quality that the system "has," we should instead understand purpose as a description of how the observer relates to the system (57). Weinberg offers an example to illustrate how a system's purpose is a description of how observers relate to that system: To a motorist, the purpose of General Motors is to manufacture cars; to a scrap metal dealer, GM's purpose is to produce scrap metal; to a stockholder, GM's purpose is to generate profits (57).

Systems theory recognizes and accounts for the interactions between observers and what they observe; in short, it provides a rich way of looking at the world that examines the looking as much as it examines the world. Composition theorists and teachers need this rich way of looking at their world, a way that does justice to the true complexity (and, indeed, the messiness) of the writing and reading processes. Unfortunately, in examining style, we often grasp at audience expectations, speculations about the writer's personality, textual features, or impressionistic labels. In doing so, we may treat style as a static list of properties possessed by, for example, certain writers or texts, instead of as a relationship among the members of the triad of writer, text, and audience.

By viewing systems as sets of relationships rather than as containers holding collections of fixed properties, we can avoid the pitfalls of essentialist thought. Weinberg illustrates this point by using another concept from systems theory: emergent properties; emergent properties are what make a system as a whole greater than the sum of the system's individual parts (1975, 60). Weinberg notes that some theorists contend that emergent properties do not exist in a system's parts, but develop in the whole; other theorists dispute this, contending that so-called emergence is simply another label for a predictable "vital essence" that can be found within the system's parts (60). Weinberg acknowledges that theorists on both sides of this debate can be correct, but he argues that they go awry when they speak in absolutes, "as if emergence were 'stuff' in the system, rather than a relationship between system and observer" (60). For this reason, Weinberg concludes that, while the simplifications of essentialist thought may "[serve] us well at certain times, on a certain scale of observation, and for certain purposes," essentialist thought is ultimately too limited because it fails to account for "the human origins of our models, words, instruments, and techniques" (61). The concept of emergent properties—how the whole is more than the sum of its parts—is crucial to a new theoretical model of style because it helps us to move beyond the essentialisms inherent in prevailing theories of style.

In his classic essay, "Theories of Style and Their Implications for the Teaching of Composition" (1965), Louis Milic describes three prevailing theories of style. These are rhetorical dualism, which holds that ideas exist apart from words and can be ornamented in a variety of ways to suit the occasion; psychological monism or individualism, in which style is seen as the expression of the writer's unique personality; and aesthetic monism, which is an organic theory holding that form and content are inseparable (67). While these three models can be expedient in the classroom, they can also approach essentialism. They fail to account fully for style's relational nature because they privilege one member of the writer-text-audience triad over the others and treat style as discrete, isolable "'stuff' in the system," instead of as an inescapably contextualized three-part relationship. For example, rhetorical dualism, with its emphasis on moving an audience to do or feel something, tends to privilege audience over the writer and the text, treating style as a menu of choices designed to achieve certain effects. Similarly, psychological monism neglects both text and audience in favor of the author by asking students to plumb personalities (theirs or others') to find the wellspring of style. Finally, aesthetic monism neglects both audience and writer by focusing on the text as a closed box students can take apart to learn how it was built.

To better account for the interrelationships and connections among writer, text, and audience, style must be theorized holistically, as a system in which each member of the triad affects—and is affected by—the other members. The following metaphor, offered by David Morley, expresses how systems theory can inform a fully developed model of prose style:

> To draw a carp, Chinese masters warn, it is not enough to know the animal's morphology, study its anatomy or understand the physiological functions of its existence. They tell us that it is also necessary to consider the reed against which the carp brushes each morning while seeking its nourishment, the oblong stone behind which it conceals itself, and the rippling of water when it springs to the surface. These elements should in no way be treated as the fish's environment, the milieu in which it evolves or the natural background against which it can be drawn. They belong to the carp itself. . . . The carp must be apprehended as a certain power to affect and be affected by the world. (1992, 183)

Like Weinberg's poets, artists who wish to draw the carp must learn a new way of looking at the world; in other words, they must learn to see the entire system of interrelationships before they can, for the first time, really see the carp. In this sense, the carp is an emergent property within the context of the system rather than a priori "stuff." Similarly, to understand style, composition teachers and students must also learn a new way of looking at the world, a way that acknowledges style's dynamic, interrelational nature. Joseph M. Williams (1986) argues that what we teach about style derives from what we believe that we can substantiate and demonstrate (i.e., in texts), but judgments about what we can substantiate and demonstrate depend on the "categories, processes, and relationships in our theory" (176). Theorizing style as the dress of thought, the expression of an individual personality, or as the marriage of form and content privileges one member of the triad over the others, much like an artist trying to draw the carp without understanding all the interlocking processes that affect and are affected by the carp—indeed, that are the carp.

Much of our discipline's talk about style reduces style to "'stuff' in the system." For example Teresa Thonney (2003) emphasizes the text when she declares that "good writing has three characteristics: clarity, precision, and elegance" (xi; emphasis added). E. B. White highlights the qualities a writer brings to the relationship; for White, style is such "an expression of self" that "style is the writer" (Strunk and White 1999, 69, 84; emphasis in original). Prioritizing audience, Edward P. J. Corbett and Robert J.

Connors (1999) shifts the focus to style's rhetorical function as a means of persuasion (338). These and similar views of style do not account fully for style's relational and emergent nature. When we make stylistic judgments, what we judge is not the forensic status of the text as proof of a meaning already made or lost, a voice present or absent, or persuasion won or botched; rather, we judge the status of the interrelationships among the triad. Without seeing the whole system as a set of interrelationships, we confound ourselves—and our students—by using a possessory vocabulary to describe what is really a relational judgment. For example, when we describe a student's paper as "clear," or "persuasive," we are not simply identifying the paper as possessing certain characteristics of clear or persuasive texts. What we are really describing are the interrelations among members of the triad and how these interrelations make and affect meaning. Unfortunately, much of our present vocabulary tends to treat style as properties held by the audience, the writer, or the text (e.g., Does the audience have certain interests or prejudices that make it more or less receptive to certain rhetorical options? Does the writer have a satiric wit? Does the text contain formal features such as Latinate diction?).

Writing that Thonney would judge clear and elegant, that White would judge as evidence of a unique authorial voice, or that Corbett would judge as persuasive "has" none of these qualities outside the interrelationships among members of the triad of writer, text, and audience. Richard Lanham (1974) highlights this dynamic process when discussing style's sacred cow, clarity: "clarity is not any single verbal configuration but a relationship between writer and reader" (32). Expanding on this notion of clarity as connection, T. R. Johnson (2003) strives for a stylistic pedagogy that teaches students to be sensitive to the "latticework of interconnected moments" that "give rise to parallel experiences of connection between reader and writer"; this "intersubjective experience" is what we characterize as clarity (37). Cybernetics, a branch of systems theory, highlights the dynamics of the interrelationships among the members of the triad and can point the way to the new theory of style that composition needs.

CYBERNETICS AND RELATIONAL CHARACTERISTICS

What is cybernetics? Systems theorists Francis Heylighen and Cliff Joslyn (2002) define cybernetics as "the science that studies the abstract principles of organization in complex systems" (155). Cybernetics is an "inherently transdisciplinary" science whose "reasoning can be applied to understand, model and design systems of any kind: physical, technological, biological, ecological, psychological, social, or any combination of those" (155). Indeed, cybernetics has even been used as a conceptual model to explain seemingly nonscientific, aesthetic processes; for example, philosophy professor Ervin Laszlo (1973) has applied cybernetics to the aesthetic problems inherent in studying the creation, performance, and appreciation of music.

Cybernetics theorizes about how systems interact and operate by using three types of informational loops: negative feedback loops, positive feedback loops, and feedforward loops (Porter 1969, 5–6; Heylighen and Josyln 2002, 163). Of these three types of informational loops, the first two involve the concept of feedback. The principle of feedback has been called "one of the most fundamental in life and in many processes and systems that man has devised" (Porter 1969, 14). Feedback arises when a system uses information about the results of its processes to alter the processes themselves; stated another way, it is "the influence of output back on input" (Richardson 1991, 128). Similarly, composition research has long recognized that writing should be conceptualized as a complex, recursive process rather than a simple, linear progression. This recursive process is rooted in varieties of feedback—the writer oscillates back and forth between planning and drafting, exploration and reformulation, using the results of each to affect the other.

Negative and positive feedback loops differ in how they use the results of the system's processes to affect the processes themselves. In a negative feedback loop, the system compares its ideal output or behavior with its actual output or behavior, and the difference is used to constrain the actual to bring it more in line with the ideal (Porter 1969, 8). An example of a negative feedback loop is the Federal Reserve's adjustments to the interest rate to affect the behavior of the national economy (14–15). A positive feedback loop is exactly the opposite. In a positive feedback loop, the system's output facilitates and accelerates input of the same type that produced it; examples of positive feedback loops include returns on investments, arms races, and the spread of viral epidemics (Heylighen and Joslyn 2002, 162).

Feedforward loops differ fundamentally from feedback loops because, in a feedforward loop, information is used to affect the results of the system's processes before, not after, those processes occur. Unlike in feedback loops, where the system uses the results of what has already happened to influence the system's future behavior, in a feedforward loop, the input is monitored, controlled, and adjusted before it enters the system (Foster 1969, 269). For example, in a manufacturing process that requires a specified amount of moisture, the manufacturer will monitor the moisture content of the raw materials so that it can add water if necessary (269). Thus, the aim of feedforward control is, at the outset, to prevent or reduce deviation from the system's ideal state. In composition, style has often been theorized as a form of feedforward control, namely, the writer's choices made with the aim of preventing or reducing deviation from a defined ideal state, such as standard academic discourse, concision, or vigorous prose.

From its inception in the 1940s, cybernetics sought to explore similarities between living systems and machines (Heylighen and Joslyn 2002, 156). In the early 1970s, a so-called second order of cybernetics arose (156). The impetus to this second order was a desire by cyberneticists to move away from mechanistic approaches to cybernetics and to account theoretically for the role of the observer in modeling and understanding systems (156). Second-order cybernetics recognizes that the system is "an agent in its own right, interacting with another agent, the observer" and that "the results of observations will depend on" this interaction; in short, "the observer too is a cybernetic system, trying to construct a model of another cybernetic system" (156–57). Because it foregrounds the role of the observer, second-order cybernetics emphasizes the concept of reflexivity, a concept that postmodern theorist N. Katherine Hayles describes as "the movement whereby that which has been used to generate a system is made, through a changed perspective, to become part of the system it generates" (1999, 8). As Hayles explains, "feedback can loop through the observers, drawing them in to become part of the system being observed" (9; emphasis in original). In other words, our models are a result of who we are and who we are is a result of our models. Any particular lens through which we view style (as the dress of thought, as the hallmark of a unique personality, or as inextricably tied to content) results from sets of assumptions about language and reality, which assumptions in turn affect not only what we see and what we value about style, but also what we don't see or value.

Finally, second-order cybernetics incorporates the concept of autopoiesis, or self-production (Heylighen and Joslyn, 2002, 161). Autopoiesis arises from the self-organizing "mutually constitutive interactions between the components of a system" (Hayles 1999, 11). Autopoietic systems are "autonomous, self-referring and self-constructing" (Cohen and Wartofsky 1980, i) and are part of a "concatenation of processes"

(Maturana and Varela 1980, 80). Thus, as Hayles points out, "the auto-poietic view shifts the center of interest from the cybernetics of the observed system to the cybernetics of the observer" (11). The second-order cyberneticist realizes that, as Hayles puts it, "we do not see a world 'out there' that exists apart from us. Rather, we see only what our systemic organization allows us to see" (11). The constructivist epistemology behind this shift carries important implications for a new theoretical model of style. Reflexivity and autopoiesis can help us to theorize style as a contextualized, mediated, relational way of seeing within a complex, dynamic network of interactions, interactions that make the whole of style more than the sum of its parts. In these interactions, each member of the triad—audience, writer, and text—occupies a position of potential flux and changing perspectives.

TOWARD A CYBERNETIC MODEL OF PROSE STYLE

Lanham argues that prose styles are not "neutral, dependable, preexistent objects that everyone sees the same way"; rather, every "prose style is itself not only an object seen but [also] a way of seeing, both an intermediate 'reality' and a dynamic one" (1974, 33). Together, reflexivity—in which the observer interacts with (and therefore is part of) the system observed—and autopoiesis—which examines systems' self-organizing and emergent natures—provide a framework for acknowledging and attempting to map the complex, dynamic flows of information and perceptions among (and within) the triad's members. So how could we redefine style to emphasize its reflexive, autopoietic nature?

As the following figure demonstrates, each member of the triad is itself a system with its own internal dynamics; in turn, each member affects the other members and the "metasystem" as a whole.

The writer is situated (as is his or her audience) within, and affected by, three major forces: the rhetorical situation, kairos, and embodiment.[1] Some definitions are in order here. In defining the first force, rhetorical situation, Keith Grant-Davie (1997) offers a useful modification to Lloyd Bitzer's three-part taxonomy of exigence, audience, and constraints. To develop a more holistic system of communication and meaning making, Grant-Davie expressly adds the rhetor (in composition, the writer); indeed, Grant-Davie contends that "the further one delves into a [rhetorical] situation, the more connections between [the elements of exigence, rhetor, audience, and constraints] are likely to appear" (269–70, 277).

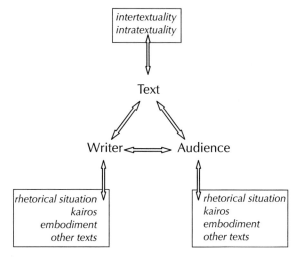

Figure 1.

The second of these forces, kairos, according to Jerry Blitefield, combines both time and place; expanding on temporal concepts such as "right timing" and the "ripe moment" (the framework within which kairos is often understood), Blitefield argues that because physical places come into and out of different states of being, they are themselves kairotic; thus, "kairoi come into existence in places, as places" (2002, 72–73; emphasis in original). As a result, "kairos is not simply a matter of rhetorical perception or willing agency: it cannot be seen apart from the physical dimensions of the place providing for it" (73). In writing, the writer and audience not only consider kairos but also help to define and construct that kairos—each is affected by and affects the other, in time and space.

The third of these forces is embodiment. Building on Elizabeth Grosz's comment that "there is no body as such; there are only bodies," Hayles draws a distinction between the body and embodiment (1999, 196). For Hayles, the body refers to a set of social and discursive practices, a complex of idealized, normative criteria; by contrast, embodiment refers to the actual instantiations of particular individual bodies; these instantiations necessarily vary from the idealized, normative criteria because they are "contextual, enmeshed within the specifics of place, time, physiology, and culture" (196). Discourses of race, gender, sexuality, age, and class all contribute to these sets of specifics and must be taken into account in a fully developed theoretical model of style. In other words, because bodies matter, the matter of bodies cannot be excised—our bodies influence and are influenced by our models of style.[2]

These three forces (rhetorical situation, kairos, and embodiment) combine to shape the writer as a system or way of looking at the world in her own right while she participates in the "metasystem" of the triad. She engages in inescapably recursive and self-making processes by composing, editing, and revising—sometimes doing all three simultaneously. Donald Murray (1980) captures the feel of these interactions: "The writer is constantly learning from the writing what it intends to say. The writer listens for evolving meaning. . . . The writing itself helps the writer see the subject" (7). In the shifting perspectives of these processes, information loops through the writer; she is part of the overall system she observes.

In style, feedforward loops—in which input is adjusted before it enters the system—arise from such elements as diction, genre and format conventions, and, especially in academic writing, the requirements and stated or implied discourse conventions of the assignment. Feedback loops—in which output affects input—arise from intertextuality (the interactions of the writer and the text in relation to other texts, including other iterations of the same text, such as drafts), intratextuality (the ways in which the text's parts relate to each other as perceived by the writer or audience), and audience response (e.g., peer or teacher comments during revision, an imagined or ideal audience, or the writer's own internal process of revising while writing).[3] Similarly, just as the text is shaped by the writer in writing and revision, it is also shaped by intertextuality and by audience response. The audience reads the text in the context of its own "internal organization"; that is, in response to other texts, and within the framework of the rhetorical situation, kairos, and embodiment.

Because second-order cybernetics emphasizes interrelationships rather than individual components, it helps to illuminate the complex dynamics of meaning at work among the triad and offers a fruitful theoretical basis for a new model of style. Like the artist who learns to see the carp as a contextualized set of relationships rather than as an isolated entity, we must learn to consider—and accord equal consideration to—all the members of the style triad holistically and dynamically. In the holistic, dynamic view, style is an ongoing emergent interaction, not a repository of isolated precepts and prescriptions. By highlighting shifting perspectives, the concatenation of processes, and the reciprocal flows of information, reflexivity and autopoiesis provide a rich theoretical framework to account for the complex, messy processes inherent in examining how and why connections or relationships are made among writers, texts, and audiences. Nonholistic models of style are limited because they privilege one member of the triad over the others by, for example, focusing on the author's choices, on the audience's reception of the text, on the writer's personality, or on the textual product itself. As a result, nonholistic models are static and fail to account for the complex interrelationships and contexts at work in style's full arena: writing, revising, and reading. As Lanham argues, "Prose style does not work in a vacuum, except in Freshman Composition. It works in a context. The context makes it what it is" (1974, 28). A cybernetic model of style would help us understand context better.

Style has often been theorized in terms of control, specifically as a feedforward loop initiated by the writer. Under this model, style is the sum of the writer's decisions on diction, tone, subject, and so on. For example, Sandra Schor argues that style should be conceptualized and taught as control, specifically control of meaning and of "one's subject" through thesis development (1986, 204, 208–9). Schor advocates discarding the term "style" as "wholly out of place" in teaching beginning writers and argues that composition instructors should "attend to control first and shelve style temporarily" (204, 211). Martha Kolln, in her *Rhetorical Grammar,* stresses the notion of rhetorical choices enacted by the writer to achieve certain effects on an audience (1999, 183). In her essay "Style as Option," Jane Walpole theorizes style as "the vast area of writer's choice" (1980, 208). In *The Writer's Options: Lessons in Style and Arrangement,* Max Morenberg and Jeff Sommers advocate that students learn to recognize language options to best "make their point" (2003, xv). Joseph Williams contends that "style is defined at least partly by how we can manipulate the categories of meaning through the categories of function and position" (1986, 181). As important as the writer's control may be, it is just one part of a complex system.

Grounded in well-developed theory about how complex systems function and interact, cybernetics provides a way for us to move beyond models of style that overemphasize the writer's choices to the detriment of the other members of the triad. Style is more than a simple feedforward loop in which students select from a menu of options intended to cause certain rhetorical effects on the audience or to comply with received notions like "concision." While writing certainly does involve some aspects of feedforward control to manage exchanges of information (e.g., punctuation, conscious word choices, arrangement), simple feedforward models are static, conceptualizing style as a whole that is exactly the sum of the parts assembled by the writer. Not only do feedforward models tend to reduce style to the icing on the cake, but they also ignore the writer's and the audience's dynamic experiences in producing, shaping, and being shaped by the text. Lanham suggests the reciprocal interaction of writer and text: "The writer controls words. Then they, as his first draft, control him. He then again, as revisor, controls them" (1974, 39). Simple feedforward models fail to account fully for how the text and the audience participate in making meaning, and how meaning may shift, change, or build upon itself to make the whole greater than the sum of its parts in ways not explainable only by appeal to "the vast area of writer's choice." Simple feedforward models only allow us to see style's emergent properties as inherent in the system's parts; in other words, when shifts in meaning occur, we can only explain them as a sort of index to the degree of the writer's control.

Contrary to Schor, Lanham believes that writing courses should push students toward "an acute self-consciousness about style"; indeed, Lanham contends that the way composition courses are usually taught is backwards: "Writing courses usually stress, not style, but rhetoric's other two traditional parts, [inventing] arguments and arranging them. Yet both, implicit in a study of style, emerge naturally only from a concentration on it" (1974, 13–14). From Lanham's perspective, focusing on control of words presupposes "a static, rather than a dynamic, model of verbal composition" in which words correlate to a fixed reality; what's more, focusing on control ignores how "the act of composition . . . oscillates from realism to idealism, and back again" (39). Lanham's "oscillation" provides a possible way for us to describe how style works within the dynamic interrelationships and interactions among the triad. These interrelated inputs, outputs, and processes combine in a series of feedforward and feedback loops through a "system of systems" involving the writer, text, and audience. Johnson describes a similar dynamic process as "interanimating" and strives to awaken students to "the micropolitics of the four-way relations between author, audience, text, and world" (2003, 5, 15). As figure 1 demonstrates, writing and reading are never conducted in isolation—instead, they are activities conducted by multiple interacting systems. This is precisely why present theories of style fail to account fully for how style works; worse, some present theories of style can even trivialize style as merely identifying a certain writer or subject matter (Genova 1979, 320; Sloan 1981, 502).

Not only is style more than a simple feedforward loop, style is also more than a simple feedback loop. Negative feedback loops are inherent in fixed notions of style as unity, coherence, and correctness, as well as in the sets of static edicts that are the hallmarks of current-traditional pedagogy. Cyberneticists sometimes call feedback control "error-controlled regulation" (Heylighen and Joslyn 2002, 163), an apt description of the ideology underlying current-traditional pedagogy. Lists of edicts, coupled with comments like "awkward" or "vague" marked on students' papers by an instructor striving to bring students' writing into compliance with the norms of "college-level English" devalue style, equating it with a simple regulatory device, such as a thermostat.

Prescriptive advice to student writers about style, especially in textbooks, often consists of what Lanham decries as "self-canceling clichés," "a tedious, repetitive, unoriginal body of dogma" (1974, 19) or "folk wisdom and exercises in the psychology of rumor" (1993, 128). For example, the fifth edition of the popular *St. Martin's Handbook,* echoing Strunk and White, exhorts students to, among other things, write concisely, favor simple sentence structures, and eliminate words that do not advance a clear meaning (Lundsford 2003, 701–2). Peter Elbow wants writing to have the "good timing," "personality," and "resonance" of a "real self" and "real voice," all in the name of, as the title of one of his best-known works declares, *Writing with Power* (1981, 292–93). Perhaps echoing Swift's dictum of "proper words in proper places," John Haynes notes that style has been commonly viewed as "a matter of the careful choice of exactly the right word or phrase, le mot juste" (1995, 3). I do not advocate simply repudiating all of the time-tested vocabulary we use to describe style; however, we must realize how judgments about whether a particular mot is juste or not, or whether a text is clear, harmonious, resonant, and powerful (or their opposites) can arise only out of the interrelationships among the triad, not to mention the cultural and historical contexts for reading and interpreting. With a holistic model of style as a system, perhaps we could blow centuries of dust off these prescriptive yet impressionistic terms and, for the first time, understand them according to their relational and emergent characteristics.

Like Lanham, I maintain that style is vital to composition pedagogy; for the same reason, Schor's position that teaching style should be deferred until the instructor decrees that control has been learned seems less fruitful to me because it treats style as an "add-on" to language. A pedagogy limiting the development of students' ideas in the name of control tends to reward bland, "safe" writing—what Lanham calls "neutral expository prose that filters out self" (1974, 116). Lanham wants to move away from the traditional focus on sincerity and authenticity in composition pedagogy and argues that students should be encouraged to experiment with a wide variety of prose styles (118). However, when Lanham argues that a "range of opinions ought to be furnished and surveyed along with a range of styles," and, if a student cannot develop his own opinions, "let him be given some," his approach starts to become too prescriptive (118).[4] With any luck, developing students' awareness of the complexities of the reading and writing processes would obviate or lessen any perceived need to furnish them with styles or opinions to get them started writing. Apart from the dangers inherent in mindless, mechanistic imitation, prescribing styles tends to overemphasize details at the most local level, for example, at the level of word choice, arrangement, and "voice." Prescribing styles fails to provide a deeper understanding of what happens within and outside the text as part of a system affected by, to use just one example, particular cultural and historical expectations of what constitutes coherent or clear prose.

In his venerable *Classical Rhetoric for the Modern Student,* Corbett, a rhetorical dualist, analyzes style in terms of grammatical competence; vocabulary; purity, propriety, and precision of diction; and sentence composition (1990, 339–59). Corbett also provides a comprehensive taxonomy of style, including kinds of diction, length of sentences, kinds of sentences, variety of sentence patterns, sentence euphony, articulation of sentences, figures of speech, and paragraphing (361–69). Corbett's compendium is thorough and his text immerses the student in a wealth of information and examples (especially as to schemes and tropes); however, the rhetorical dualist formulation of style could cause style to be misunderstood as mere ornamentation or special effects. Indeed, Corbett appears to suspect this; just four paragraphs into his 146–page chapter on style, he defends style against the charge that it is merely "the dress of thought" (338). A more serious shortcoming of the rhetorical dualist approach is that it can lead to a tyranny of the audience. If the student is primarily concerned with moving an audience to do or feel something, his writing can slip into legalisms, bombast, or sentimentality; worse, he learns to view writing as he views a can opener—as a utilitarian product assembled for a predetermined, limited purpose.

As I have argued, one of the virtues of a cybernetic model of style is that it would provide a fuller awareness of important interrelationships and contexts than existing models provide. A cybernetic model of style would enable students to see that when style works—when the text seems clear, when the words seem exactly fitted to the occasion, when the writer's voice resonates, or when the audience is persuaded—such judgments describe the state of a complex system of interrelationships and interactions, as mediated and affected by the observer's conceptual model, her way of looking at the world. This awareness could not only encourage students to take risks and to experiment with their writing, but could also make revision and editing more mindful. A cybernetic model of style would provide a more holistic view and a richer understanding of what happens when texts are made and read. This could empower students to examine the dynamic forces at play in the production and reception of texts, rather than simply exhorting them to, for example, "be clear" and "avoid the passive voice," as if being clear and avoiding the passive voice were ends in themselves (or, indeed, even cognizable at all) outside the context of the triad.

Style is more than a writer choosing particular words for particular effects or, as Elbow, the psychological monist, would have it, striving for a particular voice. Milic, a rhetorical dualist, argues that "if style is the expression of the student's mind and personality," we as teachers of composition have precious little to do besides offering our students a few exhortations about writing naturally and expressing themselves (1965, 69). By rigorously and consistently foregrounding the role of the observer and by helping students develop strategies that account for all three members of the triad, a cybernetic theory of style would avoid the charges of excessive subjectivity and privileging the writer that can be leveled against psychological monism. Indeed, it is only through heightened awareness of style's systemic nature that students can begin to understand how "style and meaning are inextricably interwoven; they reflect, express and constitute each other" (Genova 1979, 323).

By helping us to map and to understand the interrelationships and exchanges of information at work in reading and writing, a cybernetic model of style will move us beyond the shortcomings of present theoretical models. With a cybernetic model we will, for the first time, have a holistic way to theorize style's dynamic, emergent nature. We will not only know style when we see it, but will also be able to explain what it is and how it works.

18

TEACHING THE TROPICS OF INQUIRY IN THE COMPOSITION CLASSROOM

M. Todd Harper

It has been a little less than thirty years since critical theory began to entrench itself within English departments. And, yet, in those thirty years one of the most central lessons of critical theory, the lesson that inquiry is tropological, that at the bottom of discovery is figurative speech, seems largely ignored in English studies. In part, this is the result of the fact that most English departments focus on the interpretation rather than the production of texts. As a result, scholars and their students often demonstrated the malleability and indeterminacy of language within literary works while writing in an essay form that bought into positivistic assumptions about language and research, that meaning was outside the writer and that language was simply meant to reflect and represent, not shape meaning. Indeed, many of us have found ourselves in the strange position of asking for a clear and concise essay on the slippery nature of writing.

Of course, this is not altogether true. During the 1980s, rhetoricians at the University of Iowa began to examine different forms of inquiry. John Nelson, Herbert Simons, Deirdre McCloskey, and Charles Bazerman, to name a few, broadened inquiry beyond logics, linguistics, mathematics, and statistics to "share a concern for aesthetics, dialectics, politics, and other postmodern grounds of inquiry" (Nelson, MeGill, and McCloskey 1991a, 3). In his contribution to a collection on rhetoric in the human sciences, Nelson identifies several modes of inquiry: logics, poetics, tropics, topics, dialectics, hermeneutics, ethics, politics, and epistemics. Metaphor and narrative, according to Nelson, become as important as logic and mathematics for the discovery of knowledge. For example, Nelson observes that scholars of the poetics of inquiry "confine themselves to comprehending how specific figures of research arise, reproduce, and decline. Tropics of inquiry address overt and patent characters (economic man), models (free market), statistics (significant tests) and other figures of research" (1991, 409). Moreover, these different forms of inquiry frequently complement each other. As Nelson notes, "Often as not, aesthetics and dialectics produce logics and statistics, while ethics and politics govern the use of linguistics and mathematics" (409).

Because this movement was so broad, the pedagogical implications tended to focus on elements outside the relationship between style and inquiry. Theorists of social constructionist pedagogies, such as Bazerman, Paul Prior, and Cheryl Geisler, informed by the rhetoric of inquiry, tended to return to the historical relationship between dialectics and rhetoric. Writing and research was theorized as an "unending conversation" (a term borrowed from Kenneth Burke's *The Philosophy of Literary Form* [1973, 110]). Textbooks such as Bazerman and Priors's *What Writing Does* (2003) or David Joliffe's *Inquiry and Genre* (1998) advanced writing as a dialectical process. On the other hand, the relationship between style and inquiry remained unexplored as pedagogy, unless it was offered as a way for students to examine rhetorical and literary ornamentation in disciplinary writing.

This essay intends to return to the relationship of style and inquiry. Borrowing on the tradition of post-structuralist thought to examine the role of style in inquiry, I seek to develop an understanding of and pedagogy for tropic discovery. As Richard Rorty notes of Jacques Derrida, Derrida's gift is not to read literary texts as a demonstration of the literary nature of language, but rather to read philosophy and other disciplinary texts as literary. In doing so, Derrida locates the formation of meaning within rather than outside the text. Another way to theorize this is through Ian Hacking's declaration that the disciplines have different "styles of reasoning" (1982, 49). In a collection on relativism and rationality, Hacking notes that different forms of disciplinary thinking should be considered the way that we consider different stylistic systems, with their unique claims, reasoning, and evidence. In the first section, I examine Paul Rabinow, whose reflection on his own dissertation research provides a model for student reflection on research. Although Rabinow stops short of calling his experience allegorical, his reader can quickly point to how Rabinow framed his original experience and then reflected on it as an allegorical journey of self-discovery. In the second section, I discuss Cynthia Haynes and Victor Vitanza's juxtaposition of two texts, Han Kellner's "Supposing Barthes's Voice" and audio samples of Roland Barthes called "Sampling Roland Barthes," to extend the metaphor of inquiry as conversation within a musical setting. By slightly shifting the metaphor of research as a conversation, Haynes and Vitanza provide an example of how to play with style and inquiry.

DEVELOPING A TROPIC FRAMEWORK

Before suggesting strategies for teaching style as inquiry, we must first discover for ourselves what stylistic inquiry looks like. Stylistic inquiry appears at the beginning of scholarly discovery and invention, shaping and organizing the research methodology rather than its result. For example, geneticists used the patriarchal metaphor of "master gene" and the cartographical metaphor of "mapping" to investigate the human genome. Both metaphors shaped how these scientists approached and then collected data from the human genome. In fact, as many feminists have noted, including Mary Rosner and T. R. Johnson (1995), "master gene" and other patriarchal metaphors may have cost geneticists involved in the human genome project the ability to see more complex, yet subtle, relationships between the genes.

The difficulty in finding examples of style as inquiry is that we usually treat style from the perspective of reception rather than the production of texts. Far easier is it to discuss the effect of the metaphor "Double Helix" on the investigation of future scientists and readers of James Watson and Francis Crick than to speculate on to what extent Watson and Crick depended on the framework of geometrical metaphors to "comprehend" the structure of DNA. Yet, given their initial approach to researching DNA by constructing highly abstract chemical models, we should not be surprised that they name the structure of DNA with a stable geometric metaphor. In contrast, the "Warped Zipper," the name proposed by a number of scientists at the time, suggested an inquiry into the automatic process of DNA construction and not the product, the wave instead of the particle (to borrow from the metaphors of physics). Clearly, style becomes a way of thinking, as writers use a controlling trope to organize, even generate their material.

James Clifford (1986) provides an interesting description of the role of style in inquiry by locating allegory in ethnographic writing. It should be of no surprise that anthropologists, who investigate "other" cultures—that is, the "other" to their culture—would use the stylistic trope specific to the other. A combination of the Greek words allos (the other) and aggorein (to speak publicly—in the agoria), allegory is the telling of one tale while speaking another. A science fiction movie about the conflict between a sadistic, totalitarian empire (aptly described as the dark side) and a federation of rogue states becomes an allegory of the struggle between good and evil. Allegories tell two tales, one literal, one symbolic, while often speaking to two audiences, one who understands only the literal, one who understands both the literal and the symbolic. What surprises Clifford is that most anthropologists choose to ignore the fact that their ethnographies are allegorical. Instead, they choose to buy into positivistic notions of reality that maintain that the "other" culture and the anthropologist's encounter with the "other" culture can be represented simplistically—that is, one-dimensionally, literally. We often associate allegory with medieval and Renaissance Christian allegory. Sir Gawain's struggle with the Green Knight becomes an allegorical test of his character and ability to maintain his word to the host. Dante's descent into hell becomes a political and social allegory of the sins and betrayals of his time. Much less are we apt to think of allegory outside of religious allegory or within nonliterary texts. Yet, as Clifford observes, "Ethnographic texts are inescapably allegorical," in part because "allegory draws attention to the narrative character of cultural representation, to the stories built into the process itself" (100). Clifford identifies two common types of allegory in twentieth-century ethnography: ethnography as scientific lab and ethnography as personal journey. Because of anthropology's insecurity as a social science, ethnographies often become a testimony to the ethnographer as scientist and ethnography as good empirical methodology. Ethnography as scientific lab tells the tale of legitimizing anthropology while telling the story of another culture. Ethnography as personal journey, on the other hand, narrates self-discovery and awareness in the process of researching another culture. In many ways, it is the secular, academic counterpart of the earlier Christian allegories. Like *Piers Plowman* or *The Fairy Queen,* the anthropologist transforms as he or she journeys out into another culture.

Clifford's observations apply to the reception and production of texts. His principal argument is that "a serious acceptance of this fact [enthnographic texts as inescapably allegorical] changes the ways they can be read and written" (1986, 100). An example of this is Paul Rabinow, who provides an interesting glimpse into the allegorical nature of ethnographic inquiry in *Reflections on Fieldwork in Morocco* (1977). While not itself an ethnography, *Reflections* recounts Rabinow's fieldwork for his dissertation under Clifford Geertz. As a student, Rabinow observes that there are no books on conducting fieldwork, even though fieldwork is what separates the anthropologist from the anthropology student. *Reflections* attempts to fill this gap by recalling Rabinow's experience in Morocco for his dissertation. Rather than the distribution of surveys, questionnaires, and other tools often associated with anthropology, Rabinow discovers that ethnography often involves conversations over coffee, mediating disputes, providing car rides, and running errands for his informants.

The fact that *Reflections* is a reflection on ethnographic fieldwork affords Rabinow the opportunity to unpack much of the symbolic content in his ethnography, while also describing the process of its construction. Several elements within the text strongly suggest that Rabinow approaches his research as an allegorical experience of personal journey. Most notably, Rabinow views the experience within the framework of self-discovery and personal achievement. Even before he leaves for Morocco during the summer of 1968, he notes that fieldwork is what distinguishes the true anthropologist from the student. Ethnographic research, he informs us, becomes a rite of passage that he, having neared the end of his studies, still needed to accomplish. It is a badge of honor, a mark in his armor, requiring a journey into another world. And yet, what results is less Sir Galahad acquiring entrance into the Knights of the Round Table and more the sullen and inward Richard Burton cum King Arthur at the end of Rogers and Hammerstein's *Camelot*. Near the end of the experience, he meditates on "self" and "other" in terms of the anthropologist and his informant. Writing on his last informant, he observes:

> What separated us was fundamentally our past. I could understand ben Mohammed only to the extent that he could understand me—that is to say, partially. He did not live in a crystalline world of immutable Otherness any more than I did. He grew up in an historical situation which provided him with meaningful but only partially satisfactory interpretations of the world, as I did. Our otherness was not an ineffable essence, but rather the sum of different historical experiences. Different webs of signification separated us, but these webs were now at least partially intertwined. But a dialogue was only possible when we recognized our differences, when we remained critically loyal to the symbols which our traditions had given us. By so doing, we began a process of change. (1977, 162)

The Rabinow who has this epiphany is very different than the Rabinow who leaves Chicago for Morocco. However, it is Rabinow's initial approach to ethnography as a personal journey that finally leads him to this realization.

Rabinow provides other details that suggest his allegorical framework. Dates and places take on an added significance. He leaves Chicago two days before Robert Kennedy is shot and two months before the 1968 Democratic convention. He arrives in Paris shortly after the May uprising. These Western revolutions are juxtaposed with a revolution and upheaval taking place within his own circumstances as he begins to understand the other as well as himself as other. The people he meets in Morocco are like those one might meet in any modern allegorical story. The expatriate hotel owner; the small businessman; the thief; the shaman; the religious novice who finds himself other to the world he grew up in, even while wanting to preserve and maintain his culture: all become guides in Rabinow's process of self-discovery. As in an allegorical work of fiction, where they might appear as characters, Rabinow's informants are never directly located within one culture, but rather exist between multiple cultures. They easily move out of one culture and into another, although they are never at home, nor ever accepted in any one particular culture. When one of the informants can no longer answer the anthropologist's questions, he leads Rabinow to the next informant.

By approaching his fieldwork as a journey of self-discovery, Rabinow opened himself up to the possibility of learning something more than the genealogy of a small Moroccan tribe. Rather, he becomes aware that he already lives within a world of symbols and allegorical narratives that can offer up the possibility of discovery within his field and within himself. And this, of course, is among the highest of goals in a good many composition courses. More specifically, when I teach courses in writing in the disciplines, we invariably begin to understand ethnographies in terms of a subtle allegorical dimension, and we then talk about allegory as a system of metaphors, of stylistic "ornaments" that, in fact, are extraordinarily powerful machines for the production of knowledge—knowledge about self and other, of self as other.

PLAY WITHIN THE TROPIC FRAMEWORK

If Paul Rabinow provides us with a glimpse into how a realization of the tropes that inform inquiry can lead to a greater appreciation of the discovery of knowledge, then Cynthia Haynes and Victor Vitanza, editors of *The Soundz of WOOsi Writing* (2000), exploring the relationship between music and writing, demonstrate what it means to play with the tropes that inform inquiry. In their juxtaposition of Hans Kellner's "Supposing Barthes's Voice" and audio files of Roland Barthes in "Sampling Barthes'

Voice," Haynes and Vitanza place the metaphor of inquiry as rhetorical conversation within a musical context.

In *The Philosophy of Literary Form,* Kenneth Burke described rhetorical inquiry as an "unending conversation":

> Where does the drama get its materials? From the "unending conversation" that is going on at the point in history when we are born. Imagine that you enter a parlor. You come late. When you arrive, others have long preceded you, and they are engaged in a heated discussion, a discussion too heated for them to pause and tell you exactly what it is about. In fact, the discussion had already begun long before any of them got there, so that no one present is qualified to retrace for you all the steps that had gone before. You listen for a while, until you decide that you have caught the tenor of the argument; then you put in your oar. Someone answers; you answer him; another comes to your defense; another aligns himself against you, to either the embarrassment or gratification of your opponent, depending upon the quality of your ally's assistance. However, the discussion is interminable. The hour grows late, you must depart. And you do depart, with the discussion still vigorously in progress. (1973, 110)

Even before the initial stages of research and writing, the scholar must become acquainted with the conversation; the particular topic of that conversation at any one particular moment (kairos), the divisions and agreements among the speakers (stasis), and the common topics and proofs (commonplaces). In other words, inquiry occurs within a rhetorical context, rather than in a vacuum.

There are several elements that place Burke's statement within a tradition that views rhetoric in relation to dialectics and yet extends that tradition. By identifying inquiry with conversation, he locates the role of academic discovery squarely within a tradition of rhetoric and dialectics, a tradition beginning with Plato's identification of dialectics as "philosophical argument" and Aristotle's juxtaposition of rhetoric as the antistrophe of dialectics. Inquiry is an exchange between two speakers engaged in a process of defining and redefining a particular topic. By placing his "unending conversation" within the context of the parlor, Burke emphasizes the oral quality of inquiry, most notably its fleeting and temporal nature. As topics within "parlor conversations" are often brief, though heated, so are the topics of inquiry, which too often seem permanent only to be transient. Moreover, the scholar must work within the framework of the "now" in order to participate effectively in the conversation. Finally, his use of the parlor as well as masculine metaphors suggest the upper-class, white male establishment of the academy at that time.

In *The Soundzs of WOOsic Writing,* a special edition of *Pre/Text: Electra(lite),* Haynes and Vitanza deliberately play with the metaphor of the "unending conversation" within a musical setting by juxtaposing audio samples of Roland Barthes's voice with Hans Kellner's "Supposing Barthes' Voice." Seven short audio samples in French are taken from an interview Barthes granted that focused on the relationship between speech and writing. (Interestingly, Barthes's audio clips do not match up exactly with the responses that were printed in the interview.) These audio clips are "samples" in the way that they are fragments taken from a larger interview, and they are also "samplings," audio bits that provide a near musical refrain to the special edition's examination of orality and literacy implicit within the larger discussion of music and rhetoric.

The relationship of the audio to other multimedia pieces in the special edition is especially apparent in Hans Kellner's "Supposing Barthes' Voice." Kellner's multimedia essay is the only other within the collection that directly addresses Barthes and his interest in orality and literacy. Kellner takes up and analyzes Barthes's distinction between fascism that forces the speaker to speak and fascism that silences the speaker. Moreover, the essay is divided into ten parts. Each part includes text and audio recording of the text read by Kellner or Vitanza, in many ways performing the issues of orality and literacy that are addressed. By placing these two multimedia pieces in relation to one another, Haynes and Vitanza create a dialogue in which one informs and explicates the other. As a result, a third text emerges, a text not unlike a musical sampling in rap and hip-hop where two musical pieces, one that is authored by the rapper and one that is borrowed from an earlier source, are placed in relationship between each other.

The back and forth that occurs between the quote and its explication mimics the call and response that occurs in many contemporary musical samplings. On the one hand, Kellner's response is an elaboration and extension of Barthes's quote. Within the context of its utterance, Kellner begins to tease out the paradox in Barthes's identifying speech with fascism. On the other hand, Kellner sets up a dialogue with Barthes's quote, so that the original quote acts as a response within a dialogue about orality and fascisms. Kellner writes alongside, against, and with Barthes. Because this essay is placed within such close proximity of the audio sampling of Barthes, the reader/listener/viewer is allowed the interchange that takes place between a writer and his or her sources—a dialogue, Bruno Latour (33-44) asserts, that most commonly takes place in footnotes and endnotes—within the context of the musical sampling.

What is particularly striking is the way that these two texts extend Kenneth Burke's unending conversation. Like dialogue, sampling is a type of conversation. Yet, several things differentiate it from the parlor conversation that Burke describes. Whereas the parlor conversation is bound by the constraints of time and space—the listener/speaker must engage with the conversation at its present moment; he or she cannot rewind the conversation and engage with its past—sampling plays with time and space. Samples are chosen from previous works to be played and manipulated during the singer's rap. The past is folded into the present; and with current recording technology, the spontaneous play between rapper and sample is then placed on tape. (Think of the difference between early sampling, which was done only at parties or on the street, as opposed to current sampling, which is now almost always heard recorded.) Moreover, the Burkean parlor is primarily grounded in the metaphor of orality. Sampling, on the other hand, incorporates recorded technology in the use of the sample in a dialogue with the singer's voice or the musician's instrument. Finally, sampling brings Burke's conversation into the streets. What the parlor and parlor conversations were to the elite of the 1930s, 1940s, and 1950s, musical sampling is to the urban streets in the 1980s and 1990s.

What is particularly unique about the use of "sampling" for this special edition of *Pre/Text: Electra(lite)* is the role that it gives to Haynes and Vitanza. In Burke's parlor, the conversation focuses on the participants of the conversation. Not much thought is given to the facilitator of the conversation or any other aspects. In contrast, the juxtaposition of the two pieces in *Pre/Text: Electra(lite)* not only place an emphasis on the "authors" of the separate works, Barthes and Kellner, respectively, but also on Haynes and Vitanza as the facilitators of this particular musical dialogue. Likewise, musical sampling not only focuses on the different artists, but also the "DJ" who spins and manipulates the sample to facilitate the conversation between the older recording and the concurrent performance. Indeed, when any text becomes performative, we should not be surprised that the director, actors, and staff become as important, if not more important, than the playwright. Surprisingly, Burke seemed to forget this when he conceived the Burkean parlor.

THE CLASSROOM

Reflection has enjoyed attention in recent composition scholarship. Many compositionists view it as a means for students to gather their thoughts around a particular project or series of projects. Through reflection, students can think at a metacognitive level about the rhetorical and personal decisions that they made in shaping their texts. Reflection can take any form, from a student placing his or her writing within a historical and social context to a personal account of the research and writing process. Most composition scholars have tended to focus on personal reflection. In student research, this is particularly borne out in assignments such as the I-Search paper, where students discuss the sources that they chose, how they discovered those sources, why they chose those sources over others, and how they might use those sources. Although I-Search papers ask the student to record his or her journey, very few students make the observations, such as the intersubjective nature of inquiry, that Rabinow makes. (Granted, students are not expected to reflect on their writing at this level; however, they are often asked to write no more than why they chose their topic, where and how they found a source within the library, and what they learned about their topic.)

Yet, Rabinow's narrative suggests the possibility of placing inquiry within a tropological analysis. For this to occur in the classroom, the teacher must understand and be able to teach the rhetorical and literary nature of language and meaning. It is a project begun by Nietzsche, whose question "What is truth, but a mobile army of metaphors, metonymies, and anthropomorphisms?" set the stage for post-structuralist thinking, most notably Jacques Derrida, who, as Richard Rorty points out, reads philosophy as literature. (In fact, much of the post-structuralist experiment was examining the relationship between rhetorical and literary tropes and language.) Moreover, the teacher must encourage his or her students to reflect on the rhetorical quality of inquiry the way that they would examine the role of metaphor or metonymy in a poem. Finally, the student, with the help of the teacher, must be able to unearth tropes within his or her own investigation into a topic.

Haynes and Vitanza offer a more advanced alternative. Through their selection and arrangement of texts they bring to the forefront writing and research as a conversation. Interestingly, the Burkean parlor became the place within the print edition of *Pre/Text* where writers would respond to readers' comments and concerns. However, they extend that metaphor by placing it within a musical setting. By locating Kellner's essay in relation-ship to Barthes's audio samples, and then by publishing both in a special edition of *Pre/Text: Electra(lite)* examining music and writing, Haynes and Vitanza pick up on the "conversational" quality of musical sampling and the "musical" nature of academic writing. Students who become aware of the tropes that shape their inquiry—or even the tropes that constitute central concepts and topics, such as the "master gene" in genetics—can then begin to exploit, manipulate, and even turn those tropes into other possibilities of research. In the case of "research and writing as conversa-tion," Haynes and Vitanza lead the reader to ask questions, such as what is the relationship between writing and music? what happens to conver-sation when placed within a musical context? what happens when the technology of that conversation is altered? And, of course, all of these sorts of questions quickly lead to close scrutiny of particular features of a text's style.

In conclusion, as writing teachers we must begin to understand and teach the rhetorical nature of inquiry. If we don't, we risk returning our students and ourselves to positivistic notions that maintain a "language as transparent" attitude. Rather, stylistic turning exists at the very heart of all types of inquiry. When a student is able to grasp this, he or she is not only able to understand the importance of rhetorical and literary language in all the disciplines, but also the manner in which style grounds our think-ing. For reflection to be successful at this level, teachers must be able to articulate to their students the role of tropes and inquiry. This means that they must have an understanding of language as primarily figurative, and that these figures inform and shape the creation of knowledge within the disciplines. They must also have an understanding of different forms of inquiry, which, alas, many writing teachers don't have.

19

WRITING WITH THE EAR

T. R. Johnson

When a writer tinkers with the style of a particular sentence, she considers it and its different versions from a reader's point of view. She might read the sentence aloud as she wonders which version sounds best, and, as she does, she bifurcates or doubles, for only when she becomes two can an inner dialogue ensue in which one self offers some words and the other listens and responds (see Murray 1982; Johnson 2003, 52–56). The writer can facilitate this inner dialogue, as Joseph Williams (2002) suggests, and can even anticipate to some degree how readers will experience a particular sentence, if she considers the sentence in the context of various stylistic principles of "clarity and grace." These principles are tools for opening one's ear to one's own prose and thereby building a stronger link to one's reader. But this is only the beginning. In the following pages, I hope to suggest what the ear, when open, can do. And I hope to point the way toward something like an ear-oriented approach to composing.

To open the ear, to write with the ear: these are, I admit, vague, wholly metaphorical goals. But I've begun to wonder about the possibilities that might emerge if I press toward them in a spirit of literalism. I have a hunch that, by exploring these metaphors, floating back and forth between relatively rigorous theoretical reflection about the writer's ear and the more evocative flights of fancy they invite, borrowing and stitching together scraps of academic, poetic, and mystical discourses, I might manage to sensitize my own ear, render it more open, more active—and perhaps enable others to do the same.

More concretely, if the writer is constantly switching into the role of the reader, "listening" to prose in the act of producing it, then I'd like to suppose that the tension between these two roles (writer/reader) might support a yet subtler possibility, an analogous sort of tension between what, at the moment, I want to call the semantic and the auditory. While plenty of sounds have no particular meaning (the buzz of the fluorescent light above me, for example, which I no longer even notice), I'm interested in the possibility that meanings always carry traces of something like sound—that is, an eventlike energy that works on the body, potentially stirring feeling, even inciting movement. As Stephen Katz and Walter Ong have noted, even when we silently read, our vocal chords register tiny movements, perhaps sending signals to the brain and other parts of the body as part of the process of constructing meaning (Katz 1996, 137; Ong 1982, 8). And it is this auditory element in the composing process—meaning's sonic residue or resonance—that has led me to ponder the secret significance of the writer's ear as that which enables one to craft one's prose to move one's audience.

I first began to wonder about the challenge of teaching students to write with their ears when I chanced upon an article published nearly twenty-five years ago in *CCC:* Barrett Mandel's "The Writer Writing Is Not at Home" (1980). In this fascinating but too seldom cited essay, Mandel asks us to imagine how the act of writing proceeds not from consciousness—that screen crowded with the familiar, elaborately codified projections we call "reality"—but from elsewhere, a mysterious domain of intuition and sudden insight which, when we're there, seems to transport us, carry us away from the experience, say, of the chair we're sitting in, the desk we're sitting at, the buzzing fluorescent bulb we're sitting under, and all the other features of the external world that ordinarily take turns holding our attention. I found that I agreed wholeheartedly with Mandel's assertion that the writer, writing, is not at home. But I've never thought of the writer as merely "checked out" or lost in an undifferentiated daze; on the contrary, he may not be at home, but he is intensely focused, wholly absorbed. Where then, I began to wonder, does the writer, writing, go?

I've already noted the movement in which the writer shifts back and forth between the roles of writer and reader, and I think that Mandel might suggest that this regular oscillation enables a broader kind of movement, walking the writer, as it were, to different, changed sorts of perspectives, to new insights and to greater engagement with the movement that is yielding those insights. Mandel might say that listening to prose, opening the ear toward it, can open in turn that mysterious realm of intuitions, sudden insights, and greater meanings. What's more, if the writer's prose is "meaningful" enough, it can spark a roughly corresponding movement in audiences, and precisely this possibility is what writers are "listening for" when they intermittently play the role of the reader. They are listening for places in the text that are potentially powerful moments in the reader's experience of it: words, phrases, sentences, and passages that are sequenced in ways that allow language to leave behind the simple black-and-white of the printed page, to move out into the world to change things, to travel, echo, and amplify as they spread into receptive channels, like sound waves. They are listening for moments that resonate, that vibrate with the potential to lead their drafts forward and also to lead their readers to follow along in agreement. When student writers find them in their drafts, they say things like "This part sounds good—right here, I feel I'm really getting somewhere, making some headway. I want to pursue this idea in my next draft."

In other words, whenever we pause in our writing to switch for a moment to the role of the reader, we aren't so much looking at the letters and words on the page but rather we look through them in search of "fleeting vision-like sensations, inklings of sound, faint brushes of movement," and this activity, "this turning in on itself of the body, its self-referential short-circuiting of outward projected activity gives free rein to these incipient perceptions" (Massumi 2002, 139). When a writer engages issues of style by asking herself questions like "How does this sound?" or "What if I rearranged this paragraph back around the way I first had it?" she is, I think, playing with the sound of her text, manipulating matters of rhythm, tone, balance, repetition, tempo, and so on in the service of her semantic mission, ultimately to conjure the power of her meanings to move people the way music does. She is playing with the tension between the auditory and the semantic. She is, as Mandel would say, not at home, not trapped among the external coordinates of the ego like a boat tied to a dock; and I would add that in the push to create moving prose, to fill her pages like sails with propulsive energy, she is listening for places where her prose seems ready to take wing, to sing. In so doing, she has begun to pass the way of Alice through the looking glass—and into the open ocean of her own ear.

The mysteriousness of all of this is tempered, at least in Mandel's essay, with simple, practical advice for teachers. He recommends that teachers assign what he calls rote writing: "the copying of well-written prose, selected by the student . . . into a copy book" (1980, 376). Rote writing is quite similar, if counterintuitively so, to freewriting, and, in one sense, it's even better, for it allows "the student's whole organism to have the experience of producing mature prose without conceptualizing consciously at all" (376; emphasis in original). Mandel adds that two offshoots of rote writing are parodying and syntactic modeling, for, like freewriting, they create a climate in which the nonconscious phenomenon of powerful intuitions can occur, intuitions into the "general feel" of forceful prose, the "sound" of good writing, and these intuitions can become benchmarks or templates in the backs of students' minds that students can imitate or critically undermine when they draft their own work.

We can further temper this mysteriousness by turning to the history of rhetoric, for the ear's significance was perhaps not so secret to the ancient Sophists, nor, in the modern era, to Kenneth Burke. And of course, generations upon generations of poets have written about it (I'll consider some examples in a moment) and, moreover, plenty of today's students, in a curious blend of the quirky and the commonsensical, comment on its importance in their own composing processes when they say things like, "I like how this sounds." I'd like to explore some of these resources, for the mysteriousness of the ear has kept the field of rhetoric and composition from paying it much attention and, in effect, has almost entirely removed this crucial tool from what we consider the teachable repertoire of rhetorical powers. And then I hope to balance this handful of historical observations with remarks that reopen and rejuvenate the mysterious power of the ear.

SOME BACKGROUND MUSIC: THE EAR IN ANCIENT AND MODERN RHETORIC

When the ancient Sophists first began to teach the arts of rhetoric, they often did so, according to Debra Hawhee (2002), in private *palaestra*—that is, in places where their students also learned wrestling and other sporting activities. The daily activity of these wrestling schools was usually accompanied by someone playing an aulos (a reed instrument akin to bagpipes) to set "the rhythm for all gymnastic exercises," for the rhythms helped to focus the students' minds on their repeated physical movements, so that these movements, after much disciplined repetition, could become refined habits and shape their automatic responses to actual situations (145). These ancient teachers understood, moreover, that music can be motivational: as Hawhee puts it, they understood "that music has . . . [a] transformative capacity . . . that falls outside the category of reasoned, conscious learning, as rhythms and modes invade the soul, and, at times, excite the body to movement" (146). Additionally, they associated particular rhythms and tones with particular moods and, in turn, used background music in the *palaestra* to inculcate a particular ethos or character in the students, perhaps a sense of shared identity or communal belonging.

Beyond the gymnastics, the rhythms of the aulos inevitably flowed into "recitations and sophistic lectures, producing an awareness of—indeed, facilitating—the rhythmic, tonic quality of speeches" (Hawhee 2002, 146). Given this environment, the Sophists, not surprisingly, became keenly interested in the way verbal techniques of balance, repetition, and other quasi-musical, literary effects could promote a strong, inward surge of pleasure in the listener. This pleasure carried a feeling of merger with the collective, a feeling of knowledge that seemed more meaningful than the knowledge developed by strictly rational inquiry or empirical obser-vation—a feeling, finally, that, while rooted in music, was increasingly understood by the Sophists as indispensable to moving an audience with words (see Johnson 2003).

This interest of the ancient Sophists in the power of carefully organized sound to incite feeling and movement—call it e/motion—persists in modern rhetoric. In *A Rhetoric of Motives* (1962), Kenneth Burke describes the way that verbal formality, as such, has a way of inviting the reader/lis-tener to follow the contours of the form, anticipating certain sounds with a slight feeling of increased tension, and, as the anticipation is fulfilled, a corresponding release. Stylized language, he says, subliminally stirs a feeling of "collaborative expectancy," as when, for example, the reader can't help but start "swinging along with the succession of antitheses," get-ting caught up in the rhythm, anticipating its moves. This phenomenon, adds Burke, "this yielding to the form, (58)" actually paves the way for a broader assent to the content, the substance of the position associated with the musical language, and thus style plays a key role in persuading an audience. In short, Burke knew what the Sophists knew: style is more than aesthetic ornament, for it can function as a powerful rhetorical strategy. It can engender, focus, and discharge energy—a sort of textual background music that can buoy and propel the rhetorical enterprise.

I observe this phenomenon every semester. When I introduce my students to various stylistic devices that allow them to shape their sen-tences with attention to balance and rhythm, they nearly always remark that revising along these lines seems to energize them and to make their essays much stronger. One student told me that her efforts to turn her thesis sentence into a chiasmus were giving her so many new ideas for her paper that she felt as if her mind were about to "boil over." Others describe a new sort of immediacy to their prose, as if their writing had come much closer to speech and involved them in the rhetorical situa-tion where, before, they had felt relatively less connected. Some students tell me that, as they read their newly stylized papers out loud, they feel like Martin Luther King or a presidential candidate, for the formalism they've begun to dabble in has unleashed a palpable capacity for rallying and moving audiences. They are learning to stir a feeling of "collaborative expectancy," sentence by sentence, in their readers. They are learning to write with their ears—that is, to use the ear as a studio for designing and testing methods and techniques for moving audiences.

When a writer moves in this direction—toward an active engagement with the ear—he is not simply indulging feelings, but finding a new strength in relation to the whole domain of feeling, a sense of linguistic options and agency that put him, to an extent, in charge of shifting moods, states of mind, and e/motions. He has embarked on a path of empowerment, a movement that registers as exuberance. We might say that he has begun to engage the place where emotions as waves of bodily energy would seem intertwined with the waves of energy that constitute the auditory. He is playing in the dynamic between sounds and semantics. Allow me to digress, to dig into these possibilities a little further, for the issue of emotion has long vexed the field of composition and some new work by Brian Massumi has provided useful means for exploring, in particular, the exuberance my students describe when they discover style and the power of their ears.

BRIAN MASSUMI ON MOVEMENT, AFFECT, SENSATION

Every emotion, Brian Massumi says, is always comprised of two elements, "intensity" and "quality" (2002, 24-33). More specifically, an emotion is an experience that has been qualified, turned into a quality—that is, named and nailed down in the sociolinguistic codes that constitute determinate, intersubjective meaning, the discursive grid of social space. Some part of emotion, however, resists full capture and articulation, and this aspect, being a function of the feeling's strength and duration, is called intensity. This is the dimension of emotion that takes the subject out of him- or herself ("I'm beside myself!") and scrambles to some degree the codes of semantic ordering and control, as in a sigh or an "Ugh!" or a "hmmm" or in the cartoonists' standard (a)signification for angry profanity, "# % @ * X + !!" If quality is essentially information, then intensity is broadly analogous to energy, for intensity belongs to nonlinear processes that feed back or suspend or speed up the established flow of time, engendering tension and release through a rich, vibratory motion all its own, much the way music does. In fact, an emotion's intensity is to its quality just as a song's music is to its lyrics: they do not antagonize each other but instead can amplify or diminish or redirect each other, resonating with each other in an endless variety of ways.

References to singing and music are difficult to resist here, for intensity lives in the ear. More precisely, if touch is the most direct sensory medium for intensity, the ear might be understood as the place where our sense of touch is most acute and refined, for while the skin registers relative degrees of heat and cold, vicissitudes of pressure, simple textures, pain, the joy of an affectionate caress, and perhaps a handful of other basic sensations, the ear goes much farther: it can translate a seemingly infinite variety of waves of energy from the air into equally vast nuances of meaning. The ear, we might say, is the opening through which sound passes into sense, form fuses with content, and otherwise random noises can be reversed to serve the symphony of the semantic.

The ear's potential as the bridge between intensity and quality (for, again, they should not be thought of as simple opposites) seems virtually unlimited: consider the strangely humanoid ears of bats, how these ears allow bats to map miles of caves, their flight organized and guided by musical improvisations and echoing feedback in the dark spaces between the stones. Perhaps ancient poets and Pythagoreans aspired to a similar degree of openness in their ears when they spoke of listening to the music of the spheres as the basis for the intellectual work of describing reality. In the language I've been using so far, such an openness is synonymous with freeing qualities (data) to radiate intensities (energy)—and, as new qualities emerge therein, freeing the intensity in those to discover yet newer qualities, from which yet greater intensities can roll forth and so on, ad infinitum. In the most work-a-day terms of the writing classroom, this is the practice of revision.

This batlike flight into intensity is an activity of which all our senses are capable, but in which the ear leads the way, for, again, the ear is where intensity lives. In fact, the ear, as Joachim-Ernst Berendt notes (1983), is the very first of our senses to begin working/playing, for even in the womb, long before any of the other senses have been engaged, the child hears its mother's heartbeat and soon thereafter can listen to sounds from the outside world (139). Though the other senses develop soon enough, I'd like to suppose that the ear continues to play a vital and prominent, if subliminal, role in our experience of identifying and weighing values and meanings. We engage the ear precisely this way when we play around with prose style in an attempt to move our readers.

This process is, however, necessarily and paradoxically just as mysterious as it is social. For when we do the reverse, when we turn away from the ear and turn intensity into a quality, articulating it in images, diagrams, or models, we pretend to organize and trap intensity in the domain of the eye ("Now I see what this means!"), but instead we largely lose it, for we have presumed to halt an intrinsically mobile, transformative force. Intensity, in fact, might best be thought about via a version of Zeno's paradox: if a tortoise were given a head start in a race against Achilles, and Achilles reduced his distance from the tortoise only by half every five minutes, Achilles would never reach the tortoise, because he could cover only half the distance; even when he was hard upon the tortoise, he wouldn't reach it, for he could divide the distance only by half, and then by half again, for any distance is infinitely divisible. Similarly, intensity imitates or follows the infinite divisibility of space. That is, intensity is the infinite self-involution of sheer movement toward places that are in fact not places at all but rather middlings between various terms or points. Like Achilles approaching the tortoise, intensity is essentially a vibration that can emanate ever more deeply with the real but abstract energy/substance of sheer relationship, moving inward and away from the endpoints that bracket or break off relationship. It instantiates an endlessly receding interior, a whirlpool or vortex, just as Achilles does in the moment when we would expect to him pass the tortoise.

Put simply, intensity, says Massumi, cannot be described through a frozen system of fixed terms. Rather, it is a "continuously variable impulse or momentum that can cross from one qualitatively different medium into another. Like electricity into sound waves . . . or noise in the ear into music in the heart" (2002, 135). Indeed, the more we qualify it—that is, pin it down in images and concepts—the more directly we conduct it into other media through which it changes and even upsets the coordinates or qualities used to express it. Thus, a particularly successful sentence, for example, might induce a chill down the spine of one reader or a rich belly laugh in another, or, in major cases, a new political agenda for someone but not for another, or even, in rare cases, a new reality for the collective—but always only fleetingly, for not only is intensity ultimately indeterminate, it is always on the move.

The difficulty of discussing intensity's movement derives, as Massumi asserts, not simply from the sheer absence of any reliable terms for it, but precisely because terms, as such, are the opposite of movement: "term" implies endpoint, fixity, stasis. We might try to think about movement through our own bodily experience, the feeling, say, of walking or falling or embracing, but traditionally, such discussions of bodily experience have relied on a naïve empiricism or subjectivism that fails to account for the pervasive, ongoing influence of culture in shaping, even dictating such experience. More recently, as Massumi explains, we've tried to talk about the experience of the body as influenced, even constructed by culture, but, to do so, we've invoked a kind of grid made of various "discourses" of race, class, sexuality, and so on, and then we assume that each body is constituted as a point of intersection of particular discourses (see Judith Butler's *Bodies That Matter*). The problem is that we have little way of accounting for how a body moves or changes from one point on the grid to another. We might build into our grid certain discourses like those of growth, age, education, health, illness, analysis, cure, and so on, but, as Massumi insists, we still can't describe the transitions from one point on the grid to another. What's more, the mystery of how to describe the much subtler, nonphysical movements by which a person changes his or her mind or moves from a particular habit of emotion to another ("Ah, I guess I like the liberals more than I realized") would seem utterly insoluble. Faced with this mystery, Massumi dares us to follow the path initially suggested by Henri Bergson early in the last century, through which we don't simply suspend what I've been calling the discursive grid but rather come to experience all of external space itself only as a sort of retrospect, a fatigued falling away from the primary reality—the primary reality being the mysterious spark, the inward-directed, endlessly self-involuting, transformative pulse of sheer movement. Massumi challenges us, ultimately, to stop staring with such stunned fixity or vacancy at the cloud of exhaust fumes that is external space and instead to listen to and pursue this primary reality, this interior—which is always in flight.

Our problems, of course, proliferate: why, for starters, must we link movement to vague concepts of inwardness? Massumi explains that when a body is moving, it is in an unfolding relation only to its own purely abstract but intrinsic capacity for variation, an unfolding relation to its own potential for indeterminacy, its very real "openness to an elsewhere and an otherwise than it is, in any here and now" (2002. 5). This potential is real but abstract, something like breath, the expression of life, and, though incorporeal, it inhabits the living body the way energy is said to reside in matter. Like matter and energy, the body and its real-but-abstract potential for movement and change, says Massumi, are mutually controvertible modes of the same reality, inseparable fellow travelers (5). This energy, this abstract, vital, breathlike capacity for movement and change is present in every emotion, every moment in which we feel "moved."

Again, it is intensity and it lives in the ear. Intensity is what we cultivate when we write with our ears.

TEACHING INTENSITY

Rather than explicitly delineate these concepts for my students, I invite them by a variety of means to contemplate the sorts of experiences these concepts identify in the hopes that the students might begin to identify them and cultivate them in their own ways. For example, I ask them to reread and revise their papers many times, and, as they do, I require them to use a variety of stylistic principles and devices that inevitably draw attention to the sheer sound of prose, its potential for rhythm, symmetry, tonal consistency, and degrees of parallelism. Also, I try constantly to model for them what it means to have an open ear by listening with utmost attention to everything they say in discussion and by commenting on how they sound as they read their drafts aloud.

In class discussions, I encourage inquiry into the ways that the general sound of a passage reflects a particular mood, and, in turn, a certain set of moral coordinates, even political commitments. For example, I've often assigned students to read Adrienne Rich's essay "When We Dead Awaken: Writing as Revision" (1979) to get them to see how ambitious the project of listening to one's own language can become. Rich's essay is difficult, but as we work through it together, we devote special attention to how Rich casts revision and the work of listening to herself, how such activities are wholly engaged with charting subtle mood shifts and, too, broad political movements. In the essay, Rich describes how she first began to notice the tone in Virginia Woolf's *A Room of One's Own;* how she then began to consider some of her own work along similar lines; how she heard a "deliberate detachment" and a composed and apparently cool character in her work in the early 1950s, which reflected a similar sense of confinement foisted on her by that era's narrow codes for acceptable feminine roles. This tone, she began to see, was a sign that, as a poet and perhaps as a person, she was dying, for life depends on a certain freedom of mind: "freedom to press on, to enter currents of your own thought like a glider pilot, knowing that your motion can be sustained. . . . You have to be free to play around with the notions that day might be night, love might be hate, nothing can be too sacred for the imagination to turn into its opposite or call experimentally by another name. For writing is renaming" (610). She notes as well: "Revision—the act of looking back, of seeing with fresh eyes, of entering an old text from a new critical direction—is for women more than a chapter in cultural history: it is an act of survival" (604). In the terms I've been using, revision plays with the external grid, jostles it in ways that allow for the expression of intensity, and, as Rich maintains, without this freedom to express intensity, people can die.

Rich quotes several of her own poems, and I find that students like to work with this material. In fact, once they become comfortable with Rich's ideas and talking about her poems, I might devote a short unit of the semester to having students explicate via large-group discussion an assemblage of other literary texts that, together, can get them moving in these same directions toward more flexible, more moving, more lively language. I might have them discuss Robert Lowell's short poem "Reading Myself" (1977), which fades into silence with the final, chilling, elliptical line that, tellingly, has no verb: "This open book . . . my open coffin"(183). In the context of the Rich essay, Lowell's poem has a special impact. I might also have students look at the Lowell poem alongside these lines from William Blake's introduction to the *Songs of Experience:*

Hear the voice of the Bard
Who Present, Past, and Future, Sees;
Whose ears have heard
The Holy Word
That Walk'd among the ancient trees. (1966, 210)

Blake's "Holy Word" seems to be a window onto pure intensity, for it "Walk'd among the ancient trees" and entered the ears of the Bard; and the Bard, open to this pure intensity, can now range freely through time and speak to different readers at different moments. In fact, the lines are a direct command to the reader to open the ear to this pure intensity, to enter into relationship with this supremely mobile connector that would seem to enable, in turn, eternal life.

To get my students thinking about this ecstatic dimension of relationship-as-such, this sheer middling that the Holy Word incarnates, I might ask them to elaborate on the lines from Lowell and from Blake alongside these from Niyi Osundare: "The well-spoken word is the bride of the ear"(62); and "The simple word / Is the shortest distance / Between two minds" (2002, 228). I might add into the mix Walt Whitman's appeal in "The Mystic Trumpeter," in which he rhapsodizes on the layers of inter-subjective connection he hears in the playing of this "strange musician / hovering unseen in air" who "vibrates capricious tunes tonight":

Come nearer bodiless one, haply in thee resounds
Some dead composer, haply thy pensive life
Was fill'd with aspirations high, unformed ideals,
Waves, oceans musical, chaotically surging,
That now, ecstatic ghost, close to me bending, thy cornet echoing, pealing,
Gives out to no one's ears but mine, but freely gives to mine,
That I may thee translate.

Blow trumpeter free and clear, I follow thee,
While at thy liquid prelude, glad, serene,
The fretting world, the streets, the noisy hours of day withdraw
A holy calm descends like a dew upon me. . . .
Thy song expands my numbed imbonded spirit, thou freest, launchest me,
Floating and basking on heaven's lake (1953, 366-68).

I often introduce Whitman's lines by pointing out that Whitman revised *Leaves of Grass* throughout his life, and thus he understood the work of writing as Rich does, as a struggle to open the ear yet more and more, rather than to manufacture, à la Lowell, a coffin. By having my students explicate the lines from Lowell, Blake, Osundare, and Whitman in terms of each other and in the context of Rich's essay, they can begin to find their way to experiences of the sort I delineated earlier in connection with Brian Massumi and Henri Bergson—that is, toward an experience of the ear as that which triggers and directs potentially endless expenditures and expressions of energy, for it is the substance and focal point of ever-evolving relationships and interactions, their catalyst. It is the vibrating essence of the transindividual dimension, for through it, we pass out of ourselves, experience ecstasy/ex-stasis, and, as athletes put it, we "enter the zone" or go "on a roll." The ear invites us into a trance of pure creativity that, at the time, seems perpetual.

While these poems might seem too remote from the students' immediate life-worlds, I think that when the students grapple with them as a group, the poems can begin to shed light on one another and become more accessible, more useful. To get them started, I might point out that Whitman's trumpeter, in the first stanza, is cast as a great listener ("haply in thee resounds / Some dead composer") and that the power of his trumpet originated in the power of his ear; and that this power Whitman would seem to appropriate or imitate in listening so intensely, perhaps in order to become something like a trumpeter himself, as if the trumpet-generating power of the ear were floating forward from out of the past. As the students circle back and forth through these poems and their possibilities, developing a short paper, say, on the role of the ear in writing, intensity can begin to radiate among them and they might even bring new zeal to the crafting of their own prose.

Of course, I hardly intend to present these poems as a canonical set of masterworks on sound. In fact, I can readily imagine asking students to bring in other texts that offer particularly inspired insights into, examples of, or particular techniques for cultivating intensity, inspiration, and style. Thus I'd like to end or perhaps trail off (trail in?) by offering a few thoughts about the ear that teachers can contemplate or elaborate or refine or simply bear in mind as they listen to—and model the act of serious listening for—their students. In short, I offer by way of closing a handful of thoughts that can help us to open—and thereby write with—our ears.

INCONCLUSIVE CONCLUSION: TOWARD A MYSTICISM OF STYLE

One might well ask, "What can I do—what literal, practical activity can I undertake—to open my ear, to cultivate intensity?" While I can offer no simple, foolproof method, I can suggest that there is much to gain by training one's ear upon one's breathing: listen to your own breath, focus your attention on and even "read" your body's more or less rhythmic interaction with the ethereal energy that is an essential substance and expression of moment-to-moment survival. The more closely we listen to our breath, the more deliberately we engage this abstract energy, and the longer we sustain this engagement, the more "inspired" we become, the more "moved," and the more open to yet greater movement and transformation. What I'm describing, of course, has traditionally been identified as meditation, an apt word for the state of mind for the writer, who, as Mandel says, is not at home. Such focus seemingly enables us to metamorphose into a wave of energy/sound ourselves and frees us to roll indefinitely from one medium to another, breathing, as many yoga teachers say, "into it," as we leap across the divide between Self and Other to communicate with our readers—a process at once miraculous and utterly natural.

By listening to the breath and exploring this intensity, perhaps the body can resonate to the degree that its points of resistance or displeasure are drawn into contrast, conceptualized, articulated, "qualified," and, as blockage, they can then be opened and their intensity freed to rejoin the larger resonating field of the breathing body. This is probably the goal of Freud's famous "talking cure," of therapeutic writing, perhaps of all cathartic activity. Through the ear, we achieve this inward focus and flexibility; we breathe new openings back into the dancing sea of intensities, the tossing harmonies of our flesh so that they may coalesce and heighten and flow forth to move and change other bodies. In short, what might seem a private, even solipsistic, endeavor is in fact fully rhetorical, even political.

If, as Walter Pater famously put it, all art aspires to the condition of music, then we would do well, as writing teachers, to remember James Joyce's lesser-known rejoinder, which suggests that all music aspires to the condition of language (Ellman 1972, 104). In the words I've been using here, we might say that not only are intensity and quality not in conflict, but rather they aspire to the condition of each other, enabling and animating each other. To forget this point is to make the mistake that Leopold Bloom, in the "Sirens" episode of Ulysses, observes in his friend Cowley, who is lost in his love for music: "He stunts himself with it; a kind of drunkenness. Better give way only half way the way of a man with a maid. Instance enthusiasts. All ears . . . head nodding in time. Dotty. Thinking strictly prohibited" (Ellman, 108). Despite Bloom's warning, I'd like to help my students move a little closer to the experience of Cowley. And then, of course, to return from it and then drift back to it again, oscillating between the auditory and the semantic in order to intensify both.

How do I do this? I model it, I use some of Sondra Perl's (1979) exercises for accessing the felt sense, and perhaps, above all, I resist any lockstep recipe that would encumber my and my students' ability to cultivate the playful quicksilver spirit of intensity. For the ear, in a sense, is the first drum, but it needs no drummer—for it beats on its own like a heart. And, in so doing, it enables a dance, for the writer always writes in movement, a vibratory feedback loop between the role of writer and reader.

This is the humming bifurcation I described in the first paragraph of this essay: composing as a practice of play. According to Hans-Georg Gadamer (1975, 101-133), play has its own autonomy, its own discrete, independent essence. It is a to-and-fro movement, a middling or relation-as-such, and it never posits a goal that would end, once and for all, the activity of play, for the goal of play is always simply to keep playing, to move ever more deeply into the space between the endpoints that bracket the interval of play. The purpose of play, we might say, is to slip away or coalesce into an earlike whirlpool that leads to eternity.

And, as exotic as that might sound, some commonsense renditions of this same point can illustrate fairly directly how it applies to the composition classroom. If play constantly renews itself in repetition and if it might be said to use the player for its own manifestation, like an occult force that takes possession of the player to speak through him or her, then we would do well to follow the advice Matthew Parfitt offers in "Room for 'Us' to Play: The Teacher as Midwife" (2003). What can make class discussion most lively and productive, argues Parfitt, is a certain loosening of preconceived goals, an openness to the unpredictable, and specifically the use of lots of relatively low-stakes assignments that can relax students and promote substantive conversation as opposed to the hollow, stiff, obsequious grade-seeking performances that the opposite approach so often elicits.

As Massumi (2002) notes, when someone is playing soccer, for example, he or she works not just according to expectations and "unwritten" rules, but rather plays with and around these to escape codified structure and enter, instead, the realm of creativity, surprise, and intensity. Such a player, in fact, is developing a style and working with style as such. To play with style, as Massumi says, is to toss unregulated intensities into the mix that will charge the game anew, change it, and launch new vectors of becoming, all of which the referee must watch closely in case some move crosses a line or a rule that is deemed essential to the continuity of the play as such (77). The player who plays with style and develops a style is broadly analogous to the student writer, and the referee who is watching for important rule infractions is one of the roles played by the writing teacher. Of course, another role for the teacher is to encourage students to play with sound and experiment with style, for style is what makes a star.

When a writer works with style, she relaxes her concern for rules, goals, and grades, even the goal of representing some objective reality. That is, she does not polish her prose merely to ensure that it will serve as a transparent window onto some extratextual objects. Instead, she has left behind all such tensions between representations and their objects to enter the domain that Gilles Deleuze (1994) associates with the simulacrum, a place of dazzling freedom, where possibilities are endlessly put into play, a space that is Dionysian or, in a utopian sense, schizoid (67). In this sense, when we teach our students about style, we no longer have to worry that they will struggle with the blank page and complain that they don't have any ideas to write about, for writing, in this sense, is never properly "about" any particular thing any more than music is. It is writing, in a relatively pure sense, as writing. This is not an escape from meaning or the realm of qualities, not a flight into purely auditory indeterminacy (as in Carroll's *Jabberwocky* or in Joyce's *Finnegans Wake),* for intensity is no more opposed to quality than one's right leg is opposed to one's left. Rather, enhancing one's relation to this mysterious dimension or force can enhance, in turn, one's meaning: this is what goes on when one crafts one's prose in order to move readers.

Given the Dionysian/schizoid freedom that style makes available, we must also understand style as the definitive test and object of the authorial will, for working with style means breaking up comfortable habits and clichés, commonly held approaches and, finally, all that depends, unreflexively, on familiar precedents. We might even suggest that to work with style/simulacra is to practice a form of theater—what William Blake or Antonin Artaud might call the devil's theater—for in this theater the actor, notes Deleuze, has given up trying to represent some reality to herself and/or to the audience and has instead become consumed with action, with movement as an intrinsically and quintessentially subversive force, the self-involution of which fleetingly disbands the determinate grid of familiar and routine meanings in order to transform them and rejuvenate them (1994, 5-11).

When a writer paradoxically brings tremendous will to bear on style and, at the same time, suspends preconceived goals, rules, and ideals, when he plays with utmost energy with the rhythm, tempo, and harmony of his sentences, he might ultimately rework a particular run of words a thousand times—and then resolve to keep the sentence the way he originally wrote it, the final version identical to the first. Nonetheless, a giant change, a permanent change may well have blossomed very nearby—that is, in the writer. Having sifted and surveyed a considerable expanse of possibilities and synthesized their various strengths and weaknesses into a certainty that the best choice is, in fact, the one he is using, he has opened and strengthened his ear. Perhaps this is how learning works: like music, learning is a constant repetition led forward in the darkness by sparks of variation. In reworking a sentence or run of sentences repeatedly, the writer becomes involved in a playful repetition that is not, as Freud would have it, a repression of some supremely threatening, abysslike Other, but rather the very throb thereof—a kind of chant. Like the singing of bats, it builds a reliable cognitive map and a home in what might otherwise seem merely the inky darkness, the cavelike abyss of social/textual space.

Working with style turns the void into a fertile source, a primary experience of the infinitude of intersubjectivity's interior.

More specifically, if movement allows us to experience what we call time, then rhythm is the special type of movement that allows us to experience that which is beyond time, ultimately leading us to our beloved source and goal, the beautiful wisdom of that which gives. This, says Sufi mystic and musician Hazrat Inayat Khan (1996), is the primordial rhythm of being. And it permeates our moment-to-moment experience not just as heartbeat and breath but as an ordering principle in our social interaction such as a wave to a friend, a handshake, a nod of the head, an interval of speech, and, most obviously, lovemaking. We might do well to let this insistent pulse focus our lives, very broadly, on the more conceptual two-beat groove of action-and-result. The question, more pointedly, becomes what does my action give? What new actions does it engender? Like all ethical perspectives, this one implies an extremely rigorous awareness of style: How do various versions of a passage differ in what they can and cannot do? What do they give?

Consider, in these terms, the legend of Orpheus as a kind of moral fable. Orpheus was such a gifted musician that, as Robert Graves translates, he "not only enchanted wild beasts, but made the trees and rocks move from their places to follow the sound of his music" (112). On a particular hillside in Thrace, a number of ancient oaks are "still standing in the pattern of one of his dances, just as he left them" (112). So great were his musical powers that when his wife was bitten by a serpent and died, he used them to charm his way down into the underworld, the land of the dead, in order rescue her and bring her back to life. Orpheus's music had seemingly unlimited rhetorical force, for he could persuade the gods to overturn a death, and, in so doing, transgress a fundamental feature of the natural order. Orpheus, however, had to make a deal: as he conducted his beloved back into the world of the living, guiding her with the sounds of his lyre, he could not turn back to look at her, for if he did, he would lose her irretrievably to the dead. Tragically, in the final steps of his journey, Orpheus did look back, and his wife indeed vanished back into the depths.

What might this mean? In the terms I've been using here, we might suppose that the power of Orpheus's music, at its greatest, was a function of his love for his wife, and its intensity was so great that it could override the anchoring, qualitative terms of the spatial grid, those that separate life and death. Most important, it dramatizes the supreme value of the ear and the artist's need to have full faith in it, for when Orpheus turned back to look at his wife, seeking to capture the certain truth of her safe return with his eyes, his faith in his ears implicitly wobbled, and all was lost. That passage outward, where Orpheus tragically forfeits what would have been his greatest triumph, might be seen as the passage that opens the ear to the supreme intensity. What ethical axioms follow from this fable? In simplest terms, have faith in your ears, keep playing with sounds, for this, again, is the royal road to love's victory over the most ruthless tyrant on the external, qualitative grid of space: death.

The myth of Orpheus helps me think about a certain sacred, musical dimension of writing, an aspect of writing that enables people to fall in love with it and build their lives around it. As explained by Khan (1996), whenever we enjoy something, returning to play with it over time, we are essentially enjoying that something's music—that is, its refusal of stasis, its ongoing vibrations and movements. Khan adds that music is the only pure art form, for the others are alloyed with idolatry, which is to say, stasis (2-3). Only music is free to move, to reconstitute constantly, and whenever anything moves, it is vibrating, sending out music. This point is dramatized in an Eastern legend thus: when God tried to induce the human soul to take up residence in what the soul perceived as the prison house of the human body, God ultimately succeeded in getting the soul to enter by having the angels sing, as if demonstrating that a soul in a body is potentially an angel in song, supremely mobile and free, a perpetual process, an essentially and infinitely revisionary entity, vibrating pure music eternally.

Learning to play music is an apt metaphor for learning to write with style. The only purpose in learning to play music, says Khan, is to become, essentially, musical in one's thoughts and actions, ultimately to the degree that one perceives all being as musical—that is, as endlessly harmonized and rhythmically balanced processes of action and result (111). Playing music and writing with style, in this sense, are forms of healing and prayer: they seek to open the ear to release the soul so that it may express itself freely, know itself fully, and do its work in the world.

As Joachim-Ernst Berendt (1983) notes, an ancient Christian legend claims that the Virgin Mary conceived Christ through her ear, for the ear is the most spiritual of our sense organs, the one, as we saw in the myth of Orpheus, with the richest relation to the abstract capacity for moving us around in the interpersonal domain of relationship-as-such—that is, of Love. It is the organ, Berendt adds, with the most direct connection with our ultimate origin, the primal sound (140): just as Western spiritual traditions suggest that "In the beginning was the Word," so too do Eastern traditions offer similar understandings of "OM." Berendt adds that the Tibetan *Book of the Dead* is known in Tibet by the title *Bardo Thodol,* which means "Liberation by Hearing in the Intermediate State," and it is to be read in a whisper into the ear of the recently deceased to ensure the person's safe passage into eternity (145).

This activity hinges, Khan might suggest, on the fact that a soul is simply a sound. And this is also why we respond so directly to sounds and that is why we are intoxicated by music. Sound, finally, is best understood as some dimension of one's own consciousness that has become active and mobile, pouring out invisibly through the ear. This is what I mean, at the moment, by writing with the ear. When the ear opens, it teaches us that rhythm and tone are the language of the soul. Only with an open ear can we practice the science of breath, which, as Khan implies, is synonymous with a number of other interchangeable practices: the philosophy of music, the religion of humanity, the art of self-emptying, the cultivation of rhythm, the elaboration of tone. Perhaps the discipline of rhetoric trails off or comes to an end in the place where mysticism always begins: chanting the riddles of vibration and movement in their very birthplace—the temple of the writer's ear.

NOTES

CHAPTER 1. STYLE AND THE RENAISSANCE OF COMPOSITION STUDIES (TOM PACE)

1. Aristotle defines rhetoric as "an ability, in each particular case, to see the available means of persuasion" (1991, 36).

2. Two received histories of early modern rhetoric, Kennedy (1980) and Howell (1956), both dismiss style as a surface-oriented element of rhetoric that has little to do with the invention of ideas. Both texts are often cited as standard histories of the field. In their anthology *The Rhetorical Tradition,* Bizzell and Herzberg (1990) call Kennedy's history "the standard general historical source" and *The Bedford Bibliography for Teachers of Writing* call Howell's history "the standard history of this important period in the history of rhetoric" (2004, 40).

3. Some of these strategies include experimenting wildly with various types of sentences: short, one-word sentences he called crots and longer, complex sentences he called labyrinthine. Weathers also recommended writing in what he termed "double voice," a technique that allows writers to explore two sides of an argument and present the material on opposing sides of a composition. This practice reminds me of Ann Berthoff's "Double Entry Notebook" in her book *Forming, Thinking, Writing* (1982).

CHAPTER 2. WHERE IS STYLE GOING? WHERE HAS IT BEEN? (ELIZABETH WEISER)

1. These six articles were: Fleischauer's "James Baldwin's Style" (1975), Hiatt's "The Feminine Style" (1978), Lu's "Professing Multiculturalism: The Politics of Style in the Contact Zone" (1994), Pringle's "Why Teach Style?" (1983), Walpole's "Style as Option" (1980), and Winterowd's "Prolegomenon to Pedagogical Stylistics" (1983).

2. Kirsch and Sullivan's category "feminism" I changed to the broader "diversity critique" to encompass articles discussing not only gendered but also racially/ethnically influenced discourse, bias, and learning. In Kirsch and Sullivan's book, writing theory is described as particular discourses that systemically explain phenomena (i.e., generative rhetoric or tagmemic invention); textual analysis is linguistic studies that look at inherent readability; experimental research utilizes quantitative analysis (statistics, etc.); historical analysis involves archival retrieval and recovery; teacher research involves systematic intentional inquiry by teachers; case study focuses in depth on one student; ethnography describes the interrelationship between language and culture from an emic perspective; discourse analysis looks at moments when writing is talked about (workshops, tutorials, etc.); and cognitive approaches use protocol analysis to determine how students think when writing.

3. In employing a "communication triangle," I am adapting James Kinneavy's analogy of "the communication process as a triangle composed of an encoder (writer or speaker), a decoder (reader or listener), a signal (the linguistic product), and a reality (the part of the universe to which the linguistic product refers)" (2003, 134). While Kinneavy categorized the various orientations as producing corresponding types of writing (a focus on the text produces literary works, a focus on the reader produces persuasive works, etc.), in this study I use the communication triangle concept to signify what element of communication the authors are focusing on, regardless of their methodology. Thus, one article may discuss types of transitions needed for a

stylistically cohesive paragraph (focus on text), another may discuss how students learn to produce cohesive paragraphs (focus on writer), and a third may discuss how a sample of teachers grade more or less cohesive paragraphs (focus on reader). This division into reader-writer-textual orientations is admittedly arbitrary, and, as with methodologies, a number of articles employed more than one strategy. Where this was the case, I attempted to determine the article's primary focus.

CHAPTER 3. CONTEXTUAL STYLISTICS: BREAKING DOWN THE BINARIES IN SENTENCE-LEVEL PEDAGOGY (REBECCA MOORE HOWARD)

1. For useful if not unanimous overviews of the history of stylistics, see Bradford (1997); Catano (1997); Taylor and Toolan (1984); Weber (1996).
2. Ryan Stark (2001) provides a good analysis of the rise of the plain style. See also Brody (1993), 111–15.
3. Brody (1993), 48. But Agnew 1998 argues that we must differentiate Blair's rhetoric from the ways that his successors deployed it.
4. Alternatively, one might locate the beginning of the discipline with the beginning of mandatory testing, mandatory instruction, generic handbooks, professional organizations, or scholarly journals. Thus 1874, 1885, 1907, 1911, 1949, or 1950 would be plausible starting dates for composition studies. Written entrance exams were established at Harvard in 1874, and composition became a required college course there in 1885. The first college writers' handbook (Woolley) was published in 1907. NCTE was founded in 1911. The Conference on College Composition and Communication held its first meeting in 1949—but, as Crowley points out, CCCC was established not to further knowledge but to facilitate teaching (1998, 253). *College Composition and Communication* was first published in 1950. However, teaching does not by itself make a discipline, nor does publication. A discipline must have both of these but also a sense of scholarly commitment. I focus on the 1960s decade because at that time, an appreciable number of scholars began to identify not just their teaching but also their scholarship as focusing on composition.
5. My summary here is derived directly from Parks (2000, 210–33), who provides a detailed account of this phase of language politics.
6. Stanley Fish (1987) observes that in the 1983 "Reading, Writing, and Cultural Literacy," Hirsch recants his dedication to "a pedagogy based on normative notions of correctness, readability, and quantifiable effects" and takes up a "contextualist" position. He now says that language can't be taught separately from "'vast domains of underlying cultural information' and that therefore 'we cannot do a good job of teaching, reading, and writing if we neglect . . . particular cultural vocabularies'" (Fish 1987, 353). As will become obvious in my description of contextualist stylistics, Fish and I are using the word contextualist in very different ways.
7. Weber (1996) calls it "contextualized stylistics." The movement is variously labeled contextual stylistics, contextualized stylistics, and contextualist stylistics. Bradford's choice (1997) is contextualist stylistics, and it is mine, as well: the -ist morpheme hints at an agency that I find appealing and appropriate.
8. I question the first association; critical linguistics, I believe, is a parent category for (if not the larger category of) critical stylistics.
9. David Trend's edited collection (1996) is an excellent introduction to and overview of the prospects for radical democracy.
10. I am specifically not referring to the reflexive/extensive dyad that Joseph Harris (1996) attributes to the work of Janet Emig: "Reflexive writing is personal, imaginative, and artistic; extensive writing carries out the business of the world, gets things done. Emig was perhaps even more insistent than Britton that reflexive writing must

have a personal and 'contemplative' quality; it was for the insights that such writing could offer into the self that she most valued it" (58).

CHAPTER 4. STYLE REDUX (KATHRYN T. FLANNERY)

1. I am indebted to Barry Kroll's thinking about inquiry. See in particular his *Teaching Hearts and Minds* (1992).
2. This is a case I make in *The Emperor New Clothes* (1995).
3. I am thinking here of both *Amazing Grace* (1995) and *Ordinary Resurrections* (2000).
4. To protect the privacy of the writers, and with their permission, I am using pseudonyms.

CHAPTER 5. THE USES OF LITERATURE (TINA KELLEHER)

I title this essay to recall Richard Hoggart's seminal cultural studies work, *The Uses of Literacy* (1958). I am interested in the imaginative and practical ways literature and creative composition can figure in realizing cultural studies' goal of social inclusion in the classroom and how a combination of these approaches might animate a style-based writing pedagogy. For a lucid disciplinary history of how the tensions between the study of language and the study of literature emerged and evolved, resulting in (among other things) our present-day disciplinary schism between the teaching of writing and the teaching of literature, see Guillory (2002, 19–43). The volume editors conclude Guillory's "uncovering of the contested nature of an emergent discipline confirms that disciplines are always constituted in relation to, and in a kind of dialogue with other disciplines. . . . to call cultural studies an antidiscipline or even a multidiscipline is misleading insofar as disciplinarity was always defined against fields and methodologies that could not encompass its subject" (5). Following these insights, this essay specifically explores the interdisciplinary and cross-disciplinary value of style (as a tool of rhetoric) in illuminating the communicative and inventive objectives of writing in the humanities and writing across the disciplines.

1. I focus upon Smith rather than his frequently cited disciple, Hugh Blair (1783), because I am interested in how his discussion emerges from and relates to writing across the disciplines and how the category of style enables his cross-disciplinary maneuverings. I also view Smith as preeminent, because he quite literally serves as a primary proponent of writing as transcribed speech. The *Lectures* were delivered orally and transcribed by students, and Smith requested that written papers relating to his lectures be posthumously burned. The eventual publication of his lectures did not transpire until the early twentieth century, with the discovery, redaction, and synthesis of his students' notes.
2. Walter J. Ong engagingly analyzes and historicizes writing as a technology in *Orality and Literacy* (1982). See especially chapter 4: "Writing Restructures Consciousness."
3. For the purposes of this essay, I address (though ultimately bracket) disciplinary and institutional politics in order to understand how, in varying degrees, these respective positions potentially interfere with a student's ability to apprehend writing as a techne, as an interactive experience contingent upon practices of engaged reading.
4. Students encounter a range of paradoxes when being initiated to college-level writing. For example, the Advanced Placement Language and Composition exam administered to secondary school students by the College Board, for possible exemption from university humanities and writing requirements, includes literature-based essay questions falling under the rubric "style analyses"—a genre of writing assignment rarely found on most contemporary college-level composition and expository writing syllabi. How can we account for the ostensible gap between what the College Board and entering college students imagine as a necessary skill and what university writing faculty and instructors in fact prioritize? If students covet style, how might we

best respond to this perceived need, to inspire their writing and to embolden their critical thinking skills? The Johns Hopkins Center for Talented Youth (CTY), which offers distance education college-preparatory writing courses to middle and secondary school students from across the United States and parts of Europe and Asia, has responded to this trend in demand by launching in the summer of 2003 Language Rules: From Structure to Style, a course that aims to inculcate a reflective awareness of grammatical principles and how these apply to stylistic decision making in argumentative and creative forms of writing.

5. For an insightful intertextual consideration of the Scottish *belles lettres* movement and its French influences, see Warnick (1993).

6. For an informative interdisciplinary analysis of the Scottish *belles lettres* movement's origins, see Miller (1997). Also see Jones and Skinner (1992); Berry (1974).

7. The political and nationalistic implications of Smith's work come through more explicitly in an essay that derives from lecture 3, titled "Considerations concerning the First Formations of Languages and the Different Genius of Original and Compounded Languages" in Smith 1985. When differentiating Smith and Locke's theories of language (theories "designed to resolve, or at least, circumvent, the tension between private property rights and the common social consensus"), Irene Tucker notes that "[c]ommon language in [Smith's] history is not the ground of political authority, or even the medium within which it might be established, but instead is the condition of politics' elimination" (2000, 36–38).

8. Russell's insightful historical study explores four central conflicts that have characterized writing instruction in the disciplines: The first two have to do with the nature of writing and its acquisition: writing as a single elementary skill, as transparent recording of speech or thought or physical reality, vs. writing as a complex rhetorical activity, embedded in the differentiated practices of academic discourse communities; and writing acquisitions as remediation of deficiencies of skill vs. writing acquisition as a continually developing intellectual and social attainment tied to disciplinary learning. The second two conflicts center on the relation between language and the structure of mass education: academia as a single discourse community vs, academia as many competing discourse communities; and disciplinary excellence vs. social equity as the goal of writing instruction (1991, 9–10).

9. For an incisive historical analysis of the cultural studies movement in its American and British contexts, see During (1993). As I am more specifically interested in the relevance of these developments to writing pedagogy, my discussion provides only a thumbnail characterization of cultural studies' methodological tendencies. See also Gelder and Thornton (1997) for an additional sampling of cultural studies scholarship. A number of essays in these volumes notably literalize style as an object of study through the discourse and subject matter of fashion.

10. Flannery's study analyzes efforts to normalize and standardize issues of style in multifarious contexts: she explores, among other issues, the British Royal Society's attempts during the Renaissance to establish criteria for a denotative prose style to advance and disseminate findings for scientific inquiry; contemporary American initiatives to reform legal writing to prevent breaches of contract, to protect privacy and property rights, and to avoid frivolous law suits; and in addition, educational and governmental attempts to mandate literacy standards and a national prose style, amid the increasing cultural and linguistic diversity of the American population.

11. It's worth reiterating that classical rhetoric emphasized political oratory and that Smith's *Lectures* exist as transcripts of his speechifying about writing. In other words, both the old and new rhetoric hinged upon matters of speech, even if they're not necessarily taught in contemporary contexts to reflect that original intent. Reading a piece of writing aloud, for example, commonly serves as a recommended "strategy"

for proofreading. Such articulating does not in and of itself remedy or substitute for a knowledge of mechanics, but it suggests reading aloud triggers metacognitive reflection upon internalized conventions (assuming, of course, they've been already learned), and externalizing them in speech resuscitates recognition.

12.   The challenge remains integrating these issues into course content in inspired and strategic ways, so that students can recognize how such considerations influence and motivate their reading practices as well as their writing processes. A number of valuable texts already address these practical instructional concerns, but they're often used in supplementary rather than holistic ways: for example, Kolln (1999); Williams (2002).

13.   Slevin proposes, for example, that texts such as Sterne's *Tristam Shandy* and Fielding's *Tom Jones* can be profitably used, because "[c]omposition's way of reading them, by attending critically to the conventions and forms used and not used, examines the operations of language across boundaries of social differentiation and the ideologies that ground various (insightful as well as unreflective) representations of these operations" (2001, 254). In chapter 6 of this collection, Slevin also compellingly examines ways of reading style in light of Mary Louise Pratt's concept of a "linguistics of contact," which explores the knowledge yielded from exchanges and misunderstandings among different languages, social groups, and historically situated subjects.

14.   Roland Barthes cannily notes that "what the (secondary) school prides itself on is teaching to read (well) and no longer to write (consciousness of the deficiency is becoming fashionable again today: the teacher is called upon to teach pupils to 'express themselves,' which is a little like replacing a form of repression by a misconception)" (1977a, 162; emphasis in original).

15.   I stress this point not through a Luddite suspicion of information technologies, but because most students do not understand what criteria search engines use to prioritize and sort sources. Teachers should stay abreast of such developments to translate for students how and why criteria used to evaluate print sources apply to Web-based contexts.

16.   As I've noted in the previous note, technology really poses a difference in degree rather than kind: online writing workshops facilitate peer review and feedback and provide unique opportunities to encourage revision of student work. On this trend, see for example, Guernsey (2003).

17.   For a compelling historical examination of how these interrelated fields became artificially separated in ways that have obscured their mutual interdependence and shared institutional and pedagogical interests, see Quade (1992). Quade suggests a number of possible ways to establish interconnecting interests—for example, acknowledging the essay as our most democratic form of literature and regarding student writing as a kind of literature that merits close analysis and study—and I would add to this list incorporating into our pedagogy the cross-disciplinary concerns spawned by issues of style.

CHAPTER 11. STYLE: THE NEW GRAMMAR IN COMPOSITION STUDIES? (NICOLE AMARE)

1.   It is important to note here that the majority of plagiarism definitions, including the one in the WPA (Writing Program Administrators) Plagiarism Statement, do not include style or syntactical structure as plagiarism. Recently, on the WPA listserv, established compositionists like Andrea Lunsford and Chris Anson discussed the issue of copying of a published author's syntactical style as an element of plagiarism; all the professors who contributed to the listserv discussion, including Lunsford and Anson, agreed that imitating language form does not constitute plagiarism; only content does.

2.   And the rest of the class, for I do this assignment as a group activity.
3.   Provided you have the student's permission to do so.

CHAPTER 12. BALANCING THOUGHT AND EXPRESSION: A SHORT COURSE IN STYLE (LISA BAIRD)

1.   Note: References to "truth" and "scene" might suggest a Burkean undercurrent at work in this rubric. The rubric is Burkean in the way the categories aid invention, but that is the extent of the similarity. "In any given style," write Thomas and Turner, "positions will be assigned to truth, language, the writer, and the reader. Classic style is a group of closely related decisions. It defines roles and creates a distinctive network of relationships" (1994, 22).

CHAPTER 13. RETHINKING STYLISTIC ANALYSIS IN THE WRITING CLASS (WILLIAM J. CARPENTER)

1.   For the most famous example of stylistic analysis, see Corbett and Connors (1999).
2.   Patrick Hartwell systematically critiques formalist, structuralist, transformational-generative, and "stylistic" grammars on the basis of their usefulness to the teaching of writing. He concludes his essay by arguing: "At no point in the English curriculum is the question of power more blatantly posed than in the issue of formal grammar instruction" (1985, 126). In other words, teaching any of the types of grammars listed not only interferes with writing instruction but also disempowers students who cannot make their own useable knowledge of language match up with the taxonomies presented by the models.
3.   Like Hartwell, I am not arguing that other grammars are "wrong" or "bad" in some way. Other grammars simply have different priorities for their descriptions of language. That these priorities usually involve creating taxonomies of structural forms or of psychological operations in the creation of these forms makes such grammars useless in discussions of discourse production. Making meaning in language is a social operation—just as much as it is a psychological one—and any useful grammar for the teaching of writing and style must consider the social nature of language use.
4.   My use of functional terms will be limited here. Like other grammars, the functional model is as complex as it is comprehensive. I believe that only a handful of terms are needed for people to see the different kinds of information functional analysis can provide. For more detailed descriptions of functional grammar, see Thompson (1996); Halliday (1973, 1978); Collerson (1994).

CHAPTER 14. RE-PLACING THE SENTENCE: APPROACHING STYLE THROUGH GENRE (PETER CLEMENTS)

I would like to thank Anis Bawarshi and T. R. Johnson for their helpful comments on earlier drafts of this chapter.
1.   This term refers to children from immigrant families or from multilingual communities who have grown up speaking languages other than English. See Harklau, Losey, and Siegal (1999).
2.   This activity is an adaptation of an activity that was first suggested to me by Meredith Lee.
3.   This assignment sequence was originally based on ideas and materials developed by Terri Major.

CHAPTER 15. TUTORING TABOO: A RECONSIDERATION OF STYLE IN THE WRITING CENTER (JESSE KAVADLO)

1.   Indeed, Stephen North and, separately, Patricia Dunn lament how frequently this antiquated approach to process takes place in English departments, let alone in fields

that have incorporated writing only recently into their curricula. See North (1984, 1994); Dunn (2000).

2.   I have my student's permission to use her writing anonymously.

CHAPTER 16. RHETOR-FITTING: DEFINING ETHICS THROUGH STYLE (DION C. CAUTRELL)

1.   With Brenda Deen Schildgen, I recognize (and celebrate) that "current composition theory and practice are engaged in realigning philosophy and rhetoric because composition defines rhetoric to include both production and interpretation of texts" (1993, 30). Consequently, I take rhetoric to mean theorizing and enactment, textual creation, and textual reception. Similarly, discourse refers to motivated language, or rather language-in-use, regardless of who (writer or reader) is putting it to use.

2.   Susan Jarratt's *Rereading the Sophists* (1998) and Kathleen Welch's *The Contemporary Reception of Classical Rhetoric* (1990) provide thorough analyses of these traditions, their continuing importance to both stylistics and rhetoric-composition as a whole.

3.   Quintilian, as Cicero and Isocrates before him, argues that rhetoric and ethics are mutually reinforcing, that rhetorical education should produce "the good man speaking well" (*vi bonus dicendi peritus*)—see *The Orator's Education (Institutio Oratoria)* (2002), book 12. In *The Electronic Word,* however, Lanham deems this argument "the Weak Defense" of stylistic ethics and proceeds to develop the position I partially detail in coming pages (1993, 155).

4.   Mary Margaret McCabe sees the Aristotle of the *Rhetoric* as himself embodying the middle ground between the Platonic and Sophistic traditions, an authorial manifestation of competing tendencies (1994, 129, ff.). John Cooper links ethos (character, credibility), as described in the *Rhetoric,* with Aristotle's treatments of phronesis, moral virtue, and goodwill in the *Rhetoric* and *Nicomachean Ethics* (see especially 1994, 199–202).

5.   Lanham's "bi-stable oscillation" (as described in Lanham 1993) and Jean-François Lyotard's "differend" (as described in Lyotard 1988) are variations of the transformandum Burke describes.

6.   In *Counter-statement* Burke contends that a similar pairing underlies eloquence—defined as "the frequency of Symbolic and formal effects" (1953, 165): "The profuse embodiment of eloquence cannot be accomplished without coexisting discipline (resistance) and exposure (non-resistance)" (185). That "discipline" and "exposure" do not seem to be in opposition until renamed as "(non-) resistance" indicates how easily opposition becomes complementarity and vice versa.

7.   Lanham has devoted his career to challenging these attitudes, particularly as they inhibit stylistics, and as its title suggests, *Style: An Anti-textbook* (1974) radicalizes writing pedagogy by transforming style into the habit of mind central to rhetorical action. *The Electronic Word* (1993) updates and extends his position to account for both postmodernism and technological change.

8.   Avoiding the dangerous idealism of categorical imperatives (best exemplified by Platonism), the Sophists generally sought an ethics whose standard was *nomos* (social custom, received opinion) rather than *physis* (natural order or law). This change in first principles leaves rhetoric vulnerable to what some have treated as a do-it-yourself morality, but beyond any flaws it possesses, the philosophy requires interlocutors to think about who and what they engage with their discourse. Moreover, while some might choose to deceive or coerce, they (and their audiences) would know—or at least have the opportunity to know—that their choices are unethical. Actions have consequences, and those consequences may be judged. The Sophists did not redefine ethics as much as make it materially meaningful.

9.   In a similarly commonsensical fashion, Davidson addresses "whether the methods of radical interpretation [Davidson's theory] bear any serious resemblance to the way the mind works in acquiring language or grasping the sense of utterances": I confess I haven't thought much about this. I have said repeatedly that I very much doubted that my armchair speculations had much to do with how the mind actually copes with speech. I would be satisfied, I wrote, if a theory of the kind I described would suffice for understanding. (Davidson 1999a, 159).

CHAPTER 17. STYLE AS A SYSTEM: TOWARD A CYBERNETIC MODEL OF COMPOSITION STYLE (DREW LOEWE)

Without Sue Hum's endless patience, close critical readings, and insightful comments, this essay would not have been possible. In addition, I would like to thank the editors for their stimulating and productive suggestions during the revision process.

1.   I limit myself to these elements in order to have a workable initial model of what a cybernetic theory of style could look like; of course, additional inputs, outputs, and variables can exist in writing and reading.

2.   A full discussion of how discourses of the body affect and are affected by embodiment is beyond the scope of this essay. Readers wishing to further explore these ideas should read Hum (2001).

3.   Johnson calls the writer's internal process of revision while writing the "'audience within, a receptor or interlocutor we carry in our musculature and that tells us if we're writing well or not" (2003, 41).

4.   Schor takes the opposite approach. She argues that students do not need to be provided with opinions and topics because "[t]hey have plenty of their own" (1986, 210). In her view, composition teachers should train students to "recognize as topics the ideas that burden them" (210). Although Schor takes issue with Lanham for being prescriptive, her particular choices of terms (e.g., "control," "training," "burden") perhaps belie a more prescriptive approach for her pedagogy than she acknowledges.

REFERENCES

Addison, James, and Henry Wilson. 1991. From Writing Lab to Writing Center: Reinventing, Advancing, and Expanding. In *The Writing Center: New Directions*, edited by Ray Wallace and Jeanne Simpson. New York: Garland.

Agee, James, and Walker Evans. 1988. *Let Us Now Praise Famous Men*. Boston: Houghton Mifflin.

Agnew, Lois. 1998. The Civic Function of Taste: A Re-Assessment of Hugh Blair's Rhetorical Theory. *Rhetoric Society Quarterly* 28.2:25–36.

Anson, Chris M., and Robert A. Schwegler. 2003. *The Longman Handbook for Writers and Readers*. 3rd ed. New York: Longman.

Aristotle. 1984. *The Complete Works of Aristotle*. Vol. 2. Edited by Jonathan Barnes. Princeton: Princeton University Press.

———. 1991. *On Rhetoric: A Theory of Civic Discourse*. Translated by George A. Kennedy. New York: Oxford University Press.

Arrington, Phillip. 1988. A Dramatistic Approach to Understanding and Teaching the Paraphrase. *CCC* 39:185–97.

Axelrod, Rise, and Charles Cooper. *The St. Martin's Guide to Writing*. 7th ed. Boston: Bedford/St. Martin's, 2004.

Baker, Sheridan. 1997. *The Practical Stylist*. 8th ed. New York: Harper.

Barnett, Robert W., and Jacob Blumner, eds. 2001. *The Allyn and Bacon Guide to Writing Center Theory and Practice*. Boston: Allyn and Bacon.

Barthes, Roland. 1977a. From Work to Text. In *Image, Music, Text*, translated by Stephen Heath, 1998. New York: Hill and Wang.

———. 1977b. Writers, Intellectuals, Teachers. In *Image, Music, Text*, translated by Stephen Heath, 1998. New York: Hill and Wang.

———. 1988. The Death of the Author. In *Modern Criticism and Theory*, edited by David Lodge. London: Longman.

Bartholomae, David. 1986. Inventing the University. *Journal of Basic Writing* 5.1:4–23.

Bawarshi, Anis. 2003. *Genre and the Invention of the Writer: Reconsidering the Place of Invention in Composition*. Logan: Utah State University Press.

Bazerman, Charles, and Paul Prior. 2003. *What Writing Does and How It Does It: An Introduction to Analyzing Texts and Textual Practices*. New York: Lea Press.

Beason, Larry. 2002. Ethos and Error: How Business People React to Errors. *CCC* 53:33–64.

Beer, Stafford. 1980. Preface to *Autopoiesis*. In *Autopoiesis and Cognition: The Realization of the Living*, by Humberto R. Maturana and Francisco J. Varela, edited by Robert S. Cohen and Marx W. Wartofsky. Boston Studies in the Philosophy of Science 42. Dordrecht: D. Reidel.

Berendt, Joachim-Ernst. 1983. *The World Is Sound: Music and the Landscape of Conciousness*. Rochester, VT.: Destiny Books.

Berger, John. 1972. *Ways of Seeing*. London: BBC.

———. 2000. *Ways of Seeing*. Academic Discourse: Readings for Argument and Analysis. Fort Worth: Hancourt College Press, 2000. 59-82.

Berger, John, and Jean Mohr. 1982. *Another Way of Telling*. New York: Vantage International.

Berkenkotter, Carol, and Thomas Huckin. 1993. Rethinking Genre from a Sociocognitive Perspective. *Written Communication* 10:475–509.

———. 1995. *Genre Knowledge in Disciplinary Communication*. Hillsdale: Erlbaum.

Berlin, James A. 1984. *Writing Instruction in Nineteenth-Century American Colleges.* Carbondale: Southern Illinois University Press.

———. 1987. *Rhetoric and Reality: Writing Instruction in American Colleges, 1900 to 1985.* Carbondale: Southern Illinois University Press.

———. 1991. Composition and Cultural Studies. In Hurlbert and Blitz 1991.

Berry, Christopher J. 1974. Adam Smith's Considerations on Language. In *Adam Smith,* edited by Knud Haakonssen, 1998. Brookfield, VT: Ashgate.

Berthoff, Ann E. 1982. *Forming, Thinking, Writing.* Portsmouth, NH: Boynton/Cook.

———. 1990. *The Sense of Learning.* Portsmouth, NH: Boynton/Cook.

———. 1999. *The Mysterious Barricades.* Toronto: Toronto University Press.

Bickerton, Derek. 1990. *Language and Species.* Chicago: University of Chicago Press.

Bishop, Wendy. 1995. Teaching Grammar for Writers in a Process Workshop Classroom. In *The Place of Grammar in Writing Instruction,* edited by Susan Hunter and Ray Wallace. Portsmouth, NH: Boynton/Cook.

Bizzell, Patricia. 1982. Cognition, Convention, and Certainty: What We Need to Know about Writing. *PRE/TEXT* 3:213–43.

———. 1990. Beyond Anti-foundationalism to Rhetorical Authority: Problems Defining Cultural Literacy. In *Academic Discourse and Critical Consciousness,* 1992. University of Pittsburgh Press.

Bizzell, Patricia, and Bruce Herzberg, eds. 1990. *The Rhetorical Tradition: Readings from Classical Times to the Present.* Boston: Bedford/St. Martin's Press.

Blair, Hugh. 1783. *Lectures on Rhetoric and Belles Lettres.* 2005. Carbondale: Southern Illinois Univeristy Press. Edited by Linda Ferreira-Buckley and S. Michael Halloran.

Blake, William. 1966. *Complete Writings.* Edited by Geoffrey Keynes. London: Oxford University Press.

Bleich, David. 1998. *Know and Tell.* Portsmouth, NH: Boynton/Cook.

Blitefield, Jerry. 2002. *Kairos* and the Rhetorical Place. In *Professing Rhetoric: Selected Papers from the 2000 Rhetoric Society of America Conference,* edited by Frederick J. Antczak, Cinda Coggins, and Geoffrey D. Klinger. Mahwah, NJ: Erlbaum.

Bloom, Lynn Z. 1996. Freshman Composition as a Middle-Class Enterprise. *College English* 58:654–75.

Braddock, Richard, Richard Lloyd-Jones, and Lowell Schoer. 1963. *Research in Written Composition.* Urbana, IL: NCTE.

Bradford, Richard. 1997. *Stylistics.* New York: Routledge.

Brody, Miriam. 1993. *Manly Writing: Gender, Rhetoric, and the Rise of Composition.* Carbondale: Southern Illinois University Press.

Brooks, Jeff. 1991. Minimalist Tutoring: Making the Student Do All the Work. In Barnett and Blumner 2001.

Brown, Chip. 1993. Fire Levels Cult HQ after Assault by FBI. *Chicago Sun-Times,* April 19.

Bullock, Richard, and John Trimbur. 1991. *The Politics of Writing Instruction: Postsecondary.* Portsmouth, NH: Heinemann/Boynton Cook.

Burke, Kenneth. 1953. *Counter-statement.* Los Altos: Hermes.

———. 1962. *A Rhetoric of Motives.* Berkeley: University of California Press.

———. 1973. *The Philosophy of Literary Form.* 3rd. ed. Berkeley: University of California Press.

Burnett, Rebecca E. 2001. *Technical Communication.* 5th ed. Boston: Heinle.

Butler, Judith. 1993. *Bodies That Matter: On the Discursive Limits of 'Sex'.* New York: Routledge.

Butler, Paul. 2001. Toward a Pedagogy of Writing Immersion: Using Imitation in the Composition Classroom. *Journal of College Writing* 4.1:107–13.

Campbell, Kim Sydow, et al. 1999. Exploring How Instruction in Style Affects Writing Quality. *Business Communication Quarterly* 62:71–86.

Carino, Peter. 1995. Early Writing Centers: Toward a History. In Barnett and Blumner 2001.

Carpenter, William J. 2001. Re-defining Style in Composition. PhD diss., University of Kansas, 2001. Ann Arbor: UMI, 9998065.

Carver, Raymond. 1988a. Feathers. In *Where I'm Calling From*. New York: Atlantic Monthly Press.

———. 1988b. The Third Thing That Killed My Father Off. In *Where I'm Calling From*. New York: Atlantic Monthly Press.

Catano, Jones. 1997. Stylistics. *The John Hopkins Guide to Literacy Theory and Criticism.* Ed. Michael Groden and Martin Kreiswirth. Baltimore, MD: Johns Hopkins Univeristy Press, 1997.

Caudery, Tim. 2002. Increasing Students' Awareness of Genre through Text Transformation Exercises: An Old Classroom Activity Revisited. *TESL-EJ* 3.3 (2002). http://www-writing.berkeley.edu/TESL-EJ/ej11/a2.html

Challenging Tradition: A Conversation about Reimagining the Dissertation in Rhetoric and Composition. 2001. *CCC* 52:441–54.

Christensen, Francis. "A Generative Rhetoric of the Sentence." 1963. October. *CCC* 14 (p.155-161)

———.1965. The Generative Rhetoric of the Paragraph. *CCC* 16:144–56.

———. 1978. The Generative Rhetoric of the Sentence. In *Notes toward a New Rhetoric*. 2nd ed. New York: Harper and Row.

Cicero. 1949. *On Invention*. Translated by H. M Hubbell. Cambridge: Harvard University Press.

Cixous, Hélène. 1975. The Laugh of the Medusa. (Le rire de la Medusa.) Translated by Keith Cohen and Paula Cohen. In Bizzell and Herzberg 1990.

Clark, Irene, and Dave Healy. 1996. Are Writing Centers Ethical? In Barnett and Blumner 2001.

Clifford, James. 1986. On Ethnographic Allegory. In *Writing Culture*, edited by James Clifford and Herbert Marcus. Berkeley: University of California Press.

Clifford, John. 1991. The Subject in Discourse. In Harkin and Schilb 1991.

Clouse, Barbara. 2001. *Progressions with Readings: Paragraphs to Essays.* New York: Longman.

Codrescu, Andrei. 2003. Penny Post: San Francisco Noir. *Gambit-Weekly*, June 17.

Coe, Richard M. 1987. An Apology for Form; or, Who Took the Form Out of the Process? In McDonald 2000.

———. 2002. The New Rhetoric of Genre. In Johns 2002b.

Cohen, Robert S., and Marx W. Wartofsky. 1980. Editorial preface to Maturana and Varela 1980.

Collerson, John. 1994. *English Grammar: A Functional Approach*. Newtown, Australia: PETA.

Connors, Robert J. 1981. The Rise and Fall of the Modes of Discourse. *CCC* 32:444–55.

———. 1983. Static Abstractions and Composition. In Tate, Corbett, and Myers 1994.

———. 1985. Mechanical Correctness as a Focus in Composition Instruction. *CCC* 36:61–72.

———. 1997. *Composition-Rhetoric: Backgrounds, Theory, and Pedagogy*. Pittsburgh: University of Pittsburgh Press.

———. 2000. The Erasure of the Sentence. *CCC* 52:96–128.

Connors, Robert, and Cheryl Glenn. 1995. Teaching Style. In *The St. Martin's Guide to Teaching Writing*. New York: St. Martin's Press.

Cooper, John M. 1994. Ethical-Political Theory in Aristotle's *Rhetoric*. In Furley and Nehamas 1994.

Corbett, Edward P. J. 1963. The Usefulness of Classical Rhetoric. *CCC* 14.3: 162-164.

———. 1971. The Theory and Practice of Imitation in Classical Rhetoric. *CCC* 22: 243–50.

————. 1990. *Classical Rhetoric for the Modern Student.* 3rd ed. New York: Oxford University Press.

————. 1996. Teaching Style. *Selected Essays of Edward P. J. Corbett.* Ed. Robert J. Connors. Dallas: Southern Methodist Univeristy Press, 1989. Rpt. in *The Allyn and Bacon Sourcebook for College Writing Teachers.* Ed. James C. McDonald. Boston: Allyn and Bacon, 1996. 215-23.

Corbett, Edward P. J., Gary Tate, and Nancy Myers. 2000. *The Writing Teacher's Sourcebook.* New York: Oxford University Press.

Corbett, Edward P. J., and Robert J. Connors. 1999. *Style and Statement.* New York: Oxford University Press.

————. 2000. *Classical Rhetoric for the Modern Sudent.* 4th ed. New York: Oxford University Press.

Covino, William. 2001. "Rhetorical Pedagogy." In Tate, Ruppier, and Schick, 2001.

Crowley, Sharon. 1986. Current-Traditional Theory of Style. *Rhetoric Society Quarterly* 16:233-50.

————. 1989. Linguistics and Composition Instruction: 1950-1980. *Written Communication* 6:480-505.

————. 1990. *The Methodical Memory: Invention in Current-Traditional Rhetoric.* Carbondale: Southern Illinois University Press.

————. 1998. Around 1971. In *Composition in the University: Historical and Polemical Essays.* Pittsburgh: University of Pittsburgh Press.

Daiker, Donald A., Andrew Kerek, and Max Morenberg. 1978. Sentence Combining and Syntactic Maturity in Freshman English. *CCC* 29:36-41.

Daiker, Donald, Andrew Kerek, Max Morenberg, eds. 1985. *Sentence-Combining and the Teaching of Writing.* Carbondale: Southern Illinois University Press.

D'Angelo, Frank J. 1973. Imitation and Style. *CCC* 24:283-90.

————. 1974. Sacred Cows Make Great Hamburgers: The Rhetoric of Graffiti. *CCC* 25:173-80.

————. 1986. The Topic Sentence Revisited. *CCC* 37:431-41.

Daniels, Harvey A. 1983. *Famous Last Words.* Carbondale: Southern Illinois University Press.

Davidson, Donald. 1999a. General Comments. In Zeglen 1999.

————. 1999b. Reply to Roger F. Gibson. In Zeglen 1999.

Dawkins, John. 1995. Teaching Punctuation as a Rhetorical Tool. *CCC* 46:533-48.

Deacon, Terrence. 1997. *The Symbolic Species.* New York: Norton.

Deleuze, Gilles. 1994. *Difference and Repetition.* Translated by Paul Patton. New York: Columbia University Press.

Delpit, Lisa. 1988 . The Silenced Dialogue: Power and Pedagogy in Educating Other People's Children. *Harvard Educational Review* 58:280-98.

Demetrius. 1963. *On Style.* Translated with an introduction by John Warrington. New York: Dutton.

Deren, Maya. 1984. *Divine Horsemen: The Living Gods of Haiti.* New York: MacPherson.

Devitt, Amy J. 1993. Generalizing about Genre: New Conceptions of an Old Concept. *CCC* 44:573-86.

Devitt, Amy J., Anis Bawarshi, and Mary Jo Reiff. 2004. *Scenes of Writing: Genre Acts.* New York: Longman.

Dillard, Annie. 1982. *Teaching a Stone to Talk.* New York: HarperPerennial.

Duncan, David James. 2001. *My Story as Told by Water.* San Francisco: Sierra Club Books.

Dunn, Patricia. 2000. Marginal Comments on Writers' Texts: The Status of the Commentator as a Factor in Writing Center Tutorials. In *Stories from the Center: Connecting Narrative and Theory in the Writing Center,* edited by Lynn Craigue Briggs and Meg Woolbright. Urbana, IL: NCTE.

During, Simon. 1993. Introduction to *The Cultural Studies Reader*. New York: Routledge.

Ede, Lisa S. 1979. On Audience and Composition. *CCC* 30:291–95.

———. 1999. Reading—and Rereading—the Braddock Essays. In *On Writing Research: The Braddock Essays 1975–1998,* ed. Lisa Ede. Boston: Bedford/St. Martin's.

Elbow, Peter. 1973. *Writing without Teachers*. New York: Oxford University Press.

———. 1981. *Writing with Power*. New York: Oxford University Press.

———. 2002. The Cultures of Literature and Composition: What Could Each Learn from the Other? *College English* 64:533–46.

Ellman, Richard. 1972. *Ulysses on the Liffey*. Oxford: Oxford University Press.

Faigley, Lester. 1979. Generative Rhetoric as a Way of Increasing Syntactic Fluency. *CCC* 30:176–81.

———. 1986. Competing Theories of Process: A Critique and a Proposal. *College English* 48:527–42.

———. 1992. *Fragments of Rationality: Postmodernity and the Subject of Composition*. Pittsburgh: University of Pittsburgh Press.

Fakundiny, Lydia. 1991. Talking about Style. In *The Art of the Essay*. Boston: Houghton Mifflin.

Falk, Julia S. 1973. *Linguistics and Language*. Lexington: Xerox College.

Ferris, Dana. 2002. *Treatment of Error in Second Language Student Writing*. Ann Arbor: University of Michigan Press.

Fine Clouse, Barbara. *Progressions With Readings: Paragraphs to Essays*. 6th ed. San Francisco: Pearson Longman, 2005.

Fish, Stanley E. 1987. Anti-foundationalism, Theory Hope, and the Teaching of Composition. In *Doing What Comes Naturally: Change, Rhetoric, and the Practice of Theory in Literary and Legal Studies (Post-Contemporary Interventions),* 1990. Chapel Hill, NC: Duke University Press.

Flannery, Kathryn. 1995. *The Emperor's New Clothes: Literature, Literacy, and the Ideology of Style*. Pittsburgh: University of Pittsburgh Press.

Fleischauer, John F. 1975. James Baldwin's Style: A Prospectus for the Classroom. *CCC* 26:141–48.

Flynn, Elizabeth. 1988. Composing as a Woman. *CCC* 39:423–35.

Fortune, Ron. 1989. Style in Composition Research and Teaching. *Style* 23:508–29.

Foss, Sonja. 1995. *Rhetorical Criticism: Exploration and Practice*. Prospect Heights, IL: Waveland.

Foster, D. B. 1969. Cybernetics and Industrial Processes. In *Survey of Cybernetics,* edited by J. Rose. New York: Gordon and Breach.

Foucault, Michel. 1988. What Is an Author? In *Modern Criticism and Theory,* edited by David Lodge. London: Longman.

Frank, Thomas. 2003. Down and Out in the Red Zone. *The Baffler #15: Civilization with a Krag,* January 1.

Freadman, Anne. 1994. Anyone for Tennis? In Freedman and Medway 1994a.

Freedman, Aviva. 1994. "Do as I Say": The Relationship between Teaching and Learning New Genres. In Freedman and Medway 1994a.

Freedman, Aviva and Peter Medway, eds. 1994a. *Genre and the New Rhetoric*. London: Taylor and Francis.

———. 1994b. Locating Genre Studies: Antecedents and Prospects. In Freedman and Medway 1994a.

Freire, Paulo. 1970. *Pedagogy of the Oppressed*. Translated by M. B. Rames. New York: Continuum.

———. 1973. *Education for Critical Consciousness*. New York: Seabury Press.

Fuller, Mary. 1991. Teaching Style in Advanced Composition Classes. In *Teaching Advanced Composition,* edited by Katherine H. Adams and John L. Adams. Portsmouth, NH: Boynton/Cook.

Furley, David J., and Alexander Nehamas, eds. 1994. *Aristotle's Rhetoric: Philosophical Essays.* Princeton: Princeton University Press.

Gadamer, Hans-Georg. 1975. *Truth and Method.* Translated by Joel Weinsheimer and Donald G. Marshall. New York: Crossroads.

Gage, John T. 1980. Philosophies of Style and Their Implications for Composition. *College English* 41:615–22.

Gallagher, Chris. 2002. *Radical Departures: Composition and Progressive Pedagogy.* Urbana, IL: NCTE.

Gannon, John. 1995. Nice Work If You Can Get It. *Mother Jones,* March–April.

Gebhardt, Richard. 1985. Sentence Combining in the Teaching of the Writing Process. In McDonald 2000.

Gelder, Ken, and Sarah Thornton, eds. 1997. *The Subcultures Reader.* New York: Routledge.

Genova, Judith. 1979. The Significance of Style. *Journal of Aesthetics and Art Criticism* 37.3:315–24.

George, Ann. 2001. Critical Pedagogy: Dreaming of Democracy. In Tate, Rupiper, and Schick.

Gerber, John C. 1950. The Conference on College Composition and Communication. *CCC* 1:12.

Gorgias. 1990. Encomium of Helen. Translated by George Kennedy. In Bizzell and Herzberg.

Grant-Davie, Keith. 1997. Rhetorical Situations and Their Constituents. *Rhetoric Review* 15.2:264–79.

Graves, Richard L. 1974. A Primer for Teaching Style. *CCC* 25:186–90.

Graves, Robert. 2002. *The Greek Myths.* London: The Folio Society.

Guernsey, Lisa. 2003. A Young Writer's Roundtable, via the Web. *New York Times,* August 14.

Guffey, Mary Ellen. 2001. *Essential of Business Communication.* 5th ed. Mason, OH: South-Western College.

Guillory, John. 2002. Literary Study and the Disciplines. In *Disciplinarity at the Fin de Siècle,* edited by Amanda Anderson and Joseph Valente. Princeton: Princeton University Press.

Hacking, Ian. 1982. Language, Truth, and Reason. In *Rationality and Relativity,* edited by Martin Hollis and Steven Lucas. Boston: MIT Press.

Hairston, Maxine. 1982. *The Winds of Change: Thomas Kuhn and the Revolution in the Teaching of Writing.* CCC 33.1: 76-88.

Hake, Rosemary, and Joseph Williams. 1985. Some Cognitive Issues in Sentence Combining: On the Theory That Smaller Is Better. In Daiker et al. 1985.

Halliday, M. A. K. 1973. *Explorations in the Functions of Language.* New York: Elsevier.

———. 1978. *Language as Social Semiotic.* London: Edward Arnold.

Halliwell, Stephen. 1994. Popular Morality, Philosophical Ethics, and the *Rhetoric.* In Furley and Nehamas 1994.

Harding, Sandra. 1987. Is There a Feminist Method? In *Feminism and Methodology,* edited by Sandra Harding. Bloomington: Indiana University Press.

Harkin, Patricia, and John Schilb, eds. 1991. *Contending with Words: Composition and Rhetoric in a Postmodern Age.* New York: MLA.

Harklau, Linda, Kay M. Losey, and Meryl Siegal, eds. 1999. *Generation 1.5 Meets College Composition: Issues in the Teaching of Writing to U.S.–Educated Learners of ESL.* Mahwah, NJ: Erlbaum.

Harris, Joseph. 1996. *A Teaching Subject: Composition since 1966.* New York: Prentice Hall.

Harris, Joseph, and Jay Rosen. 1991. Teaching Writing as Cultural Criticism. In Hurlbert and Blitz 1991.

Harris, Muriel, and Katherine E. Rowan. 1996. Explaining Grammatical Concepts. In *The Allyn and Bacon Sourcebook for College Writing Teachers,* edited by James C. McDonald. Boston: Allyn and Bacon.

Hartwell, Patrick. 1985. Grammar, Grammars, and the Teaching of Grammar. *College English* 47:105–27.

———. 1996. *Grammar, Grammars, and the Teaching of Grammar.* In *The Allyn and Bacon Sourcebook for Writing Teachers.* Ed. James C. McDonald. Boston: Allyn and Bacon, 1996. 234-57.

Hashimoto, Irvin. 1991. *Thirteen Weeks.* Portsmouth, NH: Boynton/Cook.

Havelock, Eric. 1982. *The Literate Revolution in Greece and Its Cultural Consequences.* Princeton: Princeton University Press.

Hawhee, Debra. 2002. Bodily Pedagogies: Rhetoric, Athletics, and the Sophists' Three Rs. *College English* 65:2, 142–62.

Hayles, N. Katherine. 1999. *How We Became Posthuman: Virtual Bodies in Cybernetics, Literature, and Informatics.* Chicago: University of Chicago Press.

Haynes, Cynthia, and Victor Vitanza, eds. 2000. *The Soundzs of WOOsic Writing. Pre/Text: Electrilite* 3.1. http://www.utdallas.edu/pretext/index1a.html.

Haynes, John. 1995. *Style.* New York: Routledge,.

Heilker, Paul. 1996. *The Essay: Theory and Pedagogy for an Active Form.* Urbana, IL: NCTE.

Hemingway, Ernest. 1926. *The Sun Also Rises.* New York: MacMillan.

Heylighen, Francis, and Cliff Joslyn. 2002. Cybernetics and Second-Order Cybernetics. In *Encylopedia of Physical Science and Technology,* 17 vols., 3rd ed., edited by Robert. A. Meyers.

Hiatt, Mary. 1978. The Feminine Style: Theory and Fact. *CCC* 29:222–26.

Hillocks, George, Jr. 1986. *Research on Written Composition.* Urbana, IL: NCTE.

———. 1995. *Teaching Writing as Reflective Practice.* New York: Teachers College Press.

Hirsch, E. D., Jr. 1977. *The Philosophy of Composition.* University of Chicago Press.

_____. 1983. Reading, Writing, and Cultural Literacy. In *Composition and Literature: Bridging the Gap,* edited by Winifred Bryan Horner. University of Chicago Press.

Hocks. 2003. Understanding Visual Rhetoric in Digital Writing Environments. "Understanding Visual Rhetoric in Digital Writing Environments." CCC 54.4: 629-656.

Hoggart, Richard. 1997. *The Uses of Literacy.* New York: Transaction Publishers.

Holden, Michael. 1994. Effectiveness of Two Approaches to Teaching Writing in Improving Students' Knowledge of English Grammar. ERIC, ED 366 006.

Horner, Bruce. 1999. The "Birth" of "Basic Writing." In Horner and Lu 1999.

Horner, Bruce, and Min-Zhan Lu, eds. 1999. *Representing the "Other": Basic Writers and the Teaching of Basic Writing.* Urbana, IL: NCTE.

Howard, Rebecca Moore. 1996. The Great Wall of African American Vernacular English in the American College Classroom. *JAC: A Journal of Composition Theory* 16.2: 265–84.

———. 2000. Style, Race, Culture, Context. In *Coming of Age: The Advanced Writing Curriculum,* edited by Linda K. Shamoon, Rebecca Moore Howard, Sandra Jamieson, and Robert A. Schwegler. Portsmouth, NH: Heinemann Boynton/Cook.

Howard, Rebecca Moore, Heidi Beierle, Patricia Tallakson, Amy Taggart, Dan Fredrick, Mark Noe, Artist Thornton, Kurt Schick, and Melanie Peterson. 2002. What Are Styles and Why Are We Saying Such Terrific Things about Them? In *Teaching Writing: Landmarks and Horizons,* edited by Christina Russell McDonald and Robert L. McDonald. Carbondale: Southern Illinois University Press.

Howell, Wilbur S. 1956. *Logic and Rhetoric in England: 1500–1700.* Princeton: Princeton University Press.

Hugo, Richard. 1979. *The Triggering Town.* New York: W. W. Norton

Hum, Sue. 2001. Articulating Authentic Chineseness: The Politics of Reading Race and Ethnicity Aesthetically. *Readerly/Writerly Texts* 9.1–2:61–82.

Hunt, Kendall. 1966. Recent Measures in Syntactic Development. *Elementary English* 43:732–39.

Hunter, Susan, and Ray Wallace, eds. 1995. *The Place of Grammar in Writing Instruction: Past, Present, and Future.* Portsmouth, NH: Boyton/Cook.

Hurlbert, C. Mark, and Michael Blitz, eds. 1991. *Composition and Resistance.* Portsmouth, NH: Boyton/Cook.

"I Provide Office Solutions," Says Pitiful Little Man. 1998. *Onion*, September 24. http://www.theonion.com/onion3408/officesolutions.html.

Jarratt, Susan. 1998. *Rereading the Sophists: Classical Rhetoric Refigured.* Carbondale: Southern Illinois University Press.

Jensen, George H., and John K. DiTiberio. 1984. Personality and Individual Writing Processes. *CCC* 35:285–300.

Johns, Ann M. 2002a. Destabilizing and Enriching Novice Students' Genre Theories. In Johns 2002b.

———, ed. 2002b. *Genre in the Classroom: Multiple Perspectives.* Mahwah, NJ: Erlbaum.

Johnson, Sabina Thorne. 1969. Some Tentative Strictures on Generative Rhetoric. *College English* 31:155–65.

Johnson, Steven. 1997. Interface Culture: How New Technology Transforms the Way We Create and Communicate. New York: Basic.

Johnson, T. R. 2001. School Sucks. *CCC* 52:620–50.

———. 2003. *A Rhetoric of Pleasure: Prose Style and Today's Composition Classroom.* Portsmouth, NH: Boynton/Cook.

Jolliffe, David. 1998. *Inquiry and Genre: Writing to Learn in College.* Boston: Longman.

Jones, Peter, and Andrew S. Skinner. 1992. *Adam Smith Reviewed.* Edinburgh: Edinburgh University Press.

Kaplan, Robert. 1966. Cultural Thought Patterns in Inter-Cultural Education. *Language Learning* 16:1–20.

Katz, Stephen. 1996. *The Epistemic Music of Rhetoric.* Carbondale: Southern Illinois University Press.

Kaufer, David S., and Erwin R. Steinberg. 1988. Economies of Expression: Some Hypotheses. *CCC* 39:453–57.

Kaufer, David, and Richard Young. 1993. Writing in the Content Areas: Some Theoretical Complexities. In *Theory and Practice in the Teaching of Writing: Rethinking the Discipline*, edited by Lee Odell. Carbondale: Southern Illinois University Press.

Kellner, Hans. 2000. Supposing Barthes's Voice. In *The Soundz of WOOsic Writing*, edited by Cynthia Haynes and Victor Vitanza. *Pre/Text: Electrilite* 3.1. www.utdallas.edu/pretext/PT3.1/kellner1.html.

Kelly, Lou. 1974. Is Competent Copyreading a Violation of the Students' Right to Their Own Language? *CCC* 25: 254–58.

Kennedy, George A. 1980. *Classical Rhetoric and Its Christian and Secular Tradition: From Ancient to Modern Times.* Chapel Hill: University of North Carolina Press.

Kent, Thomas. 1993. *Paralogic Rhetoric: A Theory of Communicative Interaction.* Lewisburg: Bucknell University Press.

———. 1999. Introduction to *Post-process Theory: Beyond the Writing Process/Paradigm*, edited by Thomas Kent. Carbondale: Southern Illinois University Press.

Khan, Hazrat Inayat. 1996. *The Mysticism of Sound and Music.* Boston: Shambhala.

Kinneavy, James E. 1969. The Basic Aims of Discourse. In *Cross-Talk in Comp Theory*, edited by Victor Villanueva, 2003. Urbana, IL: NCTE.

Kirsch, Gesa, and Patricia A. Sullivan. 1992. *Methods and Methodology in Composition Research.* Carbondale: Southern Illinois University Press.

Kolln, Martha. 1981. *Closing the Books on Alchemy.* CCC 32 (May 1981): 139-151.

———. 1999. *Rhetorical Grammar: Grammatical Choices, Rhetorical Effects.* 3rd ed. New York: Longman.

Kozol, Jonathan. 1991. *Savage Inequalities: Children in America's Schools.* New York: Harper.

———. 1995. *Amazing Grace.* New York: Crown.

———. 2000. *Ordinary Resurrections.* New York: Crown.

Krause, Martin. 1992. *Surrational Images: Photomontages by Scott Mutter.* Chicago: University of Illinois Press.

Krizan, A. C., et al. 2002. *Business Communication.* 5th ed. Mason, OH: South-Western College.

Kroll, Barbara. 2001. The Composition of a Life in Composition. In *On Second Language Writing,* edited by Tony Silva and Paul Kei Matsuda. Mahwah, NJ: Erlbaum.

Kroll, Barry. 1992. *Teaching Hearts and Minds.* Carbondale: Southern Illinois University Press.

Kurland, Dan. 2000. How the Language Really Works: The Fundamentals of Critical Reading and Effective Writing. http://www.criticalreading.com.

Laib, Nevin. 1990. Conciseness and Amplification. *CCC* 41:443–59.

Lanham, Richard A. 1974. *Style: An Anti-textbook,* 2nd ed., 1978. New Haven: Yale University Press.

———. 1991. *A Handlist of Rhetorical Terms.* 2nd ed. Berkeley: University of California Press.

———. 1993. *The Electronic Word: Democracy, Technology, and the Arts.* Chicago: University of Chicago Press.

Lannon, John M. 2002. *Technical Communication.* 9th ed. New York: Longman.

Laszlo, Ervin. 1973. Cybernetics of Musical Activity. *Journal of Aesthetics and Art Criticism* 31.3:375–87.

Latour, Bruno. 1987. *Science in Action.* Cambridge: Harvard University Press. 33-44.

LeFevre, Karen Burke. 1987. *Invention as a Social Act.* Carbondale: Southern Illinois University Press.

Leki, Ilona. 1992. *Understanding ESL Writers.* Portsmouth, NH: Boynton/Cook.

Lind, Vicki R., and Elizabeth Lindsey. 2003. *Creative Collaboration: Teachers and Artists in the Classroom Pre-K–Grade 12.* Pasadena: California Alliance of the Arts.

Lindemann, Erika. 1995. *A Rhetoric for Writing Teachers.* 3rd ed. New York: Oxford University Press.

Linn, Michael D. 1975. Black Rhetorical Patterns and the Teaching of Composition. *CCC* 26:149–53.

Lorca, Federico Garcia. 1955. *In Search of Duende.* New York: New Directions.

Lowe, Ralph E. 1973. *The Writing Clinic.* Englewood Cliffs, NJ: Prentice-Hall.

Lowell, Robert. 1977. *Selected Poems.* New York: Farrar, Strauss, Giroux.

Lu, Min-Zhan. 1994. Professing Multiculturalism: The Politics of Style in the Contact Zone. In Horner and Lu 1999.

———. 1999. Redefining the Legacy of Mina Shaughnessy: A Critique of the Politics of Linguistic Innocence. In Horner and Lu 1999.

Lundsford, Andrea A. 2003. *The St. Martin's Handbook.* 5th ed. Boston: Bedford/St. Martin's.

Lyotard, Jean-François. 1988. *The Differend: Phrases in Dispute.* Translated by Georges Van Den Abeeles. Theory and History of Literature 46. Minneapolis: University of Minnesota Press.

Lyotard, Jean-François, and Jean-Loup Thébaud. 1985. *Just Gaming.* Translated by Wlad Godzich. Theory and History of Literature 20. Minneapolis: University of Minnesota Press.

MacDonald, Susan Peck. 2002. The Analysis of Academic Discourse(s). In *Discourse Studies in Composition,* edited by Ellen Barton and Gail Stygall. Cresskill, NJ: Hampton Press.

Macrorie, Ken. 1970. *Telling Writing.* Rochelle Park, NJ: Hayden.

Mandel, Barrett. 1980. The Writer Writing Is Not at Home. *CCC* 31.4: 371–77.

Markel, Mike. 2001. *Technical Communication.* 6th ed. Boston: Bedford/St. Martin's.

Martinez, Sam Burke. 1997. Problematizing Style: How Style Is Represented in College Composition Textbooks. PhD diss., Arizona State University. DAI 58.05A: 1690.

Masiello, Lea. 2000. Style in the Writing Center: It's a Matter of Choice and Voice. In *A Tutor's Guide: Helping Writers One to One,* edited by Ben Rafoth. Portsmouth, NH: Boynton/Cook.

Massumi, Brian. 2002. *Parables for the Virtual: Movement, Affect, Sensation.* Durham: Duke University Press.

Maturana, Humberto R., and Francisco J. Varela. 1980. *Autopoiesis and Cognition: The Realization of the Living.* Edited by Robert S. Cohen and Marx W. Wartofsky. Boston Studies in the Philosophy of Science 42. Dordrecht: D. Reidel.

McCabe, Mary Margaret. 1994. Arguments in Context: Aristotle's Defense of Rhetoric. In Furley and Nehamas 1994.

McComiskey, Bruce. 1997. Writing in Context: Postmodern Theory and Practice in the Composition Class. *Composition Forum* 8.2:30–38.

McCrimmon, James. 1984. *Writing with a Purpose.* New York: Houghton Mifflin.

McDonald, James C., ed. 2000. *The Allyn and Bacon Sourcebook for College Writing Teachers.* 2nd ed. Boston: Allyn and Bacon.

McQuade, Donald A., ed. 1986. *The Territory of Language: Linguistics, Stylistics, and the Teaching of Composition.* Carbondale: Southern Illinois University Press.

Milic, Louis. 1965. Theories of Style and Their Implications for the Teaching of Composition. *CCC* 16:66–69, 126.

———. 1966. Metaphysics in the Criticism of Style. *CCC* 17:124–29.

———. 1971. Rhetorical Choice and Stylistic Options. *Literary Style* ed. by Seymour Chatman. New York: Oxford Univeristy Press.

Miller, Carolyn. 1984. Genre as Social Action. *Quarterly Journal of Speech* 70:151–67.

———. 1994. Rhetorical Community: The Cultural Basis of Genre. In Freedman and Medway 1994a.

Miller, Susan. 1991. *Textual Carnivals: The Politics of Composition.* Carbondale: Southern Illinois University Press.

———. 1997. Technologies of Self?-Formation. *JAC: A Journal of Composition Theory* 17:497–500.

Miller, Thomas P. 1997. *The Formation of College English: Rhetoric and Belles Lettres in the British Cultural Provinces.* Pittsburgh: University of Pittsburgh Press.

Moore, Robert. 1950. The Writing Clinic and the Writing Laboratory. In Barnett and Blumner 2001.

Morenberg, Max, and Jeff Sommers. 2003. *The Writer's Options: Lessons in Style and Arrangement.* 7th ed. Boston: Longman.

Morley, David. 1992. *Television, Audiences, and Cultural Studies.* New York: Routledge.

Murphy, Christina. 1989. Freud in the Writing Center: The Psychoanalytics of Tutoring Well. In Barnett and Blumner 2001.

Murray, Donald. 1980. Writing as Process: How Writing Finds Its Own Meaning. In *Eight Approaches to Teaching Composition,* edited by Timothy R. Donovan and Ben McClelland. Urbana, IL: NCTE.

———. 1982. *Teaching the Other Self: The Writer's First Reader. CCC* 33.2: 140–46.

Myers, Sharon A. 2003. ReMembering the Sentence. *CCC* 54:610–28.

National Center for Education Statistics. 2000. Major Findings from the NAEP 1998 Writing Report Card. In *National Assessment of Educational Progress.* http://165.224.221.98/nation-sreportcard/writing/writing.asp.

Nelson, John S. 1991. Seven Rhetorics of Inquiry: A Provocation. In Nelson, MeGill, and McCloskey 1991b.

Nelson, John S., Allan MeGill, and Donald M. McCloskey. 1991a. Rhetoric of Inquiry. In Nelson, MeGill, and McCloskey 1991b.

————, eds. 1991b. *The Rhetoric of the Human Sciences: Language and Argument in Scholarship and Public Affairs*. Madison: University of Wisconsin Press.

Nietzsche, Friedrich. 1989. *Friedrich Nietzsche on Rhetoric and Language*. Edited and translated by Sander L. Gilman, Carole Blair, and David J. Parent. New York: Oxford University Press.

Noguchi, Rei R. 1991. *Grammar and the Teaching of Writing: Limits and Possibilities*. Urbana, IL: NCTE.

North, Stephen M. 1984. The Idea of a Writing Center. In Barnett and Blumner 2001.

————. 1994. Revisiting "The Idea of a Writing Center." In Barnett and Blumner 2001.

Odell, Lee. 1973. Responding to Student Writing. *CCC* 24:394–400.

O'Hare, Frank. 1973. Sentence Combining: Improving Student Writing without Formal Grammar Instruction. Urbana, IL: NCTE.

Ohmann, Richard. 1979. Use Definite, Specific, Concrete Language. *College English* 41:390–97.

Ong, Walter. 1982. *Orality and Literacy: The Technologizing of the Word*. New York: Methuen.

Orwell, George. 1950. A Hanging. In *Shooting an Elephant and Other Essays*. New York: Harcourt.

Osundare, Niyi. 2002. *Pages from the Book of the Sun*. Trenton, NJ: Africa World Press.

Paine, Charles. 1999. *The Resistant Writer: Rhetoric as Immunity, 1850 to the Present*. SUNY Series in Literacy, Culture, and Learning—Theory and Practice. New York: State University of New York Press.

Pang, Terence T. T. 2002. Textual Analysis and Contextual Awareness Building: A Comparison of Two Approaches to Teaching Genre. In Johns 2002b.

Paré, Anthony, and Graham Smart. 1994. Observing Genres in Action: Towards a Research Methodology. In Freedman and Medway 1994a.

Parfitt, Matthew. 2003. Room for "Us" to Play: The Teacher as Midwife. In *Conflicts and Crises in the Composition Classroom—and What Instructors Can Do about Them*, edited by Dawn Skorczewski and Matthew Parfitt. Portsmouth: Heinemann Boyton Cook.

Parks, Stephen. 2000. *Class Politics: The Movement for the Students' Right to Their Own Language*. Urbana, IL: NCTE.

Peirce, Charles. S. 1878. How to Make Our Ideas Clear. *Popular Science Monthly* 12:286–302.

Perl, Sondra. 1979. The Composing Process of Unskilled College Writers. *Research in the Teaching of English*. 13.4:317–36.

Phelps, Louise Wetherbee. 1985. Dialectics of Coherence: Toward an Integrative Theory. *College English* 47:12–29.

Pinker, Steven. 1995. *The Language Instinct*. New York: HarperPerennial.

Plato. *Gorgias*. 2003. Translated by W. R. M. Lamb. Perseus Project. http://www.perseus.tufts.edu/cgibin/.

Porter, Arthur. 1969. *Cybernetics Simplified*. New York: Barnes and Noble.

Pratt, Mary Louise. 1977. *Toward a Speech Act Theory of Literary Discourse*. Bloomington: Indiana University Press.

————. 1986. Ideology and Speech-Act Theory. In Weber 1996a.

Pringle, Ian. 1983. Why Teach Style? A Review-Essay. *CCC* 34:91–98.

Purcell, William M., and David Snowball. 1996. Style. In *Encyclopedia of Rhetoric and Composition: Communication from Ancient Times to the Information Age*, edited by Theresa Enos. New York: Garland.

Quade, Dennis. 1992. Composition and Literature Studies. In *Redrawing the Boundaries: The Transformation of English and American Literary Studies*, edited by Stephen Greenblatt and Giles Gunn. New York: MLA.

Quintilian. 1987. *Quintilian on the Teaching of Speaking and Writing: Translations from Books One, Two, and Ten of the "Institutio Oratoria."* Edited by James Jerome Murphy. Carbondale: Southern Illinois University Press.

————. 2002. *The Orator's Education*. Books 11–12. Vol. 5. Translated by Donald A. Russell. Loeb Classical Library 494. Cambridge: Harvard University Press.

Rabinow, Paul. 1977. *Reflections on Fieldwork in Morocco*. Berkeley: University of California Press.

Rankin, Elizabeth. 1985. Revitalizing Style: Toward a New Theory and Pedagogy. In *The Writing Teacher's Sourcebook*, edited by Edward P. J. Corbett, Nancy Myers, and Gary Tate, 2000, 4th ed. New York: Oxford University Press.

Raymond, James C. 1986. *Writing Is an Unnatural Act*. New York: Harper and Row.

————. 1993. I-Dropping and Androgyny: The Authorial "I" in Scholarly Writing. *CCC* 44:478–93.

————. 1999. *Moves Writers Make*. Upper Saddle River, NJ: Prentice-Hall.

Reigstad, Thoimas J., and Donald A. McAndrew. 1984. *Training Tutors for Writing Conferences*. Urbana, IL: NCTE.

Reynolds, Nedra. 2000. *Portfolio Teaching: A Guide for Instructors*. Boston: Bedford.

Reynolds, Nedra, et al. 2004. The Bedford Bibliography for Teachers of Writing. Boston: Bedford St. Martin's.

Rhetoric to Herennius. 1981. Translated by Harry Caplan. Loeb Classical Library. Cambridge: Harvard University Press.

Rich, Adrienne. 1979. When We Dead Awaken: Writing as Revision In *On Lies, Secrets, and Silence*. New York: Norton.

Richardson, George P. 1991. *Feedback Thought in Social Science and Systems Theory*. Philadelphia: University of Pennsylvania Press.

Richardson, Paul. 1994. Language as Personal Resource and as Social Construct: Competing Views of Literacy Pedagogy in Australia. In *Learning and Teaching Genre*, edited by Aviva Freedman and Peter Medway. Portsmouth, NH: Boynton/Cook.

Riley, Kathryn, et al. 1999. *Revising Professional Writing in Science and Technology, Business, and the Social Sciences*. Superior, WI: Parlay Press.

Rodriguez, Richard. 2002. The Achievement of Desire. In *Ways of Reading: An Anthology for Writers*, edited by David Bartholomae and Anthony Petrosky. Boston: Bedford/St. Martin's.

Ronald, Kate, and Hephzibah Roskelly, eds. 1989. *Farther Along: Transforming Dichotomies in Rhetoric and Composition*. Portsmouth, NH: Heinemann Boynton/Cook.

Rorty, Richard. 1982. Philosophy as a Kind of Writing. In *Consequences of Pragmatism: Essays, 1972–1980*. Minneapolis: University of Minnesota Press.

Rose, Mike. 1989. *Lives on the Boundary*. New York: Free Press.

Rosner, Mary, and T. R. Johnson. 1995. Telling Stories: Metaphors for the Human Genome Project. *Hypatia* 10:4, 104-129.

Russell, David R. 1991. *Writing in the Academic Disciplines 1870–1990: A Curricular History*. Carbondale: Southern Illinois University Press.

Ryan, Leigh. 1998. *The Bedford Guide for Writing Tutors*. 2nd ed. Boston: Bedford.

Scarry, Elaine. 1999. On Beauty and Being Just. Princeton: Princeton Univeristy Press.

Schildgen, Brenda Deen. 1993. Reconnecting Rhetoric and Philosophy in the Composition Classroom. In *Into the Field: Sites of Composition Studies*, edited by Anne Ruggles Gere. New York: MLA.

Schneider, Barbara. 2002. Nonstandard Quotes: Superimpositions and Cultural Maps. *CCC* 54:188–207.

Schor, Sandra. 1986. Style through Control: The Pleasures of the Beginning Writer. In McQuade 1986.

Selzer, Jack. 1984. Exploring Options in Composing. *CCC* 35:276–84.

Shamoon, Linda K., and Deborah H. Burns. 1995. A Critique of Pure Tutoring. In Barnett and Blumner 2001.

Shaughnessy, Mina P. 1977. *Errors and Expectations: A Guide for the Teacher of Basic Writing*. New York: Oxford University Press.

Shopen, Tim. 1974. Some Contributions from Grammar to the Theory of Style. *College English* 35:775–98.

Skorczewski, Dawn. 2000. "Everybody Has Their Own Ideas:" Responding to Cliché in Student Writing. *CCC* 52:220–39.

Slevin, James F. 2001. Beyond the Culture of Improvement: The Fate of Reading in Composition (or, Does Composition Have a Canon, and if So, What's in It, Who Says So, and Why Care?). In *Introducing English: Essays in the Intellectual Work of Composition.* Pittsburgh: University of Pittsburgh Press.

Sloan, Gary. 1981. Mistaking Subject Matter for Style. *College English* 43:502–7.

Smith, Adam. 1983. *Lectures on Rhetoric and Belles Lettres.* Oxford: Oxford University Press.

———. 1985. *Lectures on Rhetoric and Belles Lettres.* Edited by J. C. Bryce. Indianapolis: Liberty Fund, 1985.

Smye, Randy. 1988. Style and Usage Software: Mentor Not Judge. *Computers and Composition.* 06.1: 47-61.

Sommers, Nancy. 1982. Responding to Student Writing. *CCC* 33:148–56.

Spack, Ruth. 1988. Initiating Students into the Academic Discourse Community: How Far Should We Go? *TESOL Quarterly* 22:29–51.

Spellmeyer, Kurt.1991. Knowledge against "Knowledge": Freshman English, Public Discourse, and the Social Imagination. In Hurlbert and Blitz 1991.

Stark, Ryan J. 2001. From Mysticism to Skepticism: Stylistic Reform in Seventeenth-Century British Philosophy and Rhetoric. *Philosophy and Rhetoric* 34.4:322–34.

Sternglass, Marilyn S. 1974. Dialect Features in the Compositions of Black and White College Students: The Same or Different? *CCC* 25:259–63.

Stine, Elizabeth Lotz, and John Neil Bohannon III. 1983. Imitations, Interactions, and Language Acquisition. *Journal of Child Language* 10.3:589–603.

Strunk, William, and E. B. White, Jr. 1999. *The Elements of Style.* 4th ed. New York: Pearson Allyn and Bacon.

Students' Right to Their Own Language. 1974. *CCC* 25.3:1–32. http://www.ncte.org/cccc/positions/right_to_language.shtml.

Swales, John. 1990. *Genre Analysis: English in Academic and Research Settings.* Cambridge: Cambridge University Press.

Tate, Gary, Edward P. J. Corbett, and Nancy Myers, eds. 1994. *The Writing Teacher's Sourcebook.* 3rd ed. New York: Oxford University Press.

Tate, Gary, Amy Ruppier, and Kurt Schick, eds. 2001. *A Guide to Composition Pedagogies.* New York: Oxford University Press.

Talbot, Taylor and Michael Toolan. 1984. Recent Trends in Stylistics. *Journal of Literary Semantics.* 13.1: 55-75.

Thill, John V., and Courtland L. Bovée. 2001. *Excellence in Business Communication.* 5th ed. New York: Prentice Hall.

Thomas, Francis-Noël, and Mark Turner. 1994. *Clear and Simple as the Truth: Writing Classic Prose.* Princeton: Princeton University Press.

Thompson, Geoff. 1996. *Introducing Functional Grammar.* London: Oxford University Press.

Thonney, Teresa. 2003. *Qualities of Good Prose.* New York: Longman.

Tibbets, A. B. 1976. On the Practical Uses of a Grammatical System: A Note on Christensen and Johnson. In *Rhetoric and Composition: A Sourcebook for Teachers,* edited by E. Richard Graves. Rochelle Park, NJ: Hayden.

Tompkins, Jane. 2000. "Indians": Textualism, Morality, and the Problem of History. In *Academic Discourse: Readings for Argument and Analysis,* edited by Gail Stygall. Fort Worth: Harcourt College.

Trend, David, ed. 1996. *Radical Democracy: Identity, Citizenship, and the State.* New York: Routledge.

Tucker, Irene. 2000. *A Probable State: The Novel, the Contract, and the Jews.* Chicago: University of Chicago Press.

Tufte, Virginia. 1971. *Grammar as Style*. New York: Holt, Rinehart, and Winston.

Vande Kopple, William J. 1985. Some Exploratory Discourse on Metadiscourse. *CCC* 36:82–93.

Vitanza, Victor. 1997. *Negation, Subjectivity, and the History of Rhetoric*. Albany: State University of New York Press.

Vygotsky, Lev. 1986. *Thought and Language*. Trans. Alex Kozvlin. Boston: MIT Press.

Walker, Jeffrey. 2000. *Rhetoric and Poetics in Antiquity*. New York: Oxford University Press.

Wallace, David Foster. 2001. Tense Present. *Harper's*. April 2001.

Wallace, Ron. 1989. Cognitive Mapping and the Origin of Language and Mind. *Current Anthropology* 30:518–29.

Walpole, Jane R. 1980. Style as Option. *CCC* 31:205–12.

Warnick, Barbara. 1993. *The Sixth Canon: Belletristic Rhetorical Theory and Its French Antecedents*. Columbia: University of South Carolina Press.

Weathers, Winston. 1980. *An Alternative Style: Options in Composition*. Rochelle Park, NJ: Hayden.

———. 1994. Teaching Style: A Possible Anatomy. In Corbett, Tate, and Myers 1994.

Weathers, Winston, and Wendy Bishop. 1996. Talking to Winston Weathers on E-Mail—An Interview. *Composition Studies* 24.1–2:72–87.

Weathers, Winston, and Otis Winchester. 1978. *The New Strategy of Style*. 2nd ed. New York: McGraw-Hill.

Weaver, Richard. 1953. *The Ethics of Rhetoric*. Chicago: Henry Regnery.

Weber, Jean Jacques, ed. 1996a. *The Stylistics Reader: From Roman Jakobson to the Present*. New York: St. Martin's.

———. 1996b. Towards Contextualized Stylistics: An Overview. In Weber 1996a.

Weinberg, Gerald M. 1975. *An Introduction to General Systems Thinking*. New York: Wiley.

Welch, Nancy. "And Now I Know Them": Composing Mutuality in a Service Learning Course. *CCC* 54.2. 243-263.

Welch, Kathleen E. 1990. *The Contemporary Reception of Classical Rhetoric: Appropriations of Ancient Discourse*. Hillsdale: LEA.

White, E. B. 1979. Sootfall and Fallout. In *Essays of E. B. White*. New York: Harper and Row.

Whitman, Walt. 1953. Leaves of Grass. New York: Modern Library.

Williams, Bronwyn T. 2003. Speak for Yourself? Power and Hybridity in the Cross-Cultural Classroom. *CCC* 54:586–609.

Williams, Joseph. 1979. Defining Complexity. *College English* 40.6:595–609.

———. 1986. Non-Linguistic Linguistics and the Teaching of Style. In McQuade 1986.

———. 1989. The Phenomenology of Error. *CCC* 32:152–86.

———. 1997. Linguistic Responsibility. *College English* 39.1:8–17.

———. 2003. *Style: Ten Lessons in Clarity and Grace*. 7th ed. New York: Addison Wesley Longman.

———. 2003. *The Craft of Argument*. Abr. ed. New York: Longman.

Williams, Patricia. 1991. *The Alchemy of Race and Rights: Diary of a Law Professor*. Cambridge: Harvard University Press.

Williams, Terry Tempest. 1994. *An Unspoken Hunger*. New York: Pantheon.

———. 1991. *Refuge: An Unnatural History of Family and Place*. New York: Vintage.

Winterowd, W. Ross. 1970. Style: A Matter of Manner. *Quarterly Journal of Speech* 56:160–67.

———. 1983. Prolegomenon to Pedagogical Stylistics. *CCC* 34:80–90.

———. 1998. *The English Department: A Personal and Institutional History*. Carbondale: Southern Illinois University Press.

Wolfe, Don M. 1964. Grammar and Linguistics: A Contrast in Realities. *English Journal* 53:73–78, 100.

Woods, William F. 1985. Nineteenth-Century Psychology and the Teaching of Writing. *CCC* 36:20–41.

Woolley, Edwin C. 1907. *Handbook of Composition: A Compendium of Rules regarding Good English, Grammar, Sentence Structure, Paragraphing, Manuscript Arrangement, Punctuation, Spelling, Essay Writing, and Letter Writing.* Boston: D. C. Heath.

Young, Richard. 1982. Concepts of Art and the Teaching of Writing. In *The Rhetorical Tradition and Modern Writing,* edited by James J. Murphy. New York: MLA.

Zawacki, Terry Myers. 1992. Recomposing as a Woman—An Essay in Different Voices. *CCC* 43:32–38.

Zeglen, Ursula M., ed. 1999. *Donald Davidson: Truth, Meaning and Knowledge.* New York: Routledge.

Zinsser, William. 1980. *On Writing Well.* 2nd ed. New York: Harper.

CONTRIBUTORS

T. R. JOHNSON is an associate professor of English and Director of Composition at Tulane University in New Orleans. He is the author of *A Rhetoric of Pleasure: Prose Style in Today's Composition Classroom* (Heinemann, 2003) and editor of *Teaching Composition: Background Readings* (Bedford St. Martins, 2004).

TOM PACE is an assistant professor and Director of First-Year Composition at John Carroll University in Cleveland, Ohio, where he teaches first-year composition, advanced composition, graduate courses on rhetoric and composition, and courses on British writers. He earned BA and MA degrees from the University of Louisville and a PhD from Miami University of Ohio. He is also currently working on several projects on style, pedagogy, and the history of teaching writing.

ALLISON ALSUP received her BA in French Literature from the University of California and her MFA in Creative Writing from Emerson College. She has taught at Delgado Community College, El Portal Elementary School in California, and Kaplan Educational Centers in Berkeley, CA. She has taught at the University of New Orleans since 2002.

NICOLE AMARE is an assistant professor of technical writing at the University of South Alabama where she teaches technical writing, editing, stylistics, and grammar. She has written *Real Life University*, a college success guide, and has edited *Global Student Entrepreneurs* and *Beyond the Lemonade Stand*.

LISA BAIRD completed her PhD at Texas Christian University and now teaches writing at Purdue North Central University. In addition to matters of prose style, her research focuses on visual rhetoric.

WILLIAM CARPENTER is an assistant professor of English and assistant director of the writing program at Chapman College in Orange, California. He is particular interested in computer-based pedagogies, hypertext, and the genre of the literacy narrative. He is the editor of *The Allyn and Bacon Sourcebook for Writing Program Administrators,* and is currently at work on a book about teaching prose style.

DION C. CAUTRELL teaches rhetoric and writing at The Ohio State University, Mansfield Campus. He has presented and published scholarship on style as well as the relationship among invention, arrangement and revision. His other research interests include ethics, gnosticism, and the rhetorics of science.

PETER CLEMENTS is assistant professor of English at the International University of Japan where he teaches academic writing courses for graduate students. His research interests include genre theory and analysis, discourse analysis, contrastive rhetoric, and second language writing. He is especially interested in response and revision practices, and is currently at work on a longitudinal study of response in second language writing classrooms for his dissertation.

J. SCOTT FARRIN is a writer and teacher working for the University of New Orleans. He received his MFA in Creative Writing from Texas State University and has published fiction in journals such as *Puerto del Sol* and *The South Carolina Review*.

KATHRYN T. FLANNERY is Professor of English and Women's Studies at the University of Pittsburgh where she serves as Director of the Women's Studies Program. She is the author of *Emperor's New Clothes: Literature, Literacy, and the Ideology of Style* (1995), *Feminist Literacies, 1968-75* (2005), and articles on the teaching of writing, performance pedagogy, feminist poetry, and women writers.

GABE GOMEZ is a poet and ceramic artist based in New Orleans. He studied creative writing at the College of Santa Fe and St. Mary's College of California. He is an English instructor at Tulane University.

M. TODD HARPER is an Associate Professor of English at Kennesaw State University. He has explored the relationship between rhetorical tropes and writing in a number of articles, and, most recently, he has begun to explore issues of composition pedagogy in an international context.

REBECCA MOORE HOWARD earned her PhD in English at West Virginia University. She is now Associate Professor of Writing and Rhetoric at Syracuse University and the former writing program administrator at Syracuse, Texas Christian, and Colgate Universities. She is coauthor of the *1995 Bedford Guide to Teaching Writing in the Disciplines*; author of *Standing in the Shadow of Giants* (1999), a book about the cultural work of plagiarism; coeditor of *Coming of Age: The Advanced Writing Curriculum,* which won the 2000-2001 WPA Book Award; coeditor of *Authorship in Composition Studies* (2006); and author of a writers' handbook in progress for McGraw-Hill.

JESSE KAVADLO is Assistant Professor of English and Writing Center Director at Maryville University of St. Louis. He is the author of *Don DeLillo: Balance at the Edge of Belief* (New York: Peter Lang, 2004) as well as essays on contemporary American fiction, critical theory, and writing pedagogy.

TINA M. KELLEHER recently completed her PhD in English at The Johns Hopkins University, where she served as graduate fellow to the expository writing program.

MELISSA A. GOLDTHWAITE is Assistant Professor of English at Saint Joseph's University, where she teaches poetry, creative nonfiction, composition, and rhetorical theory. She is co-editor of *Surveying the Literary Landscapes of Terry Tempest Williams* (University of Utah Press, 2003) and co-author of *The St. Martin's Guide to Teaching Writing,* 5th edition.

DREW M. LOEWE is a happily reformed attorney. He is a doctoral student in English at Texas Christian University, where he holds a Radford fellowship in Rhetoric and Composition. His research interests include argument and persuasion, 20th Century rhetoric, style and stylistics, composition theory and pedagogy, and rhetorical criticism.

KEITH RHODES was the Coordinator of Composition at Northwest Missouri State University and then the Director of Developmental Writing at Missouri Western State University. He has practiced law in Baltimore and Kansas City. He will soon begin teaching English at East Buchanan High School in Gower, Missouri.

ELIZABETH WEISER is Assistant Professor of English at the Ohio State University-Newark. A historiographer, she specializes in modern rhetorical theory, public debate, and rhetoric/ poetics links. She is working on a manuscript entitled *Word Man at War: The Development of Kenneth Burke's Dramatism*, as well as articles on epideictic fiction and psychological/rhetorical theories of ambiguity.

INDEX